KINGS CANYON National Park

From the book…

Combined with the acreage from the surrounding John Muir, Golden Trout, Jennie Lakes, and Monarch wilderness areas, these protected lands create a vast, unbroken chain of exquisite backcountry. Over 800 miles of trail lure sightseers, hikers, and backpackers away from the roads and into the picturesque terrain of the parks. **–from the Introduction**

Redwood Mountain Grove: Sugar Bowl Loop (Trip 4)

The Redwood Mountain Grove is the largest intact grove of giant sequoias in the world. Despite this distinction, the area is not overrun by tourists, allowing hikers and backpackers to enjoy the magnificent trees with a modicum of peace and quiet.

Don Cecil Trail to Lookout Peak (Trip 20)

The climb up the Don Cecil Trail to the top of Lookout Peak affords hikers a bird's-eye view of Kings Canyon and an impressive vista of the peaks and ridges forming the backcountry of Kings Canyon National Park.

Blayney Hot Springs, Goddard Canyon, and Martha Lake (Trip 38)

On the far side of the South Fork is Pig Chute, where a seasonal stream pours down a narrow cleft in the rock beside a rocky, knife-edged protrusion. Farther up the trail, a spectacular waterfall spills dramatically into an emerald pool.

Sabrina Basin (Trip 56)

The main quandary when contemplating a trip to Sabrina Basin is whether you have enough time to visit all of its scenic lakes, because there is a bountiful number and nary a rotten apple in the bunch.

KINGS CANYON
National Park

A COMPLETE
HIKER'S GUIDE

MIKE WHITE

 WILDERNESS PRESS · BERKELEY, CA

Kings Canyon National Park: A Complete Hiker's Guide

1st EDITION March 2004
  2nd printing June 2006

Copyright © 2004 by Mike White

Front cover photo © 2004 by David Muench
Back cover photo © 2004 by Mike White
Interior photos, except where noted, by Mike White
Maps: Mike White and Fineline Maps
Illustrations: Danny Woodward
Cover and book design: Larry B. Van Dyke

ISBN 0-89997-335-3
UPC 7-19609-97335-5

Manufactured in the United States of America

Published by: **Wilderness Press**
              1200 5th Street
              Berkeley, CA 94710
              (800) 443-7227; FAX (510) 558-1696
              info@wildernesspress.com
              www.wildernesspress.com

Visit our website for a complete listing of our books and for ordering information.

Cover photos: Lake Reflection (Trip 27) *(front);*
                Long Lake and Mt. Goode from the Bishop Pass Trail (Trip 51) *(back)*
Frontispiece: Temple Crag towers over Second Lake (Trip 50)

SAFETY NOTICE: Although Wilderness Press and the author have made every attempt to ensure that the information in this book is accurate at press time, they are not responsible for any loss, damage, injury, or inconvenience that may occur to anyone while using this book. You are responsible for your own safety and health while in the wilderness. The fact that a trail is described in this book does not mean that it will be safe for you. Be aware that trail conditions can change from day to day. Always check local conditions and know your own limitations.

Dedication

To all our friends at Hume Lake: May God continue to use you in the lives of all who cross your paths.

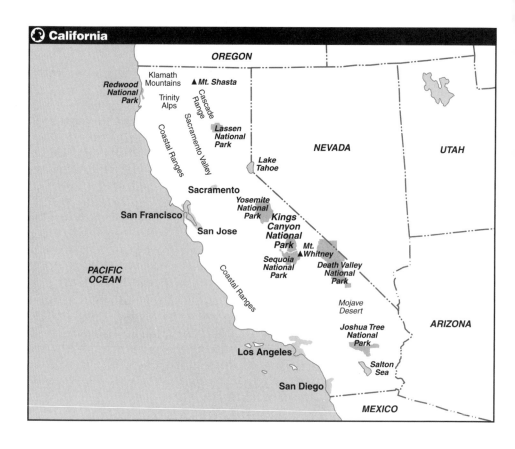

California

OREGON

Redwood National Park

Klamath Mountains

Trinity Alps

▲ Mt. Shasta

Cascade Range

Sacramento Valley

Coastal Ranges

Lassen National Park

Lake Tahoe

NEVADA

UTAH

Sacramento

Yosemite National Park

Kings Canyon National Park

San Francisco

San Jose

Coastal Ranges

Mt. ▲ Whitney

Sequoia National Park

Death Valley National Park

PACIFIC OCEAN

Mojave Desert

Joshua Tree National Park

ARIZONA

Los Angeles

Salton Sea

San Diego

MEXICO

Contents

Waterfall on Evolution Creek

Acknowledgments

First of all, I extend my thanks to the Creator for the majesty of His creation and for granting me the privilege of experiencing much of the best parts first hand. Second, none of my projects would ever realize fruition if not for the never-ending support of my wife, Robin, who believes in me even when I'm not very believable.

Then, there's the staff at Wilderness Press, including Mike Jones, Jannie Dresser, Elaine Merrill, and Roslyn Bullas, with whom I worked most directly on this project, and all the support staff who somehow fashioned my manuscript, photographs, and maps into a real book. I extend a special thanks to Tom Winnett, the founder and patriarch of Wilderness Press, who, with his usual care and expert eye, performed much of the editing. Also, thanks to David Weintraub for assisting in the editing of the manuscript.

Although I spent many a lonely night in campgrounds and backcountry campsites, there was a group of friends who blessed me with their presence on several of the many outings necessary for completion of the fieldwork. Among them are Robin White, Stephen White, Carmel Bang, Tic Long, Andy Montessoro, Bob Redding, Chris Taylor, Dal and Candy Hunter, Lisa Kafchinski, Art Barkley, Joe Tavares, Kim Small, Darrin Munson, and the youth group from RCF. Thanks for keeping me somewhat sane in the midst of so much isolation.

Several National Park and Forest Service rangers and personnel were very helpful in providing information during the course of this project. Although most of them remain anonymous, they were always courteous and informative. Special thanks are extended to Kris Fister, former Public Information Officer for Sequoia and Kings Canyon national parks, and Chief Park Interpreter, Ranger Bill Tweed, who were invaluable in providing needed help on a variety of items.

Preface

The greater Kings Canyon region remains my favorite area for backpacking. Nowhere else in the West have I found such a combination of extraordinary mountain scenery and consistently sunny weather. Obviously, many other hikers and backpackers share a love for this portion of the Sierra, as weekend quotas for many of the trails on both the east and west sides are usually filled to capacity during the height of the backpacking season. However, with the advantage of extra days beyond just a weekend, solitude and serenity are still relatively simple to come by in the heart of the Kings Canyon backcountry. With the ability to step off marked trails, these attributes are even more attainable in some of the grandest and most enchanting surroundings.

I discovered the east side of the Sierra many years ago soon after relocating to western Nevada from the Pacific Northwest. With such dramatic mountain topography within a three- to four-hour drive from home, numerous personal forays piled up over the years from the east side into the nooks and crannies of the heart of the Kings Canyon backcountry. Several years later, I became very excited about the prospect of covering all the trails in the Kings Canyon and Sequoia region for an upcoming project, which ultimately led to this book and the companion volume, *Sequoia National Park: A Complete Hiker's Guide*.

Having backpacked extensively from the east, I became very familiar with a large part of the Kings Canyon area, but the west side remained uncharted territory, due mainly to the long drive required to reach western trailheads from a home base in Reno. Despite several trips to Hume Lake, the west side of Kings Canyon and Sequoia remained to me unknown parcels of backcountry. Three years of hiking and backpacking nearly every trail in the Parks and surrounding wilderness areas have enabled me to become acquainted with the other side of the Sierra, which I found quite stunning and picturesque in its own right.

Although Kings Canyon and Sequoia national parks are two separate entities, the National Park Service manages the adjoining parks as a single area. Originally we took the same approach, with a goal of producing a single guidebook to cover the trails within both parks and the surrounding wilderness areas. However, during the process the realization dawned that there were too many trails to cram into a single book. After a bit of reorganization, *Sequoia National Park: A Complete Hiker's Guide* was published, followed shortly by this companion volume.

May our dilemma of too many trails for one book provide you with just the right number of wonderful adventures into the heart of the Kings Canyon backcountry.

—Mike White
January 2004

Early evening at State Lake

CHAPTER 1

Introduction

Although this guide and the companion volume, *Sequoia National Park: A Complete Hiker's Guide*, correspond to the federal designation of the area as two separate parks, in reality, both Kings Canyon National Park and the adjoining Sequoia National Park are managed as one entity. Encompassing 402,108 and 459,995 acres respectively, Sequoia and Kings Canyon national parks, along with the surrounding national forest lands, contain the bulk of the southern Sierra Nevada. The overwhelming majority of this area is managed by the National Park Service and the U.S. Forest Service as wilderness, providing hikers, backpackers, equestrians, and mountaineers with a virtually unlimited number of possibilities for enjoyment.

Sequoia and Kings Canyon national parks and the surrounding region are marked by extremes. Mt. Whitney, along the eastern fringe of Sequoia, is the highest mountain in the continental United States, at 14,494 feet. The 10,760 feet between the summit and the town of Lone Pine is the greatest relief between mountaintop and base in the lower 48 states. Just west of the confluence of the South and Middle Forks of the Kings River, the canyon becomes one of the deepest gorges in North America, measured at over 8000 feet from river level to the top of Spanish Mountain. Giant Forest, in western Sequoia, is home to the largest living tree on earth, the General Sherman tree, a giant sequoia with a volume of more than 52,500 cubic feet.

The entire Sierra Nevada range is some 450 miles long, between 50 and 80 miles in width, and contains 13 peaks over 14,000 feet high. In addition to its extreme physical features, the Sequoia and Kings Canyon region includes some of the most sublime country in the Sierra Nevada. Between the western foothills at the edge of the San Joaquin Valley and the high desert of Owens Valley to the east, the southern Sierra sprawls across California, reaching a zenith in altitude and in spectacular scenery. Besides Mt. Whitney, the rugged Sierra crest of Kings Canyon and Sequoia offers a dozen other peaks over 14,000 feet and scads more 12,000- and 13,000-foot mountains of equally impressive beauty.

Kings Canyon—the gorge of the South Fork Kings River from Lewis Creek upstream to Bubbs Creek—isn't the only deep canyon in the region; the major rivers of the Kern, North, and Middle Fork Kings, and Kaweah all flow down other canyons that are also thousands of feet deep. In the high country, these streams tumble down characteristic U-shaped canyons that have been carved over time through rugged granite. As they near the foothills, during peak season these rivers become rushing torrents of water, careening through deep V-shaped gorges of multi-hued metamorphic rock.

SEQUOIA & KINGS CANYON: LAND OF EXTREMES

Highest mountain in 48 states:
Mt. Whitney, 14,494 feet

Greatest relief in 48 states:
Lone Pine to Mt. Whitney,
10,760 feet

One of the deepest gorges in North America:
Kings River, 8000+ feet

Largest living tree:
General Sherman sequoia,
52,000+ cubic feet

Major rivers in the Sequoia area include the South Fork San Joaquin; North, Middle, and South Fork Kings River; North, Marble, Middle, and East Fork Kaweah River.

The only place on the entire globe where the giant sequoia (*Sequoiadendron giganteum*) occurs naturally is the western side of the Sierra Nevada, between 5000 and 8200 feet. Of the 75 giant sequoia groves in the Sierra, only eight are located outside of the region, north of the Kings River. Most of the largest trees are found within the Sequoia and Kings Canyon area, including the top five, General Sherman, Washington, General Grant, President, and Lincoln. Several of the most impressive groves and largest individual sequoias within the parks are easily accessible to both tourists and hikers.

Along with high peaks, deep canyons, and huge trees, the Sequoia and Kings Canyon landscape hosts a diverse cross-section of outstanding terrain. The foothills region in the extreme southwest corner of Sequoia is a protected pocket of oak woodland and chaparral, a habitat that is often subject to urban development in other areas of California. Lush woodlands of mixed conifers carpet the western slope of the Sierra, above the foothills. Here are the famed giant sequoia groves, and stands of

old-growth forest, wildflower-covered meadows, and gurgling streams. Above the forest belt, high mountain lakes, towering granite peaks, sharp ridges, and sweeping meadows crown the range. The southern Sierra truly offers some of the most magnificent scenery in North America.

Only a handful of roads penetrate the fringes of the Sequoia and Kings Canyon region on both the west and the east; the overwhelming majority of the area is roadless. Thanks to an extensive area of rugged terrain, no major highways cross the Sierra between the seasonally open Tioga Pass Road in Yosemite and the all-weather route of Highway 178 well south of the parks. Of the nearly 900,000 acres of land within the two parks, over 90% is managed as wilderness. Combined with the acreage from the surrounding John Muir, Golden Trout, Jennie Lakes, and Monarch wilderness areas, these protected lands create a vast, unbroken chain of exquisite backcountry. More than 800 miles of trail lure sightseers, hikers, and backpackers away from the roads and into the picturesque terrain of the parks.

The Sequoia and Kings Canyon region is a hiker's and backpacker's paradise. While much of nearby Yosemite sees a more vehicle-oriented tourist crowd, the main way to see the incredible sights in and around Sequoia and Kings Canyon is by foot or by horseback. An extensive network of short trails provides day hikers with a wide range of opportunities to explore diverse environments, from foothill canyons to giant sequoia groves to alpine lakes.

WORLD'S LARGEST SEQUOIAS:

1. **General Sherman**, 52,508 cubic feet

2. **Washington**, 47,850 cubic feet

3. **General Grant**, 46,608 cubic feet

4. **President**, 45,148 cubic feet

5. **Lincoln**, 44,471 cubic feet

However, the ultimate experience is to backpack through the mountainous terrain on some of the High Sierra's most excellent backcountry trails. Parts of two of the most famous long-distance trails are found within the region, the John Muir and the High Sierra, exposing backpackers to some of the most stupendous scenery in the range. An abundance of lesser-known routes leads travelers through deep canyons, over high divides, around spectacular meadows, and past picturesque lakes. This vast backcountry of the southern Sierra is one of the nation's most treasured resources.

Monarch butterfly

Human History

Native Americans and Early Settlement

The Native Americans who lived in the Sequoia and Kings Canyon region were divided into four separate tribes — the Monache, Tubatulabal, Owens Valley Paiute, and Yokut. These groups traveled extensively within the area, hunting, trading, and establishing summer camps. Several sites within the parks give evidence of some of these settlements; Hospital Rock is perhaps the most visited by modern-day tourists.

Early explorers, such as Jedediah Smith and John C. Fremont, avoided the difficult terrain and high mountains characteristic of the Sequoia/Kings Canyon region in favor of easier traverses across the Sierra to the north and the south. Discouraged by the rugged landscape, Europeans knew little about the area until settlers in the San Joaquin Valley began to venture into the mountains in the mid-1850s.

Hale D. Tharp, who established a ranch near the future site of Three Rivers, was perhaps the first Anglo to see the Giant Forest. In 1856 he headed east into the hills at the invitation of some friendly Potwishas to see the rumored Big Trees and scout a summer range for his livestock. He followed the Middle Fork Kaweah River to Moro Rock and then climbed up to Log Meadow in Giant Forest. A couple of years later, Tharp retraced his route to Giant Forest, continued into the Kings River area, and returned to his ranch via the East and South Forks of the Kaweah. Eventually, he grazed his cattle each summer in Log Meadow, using a fallen and burned out sequoia as a makeshift cabin.

Increased settlement in the San Joaquin Valley spelled doom for the Native Americans, as exposure to various illnesses devastated their population. Surviving members of the four tribes either crossed the Sierra to the less desired eastern desert or attempted

Eagle Scout Peak, from Elizabeth Pass Trail

to adapt to the growing culture of the white man on the west side.

As time wore on, Europeans came to Sequoia and Kings Canyon in increasing numbers, encouraged by gold discoveries to the north, the prospect of an unending supply of lumber, and the San Joaquin Valley's fertile ranchland.

Exploitation of Resources

Mining proved to be a disappointment to the hordes of miners who sought their fortune in the southern Sierra. Mineral King, perhaps the best known mineral site in the region, was imagined to be the Sutter's Mill of the south, but it never managed to produce a significant amount of minerals, and has only been commercially viable as a recreation area in the 20th and 21st centuries. The passage of time proved that the southern Sierra did not contain the mineral wealth that had sparked the gold and silver rushes in the north.

Lumbermen turned out to be equally as disappointed as the miners. The discovery of giant sequoias in the southern Sierra seemed to bode well for entrepreneurs who anticipated enormous profits from the lumber. But despite the positive speculation, the wood proved to be too brittle for most construction purposes. With the immense effort required to fell the Big Trees, logging the sequoias became a commercially nonviable enterprise. The mills that were built never made much of a profit—some even lost money—and most of the wood ended up being used for fence posts or shakes. Unfortunately, most lumber companies did not realize the poor quality of sequoia lumber until it was too late for a number of groves. Converse Basin, perhaps at one time the finest stand of the big trees in the Sierra, saw the destruction of every sequoia in the basin except for one lone survivor— the Boole Tree—which turned out to be the eighth largest giant sequoia in the world.

Cattle and sheep grazing prospered in the San Joaquin Valley, which then led to growing competition for rangeland. In order to feed their herds and flocks adequately, cattle ranchers and sheepherders went farther afield in search of green summer pasture, eventually inflicting severe environmental destruction on the western Sierra. Fires, set to clear forest debris to make easier passage for stock, ran unchecked throughout the range. In addition, thousands of hooves trampled sensitive meadows each season. The resulting erosion from the fires and the animals produced inevitable watershed degradation.

California Geographical Survey

About the same time miners and loggers were exploiting the area's natural resources, the California Geological Survey began exploration of the High Sierra under the leadership of Josiah D. Whitney. The survey's plan was to ascend high peaks and obtain measurements that would allow accurate mapping of the as yet unmapped High Sierra. As part of the 1864 survey, William H. Brewer led Clarence King, Richard D. Cotter, James T. Gardiner, and Charles F. Hoffman from Visalia to a base camp at Big Meadow. From there the party proceeded eastward into the Sierra, climbing and naming Mt. Silliman along the Silliman Crest and Mt. Brewer on the Great Western Divide.

From a campsite near Mt. Brewer, King and Cotter left the rest of the party to make a multi-day attempt on Mt. Whitney. Although they failed to reach the range's highest peak, they did manage to scale Mt. Tyndall (14,018′), a mere 6 miles northwest of Mt. Whitney. After the climb, the party reunited near Mt. Brewer before returning to Big Meadow.

Undeterred by the failed attempt to reach Mt. Whitney, King tried again, leading a small party from Three Rivers up the recently built Hockett Trail to the Kern River. They followed the Kern north for several miles before veering away toward the mountain, where their summit bid fell short by 300–400 vertical feet.

Following his second unsuccessful attempt on Whitney, King joined the resupplied and expanded survey party at Big Meadow to explore the Kings River region, which the party would compare favorably with Yosemite Valley. After explorations of the South and Middle forks and the Monarch Divide separating the two gorges, the party traveled eastward through the heart of Kings Canyon country by way of Bubbs Creek, crossing the crest at Kearsarge Pass and descending to the town of Fort Independence.

From Independence, the group journeyed north up the Owens Valley, recrossing the Sierra crest at Mono Pass (in the south) before establishing a base camp on the west side of the range at Vermilion Valley (current site of Lake Edison). The exact route is undetermined, but the survey headed south toward the LeConte Divide, from where Cotter, along with a soldier named Spratt, made a 36-hour assault on Mt. Goddard, turning back approximately 300 feet below the summit. After yet another failed summit bid, the party returned to Vermilion Valley and headed north to Wawona, concluding their survey for the year.

The Brewer Party was the first group to develop a significant understanding of the topography, botany, and geology of the High Sierra. In addition to the scientific findings, the survey named several significant features, including Mt. Whitney, the highest peak in the range and in the continental United States. The California Geological Survey made a more limited expedition along the east side of the range in 1870 before being disbanded in 1874.

Seeds of Preservation

Over his lifetime, John Muir made nine separate excursions into the backcountry of Sequoia and Kings Canyon, ultimately increasing public awareness of the beauty and majesty of the region as a whole and of the giant sequoias in particular. An increasing number of concerned citizens joined

Muir to champion the cause of protecting the unique character of the region, including George W. Stewart, the youthful city editor of one of Visalia's newspapers. Eventually national and international figures lent their voices to the idea of setting aside this area as parkland.

As ranching and farming increased in the San Joaquin Valley, so did the demand for irrigation. Watershed degradation brought on by logging, grazing, and mining in the southern Sierra conflicted with the agricultural needs of the ranchers and farmers downstream. Concern over water issues combined with a developing preservationist ethic to create growing opposition to unmitigated consumption of the region's natural resources and the destruction of recreational areas.

The first official step towards the establishment of a national park in the region occurred in 1880, when Theodore Wagner, United States Surveyor General for California, suspended 4 square miles of Grant Grove, prohibiting anyone from filing a land claim. Unfortunately, a 160-acre claim had already been filed adjacent to the grove. Wilsonia remains in private hands to this day. Although little progress was made in subsequent years, the seeds of a grand idea had been planted.

The Kaweah Colony

A group of socialist utopians from San Francisco created one of the most colorful chapters in the history of the region. Armed with a big dream, a heady dose of gumption, and a limited supply of capital, thirty-some members of the Cooperative Land and Colonization Association filed claims on nearly 6000 acres of prime timberland in Giant Forest. As a way to fund their utopian society, the colonists planned to build a road from near Three Rivers to a mill site in the vicinity of their timber claims, where they would harvest the timber and mill it for sale.

A certain amount of controversy swirled around the legality of the colonists'

land claims, which became an ongoing dilemma. Despite the brewing controversy, by the end of the summer of 1886 nearly 160 colonists were camped along the North Fork Kaweah River, ready to begin construction on their wagon road. Idealism and optimism reigned within the colony as the road was built over the next 4 years. Despite the sole use of hand tools, the construction and grade of the road were quite remarkable. The colonists coaxed a steam tractor they named Ajax to a saddle at the end of the road and erected a portable sawmill in an attempt to turn logs into lumber. However, a variety of complications prohibited the colonists from fully realizing their dream, including inexperience, internal squabbles, insufficient funds, and inability to secure full title to their land claims. By 1892, their dream had ended and the remaining trustees officially dissolved the colony.

Two Eagle Peak and Fifth Lake, one of the Big Pine Lakes

Although the utopian dream of the Kaweah Colony was short-lived, their road had a much longer life. Eventually extended by the U.S. Army from Colony Mill into Giant Forest, the road opened to one-way traffic in 1903 and served as the principal access to Sequoia for the next few decades.

Creation of Sequoia and General Grant National Parks

While the Kaweah colonists were busy building their road, political winds had shifted in Washington D.C. as a more development-oriented Department of Interior took over. The General Land Office reopened several townships west of Mineral King for private sale in 1889, which alarmed Stewart and others sympathetic toward preserving these resources. The tract included the Garfield Grove, one of the finest giant sequoia stands in the southern Sierra, and expansive Hockett Meadows. In response to this threat, Stewart vigorously courted public opinion and maneuvered through political channels to pass a bill on September 25, 1890, that set aside 76 square miles of Sierra forest as a public park.

Mystery surrounds the next step toward the creation of Sequoia and Kings Canyon national parks. Unbeknownst to Stewart and his group, another bill came before Congress to establish a national park for Yosemite, a mere six days following the passage of the original bill for Sequoia. Attached to the Yosemite measure was the addition of five townships to Sequoia, including the area around Giant Forest, and four sections surrounding Grant Grove. No one seems to know for certain who was behind this bill, or how the size of the land increased by 500% from the original proposal; however, on October 1, 1890, Yosemite National Park and General Grant National Park were born, and Sequoia National Park was greatly enlarged. Speculation pointed toward Daniel K. Zumwalt, an agent of the Southern Pacific Railroad, as being behind the bill, but the motivation remains unclear.

Management of the new parks became problematic the following spring. Captain Joseph H. Dorst and the Fourth Cavalry had the unenviable task of protecting the area, although the mission of the new national parks was not clearly defined. Most of the first summer was spent dealing with the Kaweah colonists, who had rather unjustly been denied their claims in Giant Forest. A smaller contingent resurfaced near Mineral King to log sequoias at the leased Atwell Mill. The government initially took issue with the practice, but after harassing the colonists for much of the summer, it decided that the mill was located on private land and was a perfectly legal operation. However, the colonists proved to be inexperienced and failed to turn a profit. By the time the lease on Atwell Mill came up for renewal the following year, the colony had disbanded. During the remainder of the summer and into the fall, Dorst and his troops explored the parks, dealing with problems of logging, grazing, and squatting.

Stewart, Muir, and others continued their push to put more land under federal protection. As a result, in 1893, President Harrison signed a presidential proclamation creating the Sierra Forest Reserve, which withdrew most of the central and southern Sierra from private sale. The Sierra Forest Reserve was reclassified as Sequoia National Forest in 1905 and placed under the jurisdiction of the Department of Agriculture, which was more concerned with resource management (grazing, mining, and logging) than preservation. During the first part of the 20th century, the idea of a large national park for the southern Sierra was still alive, but very little progress was made toward its creation.

With limited success, the military continued to protect the parks until 1914, when Walter Fry became the first civilian superintendent of General Grant and Sequoia national parks. By then the Colony

Mill Road had been extended into Giant Forest and the Mt. Whitney Power Company had constructed several hydro-electric power plants on branches of the Kaweah River. Aside from those improvements, the area was still virtually undeveloped. Cattle grazing, private inholdings, lack of access, and poor facilities plagued the region.

The Reign of the National Park Service

In 1916 Congress created the National Park Service and Californian Stephen T. Mather was appointed the first director. Mather was quite familiar with the Sequoia region, having organized an expedition of notable figures to traverse the range in 1915. Armed with first-hand knowledge of the area and a Park Service mandate for conservation and enjoyment of the national parks, Mather ushered in a new era in park management.

Two of the most important directives from the Park Service regarding the Sequoia area were the acquisition of private lands within the existing park and the expansion of the park boundaries to include the High Sierra and Kings Canyon. Acquiring private lands was a fairly easy proposition compared to that of park enlargement, which drew opposition from cattlemen, hunters, and Mineral King property owners. Other opponents included the Los Angeles Bureau of Power and Light, which wanted to construct hydroelectric dams at Cedar Grove and in Tehipite Valley; the San Joaquin Light and Power Company, with similar aspirations; and the Forest Service, which was reluctant to give up lands that had mineral, timber, and grazing potential. A scaled-down proposal was passed in 1926, which expanded the park eastward over the Sierra crest, but excluded Mineral King and Kings Canyon.

By 1926, the Generals Highway had opened from Ash Mountain to Giant Forest, replacing the old Colony Mill Road. Nine years later the road was extended to Grant Grove. Easier public access into Sequoia led to a dramatic rise in park visitation and a need for additional development of park infrastructure, including water, sewage, and trash systems. In addition to improving the roads and utilities, an extensive network of trails was built (including parts of the John Muir and High Sierra trails), campgrounds were improved, a variety of government and public structures were erected, and a concessionaire monopoly was created to cater to the increased tourist trade. Completion of the highway from Grant Grove to Kings Canyon accelerated development of campgrounds along the South Fork Kings River, but more intensive projects were held in abeyance until the issue of dams along the Kings River was settled.

Initially, the park improvements seemed a good and necessary way to accommodate growing numbers of tourists. However, as visitation and development continued to increase, traffic jams, congestion, and overcrowding began to characterize Giant Forest and to a lesser extent Grant Grove during the height of summer. A meteoric rise in visitors coupled with runaway development threatened the long-term health of the sequoia groves.

Additional threats to the parks surfaced in the form of vegetation and wildlife management. Fire suppression was the rule of the day, allowing a buildup of fuel for potentially disastrous future fires. The policy that prohibited cattle grazing within the parks was reversed, opening the door for inevitable damage to resources. Wildlife management suffered similar setbacks. In the 1920s, the last grizzly bear in California was shot and killed at Horse Corral Meadows, near the northwest fringe of Sequoia National Park. Increased conflicts between humans and black bears put "problem" bears at risk. The evening garbage feast at Bear Hill, where marauding bears put on a show for tourists at Sequoia's garbage dump, seemed emblematic of the times.

Colonel John R. White, superintendent of Sequoia National Park from 1920 to 1938 and 1941 to 1947, initiated a philosophical shift that was reflected in efforts to reduce visitation impact at Giant Forest. He placed limits on future development and moved many of the government structures to other areas, but he largely failed to limit the presence of concessionaires. One of his most fortuitous accomplishments in backcountry preservation was the defeat of several proposed roads, including two trans-Sierra links, one from Cedar Grove to Independence and another between Porterville and Lone Pine. Col. White also squelched the Sierra Way, a mountain highway planned to connect Yosemite and Sequoia, with a link between Giant Forest and Mineral King via Redwood Meadow.

The Creation of Kings Canyon National Park

While Sequoia National Park confronted rampant problems at Giant Forest, the fight to preserve Kings Canyon escalated. Interior Secretary Harold Ickes put forth a proposal in 1935 to create Kings Canyon National Park and manage it primarily as wilderness. Opposition came from four distinct groups. San Joaquin Valley businessmen saw extensive commercial potential in Kings Canyon, which creation of a national park would prohibit. The Forest Service favored a multiple-use approach and was reluctant to give up control of the area. Central Valley ranchers were concerned about how the park would affect steady irrigation supplies. Finally, both the Los Angeles Bureau of Power and Light and the San Joaquin Light and Power Corporation were competing for water supplies and hydroelectric-power generating sites.

Compromises were eventually made to secure passage of the bill, the potentially most significant one being the exclusion of Cedar Grove and Tehipite Valley from the park, leaving the door open for future dams on the South and Middle Forks of the Kings River. Ranchers were assuaged by the promise to construct the Pine Flat Reservoir, and commercial interests were assured of some development in Kings Canyon. After some political intrigue between two local congressmen, Franklin D. Roosevelt signed the bill that established Kings Canyon National Park on March 4, 1940, creating a vast area of protected wilderness. Included within the new park were the old General Grant National Park and Redwood Mountain. In 1965, Kings Canyon and Tehipite Valley were officially added to Kings Canyon National Park, removing the threat of hydroelectric dams on the Kings River system.

The Battle for Mineral King

After the establishment of Kings Canyon National Park, controversy began to swirl to the south. Responding to demands from the public for additional recreational facilities, in 1949 the multiple-use-oriented Forest Service began seeking proposals from private developers for a ski resort at Mineral King. A suitable developer with the necessary capital wasn't found until 1966, when the Walt Disney Company was awarded a temporary permit. Disney proposed a large-scale Swiss-style village, with 2 hotels, 14 ski lifts and parking for 3600 vehicles. The Sierra Club deemed the small subalpine valley unsuitable for such a huge project and began a series of legal battles to stop the project, acquiring a restraining order in 1969.

The Sierra Club effectively tied up the Disney Company in the courts long enough to win over public opinion. In another strike against Disney, California withdrew the proposal to build a new state highway from Three Rivers to Mineral King, which would have required that the developer come up with several million dollars for road construction and obtain all the necessary approvals for a route across state and federal lands. As environmental awareness increased among the public and within the Federal government, Disney began to lose the public-relations battle, and the concept of a Mineral King ski resort was in serious jeopardy. On November 10, 1978, President Jimmy Carter signed into law the Omnibus Parks Bill, part of which added Mineral King to the surrounding Sequoia National Park.

Recent History

The post-World War II era in the parks was characterized by an increase in visitation, improvements to park infrastructure, and the advancement of scientific research for the purpose of designing management policies. At Giant Forest, the park took steps to reduce the impact of development on the giant sequoias. By 1972 it had moved campsites, picnic areas, and most park structures to less sensitive areas. The visitor center was moved to Lodgepole and the gas station and maintenance facilities were relocated to Red Fir.

Nearly 25 more years passed before the park finally resolved the problem of commercialism at Giant Forest. After the 1996 season, the park permanently closed the historic Giant Forest Lodge complex near Round Meadow and started construction on new facilities at Wuksachi. Two years later, most of the commercial buildings had been closed and removed, with four exceptions. The old market was restored and remodeled into the Giant Forest Museum, which opened in 2001. Additional modifications at Giant Forest included trail improvements, interpretive displays, and improved parking lots. Nearby at General Sherman, the park continues construction on a new parking area and a trail and shuttle system due to open by the summer of 2004.

The recent construction of John Muir Lodge increased the number of overnight accommodations at Grant Grove, an area that had not been nearly as overdeveloped as Giant Forest. In 1978, a lodge at Cedar Grove with 18 motel rooms, a snack bar, and a grocery store was a small-scale fulfillment of the San Joaquin Valley businessmen's vision so many years before.

The Sierra Crest above Blue Lake

Unnamed tarn in Dusy Basin

Wilderness and Backcountry Issues

Since 1984, nearly 90% of Sequoia and Kings Canyon National Parks have been managed as wilderness. Combined with the surrounding John Muir, Golden Trout, Jennie Lakes and Monarch wildernesses, a vast stretch of the southern Sierra Nevada is wild.

After decades of neglect, the park developed backcountry regulations and policies to prevent overuse and restore environmental health. By 1972, backcountry permits and quotas were being used to forestall the crush of backpackers in the more popular areas of the parks. In addition, the Park Service and the Forest Service began a campaign to educate backcountry users on wilderness ethics. They put into place camping bans and stay limits in areas of severe overuse, and enforced campfire restrictions above certain altitudes and in sensitive areas. More recently, both the Park Service and the Forest Service began requiring the use of bear lockers and canisters in heavily used areas and strongly suggesting their use in others.

Postscript

Sequoia and Kings Canyon national parks have faced many challenges and undoubtedly await more trials. As more and more tourists seek temporary escape from the perils of urbanization, increased park visitation remains a management problem. Pollution from urban areas and the San Joaquin Valley is a perpetual threat to air quality and plant life, reducing visibility, threatening sequoia seedlings and other plants, and producing acid rain. Although backpacking numbers are down from their mid-1970s high point, fragile subalpine and alpine environments must still be protected. Stock use has come under increased scrutiny, but the current management plan is still flawed. The age-old question for the Park Service still remains — how does the agency manage the competing goals of park preservation and public enjoyment?

Flora and Fauna

Encompassing the change in elevation from the San Joaquin Valley floor to Mt. Whitney, the Sequoia and Kings Canyon region supports a diverse cross-section of plant and animal life and several distinct plant communities. The following divisions are general and should not be viewed as definitive descriptions. The bibliography at the end of this book suggests additional sources for information on plants and animals in the Sierra Nevada.

The Foothills

Plant life: The western fringe of Sequoia National Park includes the Sierra foothills, a low-elevation area that extends from the floor of the San Joaquin Valley eastward to roughly 4500–5000 feet. The foothill plant community is characterized by the Mediterranean climate of mild temperatures, winter rain, and dry summers. Average rainfall

Wildflowers at Golden Trout Lake

varies from as little as 10 inches per year in the lowlands to 40 inches at the upper elevations. Much of the vegetation appears parched and dry for a large part of the year, but after winter rains, early spring bursts forth, covering the hills with a vibrant carpet of green, decorated with brilliant wildflower displays.

Grasslands cover low slopes of the foothills, as they rise from the plain of the Central Valley. Non-native grasses have overtaken most of the native species. Periods of drought coupled with severe overgrazing in previous centuries have favored the invasive European annual grasses.

Diverse woodlands alternate with chaparral on higher slopes east of the grasslands. Generally, woodland occupies shady areas where the soil is damp, while chaparral grows on dry and sunny slopes. Foothills woodland is characterized by a savanna-like growth of trees and grasses, including a variety of oaks (blue oak, live oak, valley oak and canyon oak), and California buckeye, laurel, and redbud.

Dry, rocky slopes in the foothills are typically carpeted with a tangle of shrubs known as chaparral. Common plants include chamise (greasewood), manzanita, ceanothus, buckeye, flowering ash, mountain mahogany, and California coffeeberry. Fire plays an important role in chaparral communities, regularly burning areas every 10 to 40 years.

Although the foothills zone is generally considered to be a dry environment, several rivers, streams, and creeks pass through the area carrying water from the melting snows of the Sierra to the thirsty valley below. A varied plant community thrives along these watercourses, thanks to plentiful moisture. Cottonwood, willow, alder, oak, laurel, and sycamore are common streamside companions.

Poison oak is associated with both the foothills woodland and the chaparral communities. As the saying goes, "Leaves of three, leave it be." Leaves typically grow in groups of three; they are bronze and shiny in spring, green in summer, scarlet in autumn, and fall off prior to winter. Berries are white. Poison oak may grow as a creeping plant, an erect shrub, or even as a small tree under the right conditions. All parts of the plant (branches, stems, leaves, and roots) contain the oil urushiol, which causes some people to break out in a skin rash. Even a microscopic drop of urushiol is enough to trigger itching or a severe rash, and penetration of the skin by the toxin requires less than a 10-minute exposure time. If you do come into contact with poison oak, immediate washing or attempting to absorb the oil with dirt are recommended. Touching clothing that has brushed against the plant is just as potent as touching the plant itself, so wash clothes in soap and hot water as soon as possible. If a rash develops, treat with hydrocortisone cream. For severe reactions, consult a physician.

Animal life: The mild climate of the foothills region is hospitable to a wide variety of creatures. Common woodland amphibians include three varieties of salamander and the California newt, an amphibian whose interesting mating ritual begins in mid-winter and continues into spring. Several varieties of lizards often scurry across dry and rocky slopes. Snakes are quite common to the region as well, the western rattlesnake receiving the most interest from humans.

Several rodents find a home in this zone, including brush rabbit, black-tailed jackrabbit, Audubon's cottontail, gray squirrel, dusky-footed wood rat, and deer mouse. Bats can often be seen patrolling the skies at dusk in search of insects. Medium-sized mammals such as raccoon, ringtail, gray fox, skunk, and coyote are familiar residents. Larger mammals in the foothills include mule deer and the seldom seen bobcat and mountain lion.

Numerous birds reside in the foothills —far too many to list even all of the most common species here. Some familiar raptors are red-tailed hawk, golden eagle, American kestrel, and great horned owl. California quail is the most common game bird, although hunting is not allowed within the parks. The turkey vulture, the ubiquitous "buzzard" in California skies, is also common here.

Montane Forest

Plant Life: Above the foothills region, a zone of mixed coniferous forest, composed of conifers and deciduous trees, extends across the west slope of the Sierra between roughly 4500 and 7500 feet. The two most prevalent conifers in this zone are ponderosa pine and white fir. Generally, ponderosa pine is found in relatively dry areas, while white fir occupies soils with more moisture. At higher elevations of the montane forest, Jeffrey pine replaces ponderosa pine. Closely related to the ponderosa, and also with needles in clusters of three, Jeffrey pine is better able to tolerate the colder temperatures and increased snowfall at higher altitudes. A host of other evergreens intermixes with these conifers, most often including sugar pine and incense cedar. Some of the most common deciduous trees in the montane forest are dogwood and black oak.

On the east side of the range, in the rain shadow of the Sierra crest, the montane forest is found between elevations of 7000 and 9000 feet. Stands are typically less dense than their western counterparts and are much less diverse. The forest is composed primarily of Jeffrey pine and white fir, although widely scattered examples of

PONDEROSA PINE
(Pinus ponderosa)

The three-needled ponderosa pine is the most common and widespread conifer in the western montane forest. The trees reach heights between 60 and 130 feet.

other conifers intermixed with them are not uncommon.

As expected, streamside environments within the montane forest harbor many more species of trees, shrubs, and plants. On the west side, a number of deciduous trees line the banks of streams and rivers, including quaking aspen, black cottonwood, bigleaf maple, nutmeg, laurel, Oregon ash, and numerous varieties of willow. Eastside riparian zones are home to quaking aspen, Fremont cottonwood, black cottonwood, and water birch.

Animal Life: The ensantina salamander, western toad, and Pacific tree frog are the three amphibians typically found in the montane forest. Reptiles include a variety of lizards and snakes, including the western rattlesnake which is common up to around 6000 feet.

Like the foothills, the montane forest is home to many rodents, including the broad-handed mole, Trowbridge shrew, deer mouse, pocket gopher, gray squirrel, northern flying squirrel, California ground squirrel, chipmunk, and dusky-footed wood rat. Bats also frequent the evening montane forest skies. In addition to the medium and large mammals that live in the

BLACK BEAR
(Ursus americanus)

Weighing up to 300 pounds, the black bear is the largest mammal in the Sierra, and is usually cinnamon or black in color. A female typically gives birth to two cubs every other winter. She cares for them through the summer and following winter, and forces them to fend for themselves the next spring. Male bears do not participate in raising the cubs, and would possibly kill and eat them if the mother did not fiercely protect them.

foothill zone, the porcupine, long-tailed weasel, and black bear also reside in the montane forest.

A wide assortment of birds lives in this zone including songbirds, woodpeckers, and several types of raptors.

Giant Sequoia Groves

Plant Life: The giant sequoia sets the Sierra Nevada apart from the rest of the world's forests. When Europeans first reported having seen trees of such stature, their claims were largely discounted by virtually all who had not seen a specimen first hand—even some who had couldn't believe their own eyes. A few trees were chopped down, cut into pieces, and sent to expositions where they were carefully reassembled, only to be viewed as hoaxes by the disbelieving public. Few humans could comprehend that a living tree could attain such size. Unfortunately, when lumbermen realized the size of the trees, they turned a lustful gaze toward the stately monarchs. Only after hundreds of sequoias met their doom, did they find that the brittle lumber of the giant sequoias was not commercially viable, and could be used for nothing more than mere fence posts and shakes. After an arduous battle that lasted many decades, the giant sequoia received appropriate protection. Today, the Big Trees are safe and secure in three national parks, a national monument, and a handful of state parks.

Not only is *Sequoiadendron giganteum* the largest tree by volume on the planet, in California the statuesque specimen only grows in 75 groves, on the west side of the Sierra Nevada. All but eight of the groves are found within the greater Sequoia/Kings Canyon region. The largest groves are Redwood Mountain in Kings Canyon and Giant Forest in Sequoia. Most of the largest individual specimens also occur within this region, with General Sherman receiving top honors, followed by Washington, General Grant, President, and Lincoln—all five within park boundaries. The largest trees by volume on the planet, giant sequoias

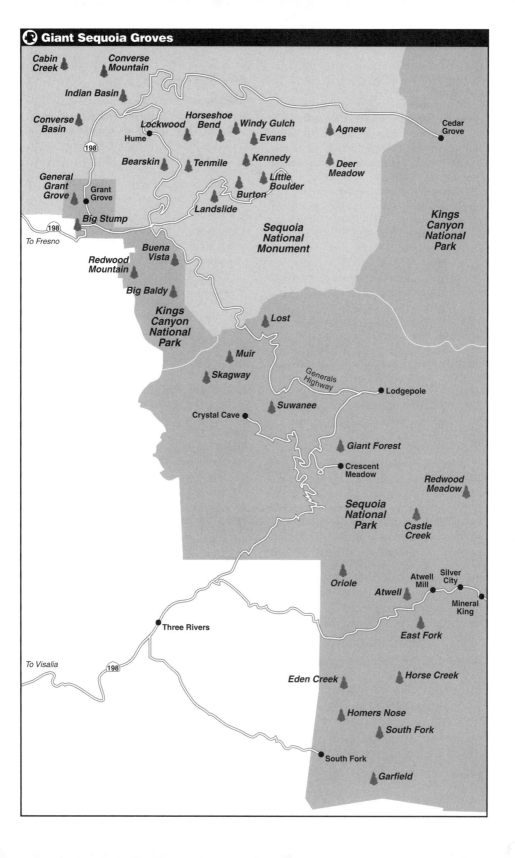

Giant Sequoia Groves

Cabin Creek
Converse Mountain
Indian Basin
Converse Basin
Lockwood
Horseshoe Bend
Windy Gulch
Agnew
Cedar Grove
Hume
Evans
198
Bearskin
Tenmile
Kennedy
Deer Meadow
General Grant Grove
Grant Grove
Little Boulder
Burton
Landslide
Big Stump
198
Sequoia National Monument
Kings Canyon National Park
To Fresno
Buena Vista
Redwood Mountain
Big Baldy
Kings Canyon National Park
Lost
Muir
Skagway
Generals Highway
Suwanee
Lodgepole
Crystal Cave
Giant Forest
Crescent Meadow
Redwood Meadow
Sequoia National Park
Castle Creek
Oriole
Atwell Mill
Silver City
Atwell
Mineral King
Three Rivers
East Fork
To Visalia
198
Eden Creek
Horse Creek
Homers Nose
South Fork
South Fork
Garfield

reach heights between 150 and 300 feet, and widths between 5 and 30 feet. The bark is cinnamon red with deep furrows; cones are 2 to 3 inches and oblong in shape.

The giant sequoia grows in mixed coniferous forests of white fir, sugar pine, incense cedar, and dogwood rather than in pure stands. Somewhat less drought resistant than other Sierra conifers, the big trees are found only in areas of moist soil, between elevations of 4500 and 8400 feet. Typical precipitation in sequoia groves varies from 45 to 60 inches per year, but the soil's ability to hold moisture throughout dry summers is perhaps a more important element to sequoia survival.

Although the sequoia has an extensive root system, their roots are generally shallow in relation to their immense size. Most trees meet their eventual demise by simply toppling over, rather than by succumbing to the more common tree maladies of disease, infestation, or forest fire. The characteristically thick sequoia bark makes the trees highly resistant to both insects and fire. Fire rarely does more than leave a black scar on the trunk.

Forest fires are in fact beneficial to giant sequoias. Their small cones require extreme heat in order to open and release the oatmeal-sized seeds. In addition, fire clears away debris on the forest floor and small plants that compete with sequoia saplings for light and moisture. Although fire suppression was the rule of the past, nowadays the Park Service intentionally sets fires in sequoia groves and elsewhere in the park to restore this natural process and to reduce the accumulation of forest fuels that feed unnaturally intense wildfires.

Animal Life: Same as montane forest zone.

Beaver

Red Fir Forest

Plant Life: Unlike the mixture of trees in the montane forest, the stately red fir is often the sole species of the climax forest on the west side of the Sierra. Growing to between 60 and 180 feet, red fir is susceptible to lightning strikes. The trees are generally 2 to 4 feet in width, and their bark is maroon-brown with red furrows. Cones are 6 to 8 inches long. The tall trees can form such dense cover that competitors and many understory plants cannot survive—any plant that does survive must be shade tolerant. Where the red fir is less dense, lodgepole pine, western white pine, Jeffrey pine, western juniper, and quaking aspen may join the forest. (One small stand of mountain hemlock occurs in this zone within the park.) White fir may intermingle along the lower edge of the zone. White and red firs are similar in appearance; the easiest way to differentiate between them is by examining the bark—maroon-brown on red fir and grayish on white fir.

Red fir prefers deep, well-drained soil, and is found in the southern Sierra between approximately 7000 and 9000 feet in elevations, from Kern County northward. The species thrives in areas of the range that receive the highest amounts of precipitation, particularly in the form of winter snowfall.

Animal Life: Inhabitants of the higher elevations of the upper forest zones must adapt to more severe weather conditions and periodically scarce food supplies. Common amphibians are limited to two varieties each of salamander, frog, and toad. Reptiles include garter snake and three varieties of lizard.

Ordinary small mammals one might expect to encounter include deer mouse, pocket gopher, vole, shrew, broad-handed mole, pika, chipmunk, chickaree, Belding ground squirrel, golden-mantled ground squirrel, northern flying squirrel, mountain beaver, white-tailed jackrabbit, and yellow-bellied marmot. Bats are quite common around lakeshores and meadows. Medium-

MULE DEER
(Odocoileus hemionus)

Mule deer are numerous in the southern Sierra, since their main predators, the grizzly bear and wolf, are now extinct in the region. Mountain lions are their most common predators today. Starvation and disease are other causes of death for mule deer. Mature males may exceed 200 pounds. Each March, males shed their antlers and start to grow them again in April.

sized animals in the upper forests include red fox, porcupine, coyote, long-tailed weasel, fisher, ermine, wolverine, badger, and pine marten. Black bear and mule deer are frequently seen larger mammals. The Sierra bighorn sheep lives in the zone but tends to be very reclusive.

Although not as numerous as in the lower zones, a vast number of birds find a home in the upper forest belt. Among some of the more interesting species are the blue grouse, the dipper, and the mountain bluebird. The most common (and occasionally obnoxious) bird known to backpackers in this zone is the Steller's jay, whose bold exploits around humans are often rewarded by a beak full of gorp.

Lodgepole Pine Forest

Plant Life: Perhaps no tree is more closely associated with the High Sierra than the lodgepole pine. The versatile lodgepole is found between 8000 and 11,000 feet in the southern Sierra, flourishing in soils where red fir struggles—either too wet or too dry. In stark contrast to red fir, which is almost exclusively Californian, the two-needled lodgepole pine is one of the most widespread trees in the American West. It is commonly found in exclusive stands, as is red fir, but intermingles with western white pine and a few whitebark pines in higher elevations, and with red fir in lower elevations. In areas of high groundwater, quaking aspen and lodgepole grow together. On the east side of the range, lodgepoles are quite common between 9000 and 11,000 feet, where western white pine is the most familiar neighbor.

Animal Life: Similar to red fir zone.

Subalpine Zone

Plant Life: Occurring between roughly 9500 and 12,000 feet, the subalpine zone straddles the Sierra crest and bridges the gap between the mighty forests of the lower altitudes and the austere realm above timberline.

The most dominant conifer in this zone is the interesting foxtail pine, with its characteristic pendulous branches. This five-needled pine is similar in appearance to the bristlecone pine. It occurs only in Inyo and Tulare counties in the southern Sierra, and in the Klamath Mountains of northern California. Trees grow to between 20 and 45 feet, and their cones are purplish and prickly, 2 to 5 inches long. The foxtail pine occasionally appears in pure stands along the eastern fringe of Sequoia National Park and along the Kern River. Its most common associate is the majestic whitebark pine.

LODGEPOLE PINE
(Pinus contorta, var. murrayana)

Tall and thin, lodgepoles are two-needled pines that reach heights of 50 to 100 feet. Their bark is pale gray and their cones are 1 to 2 inches long.

This multi-trunked tree grows in harsh conditions just below timberline, and often resembles a windblown shrub. Less common associates include western white pine, lodgepole pine, and limber pine.

Forests are only one part of the diverse subalpine region. Mountain lakes, craggy peaks, and granite boulders and slabs are other common features of the landscape. Numerous subalpine meadows harbor a vast array of wildflowers and a remarkably varied selection of grasses and sedges.

Animal Life: Similar to red fir zone.

Alpine Zone

Plant Life: The alpine zone occurs at the highest elevations of the Sierra, where the growing season is measured in weeks rather than months. Harsh conditions characterize the alpine zone, and lower temperatures and cloudier skies mean that snow lingers in here, although the alpine zone receives less snowfall than lower regions. At altitudes above 12,000 feet, frost can occur at any time during the summer and cool temperatures, nearly constant winds, and a significant lack of precipitation produce desert-like conditions. Generally poor soil, mostly granitic, further limits the number of species able to adapt to this climate.

Most alpine plants have adapted to their environment by developing a low-growing, compact, and drought-tolerant demeanor. This allows the plants to avoid the strongest winds, grow closer to the warmth of the soil and survive on small amounts of moisture. In addition, most alpine plants are perennial as opposed to annual, which means they don't have to reproduce an entire new plant each year. Vegetation in this zone can be divided into two classifications: alpine meadow and alpine rock.

Alpine meadows are common in the upper realm of the Sierra where a sufficient layer of moist soil is present. Meadows are composed principally of sedges, with alpine sedge and common sedge the most usual,

YELLOW-BELLIED MARMOT
(Marmota flaviventris)

The most common mammal in the alpine zone, marmots are often seen sunbathing on rocks. They are gray or brown on the back, dull yellow on the underside, with white around the eyes, and a dark band above the nose. Marmots utter a sharp whistle when alarmed, which accounts for the common name of "whistle pig."

and a limited number of grasses. A wide array of wildflowers put on a showy display during the brief summer, capitalizing on the greater amount of available moisture. Among them is the Sierra primrose, an alpine wildflower that prefers moist rocky soils and has reddish blossoms on a 1- to 4-inch stem. A limited variety of shrubs is found in small groupings in the alpine community. Among them are alpine and snow willows, laurel, and heather.

Vegetation grows in small patches in alpine rock communities, unlike the large swaths of foliage that are common in alpine meadows. Open gravel flats and scree areas produce a smattering of alpine plants. The protected micro-climates of boulder fields often are more suitable to the survival of a diverse group of plants; wildflowers are the most common, but a few shrubs grow in the rock community as well.

Animal Life: Aside from insects and invertebrates, there are few animals that find a home in the rarified alpine zone, where food and shelter are extremely limited. The only common residents are the heather vole, yellow-bellied marmot, and pika.

Although many different types of birds frequent the alpine zone, only the rosy finch is as common in the alpine zone as in the upper forest zones. Sierra bighorn sheep may venture to these heights during the summer, but generally prefer areas at or below timberline. Black bears that have become unnaturally accustomed to the food of backpackers may also ascend to this zone in search of treats.

Pinyon-Juniper Woodland

Plant Life: On the east side of the Sierra, between roughly 6000 and 9000 feet, lies the pinyon-juniper woodland. In the rain shadow on the east side of the Sierra crest, this zone receives little precipitation, a mere 5 to 15 inches per year. Most of the moisture falls as winter snow, with a random thunderstorm the only possibility of breaking up the usual long, dry summer. This zone is composed primarily of widely scattered, singleleaf pinyon pine, with Sierra juniper and curl-leaf mountain mahogany the two most common associates. Trees often grow in the form of large shrubs. Sagebrush, rabbitbrush, and bitterbrush commonly grow in the understory.

Spring and early summer may bring a colorful display of wildflowers to pinyon-

SINGLELEAF PINYON PINE
(Pinus monophylla)

The only single-needled pine in the Sierra, the singleleaf pinyon pine reaches between 20 and 25 feet in height; their spherical-shaped cones are 1.5 to 2 inches in length. The Piutes ate the seeds of the pinyon pine as a staple of their diet. Pine nuts, as we know them, are a gourmet food item in modern-day grocery stores.

COYOTE
(Canas latrans)

Highly adaptable and intelligent mammals, coyotes are commonly associated with the American West, but have extended their native range beyond its former borders. Although they may take a weak or sick deer on occasion, coyotes subsist as omnivores on a wide-ranging diet. Their whelps and howls are commonly heard after sundown.

juniper woodlands, including lupine, phlox, paintbrush and mule ears.

Along eastern Sierra streams at this elevation, a thick display of wildflowers, shrubs, and trees grow in stark contrast to the area immediately beyond the riparian zone. Quaking aspen, cottonwood, willow, oak, birch, and ash are common streamside trees, which may intermix with conifers from the forest zones above. Currant, wild rose, and a variety of willows are typical shrubs.

Animal Life: A wide variety of amphibians, reptiles, birds, and insects are at home in the pinyon-juniper woodland, as are a vast number of mammals. Small mammals, including a number of different species of mice, squirrel, vole, rabbit, shrew, and chipmunk, are very common. Larger mammals include coyote, skunk, badger and mule deer. Birds, including the sage grouse and red-tailed hawk, are plentiful as well.

Sagebrush scrub

Plant Life: Fortunately, only a few east side trails pass through the sagebrush scrub zone, which is often unbearably hot and dry during the usual hiking and backpacking season. This zone usually receives less than 12 inches of precipitation a year, most of which falls during the winter months. A welcome thunderstorm may water the parched ground during the summer, releasing the unforgettably pungent aroma from wet sagebrush.

At first glance, the grayish-green sagebrush creates a seemingly unbroken carpet of vegetation on the foothills above Owens Valley. A closer inspection reveals a mixture of bitterbrush, rabbitbrush, desert peach, and spiny hopsage interspersed with the sagebrush. Before overgrazing in the west replaced native perennial grasses with invasive annuals, the sagebrush zone was filled with a healthy mixture of the native bunchgrasses. Following wet winters and springs, the high desert produces a vivid display of wildflowers in late spring and early summer.

Animal Life: Similar to pinyon-juniper zone.

Geology

Although the origins of the Sequoia and Kings Canyon region may be rather speculative, as we have no human witness to the process, at least geologists can tell us with certainty the composition of the rock that forms the region's soaring peaks and deep canyons.

Even a cursory examination by the untrained eye reveals that the Sierra is overwhelmingly composed of granitic rocks. These light-colored, salt-and-pepper speckled, and coarse-grained rocks include granite, granodiorite, and tonalite (formerly called quartz diorite). They also contain varying degrees of minerals, such as quartz, feldspar, biotite and hornblende. The Sierra Nevada Batholith, as geologists commonly refer to this large mass of granitic rock, was formed when molten magma below the

Negotiating talus on the Lamarck Col cross-country route

Geologic Types	Example	Location	Access
Granitic Rocks	Moro Rock	Giant Forest	road
	Great Western Divide	Panoramic Point— Grant Grove	road/trail
	Mt. Whitney Area	Sequoia N.P.	road/trail
Metamorphic Rocks	Kaweah Peaks Ridge	Sequoia N.P.	trail
	Mineral King Peaks	Mineral King	road/trail
	Crystal Cave	West of Giant Forest	road
	Boyden Cave Sequoia N.P.	Kings Canyon, Hwy. 180	road
Volcanic Rocks	Big Pine Volcanic Field	South of Big Pine, West of US 395	road
Water-sculpted canyons	South Fork Kings River	Kings Canyon, Hwy. 180	road
	Middle Fork Kings River	North of Kings Canyon	trail
	Middle Fork Kaweah River	Ash Mountain/Foothills Area	road
Glacier-sculpted canyons	Tokopah Valley	Lodgepole	road/trail
	Kern Canyon	Sequoia N.P.—SE quadrant	trail
	LeConte Canyon/ Evolution Valley	Kings Canyon N.P.— John Muir Trail	road/trail
Glaciers	Palisade Glacier	Palisades— N. Fork Big Pine Creek	trail
	Middle Palisade Glacier	Palisades— S. Fork Big Pine Creek	trail
	Goethe Glacier	Glacier Divide— Humphreys Basin	trail

earth's surface cooled and crystallized. The batholith, over 300 miles long and more than 50 miles wide at some points, was subsequently uplifted and exposed. Today, the characteristic granite of the Sierra Nevada is evident across the range.

A much smaller proportion of the rock in the Sierra Nevada is metamorphic. Dark in color and variegated in appearance, metamorphic rocks are older than granitic rocks. Remnants of these rocks are scattered across the Sequoia and Kings Canyon region, and four distinct metamorphic terranes have been identified in the area. A number of caves, including Crystal Cave near Giant Forest and Boyden Cave near Kings Canyon, have been discovered in concentrations of marble, a type of metamorphic rock.

An even smaller percentage of the region's geologic composition includes volcanic rock. Within the park boundaries it's almost nonexistent, the lone exception being a very old intrusion occurring near Windy Peak along the Middle Fork of the Kings River. Smatterings of additional volcanic activity are evident in small pockets west of Kings Canyon and southeast of Sequoia near Golden Trout Creek. The most noticeable evidence of volcanism in the region occurs east of Kings Canyon in the Big Pine Volcanic Field, where passing motorists on Highway 395 can see cinder cones and lava flows.

The Sequoia and Kings Canyon area is home to some of the most impressive canyons in all of North America. Modern conclusions recognize the importance of both stream erosion and glaciation in the formation of these canyons. At lower elevations, the erosive power of water is clearly evident in V-shaped canyons such as the South and Middle Forks of the Kings River. At the higher elevations of Sequoia and Kings Canyon, the characteristically U-shaped canyons reflect the role of glaciation.

Speculation on the function of glaciers in the sculpting of the Sierra Nevada is as old as John Muir himself. Whatever their importance in the past, the glaciers that exist today occupy a very small percentage of territory in the uppermost realms of the High Sierra, usually above 12,000 feet on the north and east faces of the highest peaks. Despite their lack of volume, these glaciers add touches of alpine beauty to the rocky summits and dramatic faces of the range's tallest mountains. The largest glacier in the Sierra is the Palisade Glacier, a pocket of ice less than 1 square mile in size, but significant enough to qualify the surrounding Palisade peaks as part of the foremost alpine climbing area in the Sierra, luring alpinists from all over the world.

Climate

Compared to other North American mountain ranges, the Sierra Nevada is blessed with an abundance of mild, dry, and sunny weather. Summer is particularly fine, as 95% of the yearly precipitation falls between November and March. Summer thunderstorms account for the remainder, but are much more sporadic than those in other ranges, the Rocky Mountains, for instance. Summertime temperatures are generally mild, although they vary considerably from the lowlands to the alpine heights.

Because of its relatively low elevation, the foothills region provides excellent off-season hiking opportunities. Spring is perhaps the best time of year to visit, when the High Sierra is covered with the winter snowpack; grasses are green after winter rains, wildflowers are blooming, and the oak trees are leafing out. Fall is also a pleasant hiking season, when the summer heat has abated, and even winter in the foothills allows for hiking, since there are a few trails that stay snow-free all year. However, summer can be uncomfortably hot. Hikers are recommended to get an early start or plan on taking a dip in the cool waters of one of the rivers and streams during the heat of the day.

Above the foothills, snow-free hiking opportunities don't present themselves until May, when the road into Kings Canyon is opened and trails in Grant Grove and Giant Forest start to shake their winter mantle. Once the spring thaw is underway, the snow line steadily marches up the mountainsides, opening more trails along the way. By June, most west side paths are accessible into the frontcountry of Sequoia and Kings Canyon, but the High Sierra usually remains snow-covered until mid-July.

When the snow has mostly melted in the highest parts of the Sierra, backpacking season begins in earnest. Although summers in the Sierra usually bring dry, sunny days, thunderstorms are not uncommon, and backpackers should be prepared for changeable conditions, including the rare summer storm system. Afternoon highs in the summer often creep into the sixties and low seventies at the upper elevations, and if the day is sunny, the temperature will feel even warmer, thanks to the effects of increased solar radiation.

Warm weather usually persists in the High Sierra from July into September. Pleasant Indian summer conditions generally continue for another month or so, but the reliably good weather usually comes to an end at upper elevations by the end of October. Autumn is a fine time to enjoy the trails and footpaths the parks' western edge. By November of most years, the Sierra has seen the first snowfall of the season and recreationists customarily turn their attention to winter pursuits. However, some years the first snow doesn't arrive until January.

Backpackers negotiate the snow-covered trail on the way to Bishop Pass

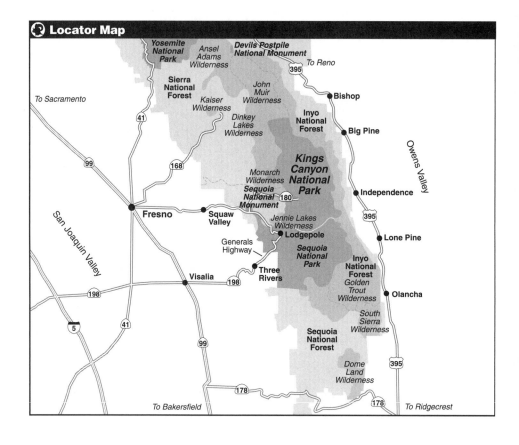

CHAPTER **2**

Traveling the Backcountry

Although this book focuses on Kings Canyon National Park and surrounding wilderness areas, the National Park service manages Kings Canyon and adjoining Sequoia National Park as a single entity. The information in this chapter regarding fees, facilities, regulations, maps, permits, and bears applies to both parks. Because of the proximity of the parks to each other, locations of visitor centers, ranger stations, and campgrounds in Sequoia National Park may be of use to visitors to Kings Canyon.

Hikers study the map above Palisade Basin

Fees

Since Sequoia and Kings Canyon national parks are managed as a unit, visitors pay a single fee to enter both parks. Fees are collected at the Ash Mountain Entrance Station where Highway 198 becomes the Generals Highway, the Lookout Point Entrance Station on Mineral King Highway, and the Big Stump Entrance on Highway 180. If you enter at a station that is not staffed, be prepared to pay the fee upon exiting.

Type of Pass	Fee	Duration	Terms
Standard Pass	$10 per vehicle $5 on foot, motorcycle, bicycle or bus	7 days	Access to Sequoia/Kings Canyon
Annual Pass	$20	1 year	Access to Sequoia/Kings Canyon
National Parks Pass	$50	1 year	Access to all national parks
Golden Eagle Pass	$65	1 year	Access to all national parks, monuments, recreation areas, historic sites & wildlife refuges
Golden Age Passport	$10 (U.S. citizens or residents 62 or over)	Lifetime	Access to all national parks
Golden Access Pass	Free (U.S. citizens or residents who are blind or permanently disabled)	Lifetime	Access to all national parks, monuments, recreation areas, historic sites & wildlife refuges

About Kings Canyon National Park and Surrounding Forest Service Lands

Tourist-related facilities in Kings Canyon and Sequoia aren't as developed or as concentrated as those in Yosemite, the more famous and more frequently visited neighbor to the north. Most hikers and backpackers will find the more sedate atmosphere of Kings Canyon and Sequoia is a definite improvement over the typical summertime zoo of Yosemite. Even so, the two southern Sierra parks offer visitors a wide range of services.

Information

Sequoia and Kings Canyon national parks:

(559) 565-3341 *(24 hours)*
www.nps.gov/seki.com

USFS Headquarters:

Sequoia National Forest
900 West Grand Avenue
Porterville, CA 93257
(559) 784-1500
(559) 565-3341
www.fs.fed.us/r5/sequoia

Sierra National Forest
1600 Tollhouse Road
Clovis, CA 93612
(559) 297-0706
www.fs.fed.us/r5/sierra/

Inyo National Forest
873 North Main Street
Bishop, CA 93514
(760) 873-2400
www.fs.fed.us/r5/inyo/

Park Service Ranger Stations and Visitor Centers:

Mineral King Ranger Station
Open daily 7 A.M. – 3:30 P.M.,
June to mid-September
Maps, books, bear canisters, first aid, wilderness permits

Ash Mountain Visitor Center
Open daily 8 A.M. – 5 P.M., summer;
8 A.M. – 4:30 P.M., winter
(559) 565-3135
Exhibits, maps, books, bear canisters, first aid, wilderness permits

Giant Forest Museum
Open daily 8 A.M. – 6 P.M., summer;
9 A.M. – 4:30 P.M., winter;
9 A.M. – 5 P.M., spring and fall
(559) 565-4480

Lodgepole Visitor Center
Open daily 8 A.M. – 6 P.M., early spring
to late fall; weekends only in winter
(559) 565-4436
Exhibits, maps, books, first aid

Lodgepole Wilderness Office
Open daily 7 A.M. – 4 P.M.,
May through September
(559) 565-3341
Wilderness permits, bear canisters, maps

Grant Grove Visitor Center
Open daily 8 A.M. – 6 P.M., summer;
9 A.M. – 4:30 P.M., spring and fall;
9:30 A.M. – 4:30 P.M., winter
(559) 565-4307
Exhibits, maps, books, bear canisters, first aid, wilderness permits

Cedar Grove Visitor Center
Open daily 9 A.M. – 5 P.M.,
May through October
(559) 565-3793
Maps, books, first aid

Roads End
Open daily 7 A.M. – 4 P.M.,
late May through September
Wilderness permits, bear canisters, maps

Forest Service District Ranger Stations

West Side	East Side
Sierra National Forest:	**Inyo National Forest:**
Pineridge Ranger District	**Mt. Whitney Ranger District**
PO Box 559	PO Box 8
Prather, CA 93651	Lone Pine, CA 93545
(559) 855-5360	(760) 876-6200
Sequoia National Forest:	**Inyo National Forest:**
Hume Lake Ranger District	**White Mountain Ranger District**
35860 Kings Canyon Road (Hwy. 180)	798 N. Main
Dunlap, CA 93621	Bishop, CA 93514
(559) 338-2251	(760) 873-2500

Lodging

A wide variety of overnight accommodations are available inside the park. Advance reservations are strongly recommended during peak season, as occupancy rates are high. A few of the park's lodges remain open all year. Communities surrounding the parks, such as Fresno, Visalia, and Three Rivers on the west side and Lone Pine, Independence, Big Pine, and Bishop on the east side, offer additional lodging options.

**Kings Canyon National Park—
Grant Grove:**

Village Cabins, Meadowcamp (KCPS)
(Open all year)
John Muir Lodge (KCPS)
(Open all year)
(559) 335-5500
www.sequoia-kingscanyon.com

**Kings Canyon National Park—
Kings Canyon:**

Cedar Grove Lodge (KCPS)
(Open May to October)
(559) 335-5500
www.sequoia-kingscanyon.com

Giant Sequoia National Monument:
(Open all year)

Montecito-Sequoia Lodge
(800) 227-9900
www.montecitosequoia.com

Stony Creek Lodge (KCPS)
(Open mid-May to October)
(558) 335-5500
www.sequoia-kingscanyon.com

Kings Canyon Lodge
(Open April to November)
(559) 335-2405

Backcountry Lodges:

Bearpaw Meadow Camp (DNPS)
(Open mid-June to mid-September)
(888) 252-5757 *(reservations required)*
www.visitsequoia.com

Pear Lake Ski Hut (SNHA)
(Open December to April)
(559) 565-3759
www.sequoiahistory.org

Campgrounds

Both parks offer an extensive array of campgrounds, and the surrounding national forests have many additional campgrounds.

Reservations (National Park Service)
(800) 365-2267 *(4 A.M. – 4 P.M. PST)*
www.reservations.nps.gov

Reservations (USFS)
(877) 444-6777
www.reserveusa.com

West Side

Sequoia National Park

Mineral King:
Atwell Mill
Cold Springs
Foothills:
Potwisha
Buckeye Flat
South Fork
Lodgepole Area:
Lodgepole
Dorst

Kings Canyon National Park

Grant Grove:
Azalea
Crystal Springs
Sunset
Cedar Grove:
Sentinel
Sheep Creek
Canyon View
Moraine

Giant Sequoia National Monument (USFS)

Hume Lake Area:
Princess
Hume Lake
Tenmile
Landslide
Big Meadows Road/Stony Creek Area:
Stony Creek
Upper Stony
Horse Camp
Buck Rock
Big Meadows

East Side

Mt. Whitney Ranger District (USFS)

Cottonwood Pass
Golden Trout
Lone Pine
Whitney Portal
Whitney Trailhead
Upper Grays Meadow
Lower Grays Meadow
Onion Valley

White Mountain Ranger District (USFS)

Sage Flat
Upper Sage Flat
Big Pine Creek
Palisade Glacier
Clyde Glacier
Big Trees
Forks
Four Jeffrey
Intake 2
Bishop Park
Sabrina
Willow
North Lake

Pack Trips

A number of private individuals and companies provide pack service for trips into the parks and the surrounding terrain. Each outfit operates with a permit from the Park Service or Forest Service agency that governs the area. It is a good idea to check with the governing agency about an outfitter's current status, as permitees may change from year to year.

West Side	East Side

West Side

Mineral King Pack Station (SNP)
(559) 561-3039 *(summer)*
(520) 855-5885 *(off season)*

Wolverton (SNP)
(559) 565-3039 *(summer)*
(520) 855-5885 *(off season)*

Horse Corral (GSNM)
(559) 565-3404 *(summer)*
(559) 564-6429 *(off season)*

Grant Grove (KCNP)
(559) 335-9292 *(summer)*
(559) 337-2314 *(off season)*

Cedar Grove (KCNP)
(559) 565-3464 *(summer)*
(559) 337-2314 *(off season)*

East Side

Mt. Whitney Pack Trains
PO Box 248
Bishop, CA 93515
(760) 872-8331
www.rockcreekpackstation.com

Cottonwood Pack Station
Star Route 1, Box 81-A
Independence, CA 93526
(760) 878-2015

Sequoia Kings Pack Trains
PO Box 209
Independence, CA 93526
(760) 387-2797 or (800) 962-0775
www.395.com/berners/

Bishop Pack Outfitters
247 Cataract Road
Bishop, CA 93514
(760) 873-8877

Glacier Pack Train
PO Box 321
Big Pine, CA 93513
(760) 938-2538

Pine Creek Pack Station
PO Box 968
Bishop, CA 93515
(800) 962-0775

Rainbow Pack Station
600 S. Main St.
Bishop, CA 93514
(760) 873-8877

Rock Creek Pack Station
PO Box 248
Bishop, CA 93515
(760) 935-4493 *(summer)*
(760) 872-8331 *(off season)*
www.rockcreekpackstation.com

Additional Park Facilities

Post Offices: Lodgepole, Grant Grove

Showers and Laundry: Lodgepole, Grant Grove, Cedar Grove

Groceries & Supplies: Lodgepole, Grant Grove, Cedar Grove

Snack Bar/Deli: Lodgepole, Grant Grove, Cedar Grove

Restaurants: Wuksachi, Grant Grove

Gasoline: To reduce environmental concerns, gasoline is no longer available within the parks, except for emergencies. Motorists approaching Sequoia or Kings Canyon from the west should fill up in Visalia or Fresno, where prices are reasonable. Closer to the parks, the cost rises considerably. Those in desperate need will find gas just outside the parks at Three Rivers, Hume Lake, Clingan's Junction, and Kings Canyon Lodge.

Eastside travelers will not find any bargain prices at gas stations in the smaller communities along U.S. 395. (You'll get charged the least in Bishop.)

Hume Lake and Kings Canyon area from Park Ridge

Wilderness Ethics and Trail Courtesy

The essence of American wilderness evokes notions of wild and undeveloped places where humans are simply visitors who leave no trace of their presence. The "Leave only footprints, take only photographs" motto of the back-to-earth 1970s embodies such a principle. The goal of every visitor, hiker, backpacker, and equestrian alike, should be to leave a wilderness area as it was found, if not better. The following backcountry guidelines should help keep the wild in wilderness.

Camping

- Camp a minimum of 100 feet from any water source.
- Choose a campsite away from trails.

- Never build improvements (fireplaces, rock walls, drainage swales etc.).
- Camp on exposed dirt or rock surfaces, not on vegetation.
- Use only downed wood for fires; never cut trees (dead or alive).
- Use only existing fire rings.
- Never leave a fire unattended.
- Fully extinguish all campfires by thoroughly soaking with water.

Sanitation

- Bury waste 6 inches deep, a minimum of 100 feet from trails, and 500 feet from water sources.
- Pack out toilet paper, or burn in areas where fires are permissible.
- Cook only the amount of food you can eat to avoid disposing of leftovers.
- Wash and rinse dishes, clothes, and yourself a minimum of 100 feet away

Great Western Divide as seen from Mitchell Peak

from water sources; never wash in lakes or streams.

- Pack out all trash—do not attempt to burn plastic or foil packaging.
- Filter, boil, or purify all drinking water.

On the Trail

- Stay on the trail—don't cut switchbacks.
- Preserve the serenity of the backcountry—avoid making loud noises.
- Yield the right-of-way to uphill hikers.
- Yield the right-of-way to equestrians—step off the trail, downhill.
- Avoid traveling in large groups.
- Because trails can change, either from natural or human causes, hikers should check with NPS visitor centers for updates before starting a hike.

Regulations for Kings Canyon and Sequoia National Parks

- Group size is limited to 15 people (10 in Redwood Canyon).
- Pets, weapons, wheeled vehicles and motorized equipment are prohibited.
- Maximum number of stock is 20.
- No pets allowed on trails.
- Campfires are restricted in many areas of the parks.
- Food must be stored so that it is completely inaccessible to bears.
- No camping within 100 feet (33 meters) of lakes or streams.
- No hunting.

Maps

USGS Topographic Maps: A number of recreational maps are available for hikers and backpackers in the popular Sequoia and Kings Canyon region, including the maps provided in this guide. The 7.5-minute quadrangles published by the United States Geological Survey are the most accurate and usable maps available. The USGS maps are available directly from the USGS or from private retailers. Park Service and Forest Service ranger stations generally sell the maps that correspond to areas within their districts. Long-distance hikers may favor maps at a larger scale, since the 1:24,000 scale of the 7.5-minute quads requires carrying numerous maps for extended backpacks.

Thanks to the advancement of computer software, programs are also available for PC users that utilize the USGS quads as a base and have numerous features for the customization of personal maps. The only disadvantage of the software versus the actual USGS maps is the inability of most computer printers to match the 22" x 29" size of the 7.5-minute maps. Recently, some outdoor retailers have installed kiosks where recreationists can select and print comparable maps onsite.

Government cutbacks may curtail or ultimately doom the services of the USGS, but until such a time recreationists can order maps and procure information from the following addresses:

USGS Information Services
Box 25286
Boulder, CO 80225
(888) ASK-USGS
www.usgs.gov/

The Map Center
1995 University Avenue
Berkeley, CA 94704
(510) 841-MAPS

USGS Map Name	Trip Numbers
1. Triple Divide Peak	26
2. Mt. Kaweah	26
3. General Grant Grove	1, 2, 3, 4, 13, 14, 15, 16, 17, 18, 19
4. Muir Grove	5, 6, 8
5. Mt. Silliman	6, 8, 9
6. Sphinx Lakes	26
7. Mt. Brewer	26, 27
8. Mt. Williamson	26
9. Hume	11, 12
10. Wren Peak	10
11. Cedar Grove	20, 29, 30, 31, 32
12. The Sphinx	21, 22, 23, 24, 25, 26, 27, 28, 33, 34, 35, 36, 42
13. Mt. Clarence King	26, 27, 28, 36, 40, 41, 42, 44, 61
14. Kearsarge Peak	39, 40, 41, 42, 43, 44
15. Slide Bluffs	32
16. Marion Peak	34
17. Mt. Pinchot	45, 46, 61
18. Aberdeen	45, 46
19. Fish Springs	46, 47, 48
20. Courtright Reservoir	37
21. Blackcap Mountain	37, 38
22. Mt. Goddard	38, 62
23. North Palisade	50, 51, 52, 61, 62
24. Split Mountain	47, 48, 49, 50, 61
25. Ward Mountain	37, 38
26. Mt. Henry	37, 38, 62
27. Mt. Darwin	56, 58, 59, 60, 62
28. Mt. Thompson	50, 51, 52, 53, 54, 55, 56, 57
29. Coyote Flat	49, 50
30. Florence Lake	38
31. Mt. Tom	60

15-minute Topographic Maps: Before the 7.5-minute maps became the USGS standard, 15-minute maps (1:62,500) were available to the general public for recreational use. Wilderness Press still offers one 15-minute quad in the Sequoia and Kings Canyon area, *Mt. Pinchot*, which is printed on plastic and covers the same scope as four 7.5-minute maps: *Mt. Pinchot, Aberdeen, Mt. Clarence King, Kearsarge Peak.*

The 15-minute *Mt. Pinchot* map may be purchased from:

Wilderness Press
1200 5th Street
Berkeley, CA 94710
(800) 443-7227
www.wildernesspress.com

Forest Service Maps:

John Muir Wilderness, Sequoia and Kings Canyon Wilderness. ($10, 1:63,360) The USFS publishes a 3-sheet set of topographic maps at 1 inch = 1 mile that backcountry travelers may find useful for trip planning or trail use. These three large maps cover nearly all of the trails described in this book and its companion guide to Kings Canyon, with the exception of the Grant Grove and Redwood Mountain regions of Kings Canyon.

A Guide to the Monarch Wilderness & Jennie Lakes Wilderness ($6, 1:36,180) A 1 inch = .5 mile topographic map of the two wilderness areas on the southwest of Kings Canyon National Park.

Golden Trout Wilderness, South Sierra Wilderness ($6, 1:63,360) A 1 inch = 1 mile topographic map of the wilderness areas south of Sequoia National Park.

Inyo National Forest ($6, 1:126,720) A .5 inch = 1 mile map of the forest lands east of Sequoia and Kings Canyon national parks.

Sequoia National Forest ($6, 1:126,720) A .5 inch = 1 mile map of forest lands west of Sequoia and Kings Canyon national parks.

Sierra National Forest ($6, 1:126,720) A .5 inch = 1 mile map of lands west of Kings Canyon National Park.

Sequoia Natural History Association Maps: The SNHA publishes a set of small foldout maps with concise descriptions of dayhikes for popular areas of the parks, including Mineral King, Giant Forest, Lodgepole, Grant Grove and Cedar Grove. These maps, available from park visitor centers and stores, at the time of writing were selling for $2.50 apiece.

Tom Harrison Maps: Tom's maps are some of the best recreational maps available from the private sector. Maps pertaining to the Sequoia and Kings Canyon region include *Bishop Pass* ($8.95, 1:47,520), *John Muir Trail Pack* ($18.95. 1:63,360), *Kings Canyon High Country* ($8.95, 1:63,360), *Mt. Whitney High Country* ($8.95, 1:63,360), *Mt. Whitney Zone* ($8.95, 1: 31,680), *Sequoia & Kings Canyon National Parks* ($8.95, 1:125,000). Maps for the Golden Trout Wilderness, Sierra National Forest, and Sequoia National Forest are in the works. Check out the website at www.tomharrisonmaps.com/.

Wilderness Permits

Dayhikers

Hikers will not need a permit to enter Kings Canyon National Park or the surrounding wilderness areas for one-day excursions.

Overnight Backpackers

Sequoia and Kings Canyon National Parks

All overnight users entering the park backcountry must obtain a valid wilderness permit from the ranger station closest to the trailhead.

Reserved Permits: Approximately 75% of the daily trailhead quota may be reserved ahead of time for a $15 charge, starting March 1 and until three weeks prior to departure. Remaining permits are available on a first-come, first-served basis. Reserved permits may be picked up after 1:00 P.M. on the afternoon preceding the beginning of the hike and will be held until 9:00 A.M. the morning of the hike. If you know you will be delayed past 9:00 A.M., call the ranger station to hold your reserved permit.

Walk-in Permits: Walk-in permits may also be obtained beginning 1:00 P.M. the day before the start of the trip. More openings may be available after 9:00 A.M. the morning of the trip if there are any unclaimed reservations. As a rule, permits will not be written late in the afternoon since distances to the first campground on most trails require several hours of hiking.

> **Wilderness Permit Reservations**
> Sequoia and Kings Canyon N.P.
> HCR 89 Box 60
> Three Rivers, CA 93271
> (559) 565-3708
> Fax: (559) 565-4239

Inyo National Forest— East Side Entry for John Muir and Golden Trout Wildernesses

Wilderness permits are required throughout the year for all overnight visits. All trails entering the wilderness have quotas in effect between May 1st and November 1st. Outside the quota period, backpackers may self-issue a wilderness permit at Inyo National Forest ranger stations or visitor centers.

Reserved Permits: Approximately 60% of the trailhead quota is available through advanced reservations for a fee of $5 per person. Remaining permits are available on a walk-in basis. Reservation requests will be accepted by mail, phone, or fax six months prior to the date of departure (email reservations may be accepted in the near future). A confirmation letter will be sent upon acceptance of the reservation, which can be turned in for an actual permit at a ranger station near the trailhead. Advanced reservations can be made up to two days before the date of the trip.

Walk-in Permits: Walk-in permits are available starting at 11 A.M. the day before a trip. Unclaimed reservations become available for walk-in permits at 10 A.M. on the day of a trip.

> **Inyo National Forest**
> **Wilderness Permit Office**
> 873 North Main Street
> Bishop, CA 93514
> (760) 873-2483
> Fax: (760) 873-2484
> www.fs.fed.us/r5/inyo/passespermits/
> index/html

Sierra National Forest— West Side Entry for John Muir Wilderness:

Reservations for permits are available by mailing the application and fee payment ($5 per person, check or money order) to the Pineridge/Kings River Ranger District. Mail the reservation application at least three weeks prior to the trip to ensure sufficient time for processing. A confirmation of your reservation will be sent, along with instructions on how to redeem the confirmation card for an actual Wilderness Visitors Permit. Reservations may also be made in person at the ranger stations. Phone, fax, or e-mail reservations are not available at this time. For general information call the appropriate Ranger District office.

Pineridge/Kings River Ranger District
PO Box 559
Prather, CA 93561
(559) 855-5360

Sequoia National Forest— Jennie Lakes and Monarch Wildernesses:

At the time of research, overnight visitors to the Sequoia National Forest were not required to obtain a wilderness permit for trips entering either Jennie Lakes or Monarch wildernesses. However, if your trip ultimately ventures into Kings Canyon or Sequoia national parks, you will be expected to have a valid wilderness permit. Permits for trips originating in either wilderness area into the parks can be obtained at both Sierra National Forest and Park Service ranger stations. Backpackers traveling exclusively within Jennie Lakes and Monarch wildernesses do not need a wilderness permit, but they do need a free campfire permit, even if using gas stoves exclusively. Campfire permits may be obtained in person or by mail from any Sequoia National Forest ranger station.

Sequoia National Forest
Hume Lake Ranger District
35860 E. Kings Canyon Rd.
Dunlap, CA 93621
(559) 338-2251

Wilderness Regulations

- Select campsites at least 100 feet from lakes, streams, and trails where terrain permits.
- Body waste and all wash water should be buried at least 100 feet from lakes and streams. Bury body waste in at least 4 inches of soil. Pack out sanitary napkins and disposable diapers
- Pack out all that you pack in. Burnable refuse may be burned if fires are allowed. Do not burn aluminum or glass. Try your skills at "No Trace" camping and leave the wilderness cleaner than you found it.
- Maintain water quality. Soap or detergent, even bio-degradable, should not be used in lakes or streams.
- Shortcutting switchbacks causes trail erosion and resource damage costing tax dollars to repair. Stay on existing trails.
- Cutting or defacing standing trees, dead or alive, is not permitted.
- Dogs or other pets are not allowed in the California Bighorn Sheep Zoological Area or in National Park Wilderness. They are allowed in National Forest Wilderness if kept under confinement.
- Motorized vehicles and mechanized equipment, including bicycles, are prohibited.
- Construction of improvements such as rock walls, large fireplaces, boughbeds, and tables is not permitted.
- Tying of pack and saddle stock within 100 feet of lakes, streams, trails, and campsites is not permitted except while loading and unloading.
- Maximum group size is 15 persons.
- Use of campsites is limited to a maximum of 15 persons per night.
- Maximum number of pack and saddle stock is limited to 25 head.

Winter in Kings Canyon and Sequoia

Hiking and Backpacking

Although Kings Canyon National Park and the surrounding areas don't provide many off-season hiking and backpacking opportunities, a few possibilities do exist. Thanks to its relatively lower elevation, the foothills region on the southwest side of Sequoia National Park offers a handful of year-round snow-free trails. At least one of the nearby campgrounds remains open all year, and lodging is available within Sequoia National Park at Wuksachi and outside the park in the town of Three Rivers (See *Sequoia National Park: A Complete Hiker's Guide*).

Snowshoeing and Cross-Country Skiing

During years of average snowfall, snowshoers and cross-country skiers can enjoy the parks from December through March. Marked trails around Grant Grove in Kings Canyon National Park and in the Giant Forest and Lodgepole areas of Sequoia National Park lure snow lovers to the parks each winter. Motorists must carry chains, which may be required at any time. Anyone wishing to spend a night or more in the backcountry is required to secure a wilderness permit from one of the visitor centers. Be sure to check with park officials about camping restrictions, as some areas are off limits to overnighters.

In Kings Canyon National Park, Highway 180 remains open in winter to Grant Grove and beyond to the Hume junction. The Azalea Campground is open all year, and lodging is available during the winter in cabins at Grant Grove and at the John Muir Lodge. The market at Grant Grove handles snowshoe and ski rentals. The grove has a good system of marked trails, as do Cherry Gap, Big Meadows, and Montecito-Sequoia, nearby.

In Sequoia, the Generals Highway is kept open from the Ash Mtn. Entrance through Giant Forest to Wolverton, Lodgepole and Wuksachi Village. Year-round camping is available at Lodgepole and lodging at Wuksachi. Snowshoe and ski rentals are available from the market at Lodgepole or at Wuksachi Village. A number of marked routes provide wide-ranging alternatives through the Giant Forest/Lodgepole area for snowshoers and skiers of all skill levels. The most challenging marked route is the trip to the Pear Lake ski hut, where overnighters must have advanced reservations. For information call (559) 565-3759 or go to www.sequoiahistory.org.

Generals Highway between Grant Grove and Wuksachi Village is subject to closures during and after snowstorms. The National Park Service does not routinely plow this section of highway, so winter visitors should not expect to travel between Kings Canyon and Sequoia national parks unless conditions are favorable.

CHAPTER 3

About this Guide

This guide is designed for hikers in search of dayhiking opportunities in and around Sequoia National Park, and for backpackers looking to explore the majesty of the Sierra on short weekend trips, multi-week excursions, and anything in between. Some aspects of the evaluations of the following trails are subjective, but every effort was made to insure that the descriptions are meaningful to the average hiker and backpacker.

The 62 trips in this guide are divided into two sections. West Side Trips includes 52 hikes or backpacks in 6 regions. East Side Trips covers 10 trips in the Mt. Whitney area. A brief introduction to each region will familiarize you with the featured area. You'll find information about access, services, campground locations and facilities, and the nearest ranger station, and helpful tips specific to the area.

Individual trip descriptions follow the regional introductions.

SYMBOLS: Each description begins with a display of symbols, denoting the following characteristics:

Trip difficulty

E = easy

M = moderate

MS = moderately strenuous

S = strenuous

Type of trip

↗ = out and back

↗ = point to point (shuttle required)

◯ = loop

♄ = semi-loop

Duration

DH = dayhike (single-day outing)

BP = backpack (overnight or long weekend backpack)

BPx = extended backpack (backpack longer than 3 days)

X = cross-country route (backpack requiring some cross-country travel)

WC = wheelchair access

DISTANCE: Distances are given in miles. Mileages for out-and-back trips are one-way. Point-to-point, loop and semi-loop trips give total mileage.

ELEVATION: Elevations are given in feet. The first set of numbers represents the starting elevation, followed by significant high and low points.

The second set of numbers represents the total elevation gain and loss. Again, the elevations listed are one-way for out-and-back trips, and total for point-to-point, loop and semi-loop trips. (To convert feet to meters, multiply by 0.3048.)

SEASON: Conditions vary from year to year; this entry gives the general period when the trail should be open and also mostly free of snow.

USE: This entry gives you an idea of the trail's popularity (light, moderate, or heavy).

MAP: This entry lists the USGS 7.5-minute quadrangles that cover the trip. Occasionally, supplemental maps are recommended.

THE MAIN BODY of the trip description includes an introduction, directions to the trailhead, and a detailed guide to the trail.

In the margins beside the main text, you'll find quick-reference icons indicating various features found along the trip route:

🏕 = campsites

🌳 = giant sequoias

〰 = swimming areas

👁 = noteworthy views

❀ = seasonal wildflowers

Additional entries accompany the main description:

O **OPTIONS** for extending or varying your trip, sidetrips, additional cross-country routes, and peaks to climb in the vicinity.

R **REGULATORY INFORMATION** concerning permits, quotas, and any specific restrictions.

Map Legend

Trail Maps

— Trail

T Trailhead

P Parking

A Campground

A Ranger Station

? Information

S Fee Collection Gate

▲ Mountain

Regional and Trailhead Maps

T Trailhead

P Parking

A Campground

A Ranger Station

? Information

S Fee Collection Gate

▲ Mountain

A Picnic Area

National Park

National Monument;
Wilderness Area

National Forest

5 Interstate

395 US Highway

41 State Highway

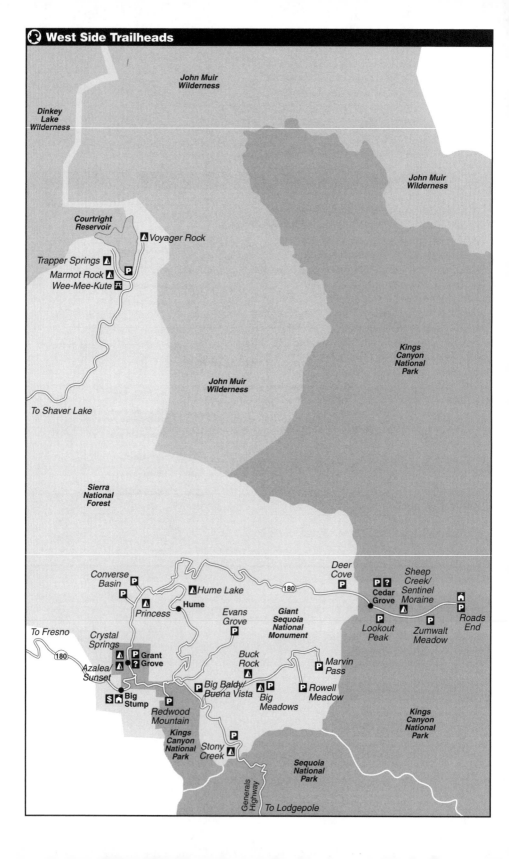

John Muir
Wilderness

Dinkey
Lake
Wilderness

John Muir
Wilderness

Courtright
Reservoir

Voyager Rock

Trapper Springs

Marmot Rock
Wee-Mee-Kute

Kings
Canyon
National
Park

John Muir
Wilderness

To Shaver Lake

Sierra
National
Forest

Deer
Cove

Sheep
Creek/
Sentinel
Moraine

Converse
Basin

Hume Lake

180

Cedar
Grove

Roads
End

Hume

Princess

Evans
Grove

Giant
Sequoia
National
Monument

Lookout
Peak

Zumwalt
Meadow

To Fresno

Crystal
Springs

180

Buck
Rock

Marvin
Pass

Azalea/
Sunset

Grant
Grove

Big Baldy/
Buena Vista

Rowell
Meadow

Kings
Canyon
National
Park

Big
Stump

Big
Meadows

Redwood
Mountain

Kings
Canyon
National
Park

Stony
Creek

Sequoia
National
Park

Generals
Highway

To Lodgepole

CHAPTER 4

West Side Trips

The west side of the Sierra Nevada rises steadily from the plain of the San Joaquin Valley toward the protected lands of Kings Canyon National Park. As you head east, the verdant agricultural land of the San Joaquin gives way to the grasslands and chaparral of the foothills zone, followed by the dense timber of the mid-elevation forests. A few roads penetrate into these areas of towering conifers and isolated groves of giant sequoias, but auto-bound visitors to the park must stop well below the granite cirques and jagged peaks that are so closely associated with the High Sierra. Steadily rising, roadless terrain continues through the red fir and lodgepole pine forests into the subalpine and alpine zones, eventually culminating at the Sierra crest along the extreme eastern border of the park.

Recreationists entering Kings Canyon National Park from the west will experience a wide range of topography, flora, and fauna. The Kings Canyon area of the park offers hiking opportunities along the Middle Fork Kings River from late April to mid-November. Once Grant Grove is snow free, usually by June 1, hikers are blessed with splendid opportunities to stand beneath a majestic giant sequoia, stroll along a tumbling stream, or gaze across a verdant, flower-filled meadow. Mid-summer, the height of the season, lures backpackers with the siren call of the magnificent backcountry found within Kings Canyon National Park.

Colby Lake, along the Circle of Solitude

Introduction to Redwood Mountain

When General Grant and Sequoia were established as national parks in 1890, the Redwood Mountain Grove was not included. In fact, 50 more years would pass before federal protection was extended to include this land in Kings Canyon National Park. Today the area is a vital national treasure—the largest intact grove of giant sequoias in the world. In spite of such stature, the grove receives far fewer visitors than one would expect, because an inauspicious, unsigned dirt road leads to the trailhead. Hikers and backpackers who do find the trailhead and walk the trails will find the magnificent monarchs in a secluded setting. A pair of vista points are also included in this section, Big Baldy and Buena

Vista Peak, accessed by two short trails that promise good westward views, providing that the air above the San Joaquin Valley is not too hazy.

ACCESS: *(Subject to winter closures)* Generals Highway accesses Redwood Mtn. and the surrounding area. Snowfall may close the highway during winter between the Y-intersection with Highway 180 and the gate north of Wuksachi. The road to Redwood Saddle leaves the Generals Highway at Quail Flat, 4.7 miles from Highway 180 and 41.3 miles from the Ash Mtn. Entrance.

AMENITIES: Note: mileages shown in parentheses are from Quail Flat. The nearest Park services are at Grant Grove (5.6 miles) and Lodgepole (20.7 miles). Along with facilities at Grant Grove, lodging is offered at Montecito-Sequoia Lodge (4.2

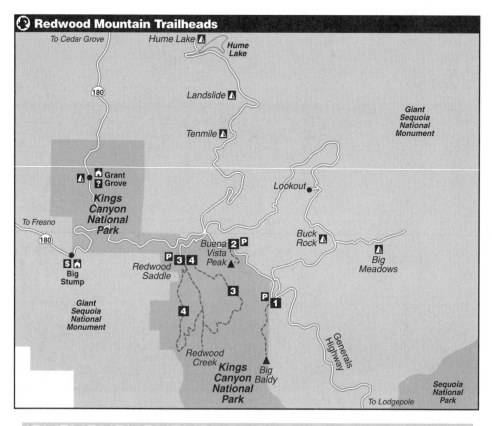

miles) and Stony Creek Village (7.8 miles), southeast of Quail Flat on Generals Highway. Hume Lake (10 miles), with general store, gasoline, picnic areas, and campground, is north of Quail Flat via Tenmile Road.

CAMPGROUNDS: Nearest Park Service campgrounds are at Grant Grove and Dorst Creek (12.6 miles). Forest Service campgrounds are located at Stony Creek (8.3 miles) on Generals Highway, and down the Big Meadows and Tenmile roads.

RANGER STATIONS: Grant Grove and Lodgepole.

Unnamed creek on Redwood Mountain

TRIP **I**

Big Baldy

M ↗ DH

DISTANCE: 2.2 miles one way

ELEVATION: 7630/8209, +975'/-445'

SEASON: June to mid-October

USE: Light

MAP: *General Grant Grove*

INTRODUCTION: A number of exposed granite domes rise from the western mountains of Kings Canyon and Sequoia, providing inspirational views of the Sierra and the San Joaquin Valley from their summits. Big Baldy is no exception, because the 8209-foot dome offers hikers a 360°-vista as a bountiful reward for the straightforward, 4-mile-plus hike. Remember to fill your water bottle prior to departure, as there is no water available at the trailhead or along the trail.

DIRECTIONS TO THE TRAILHEAD: Follow Generals Highway to the trailhead, 6.3 miles east of the Y-intersection with Highway 180, or 16.9 miles northwest from Lodgepole. Park your vehicle along the shoulder of the highway as space allows.

DESCRIPTION: Find the beginning of the trail near a wooden trailhead sign on the west side of the highway. You walk away from the road on a single-track trail through sparse fir forest, quickly crossing the boundary into Kings Canyon National Park. The path generally follows near the crest of a ridge that bends south on a mildly undulating route. Near the 0.5-mile mark, atop an outcrop of granite, you encounter a break in the trees that provides a fine view down into Redwood Canyon.

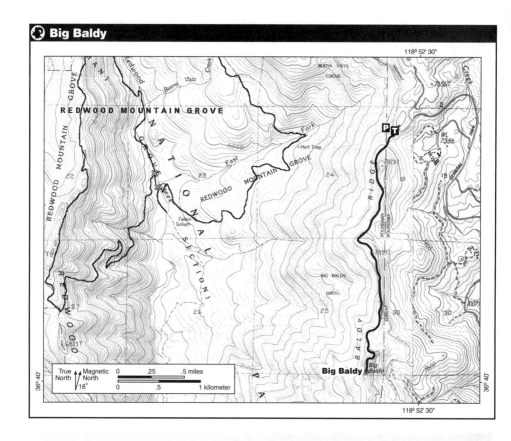

View from the top of Big Baldy

For the next 1.5 miles, you continue along the ridge, in and out of light mixed forest, with sporadic breaks in the trees offering incomplete views, tantalizing you onward toward the promise of an unobstructed vista from the top. Approaching the summit, you pass above a TV tower and a concrete-block building to make the final, winding climb up over rocks to the crest of the exposed dome.

As billed, the view from the apex of Big Baldy is grand. To the east beyond Little Baldy lie the serrated summits of peaks belonging to the Kings-Kaweah and Great Western divides. Westward, the view is across Redwood Canyon and Mountain to the foothills, the San Joaquin Valley and, on those rare clear days, the coastal hills.

GENERALS HIGHWAY TRAILHEAD

TRIP **2**

Buena Vista Peak

E ↗ DH

DISTANCE: 1.0 mile one way

ELEVATION: 7230/7605, +475'/-0'

SEASON: May to November

USE: Heavy

MAP: *General Grant Grove*

INTRODUCTION: A short hike leads to the top of Buena Vista Peak, from where you have a fine view of the western part of Kings Canyon National Park. The relatively easy one-mile trail, combined with trailhead access from the Generals Highway, makes this a very popular hike. Even the ubiquitous, overweight, artery-blocked, camcorder-carrying sightseer seems readily to accept the challenge of the moderate ascent of Buena Vista Peak. However, don't let the potential for crowds deter you, because the short climb is an enjoyable way to spend an hour or two, and the view can be quite inspiring, particularly when a

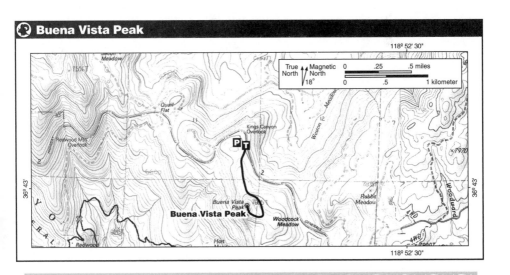

recent shower has cleared the air in the western valleys.

DIRECTIONS TO THE TRAILHEAD: The trailhead is found along Generals Highway, approximately 5 miles from Grant Grove Village, 1.0 mile southeast of the junction with Tenmile Road at Quail Flat. Parking is available in a small lot just south of the Kings Canyon Overlook, on the opposite shoulder of the highway.

DESCRIPTION: Follow a dirt path on a moderate climb through mostly open terrain dotted with large boulders, pockets of manzanita, and an occasional incense cedar or fir. Drawing nearer to the dome-like summit of the peak, you scamper over granite slabs and make an ascending traverse around the east side of the ridge through a light fir forest. A series of switchbacks leads up the southeast ridge to the top of the 7605-foot peak. On a rare smogless day, the view west from the summit of Buena Vista Peak can be quite splendid, extending across the San Joaquin Valley to the coastal hills. During periods of less idyllic atmospheric conditions, summiteers will still enjoy an array of nearby landmarks, including Redwood Mtn., Mt. Baldy, Buck Rock, and the deep cleft of the lower Kings River to the northeast.

REDWOOD MOUNTAIN TRAILHEAD

TRIP **3**

Redwood Mountain Grove: Hart Trail Loop

Ⓜ Ⓠ DH/BP

DISTANCE: 7.25 miles

ELEVATION: 6250/6445/5485/6250, +2065'/-2065'

SEASON: Late April to November

USE: Light

MAP: *General Grant Grove*

TRAIL LOG:

1.9	Hart Meadow
2.4	Fallen Tunnel Tree
3	East Fork Redwood Creek Hart Tree
4.75	Fallen Goliath
5.25	Redwood Creek Trail Jct

INTRODUCTION: The Redwood Mountain Grove is the largest intact grove of giant sequoias in the world. Such a distinction would seemingly make the area an extremely popular tourist attraction, yet the trails are lightly used. Without a paved road to the parking lot, the hoopla of road signs pointing the way, and the convenience of a motorized tram similar to the one that transports tourists through the Mariposa Grove in Yosemite, this stand of magnificent trees can be experienced sans crowds. Here you can walk among the towering monarchs in relative tranquility, basking in the presence of the world's largest trees. This route is an approximately 7-mile loop through the grove's eastern side. For those who crave even more time with the big trees, a nearly 9-mile loop is possible (see Options, below).

The giant sequoias are usually sufficient rewards to lure most discerning hikers to take this trip, but the Hart Trail Loop offers much more. Along the way you encounter lush riparian environments, where wildflowers and ferns line the banks of a number of enchanting tributaries of Redwood Creek. Although the majority of time is spent in the cool shade of the forest, occasionally the trees part enough to reveal pleasant views of the surrounding peaks. Hart Meadow is a fine example, where the stunning west face of Buena Vista Peak backdrops the verdant meadow. Backpackers will enjoy a nice selection of campsites farther down Redwood Creek.

DIRECTIONS TO THE TRAILHEAD: Follow Generals Highway to Quail Flat, 3.4 miles from the Y-intersection with Highway 180. At Quail Flat (directly opposite Tenmile Road) turn south and follow an unmarked, single-lane dirt road with turnouts to a Y-junction, 1.7 miles from the highway. Bear

left at the junction, following a sign for REDWOOD MOUNTAIN GROVE and immediately enter the large parking area at Redwood Saddle, 0.1 mile from the Y-junction.

DESCRIPTION: Near the trailhead signboard, you follow the left-hand trail, marked HART TREE, REDWOOD CANYON TRAIL, and, heading north, descend into a mixed forest of giant sequoias and firs. The winding descent follows the course of an old roadbed to a small ravine and a junction 0.3 mile from Redwood Saddle. Bear left at the junction, and proceed under the cool shade of the forest on the soft tread of a dirt trail through lush groundcover. You wind down to an easy boulderhop of a wildflower-and-fern-lined tributary of Redwood Creek, and then begin a mild, 0.3 mile climb to the next wildflower-lined

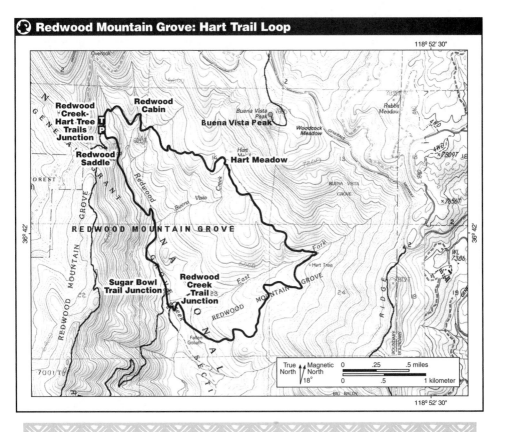

Redwood Mountain Grove: Hart Trail Loop

REDWOOD CABIN

The "cabin" is actually a fallen giant sequoia, naturally hollowed out (in part by fire) and fashioned into a cabin by some enterprising human in the late 1930s. At one time, rock fireplaces occupied both ends. Nowadays, the remains of Redwood Cabin provide an interesting curiosity for adults and a great play fort for kids.

branch. Just on the other side of the delightful stream is Redwood Cabin.

A mild climb continues for 0.2 mile to the next stream crossing. Beyond the tiny stream, you leave most of the redwoods behind as a more moderate climb begins. Through gaps in the forest, you catch an occasional glimpse of Redwood Mtn. to the west. You step across a tiny seasonal creek and climb up to an outcrop of granite, from where you now have an unobstructed view of Redwood Mtn. across the canyon, and of the bare rock summit of Big Baldy to the southeast. A mild climb from the outcrop leads to the fringe of Hart Meadow (6400'±), 1.9 miles from the trailhead. The sloping glade is picturesquely backdropped by the west face of Buena Vista Peak. You step across the twin channels of Buena Vista Creek draining the meadow and bid farewell to this pastoral scene.

Beyond the meadow, you follow the trail on a general descent back into the presence of the mighty trees for about 0.5 mile to the Fallen Tunnel Tree, so named because the route heads straight through the hollowed core of the tree. The mostly gentle decline continues through the cool shade of the forest. Eventually, you come alongside the trickle of a seasonal stream and then to the East Fork Redwood Creek (6120'±), about 3.0 miles from the trailhead. The lushly lined creek spills over moss-covered rocks and into pools, creating a lovely forest scene.

A brief climb from the East Fork brings you to the junction with a short, steep spur leading to the Hart Tree, one of the 20 largest giant sequoias in the world. Black scars 30 to 40 feet up the trunk give evidence that the immense redwood has withstood many significant fires in the past. A gentle stroll leads over to a tiny seasonal stream where a thin ribbon of water cascades down a rock cleft into an appealing pool surrounded by lush foliage and wildflowers. On a gentle descent, you continue through a mixed forest of incense cedars, firs, and widely scattered sequoias, and then briefly enter a sunny area of drier vegetation. Now back to the trees, you continue the mild and then moderate descent to a signed junction with a side trail that wanders around the huge downed sequoia known as the Fallen Goliath. Another 0.5 mile takes you down to a crossing of Redwood Creek, 5.25 mile from Redwood Saddle. The crossing may be difficult in

Giant Sequoias, Redwood Mountain Trail

early season. Just across the creek is a signed junction with the Redwood Creek Trail (5510'±). Backpackers should turn left (south) on the Redwood Creek Trail, following the creek to campsites farther down the canyon.

From the junction, you turn right and follow the Redwood Creek Trail upstream on a mild climb through a lush understory and beneath towering sequoias. At 5.3 miles, you pass a signed junction with the Sugar Bowl Trail on your left. The beautiful hike proceeds upstream along the creek and continues past some magnificent sequoias for another 0.75 mile, until the trail forsakes the creek in favor of an ascent along the hillside above the stream. At 6.9 miles, you close the loop by reaching the junction of the Redwood Creek and Hart Tree trails. From there, retrace your steps 0.3 mile to the parking lot at Redwood Saddle.

[O] By combining the Hart and Sugar Bowl trails, you can create a slightly longer loop of 8.9 miles. At the junction of the Redwood Creek and Sugar Bowl trails, 5.3 miles from the trailhead, turn left (southwest) and follow the Sugar Bowl Trail as described in Trip 4 back to Redwood Saddle.

[R] **PERMITS:** Wilderness permit required for overnight stays (quota: 15 per day).

CAMPFIRES: Not permitted in Redwood Canyon.

CAMPING: Two-night limit. Maximum group size of 10. No camping within 1.5 miles of trailhead.

TRIP **4**

Redwood Mountain Grove: Sugar Bowl Loop

(M) ↻ DH/BP

DISTANCE: 6.6 miles

ELEVATION: 6250/5520/6995/6250, +2130'/-2130'

SEASON: Late April to November

USE: Light

MAP: *General Grant Grove*

TRAIL LOG:

2   Sugar Bowl Trail Jct.
4.75 Redwood Mtn. High Pt.

INTRODUCTION: The Redwood Mountain Grove is the largest intact grove of giant sequoias in the world. Despite this distinction, the area is not overrun by tourists, allowing hikers and backpackers to enjoy the magnificent trees with a modicum of peace and quiet. This description, which follows the western loop through the grove, lacks the number of noteworthy individual trees that appear in Trip 3. But you will see countless examples of the stately trees along with an interesting work in progress —a hillside covered with Christmas-tree-sized sequoias on the site of an old burn. Biologists learned a great deal about the relationship between fire and the giant sequoias through experimental burns performed in research areas within the Redwood Mountain Grove.

Other features of this trip include a stroll along delightful Redwood Creek, where the pleasant stream tumbles down the canyon amid lush foliage and towering sequoias. Backpackers can wander farther downstream to fine campsites, where they can drift off toward slumber while listening to the soothing sound of the creek. Away from the creek, the climb up Redwood Mtn. and the traverse along its crest offer a number of excellent vistas, including views of nearby landmarks such as Buena Vista Peak and Big Baldy.

DIRECTIONS TO THE TRAILHEAD: Follow Generals Highway to Quail Flat, 3.4 miles from the Y-intersection with Highway 180. At Quail Flat (directly opposite Tenmile Road) turn south and follow an unmarked, single-lane dirt road with turnouts to a Y-junction, 1.7 miles from the highway. Bear left at the junction, following a sign for REDWOOD MOUNTAIN GROVE and immediately enter the large parking area at Redwood Saddle, 0.1 mile from the Y-junction.

DESCRIPTION: Near the trailhead sign-board, you follow the left-hand trail, marked HART TREE, REDWOOD CANYON TRAIL, and descend into a mixed forest of giant sequoias and white firs. The winding descent follows the course of an old roadbed to a small ravine and a junction, 0.3 mile from Redwood Saddle. You bear right at the junction, and follow the Redwood Creek Trail briefly on a gentle grade, until a moderate descent takes you into the canyon of Redwood Creek. At 1.25 miles, you wind down to the enchanting creek and proceed downstream through lush vegetation past a number of stately sequoias.

The trail stays close to the creek for a while, then veers away briefly before returning to its banks and reaching the Sugar Bowl Trail junction at the 2-mile mark. Backpackers will want to continue on the Redwood Creek Trail to campsites farther down the canyon. Turn right (southwest) at the junction and make a

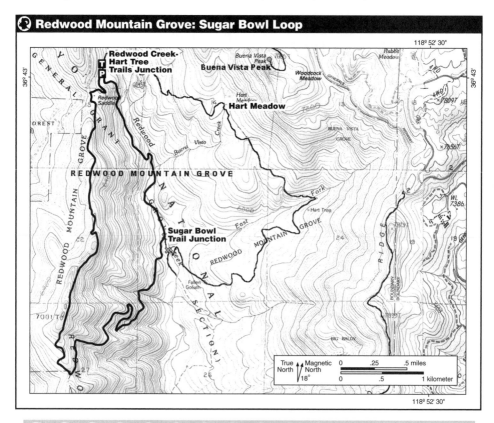

Redwood Mountain Grove: Sugar Bowl Loop

Redwood Mountain Grove, home of stately giant sequoias

moderate climb up the hillside. After a pair of short switchbacks, you ascend across the hillside through myriad young sequoias carpeting the slope amid a few widely scattered old giants. Over the tops of the short trees, a nice view of Big Baldy appears across the canyon. You reach a seasonal stream at 2.5 miles, where an increase in vegetation provides some momentary shade. Beyond the creek, you resume climbing in the open and follow a series of switchbacks up the hillside through vegetation more characteristic of the drier conditions, such as manzanita, oak, and ponderosa pine. As you climb, the views continue to improve of Big Baldy, Buena Vista Peak, and the surrounding terrain. Near the 4-mile mark, your moderate climb ends as you crest the ridge of Redwood Mtn.

Now the trail turns north and follows the ridge as you enter the cover of a mixed forest, where giant sequoias once again tower over the landscape. As you travel amid the monarchs on a soft tread, you notice the abrupt end of the big trees near the east edge of the ridge, evidence that sequoias require special conditions for their growth and survival. Most likely, the soil on that side of the ridge doesn't receive or at least husband a suitable amount of moisture. You climb mildly for 0.75 mile to the high point of your journey, weaving in and out of forest cover along the way. In clearings, you have splendid views across the canyon of Redwood Creek to Big Baldy and Buena Vista Peak. Beyond the high point, you begin a mild descent toward Redwood Saddle through mixed forest. After 1.75 miles of general descent, you close your loop at the parking area.

By combining the Sugar Bowl and Hart trails, you can create a slightly longer loop of 8.9 miles (see Trip 3).

PERMITS: Wilderness permit required for overnight stays (quota: 15 per day).

CAMPFIRES: No fires in Redwood Canyon.

CAMPING: Two-night limit. Maximum group size of 10. No camping within 1.5 miles of trailhead.

Introduction to Giant Sequoia National Monument and Jennie Lakes Wilderness

A relatively small section of Sequoia National Forest rests to the northwest of Sequoia National Park, virtually surrounding the thin, westernmost finger of Kings Canyon National Park. A 10,500-acre section of the forest was designated in 1984 as the Jennie Lakes Wilderness. Most of the remaining acreage was declared part of Giant Sequoia National Monument in 2000.

Jennie Lakes Wilderness is a compact pocket of land, somewhat forgotten next to the more famous parks. The area is lightly used, providing hikers and backpackers with wide-ranging opportunities for serene hikes and pleasant overnight trips on 26 miles of maintained trail. A good network of connecting trails provides access to the Kings Canyon and Sequoia national parks backcountry. Despite the wilderness area's relatively small size, its topography is diverse, with a fine mixture of scenic lakes, quiet forest, rushing streams, grassy meadows, and craggy peaks. Early season here brings the added bonus of an excellent array of wildflowers.

Giant Sequoia National Monument is an eclectic mixture of development and neglected forest in a state of flux due to recent changes in federal protection. While backcountry excursions are virtually nonexistent, a few little-used hiking trails lead to some interesting features. As time passes and roads are closed, logging is curtailed, and funding becomes available for improv-

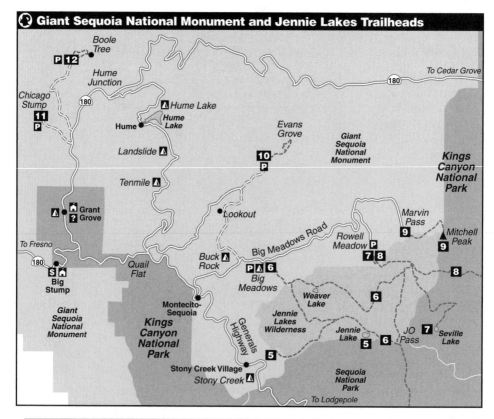

CAMPGROUNDS

Campground	Fee	Elevation	Season	Restrooms	Running Water	Bear Boxes	Phone
STONY CREEK (Generals Hwy., 13.0 miles SE of Y)	$16	6400'	Open late May to November	Vault Toilets	Yes	Yes	Yes
UPPER STONY CREEK (Generals Hwy., 13.0 miles SE of Y)	$12	6400'	Open late May to November	Vault Toilets	Yes	Yes	Yes
BUCK ROCK (0.5 mile north of Big Meadows Rd.)	free	7500'	Open late May to November	Vault Toilets	No	No	No
BIG MEADOWS (Big Meadows Rd., 4.0 miles east of Generals Hwy.)	free	7600'	Open late May to November	Vault Toilets	No	No	Yes
TENMILE (Tenmile Road)	free	5800'	Open late May to November	Pit Toilets	No	No	No
LANDSLIDE (Tenmile Road)	$8	5800'	Open late May to November	Pit Toilets	No	No	No
LOGGER FLAT (Group site on Tenmile Road)	$85	5300'	By reservation		Yes		
ASPEN HOLLOW (Group site on Tenmile Road)	$165	5300'	By reservation		Yes		
HUME LAKE (North shore of lake)	$16	5200'	Open late May to November	Flush Toilets	Yes	No	Yes
PRINCESS (Hume Jct.)	$12	5900'	Open late May to November	Pit Toilets	Yes	No	No

ing recreational opportunities, hopefully more hiking paths will be available within the monument.

ACCESS: *(Highway 180 open all year to Hume Junction; Generals Highway subject to winter closures)* The most direct entry to these National Forest lands is via the Big Stump Entrance. Roads branching from both Highway 180 and Generals Highway access trailheads. Highway 180, known as the Kings Canyon Highway, remains open year-round to Hume Junction, 10.3 miles north of the Y-intersection with Generals Highway, but is closed at that point from mid-November to late April. Generals Highway from Highway 180 south to Wuksachi is subject to closures depending on road conditions during winter.

AMENITIES: Grant Grove is not far from most of the trailheads in this section. Facilities open to the public at Hume Lake include general store, gasoline, gift shop, snack bar, and boat rentals. The lake may be accessed either from Generals Highway via Tenmile Road at Quail Flat, or by Hume Road from its junction with Highway 180, 10.3 miles north of the Y. Along Generals Highway, Montecito-Sequoia Resort, 8.9 miles southeast of the Y, offers year-round lodging: (800) 227-9900, www.montecitosequoia.com. Stony Creek Village, 12.5 miles southeast of the Y, has motel-style rooms and a general store, open between mid-May and mid-October, (559) 335-5500.

RANGER STATION: The nearest Sequoia National Forest ranger station is the Hume Lake Ranger Station, located in Dunlap on Highway 180. At the time of research, wilderness permits were not required for overnight stays unless you were also entering the national parks. However, a fire permit was necessary for campfires. National Forest personnel can issue wilderness permits for parties originating in the national forest and subsequently entering the national parks.

GOOD TO KNOW BEFORE YOU GO:

1. Information on trails and backcountry use in this fairly new national monument can be hard to find.

2. At the time of research, wilderness permits were not required for overnight stays within the Jennie Lakes Wilderness. However, if you plan to enter the adjoining national parks and spend one or more nights there, you must obtain a wilderness permit. The closest place to the trailheads to obtain a permit is from the Park Service at Grant Grove, but Forest Service personnel can issue a permit for the parks.

Jennie Lakes Wilderness sign

TRIP **5**

Stony Creek Trail to Jennie Lake

S ↗ DH / BP

DISTANCE: 5.75 miles

ELEVATION: 6575/9185/9015, +2875'/-405'

SEASON: Mid-June to early October

USE: Light

MAP: *Muir Grove*

INTRODUCTION: Jennie Lakes Wilderness is a nearly forgotten parcel of the western Sierra tucked between two popular national parks. The Generals Highway provides trouble-free access to this gem via the Stony Creek trailhead. Once the trail begins, however, the easy part of this trip ends as hikers and backpackers make a stiff 4.25-mile climb to appropriately named Poop Out Pass. The upper part of the steep ascent offers fine views of the surrounding terrain, which make the pain and suffering of the climb a bit more bearable (an early start would further reduce the stress by letting travelers avoid the heat of the day during the ascent). Beyond the pass, the final 1.5-mile forested journey to Jennie Lake is over gentler terrain. The lake is quite scenic, a worthy reward for the labor involved in getting there.

DIRECTIONS TO THE TRAILHEAD: Drive on the Generals Highway to the turnoff for Upper Stony Creek Campground, 11.3 miles southeast of the Y-intersection with Highway 180 or 12.2 miles northwest of the Lodgepole turnoff. Proceed to the upper end of the campground and the small parking area at the Stony Creek trailhead, where a nearby walk-in section of the campground provides a first-night option for backpackers desiring an early morning start.

DESCRIPTION: From the trailhead, the Stony Creek Trail attacks the slope above with a vengeance, climbing continually at a moderately steep grade. Along the way you pass through a scattered-to-light mixed forest, which initially consists mainly of red firs, with a smattering of western white and Jeffrey pines. Although the trail bears the name Stony Creek, you spend very little time near the stream, as the path climbs high above the floor of the canyon. At 0.5 mile from the campground, you cross into signed Jennie Lakes Wilderness.

The long, steady ascent continues as the trail weaves along the boundary between Sierra National Forest and Kings Canyon National Park. As you climb, you begin to hear the roar of a waterfall, formed where Stony Creek spills precipitously over a slab

of granite. Unfortunately, the forest cover never allows a good view of this picturesque cascade, unless you leave the trail and walk across the steep hillside to a better vantage point. However, farther up the trail you reach an exposed, rocky section of a ridge, from where you have a nice view of the Kings-Kaweah Divide ahead and out across the foothills to the San Joaquin Valley behind. Discernible path vanishes for a bit as you walk over rock, but just follow the ridgecrest until a more defined trail resumes farther up the ridge. As you return to the cover of light forest, the grade of ascent finally eases as the trail bends away from the crest and heads over to a crossing of twin-channeled Stony Creek, 3.25 miles from the trailhead.

This pleasantly graded stretch of trail is quickly left behind as beyond the creek you once again climb moderately steeply up the hillside through mixed forest. The steady

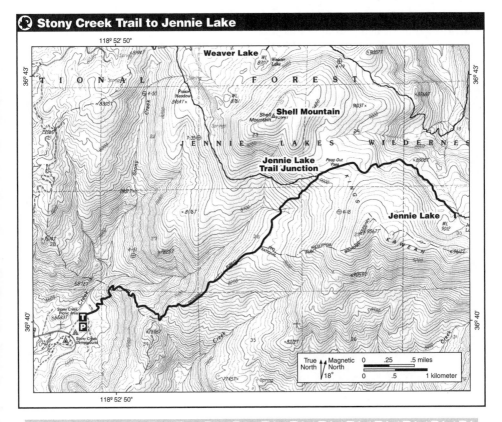

Stony Creek Trail to Jennie Lake

ascent leads to a T-junction, 3.85 miles from Stony Creek Campground, with the Jennie Lake Trail, which originates in Big Meadows.

As you veer right and proceed up the Jennie Lake Trail from the junction, an easier stretch of climbing brings you to the forested saddle of Poop Out Pass (9140'), aptly named in light of your steep 4.25-mile ascent. The pass offers no view, but the 0.8-mile, 450-foot climb of nearby Shell Mtn. (9594') will reward you with a superb vista from the easily obtained summit, which is northwest of the pass.

For the next mile, you gratefully leave the climbing behind and enjoy the pleasures of a mostly mild descent. You drop moderately from the pass, hit a switchback, and then begin an arcing, mildly descending traverse across exfoliating granodiorite slopes. Occasional views of rugged Sierra peaks propel you onward. A final, gently rising ascent leads through the trees to an unmarked junction, 5.7 miles from the trailhead. Turn right (south) and follow a short spur trail to the north shore of beautiful Jennie Lake (9012').

Jennie, named in 1897 by S.L.N. Ellis of the Sierra Forest Preserve for his wife, is a kidney-shaped lake cradled in a basin at the talus-covered foot of an exfoliating granite peak with a pyramidal summit. A light forest of lodgepole pines and red firs shelters pleasant campsites near the lake's outlet. Anglers can test their skill with the resident rainbow trout.

O Jennie Lakes Wilderness has a fine system of trails that offer a variety of possibilities for extending your journey. A straightforward extension follows the loop described in Trip 6. Other trails offer connections to routes in the adjoining national parks.

R **PERMITS:** Wilderness permits are not required.

CAMPFIRES: Fires permitted within Jennie Lakes Wilderness.

Jennie Lake

BIG MEADOWS ROAD TRAILHEADS

TRIP **6**

Jennie Lakes Loop

Ⓜ Ↄ BP

DISTANCE: 17.8 miles

ELEVATION: 7615/9465, +4135'/-4135'

SEASON: Mid-June to early October

USE: Light

MAPS: *Muir Grove, Mt. Silliman,*
Monarch Wilderness and
Jennie Lakes Wilderness,
USFS

TRAIL LOG:

2.0	Loop Junction
3.0	Weaver Lake Jct.
7.5	Rowell Mdw. Jct.
10.1	JO Pass
11.5	Jennie Lake
15.8	Loop Junction

INTRODUCTION: Pleasant lakes with craggy backdrops, rushing streams, grassy meadows, and shady forests lure the faithful away from the scenic drama of Kings Canyon and Sequoia national parks and into lightly used Jennie Lakes Wilderness. The 18-mile Jennie Lakes Loop is perhaps the ultimate way to experience the 10,500-acre wilderness. The loop is well suited to a weekend journey for backpackers in reasonable shape, although an extra day or two could easily be spent languishing along the shore of either Jennie or Weaver Lake. Throw in some good views from various points along the trail and you've got the makings of a wonderful backcountry adventure.

DIRECTIONS TO THE TRAILHEAD: Leave Generals Highway 6.4 miles southeast of the Y-intersection with Highway 180, and follow Big Meadows Road northeast 3.5 miles to the turnoff for the Big Meadows trailhead. Park in the trailhead parking lot, equipped with pit toilets and a pay phone nearby.

DESCRIPTION: Near the restroom, a sign points the way up a wooded hillside and across the paved access road. Descend the slope to a plank bridge that spans a sluggish stretch of Big Meadows Creek and come to a trail sign and register. On the mild, sandy Jennie Lake Trail, you traverse the base of a granite hump and then curve alongside a delightful, spring-fed tributary of Big Meadows Creek. Through a mixed forest of red firs, lodgepole pines, and Jeffrey pines, you briefly follow this stream before crossing it via some large boulders. The trail now leads you on a moderate climb around an exposed ridge. You break out of the forest momentarily to enjoy fine views over lupine and manzanita of the Monarch Divide and Shell Mtn. Continuing the arc around the ridge, you encounter verdant Fox Meadow and then climb to a junction near a stream, 2.0 miles from the trailhead. At the junction you begin a nearly 14-mile loop through the heart of the Jennie Lakes Wilderness.

Proceed straight across the stream from the junction, enter Jennie Lakes Wilderness, and follow the trail through alternating sections of scattered-to-light forest and shrub-covered clearings. At 3.1 miles, you reach the lateral to Weaver Lake, where you turn right.

You wind uphill through mixed forest and boulders to the lakeshore, 0.2 mile from the junction. The shoreline of Weaver Lake (8707'), shaded by lodgepole pines and firs, harbors a boulder-studded forest floor carpeted with patches of azalea, red heather, and Labrador tea. The whitish granite of Shell Mtn. creates a fine backdrop, mirrored in the placid surface of the lake. An array of campsites pepper the shoreline of this easily reached lake, the least crowded ones being on the south shore amid small groves of trees. Anglers can fish for brook trout, but the popular lake receives a lot of pressure on its fish population.

Back at the Weaver Lake junction, veer right (northeast) and follow a less-used path toward Rowell Meadow on a moderate climb through a mixed forest of firs, lodgepole pines, and silver pines to the crests of a pair of saddles. You head downhill from the second saddle, gently at first and then more steeply, to the head of Boulder Creek canyon and multiple crossings of its tributaries. Beyond the final crossing, you make a moderate climb angling up the canyon's west-facing side. The shade from a scattered-to-light forest greets you where the trail bends east over the crest of a ridge and drops to a Y-junction with the trail to Rowell Meadow, 7.5 miles from the trailhead.

Angle sharply right from the junction following the path signed JO PASS and head south on a mild climb to the crest of a rise.

Descend gently, then moderately, with occasional glimpses of Shell Mtn. through the trees, to recross a lushly lined tributary of Boulder Creek that you already crossed below. A lengthy climb ensues past slabs and boulders and over a small stream that drains a hidden pond 0.1 mile east of the trail. Eventually, the ascent brings you to JO Pass (9444') and a junction, 10.1 miles

JO PASS

As the story goes, S.L.N. Ellis of the Sierra Forest Preserve (the man who named Jennie Lake after his wife), named the pass after John Wesley Warren. Warren reportedly started to carve his name on a nearby tree, but finished only the first two letters.

Jennie Lakes Loop

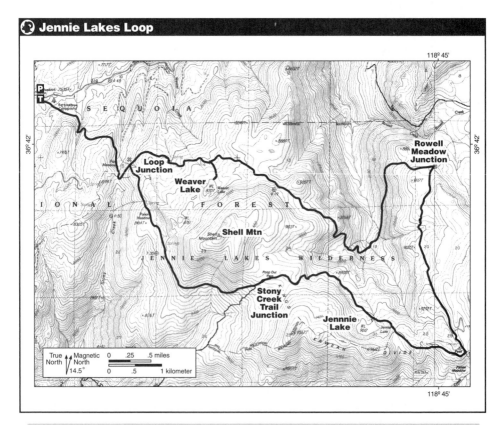

Weaver Lake on the Jennie Lakes Loop

from the trailhead. Thanks to the trees, don't expect much of a view from the pass.

The JO Pass Trail continues south 2.25 miles to a union with the Twin Lakes Trail (see Trip 46, *Sequoia National Park: A Complete Hiker's Guide*). From the pass, your route bends right (west) to follow the crest of a mildly undulating ridge. Soon, as you follow switchbacks down the hillside, you catch glimpses of Jennie Lake through the trees. At 1.4 miles from the pass, you reach a short lateral to Jennie Lake (9012'). Larger than Weaver Lake, Jennie Lake is also backdropped by impressive granite cliffs and rimmed by a light forest of red firs and lodgepole pines. Campsites are on either side of the driftwood-choked outlet. Anglers may have better luck here than at Weaver, since Jennie is twice as far from the nearest trailhead and fishing pressure is lower.

Continue on the mild trail from the Jennie Lake lateral, first on a gentle decline, then on an ascending traverse around exfoliated granodiorite slopes. Along this traverse through scattered forest, you have fine views of the Monarch Divide. A steeper, winding climb takes you up to Poop Out Pass (9180'), followed by a short descent to a Y-junction at 13.4 miles with the Stony Creek Trail (see Trip 5).

Veer right at the junction and continue on a moderate descent across the south slopes of Shell Mtn. to a crossing of a nascent, twin-channeled tributary of Stony Creek. You make a mild ascent around the nose of a ridge and then traverse across the west slope of Shell Mtn. Mostly open terrain provides excellent views of Big Baldy, Chimney Rock, and the San Joaquin Valley until you reenter forest cover. After the crossing of a lushly lined, spring-fed brook, you begin a more moderate descent, which leads past a second rivulet and then to verdant Poison Meadow. Beyond the meadow, you cross a third brook, pass over the wilderness boundary, and come to the trail junction at the close of the loop, 15.8 miles from the parking lot. From here, retrace your steps 2.0 miles to the Big Meadows trailhead.

O With an extensive system of connecting trails, you can easily extend your wanderings in the Jennie Lakes Wilderness into the adjoining national parks.

R **PERMITS:** Wilderness permits are not required.

CAMPFIRES: Campfires permitted within the Jennie Lakes Wilderness.

TRIP **7**

Seville Lake

M ⟋ DH / BP

DISTANCE: 6.6 miles one way

ELEVATION: 7925/9145/8410, +1455'/-955'

SEASON: July to mid-October

USE: Light

MAPS: *Muir Grove, Mt. Silliman, Monarch Wilderness and Jennie Lakes Wilderness, USFS*

INTRODUCTION: A little-used trail through Jennie Lakes Wilderness leads to a secluded lake just inside the western boundary of Kings Canyon National Park. Hikers pass verdant meadows and wildflower-lined streams on the way to cirque-bound Seville Lake, nestled beneath the rugged cliffs of the Kings-Kaweah Divide. Pleasant campsites and good fishing at the lake offer excellent rewards for the labor.

DIRECTIONS TO THE TRAILHEAD: Leave the Generals Highway 6.4 miles southeast of the Y-intersection with Highway 180, and follow Big Meadows Road 8.5 miles northeast to the signed turnoff for the Rowell Meadow trailhead. Drive south 2.0 miles to the campground loop and park as space allows. The no-fee, walk-in campground has fire pits and a pit toilet, but no picnic tables.

DESCRIPTION: The trail begins opposite the trailhead signboard at the lower end of the campground loop road, near a trail sign and register. Begin climbing up a heavily vegetated slope carpeted with grasses, wildflowers, and shrubs such as Labrador tea, currant, manzanita, and chinquapin. The foliage lessens a bit as you switchback up the hillside and enter a mixed forest of red firs, lodgepole pines, and Jeffrey pines. You cross into Jennie Lakes Wilderness, climb around the nose of a ridge, and come alongside a tributary of Rowell Creek. Eventually, you step across the tributary and follow gentle trail to a three-way junction, 2.0 miles from the trailhead.

Continue straight at the junction, passing flower-bedecked Rowell Meadow to your right. A faint path branches off to a snow-survey cabin before you reach a crossing of Rowell Creek on a wood plank bridge. Immediately after the creek are some campsites off to the right of the trail. Near the far end of the meadow, you reach another junction, at 2.3 miles.

Bear right (southeast) from the junction and make a mild climb through lodgepole pines to a crossing of flower-lined Gannon Creek. A more moderate ascent then leads to the crest of a forested ridge and the

signed Kings Canyon National Park boundary, 4.0 miles from the trailhead.

Descend moderately steeply from the ridge on a dusty trail through a forest of lodgepole pines and red firs to a tiny brook. Wildflowers, including lupine, blue lips, and columbine, carpet a meadowland of foliage near the rivulet. Raised sections of trail take you past a particularly marshy segment. The descent continues, as you leave the lush area behind and drop to a junction, 5.4 miles from the trailhead.

Turn right (east), step across a tributary of Sugarloaf Creek, and proceed on a gently graded path through mixed forest, following the creek upstream through Belle Canyon. As you continue, the cliffs of the Kings-Kaweah Divide, which form Seville Lake's cirque, begin to appear over the treetops. Soon you reach the north shore of lovely Seville Lake (8408'), one of the Sheep Camp Lakes.

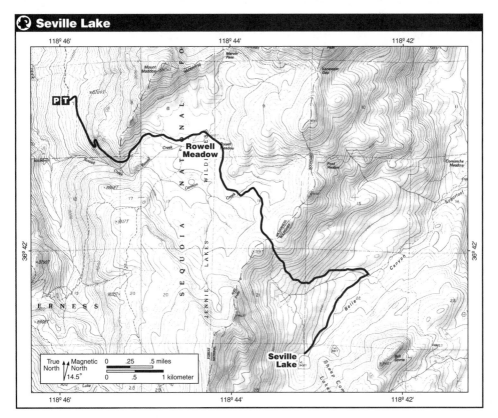

Seville Lake

Seville Lake

Granite cliffs rise above the south shore of the lake, culminating at 10,041-foot Kettle Peak, along the crest of the Kings-Kaweah Divide. The marshy shoreline is rimmed by lodgepole pines and red firs, which shade a number of pleasant campsites. Plenty of rainbow and brook trout will tempt the angler.

From a base camp at Seville Lake, off-trail enthusiasts can readily explore routes to other Sheep Camp Lakes, including a connection to Lost Lake. Kettle Peak, southwest of Seville Lake on the Silliman Crest, provides a nice scramble for mountaineers.

Rather than simply returning to the trailhead by the same trail, a semi-loop trip follows a different route through Comanche Meadow (see Trip 8).

PERMITS: Wilderness permits are required for overnight stays in Kings Canyon National Park.

CAMPFIRES: Campfires are permitted in Jennie Lakes Wilderness and at Seville Lake.

BIG MEADOWS ROAD TRAILHEADS

TRIP **8**

Rowell Meadow to Giant Forest

Ⓜ ↗ BPx

DISTANCE: 38 miles

ELEVATION: 7925/9285/7095/11,370/
6720, +9450'/-10,675'

SEASON: Mid-July to early October

USE: Light

MAPS: *Muir Grove, Mt. Silliman*

TRAIL LOG:

6.25   Comanche Meadow
7.75   Sugarbowl Meadow Camp
13.25 Roaring River
19.3   Upper Ranger Meadow
22.6   Elizabeth Pass
25.3   Tamarack Lake Jct.
27.4   Bearpaw Camp
32.4   Mehrten Creek

INTRODUCTION: This 38-mile trek allows backpackers to sample a cross section of the characteristic grandeur of the western side of Kings Canyon and Sequoia national parks. Journeying across a wide range of elevation, travelers pass through a variety of environments, including mid-elevation forest, subalpine, and alpine. The topography is equally diverse, with a bounty of flower-laden meadows, glaciated canyons, and high alpine basins. Views from the trail — of soaring peaks, precipitous canyon walls, and airy spires — augment the extraordinary scenery. An added bonus to this excursion is the potential for solitude: between the trailhead and Bearpaw Meadow you may see very few people. Once you reach the High Sierra Trail, the number of trail users will increase significantly as you approach Giant Forest.

Backpackers will have to exert a hearty effort, as the extended loop crosses the Kings-Kaweah Divide at 11,370-foot Elizabeth Pass. Most of the trail is usually in good shape, but the condition of the route on the south side of Elizabeth Pass leaves something to be desired. With extra days, forays to other interesting locales are possible (see Options).

DIRECTIONS TO THE TRAILHEAD:

START: Leave the Generals Highway 6.4 miles southeast of the Y-intersection with Highway 180, and follow Big Meadows Road 8.5 miles northeast to the signed turnoff for the Rowell Meadow trailhead. Drive south 2.0 miles to the campground loop and park as space allows. The no-fee, walk-in campground has fire pits and a pit toilet, but no picnic tables.

END: From the Generals Highway near the Giant Forest Museum in Sequoia National Park, turn onto the narrow Crescent Meadow Road and drive 1.2 miles to the junction with the road to Moro Rock. Continue on Crescent Meadow Road another 1.3 miles to the end of the road at the Crescent Meadow parking lot. The well-signed High Sierra Trail begins near the restroom.

DIRECTIONS: The trail begins opposite the trailhead signboard at the lower end of the campground loop road near a trail sign and register. Begin climbing up a heavily vegetated slope. The foliage thins a bit as you switchback up the hillside and enter a mixed forest of red firs, lodgepole pines, and Jeffrey pines. You cross into Jennie Lakes Wilderness, climb around the nose of a ridge, and come alongside a tributary of Rowell Creek. Eventually, you step across the tributary and follow gentle trail to a three-way junction, 2.0 miles from the trailhead.

Continue straight at the junction, passing flower-bedecked Rowell Meadow to your right. A faint path branches off to a snow-survey cabin before you reach a crossing of Rowell Creek on a wood plank bridge. Immediately after the creek are

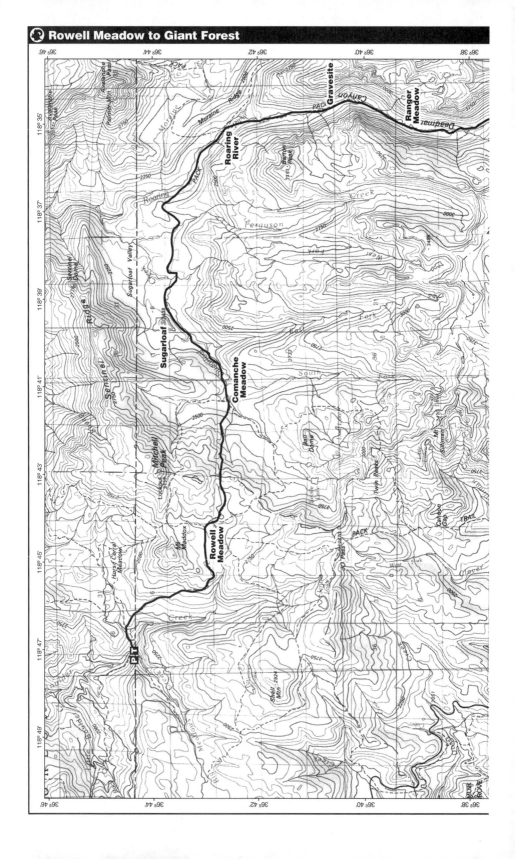

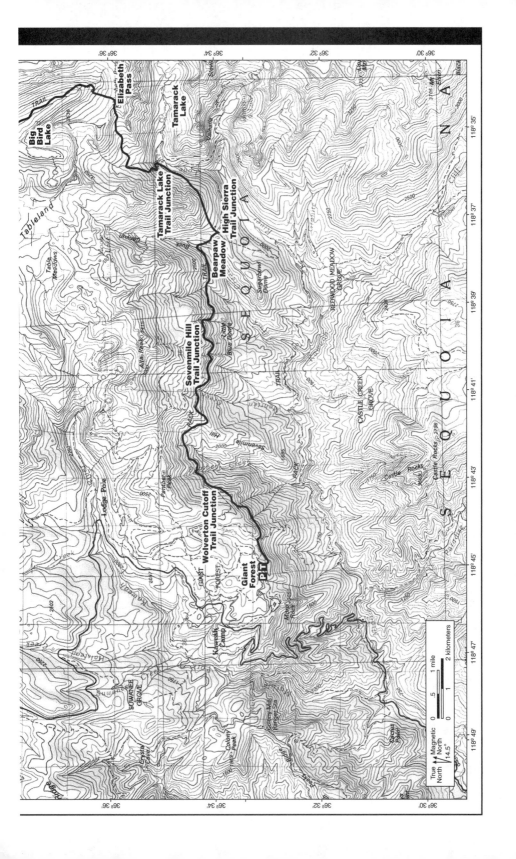

some campsites off to the right of the trail. Near the far end of the meadow, you reach another junction, at 2.3 miles.

Following a trail signed ROARING RIVER, go straight at the junction and soon climb across a sloping, flower-filled meadow. Continue the ascent to the crest of a hill, from where you follow gently graded trail on a traverse around a hillside to the crossing of a pleasant rivulet. Just beyond the rivulet, you climb to the crest of a forested ridge and meet the Kings Canyon National Park boundary, 3.7 miles from the trailhead.

Descending from the crest, you cross another delightful stream and come to a clearing, from where you have a good view of the Great Western Divide to the east, and a partial view of the Silliman Crest to the southeast. Soon you enter a moderate forest of firs, lodgepole pines, and Jeffrey pines, and continue the moderate descent to a crossing of another small stream. Beyond it, the trail winds down a forested hillside past a pocket of lush vegetation to a signed junction, on your left, with a trail to Williams Meadow (not shown on the *Mt. Silliman*

quad). A short distance ahead, you encounter a major trail junction, 6.1 miles from the Rowell Meadow trailhead.

At the junction, head east, following signs for SUGARLOAF and ROARING RIVER. Soon you encounter willow- and aspen-lined Comanche Meadow (7800±). Near the far end of the meadow, a path leads to campsites with bear box, and to use-trails leading down to Sugarloaf Creek.

Resume the downhill jaunt, through lush foliage to a crossing of the stream draining Williams Meadow. Beyond the stream, you pass into the markedly drier surroundings of a Jeffrey pine forest, which still shows clear evidence of an extensive 1974 fire. You pass through a gap in a drift fence and drop into Sugarloaf Valley, with fine views through scattered trees, and over clumps of manzanita to the prominent hump of granite for which the valley is named. Milder trail, on the valley floor, leads to a lateral marked simply BEAR BOX, at 7.75 miles. This short path heads over to a camping area south of wildflower-laden Sugarloaf Meadow (7240'±), where pines shelter a few campsites with a bear box, a

Cleft of outlet from Big Bird Lake, Deadman Canyon Trail

hitching post, and a small stream to cool your feet in.

Beyond the campsite lateral, you cross a stream and then proceed on a gently graded, dusty trail through Sugarloaf Valley, along the base of Sugarloaf, to a ford of Sugarloaf Creek. This is the lowest elevation of the journey. Even during low water, you should plan on getting your feet wet at this crossing. A couple of primitive campsites can be found above the far shore.

Mild trail takes you from Sugarloaf Creek through denser forest and across rivulets as you saunter toward tumbling Ferguson Creek. A stiff, 0.5-mile climb leads to the top of a manzanita-covered and pine-dotted moraine at the lip of the Roaring River canyon. The view includes Palmer Mtn., the Sphinx Crest, and summits along the north end of the Great Western Divide. Living up to its name, you can hear the tumultuous Roaring River below.

A 0.75-mile-long descent takes you from the lip to the floor of the canyon through a variety of vegetation. You pass through a gap in another drift fence and then begin the steady climb up the drainage, sometimes right next to the frothy Roaring River tumbling down its boulder-strewn canyon. Just beyond another fence, you cross a side stream and encounter the grassy clearing of fenced Scaffold Meadows, followed by a T-junction near the solar-powered Roaring River Ranger Station, 13.25 miles from the trailhead. Campsites with bear boxes are near the river, both left and right.

From the ranger station, veer right and head up the canyon, remaining on the west side of Roaring River to a fork in the trail, where you follow the fainter, right-hand trail toward Deadman Canyon and Elizabeth Pass. The more distinct path on the left leads to additional campsites for backpackers and stock parties. A short, steep climb leads to milder trail through a light forest of Jeffrey pines, incense cedars, and red firs, eventually taking you southbound into Deadman Canyon. After passing through an opening in a three-pole gate, you continue upstream on mild trail to campsites just before the ford of Deadman Canyon Creek, 1.6 miles from Roaring River.

Beyond the creek, you pass through a pleasant, wildflower-covered meadow with good views of the steep cliffs and granite walls of the canyon. For the next 1.5 miles, the landscape alternates between groves of mixed forest and pockets of clearing, where wildflowers and views of the glacier-carved canyon provide visual delights. Sporadic swaths of young aspens testify to the numerous avalanches that have roared down the hillside.

You encounter a long meadow where the creek glides sinuously through grasses and flowers. A path branches over to campsites at the north end of the meadow; farther up the trail is the gravesite from which the canyon received its name.

DEADMAN CANYON

Before the current designation, this area was known as Copper Canyon after the copper mine near the head. An old sign with the cryptic, deteriorating inscription, HERE REPOSES ALFRED MONIERE, SHEEPHERDER, MOUNTAIN MAN, 18–1887, marks the grave. Little else is known about the deceased, and this has fueled a variety of interesting tales. One version has the Basque sheepherder murdered, while a less-dramatic account has him taking ill and passing away before his partner could make the two-week round trip to Fresno for a physician. Whatever the cause of death, a better site for one's grave is hard to imagine, as the flower-carpeted, tree-studded meadow is blessed with a sweeping panorama of a granite cathedral. Columbine, delphinium, daisy, Mexican hat, penstemon, pennyroyal, and shooting star are among the flowers that grace the surroundings.

You ford the creek again and then continue upstream on a mild ascent through boulders, shrubs, and flowers to a picturesque location where the creek spills across a series of slabs. Past another drift fence, you ascend through more lush foliage to where the trail eases in a stand of lodgepole pines and firs. Soon you break out of the trees and enter the extensive grasslands of Ranger Meadow. Steep canyon walls and peaks at the head of the canyon combine to create an awesome view across the flower-bedecked expanse.

At the south end of lengthy Ranger Meadow, you make a moderate climb amid scattered lodgepole pines to a crossing of a lushly lined tributary. The steady ascent continues across rocky slopes dotted with heather to a ford of the vigorous main channel of Deadman Canyon Creek. A moderate climb leads through a rock garden and past another drift fence to the lip of upper Ranger Meadow (9210'±). Just off

the trail to the right, in a grove of pines, are two good campsites, 6.1 miles from Roaring River.

CROSS-COUNTRY ROUTE TO BIG BIRD LAKE: From the campsites in upper Ranger Meadow, cross the main channel of the creek and climb up a steep hillside, staying well to the left of the deep cleft of the outlet stream from Big Bird Lake. Parts of a boot-beaten path may be evident, but if not, the route is straightforward although quite steep. Work your way up to a bench overlooking the lake and several small ponds to its north. From there the route drops easily to the lakeshore. Big Bird Lake (9765') is long and narrow, cradled in a U-shaped alpine cirque below the crest of the Kings-Kaweah Divide. A few wind-battered lodgepole pines cling tenuously to the sparse soil around the lake, affording little protection to the exposed campsites on sandy flats near the north shore. The view down Deadman Canyon is quite dramatic. **END OF SIDE TRIP**

From Upper Ranger Meadow, follow gentle trail southeast through sagebrush, grasses, sedges, and wildflowers. The grade increases as you progress up the canyon and draw near the creek, which is lined with low-growing willows and clumps of flowers. As you approach a headwall beneath Elizabeth Pass, the climb becomes more pronounced and a series of switchbacks leads you up a rocky slope. After crossing the creek, the trail veers southwest to ascend a talus- and boulder-filled cirque on an interminable set of switchbacks. Finally, the goal comes into view and you zigzag up dirt trail to Elizabeth Pass (11,370'±), on the Kings-Kaweah Divide, 9.4 miles from Roaring River. The divide marks the boundary between Kings Canyon and Sequoia national parks.

Although the 2100-foot ascent is now behind you, perhaps a more difficult challenge awaits as you begin a knee-wrenching 3300-foot descent to the Tamarack Lake Trail junction. Although recently constructed switchbacks wind up the northeast side

Lonely Lake Creek, Elizabeth Pass Trail

A TURTLE NO MORE

Elizabeth Pass was once known as Turtle Pass, named after a rock about 4 feet long near the east side of the pass that bears a striking resemblance to a turtle. In 1905 author Stewart Edward White, along with his wife and another man, traveled up Deadman Canyon, crossed the Kings-Kaweah Divide at the pass, and then descended steep cliffs to Lone Pine Meadow. Their adventure was originally told in *Outing* magazine, and later in White's book *The Pass*. Turtle Pass was subsequently renamed to honor White's wife.

of Elizabeth Pass, the southwest side has a very poor trail that seemingly hasn't seen any maintenance since the General Sherman tree was a sapling. Much of the way is more reminiscent of a popular cross-country route than a bona fide trail, following the course of erosion gullies and washed-out sections of trail. Route finding on the descent is aided by numerous cairns and ducks (small rock piles), but the general route down the glacier-scoured trough is fairly obvious, even if the actual trail isn't always clear. Initially you're cheered by views of Moose and Lost lakes from just below the pass, and later on by a profusion of wildflowers on more hospitable slopes below. Farther down, as trail conditions improve, vistas of Lion Rock, Mt. Stewart, and Eagle Scout Peak issue a siren call luring backpackers up trails to the mountainous terrain surrounding Tamarack and Hamilton lakes. At 2.7 miles from the pass and 12.1 miles from Roaring River, after more switchbacks, the descent eases at the Tamarack Lake junction (8180'±).

□ **SIDE TRIP TO TAMARACK LAKE:** Head east from the Tamarack Lake junction across a boulder field to a ford of Lonely Lake's outlet. Just beyond the stream, a use-trail branches to campsites. Soon the grade of the trail increases as you climb above a scenic stair-step falls on Lone Pine Creek to sloping Lone Pine Meadow, backdropped regally by Lion Rock and Mt. Stewart, as well as by a bounty of unnamed towers and ramparts along the canyon rim. Continue the climb, initially through a tangle of ferns, grasses, and flowers, then through drier vegetation of manzanita and sagebrush. You reach the pleasant surroundings of Tamarack Meadow and stroll amid wild- flowers to the far end, where you'll find a triple-branched crossing of Lone Pine Creek. A short climb up a lodgepole pine-covered hill leads to Tamarack Lake, 1.8 miles from the junction, nestled in an impressive rock amphitheater topped by Mt. Stewart and Lion Rock. Plenty of campsites are scattered around the lonely lake (no fires). Brook trout will tantalize anglers. **END OF SIDE TRIP**

From the Tamarack Lake junction, you make a short, mild descent to another junction, this one between your route, the Over the Hill Trail, and a trail connecting with the High Sierra Trail. Veer right and begin a stiff climb up a hillside. Where the slope is open you have incredible views east, initially of the rugged terrain surrounding Lone Pine Creek canyon, and later on, past an intervening stretch of forest, of dramatic vistas up the Hamilton Creek drainage. The grade eases as you traverse around the brow of the slope through lush vegetation, and then descend amid thickening fir forest. Eventually, 2.1 miles from the Tamarack Lake junction, you reach a signed T-junction with the High Sierra Trail. A ranger station and the Bearpaw Meadow High Sierra Camp lie approximately 200 yards to the left (east), while the lateral trail to the Bearpaw Meadow backpacker camp is about the same distance to the right (west).

The overused backpacker camp, sheltered by dense timber, has numbered sites bear boxes, pit toilets, and a spigot with untreated water. Open fires are not allowed. Bearpaw Meadow High Sierra Camp and the A-frame ranger station near-

Giant Sequoia, Wolverton Cutoff Trail

by are situated at the lip of the deep cleft of Middle Fork Kaweah River canyon. Unlike the claustrophobic backpacker camp, Bearpaw Meadow High Sierra Camp has excellent views of the glacier-scoured surroundings, including Eagle Scout Peak and Mt. Stewart on the Great Western Divide, the Yosemite-esque cleft of Hamilton Creek, and Black Kaweah above Kaweah Gap. Similar to arrangements at the famed High Sierra Camps of Yosemite, guests at Bearpaw Meadow High Sierra Camp sleep in tent cabins and enjoy hot meals for breakfast and dinner (all by reservation only).

For the next leg of your journey, you'll be following the famed High Sierra Trail, second in renown only to the John Muir Trail. Begin by making a switchbacking descent through a forest of sugar pines and firs to a bridged crossing of Buck Creek. You ascend the mostly open slope of Buck Canyon and then bend around to a twin-branched tributary with nice campsites complete with a bear box. A long, rolling traverse follows, which leads across the north slope of the Middle Fork Kaweah River canyon, crossing several refreshing brooks along the way. Through periodic gaps in the forest, you have excellent views of the canyon and of Little Blue Dome, Sugarbowl Dome, and Castle Rocks. At 4.6 miles from Bearpaw Meadow, you pass the Sevenmile Hill Trail junction and then continue another 0.4 mile to the crossing of Mehrten Creek (7600±). On the west side of the creek, a use-trail leads steeply up the hillside to the last legal campsites along the High Sierra Trail (bear box).

Away from Mehrten Creek you make a 0.75-mile descent over Sevenmile Hill to the first branch of Panther Creek. For the next couple of miles you follow the mildly undulating trail in and out of the seams of the tributaries of Panther Creek. At 0.2 mile beyond the last crossing, you continue past a junction with the Wolverton Cutoff trail and proceed through light forest on a short, moderate climb.

Following the climb, four short switchbacks lead to easier travel as you traverse across a south-facing hillside. Along this traverse, you alternately pass through open areas with great views, and stretches of mixed forest composed of black oaks,

THE BUCKEYE FIRE

In October of 1988, a chaparral-covered slope below Eagle View was the site of the Buckeye Fire, ignited by a cigarette discarded at the bottom of the canyon. After a cost of 2.5 million dollars and the efforts of 1200 firefighters, the weeklong blaze was extinguished, but not before it consumed over 3000 acres. A policy of controlled burning in Giant Forest, which reduced forest fuels, was credited with slowing the advance of the fire into the Big Trees.

white firs, Jeffrey pines, and incense cedars. Nearly level hiking brings you to aptly named Eagle View. From this aerie 3300 feet above the Middle Fork Kaweah River, you have a grand view of the river's canyon, Moro Rock, Castle Rocks, and the glacier-sculpted peaks of the Great Western Divide.

Continuing westbound from Eagle View, you follow the trail away from the Middle Fork and into Giant Forest to a junction near a giant sequoia referred to as the Burial Tree. Remain on the High Sierra Trail and proceed another 0.5 mile to the parking lot at Crescent Meadow.

⊙ Side excursions to Seville, Lost, and Ranger lakes are easily accomplished via short trails (see Trip 7).

⊙ From Bearpaw Meadow, the strikingly beautiful Hamilton Lakes and the equally distinctive Nine Lakes Basin are worthy trip extensions. If a shuttle can't be arranged, backpackers can make a complete loop back to the Rowell Meadow trailhead by following trails back to Lodgepole, and then using the Twin Lakes and JO Pass trails back to Jennie Lakes Wilderness.

R **PERMITS:** Wilderness permit required for overnight stays.

CAMPFIRES: Prohibited at Bearpaw Meadow and above 10,400 feet.

CAMPING: At Bearpaw Meadow, designated sites only.

BIG MEADOWS ROAD TRAILHEADS

TRIP 9

Mitchell Peak

Ⓜ ↗ DH

DISTANCE: 3.25 miles one way

ELEVATION: 8330/10,365, +2090'/-55'

SEASON: July to mid-October

USE: Light

MAPS: *Mt. Silliman, Jennie Lakes Wilderness and Monarch Wilderness, USFS*

INTRODUCTION: Mitchell Peak, straddling the border of Jennie Lakes Wilderness and Kings Canyon National Park, provides one of the best viewpoints accessible to hikers on the western side of the greater Kings Canyon and Sequoia national parks region. Seemingly, such a grand vista would attract more devotees, but alas, the summit is seldom visited. What's a loss to some is a bonus to others, as hikers who do make the 3.25-mile climb can expect to enjoy the scenery in solitude.

DIRECTIONS TO THE TRAILHEAD: Leave Generals Highway 6.4 miles southeast of the Y-intersection with Highway 180, and follow Big Meadows Road east 9.7 miles to the signed turnoff for the Marvin Pass Trailhead. Turn onto a single-lane, dirt road and travel 2.5 miles to the signed trailhead, remaining on the main road at all intersections.

DESCRIPTION: Begin hiking up an old road to a trail sign, where you turn onto a single-track trail and climb up a hillside through scattered fir and shrubs, including manzanita, chinquapin, and currant. A moderate climb brings you to a small, fern- and flower-lined rivulet amid thicker forest. Now you pass above a pocket of foliage carpeted with an array of wildflowers,

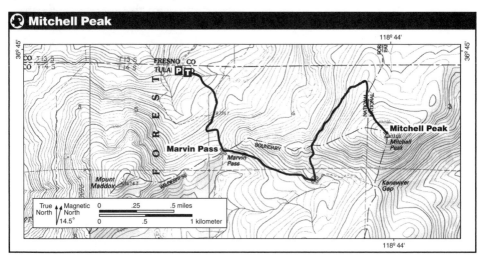

including shooting star, corn lily, buttercup, and monkey flower. Away from the lush surroundings, the steady ascent continues as the trail switchbacks up to the signed wilderness boundary and a junction at Marvin Pass (9115'±).

Turn left (southeast) and follow the Kanawyer Gap Trail across the south side of a ridge through scattered-to-light forest, shrubs, and boulders. Lupine and paintbrush add a splash of color. A mellow 0.75-mile traverse leads to a junction amid a field of chinquapin, where you turn left (north) and climb a mostly open slope back to the ridgecrest. Once across the crest, you veer northeast and make an ascending traverse along the northwest side of Mitchell Peak through a light, mixed forest of western white pines, red firs, and lodgepole pines. Eventually the grade increases as you make a winding climb toward the blocky summit. Leaving the last of the trees behind, you weave southeast among boulders to the summit and a commanding vista.

Perhaps the most impressive sight from the top of Mitchell Peak is the foreground terrain plummeting steeply northeast into the deep cleft of Kings Canyon, backdropped majestically by the towering crest of the Monarch Divide.

A vast array of Sierra Nevada summits can be seen as well, including the Palisades and Mt. Goddard along the horizon to the northeast, a multiplicity of peaks along the spine of the Great Western Divide, and the multi-colored Kaweah Peaks to the southeast. Pieces of the old fire lookout lie scattered around the summit, a silent reminder that in former days rangers had the daily privilege of this incredible view.

Labrador tea on the Marvin Pass Trail

KENNEDY MEADOWS TRAILHEAD

TRIP **10**

Evans Grove

M ↗ DH

DISTANCE: 2.0 miles one way

ELEVATION: 7430/6750, +595'/-920'

SEASON: Early June to mid-October

USE: Light

MAP: *Wren Peak*

INTRODUCTION: A virtually forgotten trail in a remote section of Giant Sequoia National Monument allows hikers the opportunity to stand among the giant monarchs of the forest in serenity and solitude. If you want to avoid the crowds around the more popular groves in the nearby national parks, this short hike is an excellent choice.

DIRECTIONS TO THE TRAILHEAD: Follow Generals Highway to Quail Flat, 3.4 miles southeast of the Y-intersection with Highway 180. At Quail Flat, head northeast on paved, single-lane Forest Service Road 14S02, which is one of four roads branching away from the flat. Follow

Giant Sequoia in the Evans Grove

14S02 for 5.1 miles to a junction and turn left onto Road 13S26, heeding a sign for the Kennedy Meadow trailhead. At 1.4 miles, you reach a Y-junction, where you

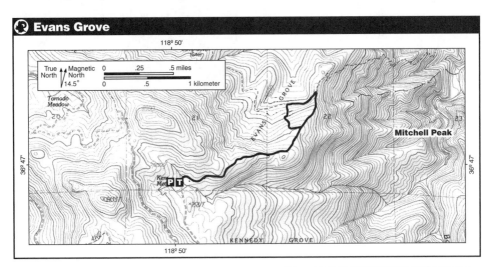

turn right onto Road 13S25, where another sign reads NATIONAL FOREST TRAILHEAD. The trailhead is in a wide clearing 0.5 mile ahead.

DESCRIPTION: Begin hiking down an old roadbed through scattered firs to a culvert draining a spring-fed tributary of Boulder Creek. Climb away from the stream on a single-track trail, pass through an old gate, and then ascend to the crest of a manzanita-covered ridge, from where you have fine views to the southeast of Shell Mtn. and the surrounding terrain. Continue along the ridgecrest until a pronounced descent takes you back into forest cover. Soon, giant sequoias begin to appear as you wind down to an unsigned junction, just over a mile from the trailhead.

Veer left at the junction, following a path downhill through the big trees. After the short, steep descent, you intersect an old road. Turn right and follow the mild grade of the roadbed, which is lined with thimbleberry, lupine, and paintbrush. After an easy 0.3 mile, leave the road at the next junction and climb steeply up a single-track trail past more sequoias. A 0.3-mile climb brings you back to the first junction. From here, retrace your steps to the trailhead.

TRIP **11**

Chicago Stump

E ↗ DH

DISTANCE: 0.3 mile one way

ELEVATION: 6645/6610, +60'/-95'

SEASON: Late May to November

USE: Light

MAP: *Hume*

INTRODUCTION: A short, easy hike leads to one of the curiosities of Giant Sequoia National Monument. In 1893, the General Noble Tree, one of the supreme monarchs of the Converse Grove, was cut down in segments, shipped to the Chicago World's Fair, and reassembled for exhibition to a skeptical audience. Most observers doubted that the existence of such large trees was

Chicago Stump

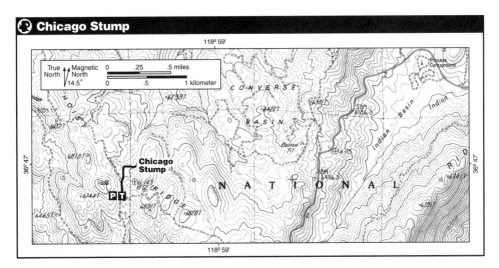

Chicago Stump

plausible, calling the oddity the "California Hoax." Along with all the other large sequoias in Converse Basin, the Noble Tree perished, its stump named for the tree's final resting place.

DIRECTIONS TO THE TRAILHEAD: Drive on Highway 180 about 3.0 miles north of Grant Grove Village to Forest Service Road 13S03 at Cherry Gap. Past a gate and a large wooden sign about the history of Converse Basin, turn left and travel north on Road 13S03 for 2.0 miles to a signed trailhead, where a small parking area is on the right (east) shoulder.

DESCRIPTION: Begin hiking down an old roadbed through Jeffrey pines and shrubs to the edge of a lengthy, verdant meadow bordered by red firs, azaleas, ferns, and a number of young sequoias. Proceed down the road to a fork and follow either path to the stump, where placards provide information on the history of the fallen tree.

THE NOBLE TREE

This giant was estimated to be the largest sequoia ever cut, requiring 18 men with outstretched arms to encircle its base. Although lumberjacks needed only several days to fell the monarch, 3200 years had been necessary for the big tree to reach such size. Modern-day hikers will gaze at the stump in awe of the former immensity of the now-truncated tree, secure in the knowledge that future giants are protected from meeting with a similar fate.

CONVERSE BASIN TRAILHEADS

TRIP 12

Boole Tree

E ↻ **DH**

DISTANCE: 2.25 miles

ELEVATION: 6265/6765, +740'/-740'

SEASON: Late May to November

USE: Light

MAP: *Hume*

INTRODUCTION: Sometimes size has advantages, and such was the case with the Boole Tree. While hundreds of giant sequoias met the ax in Converse Basin, this lone survivor received a stay of execution due to its immensity. Eventually known as the third largest sequoia in existence, the Boole Tree was spared the fate of its less fortunate neighbors. Although this impressive monarch has the largest base circumference of any sequoia (113 feet), its height of 269 feet and its volume of 42,472 cubic feet ultimately ranked the tree as the eighth largest giant sequoia. Ironically, the tree was named for the Converse Basin mill superintendent, Frank Boole, who oversaw

the demise of the rest of the sequoias in the area.

Hikers not only have the privilege of seeing such a notable tree, but the 2.25-mile loop offers them the chance to see eight other conifer species, including lodgepole, western white, Jeffrey and sugar pines; as well as red and white firs; and incense cedar. Although the trail is short, hikers pass through a variety of flora and terrain. In addition, the trail offers excellent views of the Kings River area from an open ridgecrest.

DIRECTIONS TO THE TRAILHEAD: Drive on Highway 180 about 4.25 miles north of Grant Grove Village to Forest Service Road 13S55 and head north 0.25 mile to a triple junction. Proceed straight, staying on 13S55 through Stump Meadow, and arrive at a large trailhead parking area with pit toilets and picnic tables, 2.5 miles from Highway 180.

DESCRIPTION: Pass through a wooden gate and walk uphill from the parking area through a thick canopy of mixed forest. Follow the trail on a moderate climb up switchbacks and log steps, followed by a short descent to a T-junction. A very short drop from the junction leads to the Boole Tree, 0.9 mile from the parking lot.

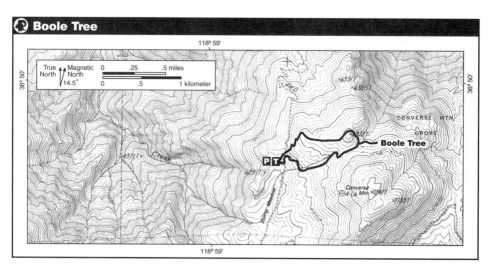

Introduction to Grant Grove

The Boole Tree, eighth largest giant sequoia in the world

After admiring the huge monarch, return to the junction and ascend a hillside to a viewpoint overlooking the deep gorge of the Kings River. You'll notice a significant change in the foliage, as the drier vegetation of manzanita, mountain misery, and scattered Jeffrey pine covers the hilltop. Heading west, you follow a ridge downhill to a series of switchbacks, with more fine views of the Kings River country along the way. Continue the descent southwest to the parking area.

Grant Grove's giant sequoias were some of the first big trees to come to the attention of early Californians, and the grove was also one of the first to receive limited federal protection. In 1890, four sections of land were set aside as General Grant National Park in the bill establishing Yosemite and Sequoia national parks. The expansion of parkland to the area we see today didn't come until the creation of Kings Canyon National Park in 1940. The private inholding of nearby Wilsonia is the lone piece of property the government failed to acquire from old land claims that were filed during the late 1800s, despite a reasonable offer to purchase it, along with other inholdings, in 1903 for an average price of $19 per acre. The shanties and cabins of Wilsonia remain a blight on the otherwise pristine Grant Grove area.

Of course, the focal point of Grant Grove has always been the General Grant Tree, third largest in the world at 46,608 cubic feet, with a height of over 268 feet and the largest base diameter of any sequoia at 40.3 feet. Named by Lucretia Baker in 1867 for Ulysses S. Grant, commanding general of the Union Army during the Civil War and subsequently president of the U.S., the tree was "discovered" by Joseph Hardin Thomas in 1862, although it certainly had been seen before that by local Monache Indians. In the 1920s, President Calvin Coolidge declared the Grant Tree "The Nation's Christmas Tree," and, in the 1950s, President Dwight D. Eisenhower proclaimed it a living national shrine, in memory of Americans who perished during wars. Today, hundreds of visitors pay tribute to the grand giant each day from spring through fall.

While backpacking opportunities around Grant Grove are virtually nonexistent, the area affords dayhikers plenty of diversions. An excellent network of trails covers the grove, offering myriad connections and loop possibilities. Aside from the obvious attraction of the Big Trees, hikers may enjoy quiet forest strolls accented by pocket meadows, vista points, waterfalls, and dancing streams. You can even learn and a bit of history on the Big Stump Grove Trail. Although the General Grant Tree Trail is usually packed with tourists, many of the other trails in the grove are lightly used, inviting hikers to experience the majesty of the Big Trees in relative solitude.

ACCESS: *(Open all year)* The Grant Grove area is easily accessed via Highway 180. From the Y-intersection with Generals Highway, Grant Grove Village is a mere 0.9 mile north. Access from the south via Generals Highway is subject to storm closures during winter.

AMENITIES: Grant Grove Village offers a wide assortment of visitor services including visitor center, general store, gift shop, restaurants, post office, and public showers. Lodging runs the gamut from rustic

CAMPGROUNDS

Campground	Fee	Elevation	Season	Restrooms	Running Water	Bear Boxes	Phone
AZALEA	$18	6500'	Open all year	Flush Toilets	Yes	Yes	Yes
CRYSTAL SPRINGS	$18	6500'	May–September	Flush Toilets	Yes	Yes	Yes
SUNSET	$18	6500'	May–September	Flush Toilets	Yes	Yes	Yes

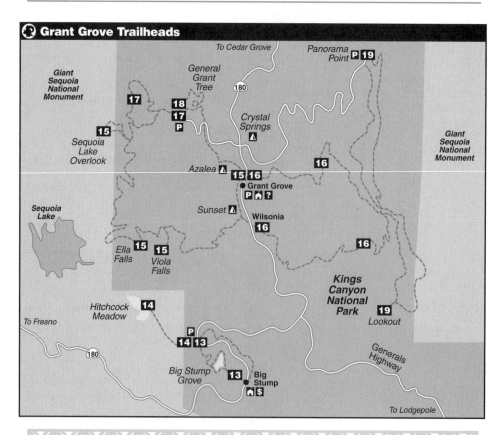

cabins to lodge rooms and suites at the John Muir Lodge. Other than in the tent cabins and rustic low-end wood cabins, lodging is available year-round. Reservations: (866) 522-6966, (559) 452-1081 or (559) 335-5000.

RANGER STATION: Wilderness permits and backcountry information can be obtained at the Grant Grove Visitor Center.

GOOD TO KNOW BEFORE YOU GO:
   1. Water is scarce on many of the trails in Grant Grove, particularly from mid to late season, so carry plenty of water in your pack.
   2. With elevations ranging between 5400 feet and 7600 feet, Grant Grove typically becomes snow-free well before the neighboring backcountry, providing early-season opportunities to enjoy the outdoors.

General Grant Tree

GRANT GROVE TRAILHEADS

TRIP **13**

Big Stump Grove

E ↻ DH

DISTANCE: 2.0 miles

ELEVATION: 6355/6155/6405, +325'/-325'

SEASON: Late May to late October

USE: Moderate to heavy

MAP: *General Grant Grove*

INTRODUCTION: Explore a slice of history on this trail, which exposes hikers to an ethic of a bygone era. In the late 1800s, when the resources of the western U.S. seemed inexhaustible, loggers came to the Sierra sequoia groves in search of jobs and big-time profits. Although the lumber from the giant sequoias would eventually prove inferior to that of other conifers, just about every big tree in this grove was sacrificed, ironically to be used for nothing more than shakes and fence posts. Visitors in the modern era will bear witness to the results: countless giant stumps spread throughout Big Stump Grove—a vivid reminder of a shortsighted vision. What could have been one of most impressive sequoia groves for Park visitors is now nothing more than a graveyard of fallen monarchs.

   Although the Big Stump Trail is quite popular with tourists, few of them go beyond the loop around Big Stump Meadow, leaving the greater part of the trail to the willing souls who don't mind the 2-mile hike.

DIRECTIONS TO THE TRAILHEAD: Drive on Highway 180 to the Big Stump Picnic Area parking lot, 0.6 mile past the Big Stump entrance to Kings Canyon National Park.

DESCRIPTION: The Big Stump Trail begins at a signboard near the restrooms on the

Big Stump Grove

south side of the parking lot. You head downhill on a wide, well-graded trail through pockets of manzanita and a forest of incense cedars, Jeffrey pines, sugar pines, and firs. Soon you encounter the first notable monarch, the Resurrection Tree, a topless sequoia still thriving despite having been struck by lightning. The winding descent brings you down to a Y-junction, 0.3 mile from the parking lot.

Veer left at the junction and circle Big Stump Meadow, site of the abandoned Smith Comstock Mill, which occupied the clearing in the late 1800s. A number of large sequoia stumps and piles of redwood sawdust litter the otherwise verdant clearing. Part way around the meadow, you encounter the Burnt Monarch, a huge

FEATHER BEDS

Since the brittle sequoias tend to burst into pieces when felled, loggers used to dig a trench and line it with boughs and branches in an attempt to cushion the blow and keep a big tree intact. The "feather bed" here is overgrown with a tangle of willows and shrubs, a jumble that belies its former purpose.

sequoia that succumbed to fire but remains standing. Just beyond is a pair of sequoias planted in 1888 by Jesse Pattee, a lumberjack who occupied a nearby cabin during the logging heyday. A cursory glance at these two young trees reveals their limited stature compared to the massive stumps of their felled neighbors. Nearing the close of the loop around the meadow, you reach a lateral leading to the Feather Bed.

Whether by the Feather Bed lateral or the trail around the meadow, you soon reach a junction with the main trail.

In order to see the Shattered Giant, you will have to walk west, back toward the trailhead, and around the south side of the meadow to a small creek. Rather than follow the standard logging practice of felling trees uphill to minimize the impact, loggers dropped this particular tree down-slope and watched the giant sequoia fragment into a hundred useless pieces, which still lie in waste across the streambed. After you have marveled at the remains, retrace your steps to the junction near the east end of the meadow. Continuing east, you cross a bridge and quickly reach the Mark Twain Stump.

Away from the Mark Twain Stump, the trail leads you through a narrow meadow toward Highway 180. Just north of the Big Stump entrance station, 1.0 mile from the

MARK TWAIN STUMP

Instead of being chopped down for lumber, in 1891 this tree was meticulously disassembled and the segments transported to the American Museum of Natural History and the British Museum in London for exhibition. Thirteen days of chopping, sawing, and wedging were necessary to drop the tree. Nowadays, a stair takes hikers to the top of the stump, from where they can gain a better appreciation for the immensity of this giant sequoia.

trailhead, you follow an angling crosswalk across the highway and over to the resumption of trail. A moderate climb ensues as you walk through mixed forest, roughly paralleling the highway. Beyond the bridged crossing of a tiny creek, you come to a junction with a short but steep lateral that leads you up a hillside to the Sawed Tree. Loggers attempted to cut down this massive sequoia, but they eventually gave up, perhaps deeming the project too difficult. Since the bark wasn't completely severed, life-giving nutrients continued to travel up the tree and the giant sequoia was spared.

Back on the main trail, the ascent continues as you pass by more stumps. Soon, the grade eases as you veer southwest toward the highway. A tunnel leads underneath the road and at the far end is a junction with the Hitchcock Meadows Trail. Turn left and head uphill, soon closing your loop at the Big Stump parking lot.

The Burnt Monarch in the Big Stump Grove

GRANT GROVE TRAILHEADS

TRIP 14

Hitchcock Meadow

E ↗ DH

DISTANCE: 0.6 mile one way

ELEVATION: 6360/6090, +20'/-290'

SEASON: Late May to late October

USE: Light

MAP: *General Grant Grove*

INTRODUCTION: A short hike to a small picturesque meadow on an infrequently used trail will tempt hikers away from the more popular Big Stump Loop nearby. If sequoia stumps pique your interest, don't despair, because the Hitchcock Meadow Trail travels past a number of the old remnants. If a longer hike is desired, the trail continues past Hitchcock Meadow, providing opportunities for further wanderings.

DIRECTIONS TO THE TRAILHEAD: Drive on Highway 180 to the Big Stump Picnic Area parking lot, 0.6 mile past the Big Stump entrance to Kings Canyon National Park.

DESCRIPTION: The Hitchcock Meadow Trail begins by a trailhead sign at the northeast end of the parking lot. You immediately descend to an intersection with the Big Stump loop, which passes through a tunnel beneath the highway to your right. Veer left at this junction and proceed through light mixed forest on a moderate descent. As you drop into the forest, a number of stumps appear, remnants of the logging era of the late 1800s, which claimed just about every large sequoia in this area. The nearly continuous descent brings you to Hitchcock Meadow, a thin ribbon of luxurious grasses, plants, and wildflowers near a small stream that flows northwest into nearby Sequoia Lake. Scattered around the meadow are more sequoia stumps.

You may elect to continue your journey by following the trail past Hitchcock Meadow to a junction with the South Boundary Trail at 0.75 mile.

The trail's right-hand branch heads east for 1.1 miles to Generals Highway and a connection with the Azalea Trail, 0.1 mile farther (see Trip 16). Perhaps a more interesting alternative would be to bear left at the junction and head north to Sequoia Creek and Viola Falls, 2.0 miles from the trailhead (see Trip 15).

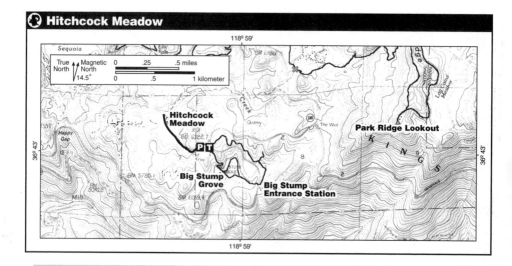

GRANT GROVE TRAILHEADS

TRIP 15

Sunset Loop Trail: Viola and Ella Falls, the Dead Giant, and Sequoia Lake Overlook

M ⟳ DH

DISTANCE: 5.75 miles

ELEVATION: 6650/5440/6650, +1885'/-1885'

Season: Late May to mid-October

USE: Light

MAP: *General Grant Grove*

TRAIL LOG:

1.5	Viola Falls Jct.
2.0	Ella Falls
4.0	Dead Giant/Sequoia Lake Overlook
4.25	North Grove Jct.
4.6	North Grove Jct.

INTRODUCTION: Waterfalls, vistas, and big trees are the chief attractions of this fine loop through the western fringe of Grant Grove. While busloads of tourists rub elbows along the ever-popular General Grant Tree Nature Trail, hikers can revel in the relative quiet and solitude found nearby along the Sunset Trail. Viola and Ella falls are best viewed in spring and early summer when snowmelt fills Sequoia Creek. During this period, Ella Falls is a raging torrent that thunders over a sheer cliff, whereas the multiple cascades of Viola Falls tumble delightfully into picturesquely sculpted pools. Farther along the loop, the Sequoia Lake Overlook provides a fine view of the artificial lake and the surrounding country-side. Although other trails in the Park provide access to more sequoias, there are a

number of interesting giants along this route, including the Dead Giant, a visible reminder of a less environmentally sensitive era. For those who desire more of the Big Trees, the nearly mile-long North Grove Trail is an easily added attraction (see Trip 17).

DIRECTIONS TO THE TRAILHEAD: Drive on Highway 180 to Grant Grove Village, 1.5 miles north of the Y-intersection with Generals Highway. Park in the visitor center parking lot.

DESCRIPTION: To locate the beginning of the Sunset and Azalea trails, follow the crosswalk directly opposite the visitor center across Highway 180 to the west side of the road, where a sign reads GRANT TREE TRAIL, GRANT TREE 0.1. A very short section of trail leads downhill to a marked junction. Turn left on a trail signed SUNSET CAMPGROUND and follow it parallel to the highway through light forest. Soon you must cross the campground access road and continue to a signed T-junction, 0.3 mile from the trailhead. Here the Azalea Trail continues straight ahead, but you turn right and follow the Sunset Trail over a low hill. A short, mild descent on indistinct trail leads to a swale. After a very brief climb of a hillside from the swale, you emerge into a small opening in the forest where manzanita lines the path. From here, the route becomes more evident as you begin a steady descent that will last until you reach the Park boundary near Sequoia Lake.

Weave down the hillside over slabs and around boulders through a light, mixed forest to a bridged crossing of an unnamed tributary of Sequoia Creek. At 1.5 miles, you reach a signed four-way junction with the old road from the Swale Work Center.

⌷ **SIDE TRIP TO VIOLA FALLS:** To reach Viola Falls, turn left (south) at the junction and follow the old road on a mild decline through moderate forest for 0.2 mile, to where the road curves east. A small sign marked VIOLA FALLS directs foot traffic straight ahead onto a single-track trail that

Sunset Loop Trail

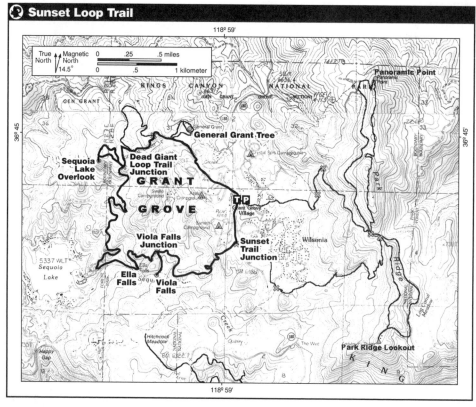

quickly leads alongside Sequoia Creek. The narrow path ends at the base of a hill, from where you can work your way to an overlook directly above the falls. Don't expect the drama of a Yosemite waterfall, as Viola Falls is actually a series of short cataracts that pour swiftly down a narrow channel into swirling pools in basins scoured out of the solid rock. Early season flowers add a touch of color to the stream banks. **END OF SIDE TRIP**

From the four-way junction, continue straight ahead on a steady descent through light to moderate mixed forest. A series of switchbacks take you across a seasonal stream, over a seep, and down to Ella Falls, 2.0 miles from the Visitor Center. While Viola Falls seems rather tame, Ella presents the sights and sounds one expects from a significant waterfall. In spring and early summer, Sequoia Creek plunges raucously down a sheer face into a whirling pool before resuming its cacophonous journey toward Sequoia Lake.

Proceed for another 0.25 mile beyond the falls to a junction near the boundary between Kings Canyon National Park and the private property of YMCA camps surrounding Sequoia Lake. The YMCA has granted permission for hikers to continue straight ahead, passing over their property to an overview of the lake, provided hikers remain on the trail and do not enter the camps. To remain on the Sunset Loop Trail from the junction, follow a trail, signed GRANT TREE, which angles away from the path to Sequoia Lake.

Climb moderately steeply up to the old Park access road from Sequoia Lake. Once on the road, turn right and begin the long climb back to Grant Grove. You follow broken asphalt on a steady, winding ascent through the partial shade of a mixed forest.

Near the 3-mile mark, you encounter a road on the left that comes up from Sequoia Lake. About 0.25 mile farther, an unmarked single-track trail, coming from Sequoia Lake, merges with the road on the left. Continue the climb to the top of a hill, 4.0 miles from the Visitor Center, where you reach a signed junction with the Dead Giant Loop Trail, which goes to the Sequoia Lake Overlook.

SIDE TRIP TO THE DEAD GIANT AND SEQUOIA LAKE OVERLOOK: From the junction, take the lower trail across a lightly forested hillside above verdant Lion Meadow. Continue a short distance past the far edge of the meadow to the Dead Giant. This very large sequoia met an untimely demise at the hands of axe-wielding loggers. Careful inspection of the trunk reveals axe marks encircling the tree that effectively sheared off the cambium layer, permanently interrupting the flow of nutrients up the tree. Without life-giving sustenance the tree ultimately died, providing a visible memorial to an age-old truth: nature's greatest enemy is man himself.

Leaving the Dead Giant behind, you climb the hillside to the crest of an open ridge and follow this spine southwest to an unmarked junction. Continue straight ahead for a short distance to where the ridge begins to drop, arriving at the Sequoia Lake Overlook. Although the attractive body of water before you appears natural, Sequoia Lake was actually created in the late 1800s as a millpond supplying water to a flume that took lumber to Sanger, in the San Joaquin Valley. Today, the lake is home to a number of summer camps.

Once you have enjoyed the view, backtrack to the junction. Now following a sign marked simply TRAIL, you proceed eastbound on the return leg of the loop and soon arrive back at the old road. **END OF SIDE TRIP**

From the Dead Giant Loop Trail junction, resume your climb along the roadbed toward the Grant Tree, passing around the

edge of Lion Meadow. About 0.25 mile from the junction, you pass the first intersection with the North Grove Trail (see Trip 17). Another 0.3 mile of climbing along the old road brings you to the other end of the North Grove Trail. A short distance from the second junction, you reach the edge of the large parking lot for the popular General Grant Tree complex. In contrast to the relative solitude of the last several miles, the bustling activity around the Grant Tree can be a bit overwhelming. Proceed past the trailhead for the General Grant Tree Trail to the far end of the parking lot and find the continuation of your route to the Grant Grove Visitor Center to the left of the restrooms. Look nearby for a stand of five stately sequoias known as the Happy Family.

You walk along a split-rail fence just to the left of a delightful rivulet known as Big Tree Creek. Soon, you cross the tiny stream on a plank bridge and stroll past the Michigan Tree, a huge, fallen sequoia that reposes in broken sections beside the trail.

Ella Falls

Just beyond this tree the fence ends, and you continue up the trail to a crossing of the Grant Tree access road. A short climb away from the road takes you along a stream through light forest past the Columbine Picnic Area and into the Azalea Campground. Pass through the campground, negotiating a number of access-road crossings along the way. After stepping across the last road, you cross the creek on a plank bridge, and ascend the hillside beyond to the junction near the visitor center. Turn uphill at the junction and retrace your steps to the visitor center parking lot.

GRANT GROVE TRAILHEADS

TRIP **16**

Azalea – Manzanita Loop Trail

M ○ DH

DISTANCE: 4.6 miles

ELEVATION: 6650/7495/6650, +1200'/-1200'

SEASON: Mid-June to mid-October

USE: Moderate

MAPS: *General Grant Grove Grant Grove Trail Map & Guide, SNHA*

INTRODUCTION: This trip offers a short, pleasant hike on a little-used trail away from the teeming masses around the General Grant Tree. Along the way, you get to sample a wide variety of terrain, from azalea- and fern-lined brooks to dry, manzanita-covered hillsides.

DIRECTIONS TO THE TRAILHEAD: Drive on Highway 180 to Grant Grove Village, 1.5 miles north of the Y-intersection with Generals Highway. Park in the visitor center parking lot.

DESCRIPTION: To get to the beginning of the Azalea trail, follow the crosswalk directly opposite the visitor center across Highway 180 to the west side of the road, where a sign reads GRANT TREE TRAIL, GRANT TREE 0.1. A very short section of trail leads downhill to a marked junction. Turn left on a trail signed SUNSET CAMPGROUND and follow it parallel to the highway through light forest. Soon you must cross the campground access road and continue to a signed T-junction, 0.3 mile from the trailhead. Here the Azalea Trail continues straight ahead, while the Sunset Trail goes off to your right.

Through scattered to light forest, continue straight from the junction, roughly paralleling Highway 180, which is to your left. You walk across the highway just before the 0.5-mile mark, climb up a low hill, and then descend to a lushly lined seasonal stream. A mild descent within earshot of the highway leads you to a crossing of another pleasant stream and then across the access road to the private development of Wilsonia. Look for the continuation of the trail a short distance down the road, and then follow the trail on a mild descent to the crossing of yet another picturesque stream. A short distance farther is the junction with the South Boundary Trail, 0.9 mile from the visitor center.

Following a sign reading AZALEA TRAIL, PARK RIDGE, 2, you bend to the left and climb moderately up the trail through patches of the namesake shrub. Just as you pull away from the din of traffic along the highway, the appearance of power lines and cabins from the Wilsonia settlement further

inhibits the potential for a wilderness ambience. Ignoring the clutter, you ascend at a moderate grade for the next mile, strolling alongside the attractive stream that you previously crossed and leaving the signs of civilization behind as you proceed toward Park Ridge. Along the way, you cross the creek a couple of more times on wooden bridges. Eventually, the trail pulls away from the drainage and switchbacks up to the crest of Park Ridge. At 2.5 miles from the visitor center, you reach a signed junction of the Manzanita Trail, the Park Ridge Trail (see Trip 19), and an extremely short lateral to the Park Ridge Fire Road. A trip from the junction to the lookout and back will add 2.0 miles to your overall journey.

From the junction, bear left (northwest) on the nearly level track of the Manzanita Trail, paralleling the fire road briefly before bending away on a mild descent across the west face of Park Ridge. On sandy trail,

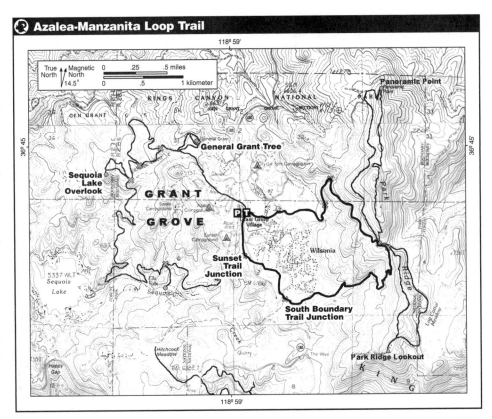

you break out into the open amid widely scattered conifers and clumps of manzanita. Farther down the trail, the trees nearly disappear where the hillside is covered with the trail's namesake shrub. Along this stretch of trail, on those rare days when the sky gets a respite from the customary haze, you have nice views across the open slope through the foothills and out to the San Joaquin Valley.

DEAD TREES

Cursory observation will reveal a number of dead white firs downslope at the fringe of the manzanita. Although fires have affected the forest on Park Ridge in the past, these trees were victims of a tussock moth infestation in the mid-1990s.

Eventually you leave the open slopes behind and enter a stand of the dead trees on the way to a Y-junction, 3.3 miles from the trailhead.

No signs point the way to Grant Grove, but from this junction you angle back down-slope to the left and continue the descent, dropping into thicker cover from a mixed forest filled with a bounty of cedar saplings. At 3.6 miles, you encounter a Y-junction with a lateral to Crystal Springs Campground. Continue straight ahead from this intersection, curving around a large water tank to an access road. You follow the road downhill toward some metal-roofed cabins for Park Service employee housing. Just before these old structures, follow a single-track trail veering off to the left to bypass the housing area. Soon the trail ends at a service road which leads you back to the edge of the Grant Grove Village. Complete the loop by strolling across the Village grounds to the visitor center parking area.

GRANT GROVE TRAILHEADS

TRIP **17**

North Grove Loop

E ↻ DH

DISTANCE: 1.5 miles

ELEVATION: 6320/5965, +355'/-355'

SEASON: Late May to mid-October

USE: Light

MAPS: *General Grant Grove*
Grant Grove, SNHA

INTRODUCTION: A reasonably short trail leads hikers away from the hubbub around the General Grant Tree down into a secluded grove of giant sequoias. Initially, the route follows the course of the old paved road that used to provide automobile access from Sequoia Lake. Nowadays, the cars are completely gone, as are the majority of tourists. The old road leads to a forested descent into the big trees of the North Grove. Those with extra time and energy can easily add the 0.75-mile Dead Giant Loop or the much longer Sunset Trail to their itinerary (see Trip 15).

DIRECTIONS TO THE TRAILHEAD: Just north of the Grant Grove visitor center, turn west from Highway 180 onto the General Grant Tree access road. Follow this road 0.7 mile to the parking lot.

DESCRIPTION: You begin your hike by heading west from the General Grant Tree parking lot, through the tour-bus and RV parking area to the closed road at the far end. Continue down the closed road for 0.1 mile to a signed junction with the North Grove Trail. Leaving the closed road, turn right (west) and begin a moderate, winding descent through a mixed forest of sugar pines, white firs, and incense cedars. Eventually, you draw near a trickling creek to your left that seems to provide sufficient

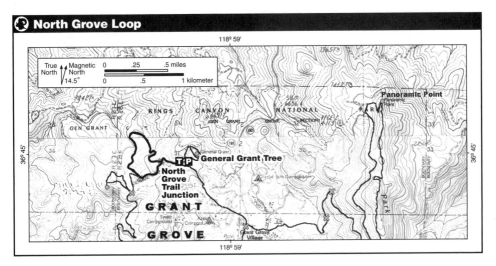

North Grove Loop

moisture for a number of large sequoias, as well as for a nice collection of shrubs and seasonal wildflowers. At the bottom of the descent, the trail veers west and you come to an overgrown wagon road heading into the trees on your right.

Now the task is to regain all that lost elevation as you head back toward the road. As you climb, the giant sequoias fade into memory, replaced by less majestic species such as pine, fir, and incense cedar.

Just past the 1-mile mark, your climb abates as you intersect the old road and follow it back on a milder ascent toward the General Grant Tree parking lot.

WAGON ROAD

Lumbermen used to travel this road to Millwood, site of two mills built by the Sanger Lumber Company in 1889. The company also built a 54-mile flume that took lumber to the San Joaquin Valley. Just beyond the old road is a rare sight—a mature giant sequoia that succumbed to a forest fire. Most sequoias of this size are able to withstand the ravages of the average forest fire quite well. In fact, their reproductive cycle benefits from such calamities, because heat from fire opens up the tree's cones, allowing seeds to fall to the ground. To see a sequoia of this size unable to survive fire is indeed rare.

GRANT GROVE TRAILHEADS

TRIP **18**

General Grant Tree Trail

E ⟳ DH

DISTANCE: 0.5 mile loop

ELEVATION: 6320/6415, +100'/-100'

SEASON: Mid-May to mid-October

USE: Heavy

MAPS: *General Grant Grove Grant Grove, SNHA, General Grant Tree Trail, SNHA*

INTRODUCTION: At a height of 267 feet and with a base diameter of over 40 feet, the General Grant Tree is the third largest living tree in the world. Additional prestige is attached to the Grant Grove area as being the oldest section of Kings Canyon National Park, set aside as General Grant National Park in 1890 by the same congressional bill that established Yosemite National Park and greatly enlarged Sequoia National Park. Such notoriety has resulted in making Grant Grove one of the Park's most popular tourist attractions. While the

General Grant Tree Trail takes visitors to the base of the namesake tree and past a stellar assortment of other giants, the resulting crowds create an atmosphere reminiscent of a theme park.

The best bet for minimizing the effects of the tourist season is to pay homage to the Grant Tree early in the morning or late in the afternoon, or some time other than between Memorial Day and Labor Day. Crowds aside, the General Grant Tree Trail invites visitors to experience the awe-inspiring majesty of one of the world's largest living creatures in one of the finest groves of giant sequoias on the planet.

DIRECTIONS TO THE TRAILHEAD: Just north of the Grant Grove visitor center, turn west from Highway 180 onto the General Grant Tree access road. Follow this road 0.7 mile to the parking lot.

DESCRIPTION: Improvements at Grant Grove include wayside exhibits that have replaced the pamphlets formerly available at the trailhead.

Beyond the trailhead, you proceed counterclockwise along the paved trail, winding your way up to the centerpiece of the area, the General Grant Tree. A short climb from here takes you past the Gamlin Cabin, and then a mild descent leads you beside more giant sequoias and back to the

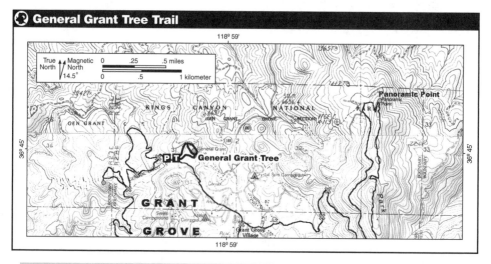
General Grant Tree Trail

trailhead. Trail extensions north of the grove are far less traveled, providing options for further wanderings.

TRIP **19**

Park Ridge Lookout

Ⓔ ↻ DH

DISTANCE: 5.6 miles

ELEVATION: 7415/7600, +1430'/-1430'

SEASON: Late May to late October

USE: Moderate

MAPS: *General Grant Grove*
         Grant Grove, SNHA

INTRODUCTION: This pleasant loop trip utilizes a hiking trail and a fire road to access one of the few remaining fire lookout towers in the Sierra. Hikers are not

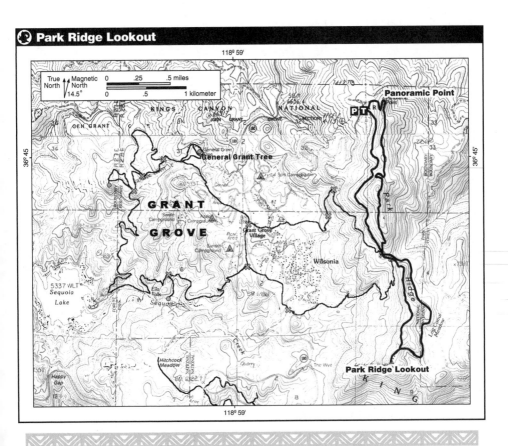

only treated to excellent views of the Great Western Divide and the San Joaquin Valley from the lookout, but, near the trailhead, to an extraordinary vista from Panoramic Point as well. Alternating between mixed forests and clearings, the route is mildly graded, following Park Ridge from the trailhead to the lookout.

DIRECTIONS TO THE TRAILHEAD: Drive on Highway 180, north past Grant Grove Village 0.25 mile to the signed Panoramic Point Road. Turn right and follow the paved road 2.3 miles to the trailhead at the end of the road, where you'll find picnic tables and restrooms.

DESCRIPTION: You begin the hike by following a paved trail, bordered by a split rail fence, for some 300 yards to Panoramic Point, where you are greeted by an excellent view that encompasses many Sierra landmarks. Here you'll see the Monarch Divide, the Great Western Divide, and a vast array of peaks along the Sierra crest. A metal sign identifies many of the significant features visible from this viewpoint.

Leaving the majority of sightseers behind, you continue up the trail away from Panoramic Point and follow a winding climb in and out of a scattered to light forest with an understory of manzanita and azalea. Scarred trunks on many of the conifers give evidence of a recent fire. Where the forest parts, you have alternating views—northeast, of the Monarch Divide; southeast, of the Great Western Divide; and west, toward the San Joaquin Valley. A little over a mile from the trailhead, you reach the crest of a knoll and begin a moderate descent down to a junction with a fire road, 1.6 miles from the parking lot.

Hike the road for about 50 yards to a signed trail junction, where you go straight on single-track trail toward the Park Ridge lookout. Follow minor ups and downs for another mile to a junction with the fire road, and then head up the road for approximately 250 yards to the fire lookout tower, 2.75 miles from the trailhead.

Transformers, power poles, communication towers, and weather equipment litter the edge of the ridge, along with a concrete-block building. Despite the man-made apparatus, the view from the lookout—from the San Joaquin Valley to the Great Western Divide and points in between—is quite rewarding.

You can easily vary your return by following the fire road back to the trailhead. Begin by retracing your steps to the junction of the road and the trail. Continue on the gently graded road through a light, mixed forest, wrapping around the hillside above Log Corral Meadow. At 1.3 miles from the lookout, you encounter the junction where you first met the fire road. Here you continue on the fire road. Fire-scarred trees and an open hillside covered with shrubs present more evidence of a previous fire as you make a general ascent. A final, 0.5-mile descent leads past a small meadow to a closed gate. From the gate, walk a short section of paved road back to the parking lot.

The Park Ridge Lookout

Introduction to Cedar Grove

The South Fork Kings River canyon, one of the deepest gorges in North America, is an undeniably spectacular sight, luring admirers from far and wide. Rivaling Yosemite Valley in many ways, Kings Canyon boasts towering rock walls, monolithic spires, and photogenic meadows. The Whitney Survey published the first written account of the canyon, which described the area as follows:

> The canyon here is very much like the Yosemite. It is a valley from half a mile to a mile wide at the bottom, about eleven miles long and closed at the lower end by a deep and inaccessible ravine like that below the Yosemite, but deeper and more precipitous. It expands above

and branches at its head, and is everywhere surrounded and walled in by grand precipices, broken here and there by side canyons, resembling the Yosemite in its main features. The Kings River canyon rivals and even surpasses the Yosemite in the altitude of its surrounding cliffs, but it has no features so striking as Half Dome, or Tutucanula (El Capitan), nor has it the stupendous waterfalls which make that valley quite unrivaled in beauty.

While a second-place finish to Yosemite in magnificence may be an arguable matter, devotees of Kings Canyon happily concede to a lower ranking in the number of tourist visits, especially by the multiple-camera-toting, polyester-clad, bus-riding variety.

Not simply picturesque in its own right, Kings Canyon is also a gateway to some of the High Sierra's finest scenery, issuing a siren call to hikers and backpackers of all stripes. Myriad trails radiate from Kings

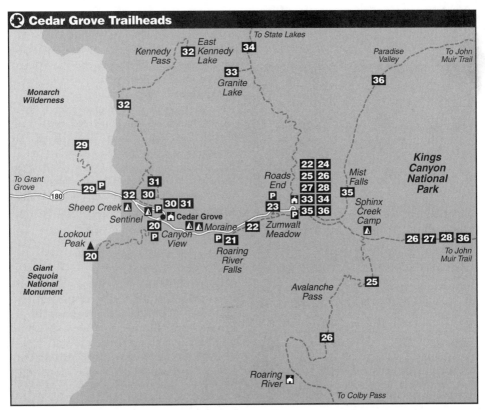

CAMPGROUNDS

Campground	Fee	Elevation	Season	Restrooms	Running Water	Bear Boxes	Phone
SENTINEL (at Cedar Grove)	$18	4600'	Late April– Mid-November	Flush Toilets	Yes	Yes	Yes
SHEEP CREEK (at Cedar Grove)	$18	4600'	As Needed: Late April– Mid-November	Flush Toilets	Yes	Yes	Yes
CANYON VIEW (0.5 mile east of Cedar Grove)	$18	4680'	Late April– Mid-November	Flush Toilets	Yes	Yes	Yes
MORAINE (0.75 mile east of Cedar Grove)	$18	4750'	As Needed: Late April– Mid-November	Flush Toilets	Yes	Yes	Yes

Canyon, most requiring stiff climbs of great elevation change in order to reach the high country beyond. The only trails that don't assume a significant grade are nature trails and short paths that never leave the valley floor. The prospect of a major ascent doesn't seem to deter too many recreationists from some of the trails leaving Roads End, especially the Woods Creek and Bubbs Creek trails, which are often combined as

The South Fork Kings River, backdropped by massive North Dome

part of the popular Rae Lakes Loop. Wilderness permits for such trails are often at a premium, especially during busy summer weekends. Other routes emanating from Kings Canyon are quiet and lonely, offering true wilderness experiences that are scenic and serene.

ACCESS: *(Late April to mid-November)* Paved, two-lane Highway 180 provides the sole vehicle access into Kings Canyon. Plan on a one-hour drive from the Big Stump Entrance, as sections of the 40-mile road are steep and winding. The highway dead-ends at appropriately named Roads End, forcing motorists to return the same way they entered the canyon. The highway is generally open from late April to mid-November. (Note: the following mileages shown in parentheses are calculated from the Y-intersection of Highway 180 and Generals Highway, 1.7 miles from the Big Stump Entrance).

Highway 180 continues from the Y-intersection with Generals Highway past the Grant Grove area, out of Kings Canyon National Park and into Sequoia National Forest, reaching the road's crest at Cherry Gap (5.8). The Hume Lake junction (10.3) provides access to picnic areas and campgrounds around the lake, as well as to Hume Lake Christian Camps. Beyond the Hume junction, where a gate closes the road from mid-November to late April, a long, winding descent plummets toward the

South Fork Kings River canyon. Excellent vista points of the deep chasm are passed on the way to Yucca Point (18.0), where motorists enter the inner gorge of the South Fork canyon. The highway leads past the steep-walled cliffs of Horseshoe Bend (22.6), then follows the turbulent river upstream to reenter the Park (32.5).

Once inside the Park, now within Kings Canyon proper, motorists quickly arrive at the turnoff into Cedar Grove (34.3), the center of activity in the canyon, providing services, campgrounds, and administrative facilities. Gently ascending the valley floor, the road continues past additional camp-grounds and points of interest, to the ter-minus of the highway at Roads End (39.8).

AMENITIES: Facilities at Cedar Grove include visitor center, general store and gift shop, snack bar, laundromat, public show-ers, horseback riding, and pack trips. Motel-style lodging is available at the Cedar Grove Lodge, (559) 335-5500. Gasoline is not available inside the Park.

Outside the Park, 17.5 miles from the Y-junction, rustic Kings Canyon Lodge offers cabin rentals, dining, and high-priced gasoline.

RANGER STATION: Wilderness permits, bear canister rentals, and backcountry information, are available from seasonal rangers at the wilderness permit station cabin at Roads End.

GOOD TO KNOW BEFORE YOU GO:
1. The low elevation and reflective walls of Kings Canyon in combination with the typically sunny Sierra sky create hot temperatures during the summer months. Hikers and backpackers should get an early start, especially on south-facing routes and trails with a lack of forest cover.
2. As in other areas in the parks, food and scented items should not be left in vehi-cles overnight in Kings Canyon, as bears may be active. Food lockers are available at trailheads, but reducing such items before arrival will minimize the amount of space needed.

CEDAR GROVE TRAILHEADS

TRIP **20**

Don Cecil Trail to Lookout Peak

(MS) ✏ DH

DISTANCE: 5.0 miles one way
ELEVATION: 4665/8485, +4000'/-225'
SEASON: June to mid-October
USE: Light
MAP: *Cedar Grove*

INTRODUCTION: The climb up the Don Cecil Trail to the top of Lookout Peak affords hikers a bird's-eye view of Kings Canyon and an impressive vista of the peaks and ridges forming the backcountry of Kings Canyon National Park. A few tourists will hike the first mile of trail to the cool grotto of Sheep Creek, but most of the remaining 4.0 miles are lightly used, despite the rewarding vista from the summit. The steady 3820-foot climb is probably enough of a deterrent for the average park visitor, but hikers in reasonable shape should be able to complete the ascent in a few hours or so. Get an early start to avoid climbing during the heat of the day, which at a start-ing elevation below 5000 feet, can be quite oppressive.

DIRECTIONS TO THE TRAILHEAD: Drive on Highway 180 into Kings Canyon and find the trailhead along the shoulder of the highway, 0.15 mile east of the turnoff to Cedar Grove Village.

DESCRIPTION: You climb up the hillside above the highway on a moderately steep grade through a light, mixed forest of black oaks, cedars, ponderosa pines, and white firs. Close inspection of their trunks will reveal that this area has seen its share of forest fires in the past. A quarter mile from the highway, you bend west and cross a

The Monarch Divide from Lookout Peak

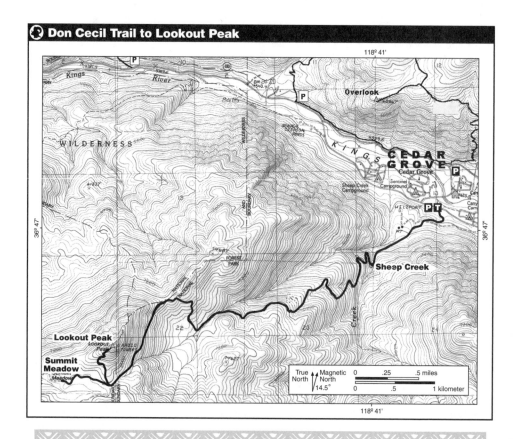

road that leads to the Cedar Grove heliport. Beyond the road, the forest provides a modicum of shade as you continue the climb up the hillside. After a steady climb, the trail abruptly levels and then makes a short descent to the cool, refreshing waters of Sheep Creek cascading over a series of rock slabs, 0.9 mile from the highway. Most sightseers tend to go no farther than the bridge over Sheep Creek, the water source for Cedar Grove Village. While enjoying the pleasantly shaded stream, take care not to contaminate the water in any way.

Beyond the creek, you ascend via a series of switchbacks through scattered forest, with periodic views of Kings Canyon below, the Monarch Divide to the north, and the Sierra crest to the east. Over the next couple of miles, the steady climb continues through the scattered trees until the forest thickens a bit as you approach the west branch of Sheep Creek. You briefly draw alongside the pleasant little stream, which is lined with a verdant assortment of wildflowers, ferns, and other small plants, before crossing it on a flat-topped log, 3.0 miles from the highway.

After following the far bank of the stream for a while, the trail bends away and leads you on a climb out of the drainage and across a slope covered with drier vegetation below Lookout Peak. Through gaps in the trees you catch glimpses of the peak above. A lengthy climb below the east face takes you up to a saddle and the signed boundary between Kings Canyon National Park and Sequoia National Forest, 4.3 miles from the highway.

Beyond the boundary, the condition of the trail deteriorates to a faint path that leads up to the crest of a ridge and then turns right (north) toward the top. In the absence of a well-defined trail, small ducks may help guide you up the ridge, but the route to the top is fairly obvious. The path becomes more distinct as you make a short dip, wind across the shrub-covered hillside, and then zigzag tightly toward the top. Just below the actual summit, you pick your way around large slabs and over boulders to emerge triumphantly on top of Lookout Peak.

Although the large microwave telephone reflector anchored to the top of Lookout Peak may detract from the sense of wildness at the summit, the view is dramatic. Nearly 4000 feet below is the South Fork Kings River tumbling through the rugged and deep cleft of Kings Canyon. Across the canyon to the north, the Monarch Divide cuts a jagged profile against the azure Sierra sky. Looking east, the peaks of the Sierra crest span the horizon. If you're fortunate enough to be on top of Lookout Peak on a rare, clear day following a cleansing summer rain, even the view toward the lowland west can be quite impressive.

By traveling west from the boundary between the National Park and Forest Service lands on an old road, you can quickly access Summit Meadow, where the wildflower display can be stunning.

CEDAR GROVE TRAILHEADS

TRIP **21**

Roaring River Falls

E ↗ DH/WC

DISTANCE: 0.25 mile one way

ELEVATION: 4850/4995, +100'/-100'

SEASON: May to November

USE: Heavy

MAPS: *The Sphinx*
Cedar Grove, SNHA

Roaring River Falls in autumn

INTRODUCTION: Although the short walk to the Roaring River Falls viewpoint can hardly be considered much of a hike, the falls are impressive and should be seen at least once by anyone visiting Kings Canyon. The falls are particularly stirring in early season, when peak snowmelt from the mountains above has turned the river into a wild torrent and the falls into a turbulent, raging, two-tiered cascade catapulting through a narrow granite chute into a deep chasm. Even in autumn or dry years the falls are still reasonably exciting, as Roaring River always seems to have a dependable flow of water.

Two separate paths lead to viewpoints on either side of the river. The trail most visitors use is a paved, wheelchair-accessible route on the east side, which is described below. The alternative is a dirt path beginning near the west side of the

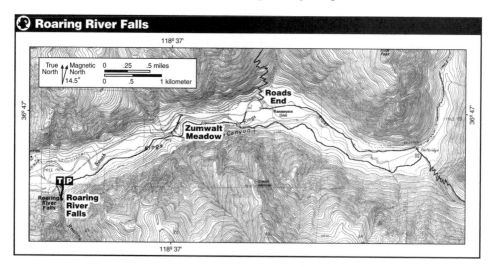

highway bridge. The trail heads above the west bank to a series of rock steps leading down to a fenced viewpoint. Hikers wishing to enjoy the view without a lot of company should opt for the west path. Only the lower section of the falls is visible from either viewpoint, and neither trail continues any farther up the canyon.

Those looking for a longer jaunt can combine the River Trail and/or the Kanawyer Loop Trail with a visit to Roaring River Falls (see Trips 22, 24).

DIRECTIONS TO THE TRAILHEAD: Drive on Highway 180 into Kings Canyon and find the parking area 2.8 miles east of the Cedar Grove turnoff.

DESCRIPTION: From the parking area, follow a paved path through mixed forest and typical canyon foliage. Your mild climb takes you to a junction on your left with the River Trail. A short walk from the junction leads to the viewpoint.

CEDAR GROVE TRAILHEADS

TRIP 22

River Trail, South Fork Kings River

E ↗ DH

DISTANCE: 1.25 miles one way to Zumwalt Meadow; 2.5 miles one way to Roaring River Falls

ELEVATION: 5040/4995, +35/-80 5040/4850, +35/-225

SEASON: May to November

USE: Heavy

MAPS: *The Sphinx* *Cedar Grove, SNHA*

INTRODUCTION: The River Trail provides hikers an easy opportunity to experience the unique environment along the South Fork Kings River. The pleasant scenery alongside the banks of the river is complemented dramatically by the towering granite walls of Grand Sentinel and North Dome—features which, in the minds of many, rival the more renowned Yosemite

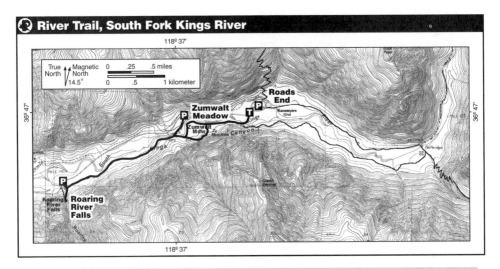

River Trail, South Fork Kings River

domes. With arrangements for a car shuttle, the gently descending trail can be followed one way, downstream to either Zumwalt Meadow or Roaring River Falls. Even without a shuttle, the distances are short enough that most hikers can easily backtrack to Roads End. Away from Zumwalt Meadow and Roaring River Falls, the trail is generally deserted, allowing visitors to experience most of the trip in quiet serenity.

DIRECTIONS TO THE TRAILHEAD: Drive on Highway 180 into Kings Canyon and to the day-use parking area at Roads End, 5.0 miles after the turnoff to Cedar Grove.

DESCRIPTION: Find the trailhead immediately southwest of the day-use parking lot, near a sign marked ZUMWALT MEADOW 1.1, BUBBS CREEK 2.6, ROARING RIVER FALLS 2.7. Follow the path through mixed forest and lush ground cover to a steel-and-wood bridge spanning the South Fork Kings River. From the bridge on an average summer day, you should see a variety of swimmers and waders contemplating a dip into the refreshing water, or a few anglers plying the river in search of the elusive trout. Just beyond the far side of the bridge, you encounter a signed three-way junction of the Kanawyer Loop Trail, left, and the River Trail, right.

Turn right from the junction and head downstream, following the River Trail toward Zumwalt Meadow, passing beside a mixture of giant boulders and broken rock deposited at the base of the mighty Grand Sentinel. The vertical wall of the granite monolith rises nearly 3500 feet above you. A mild descent leads through incense cedar, black oak, and ponderosa pine, alongside the bank of the river to a junction near the grassy flat of Zumwalt Meadow, 0.6 mile from Roads End.

At the junction, you have the option of following either branch of the Zumwalt Meadow Trail, as the paths will converge again beyond the west edge of the clearing, 0.4 mile downstream.

Near where the paths come back together, you have a fine view across the canyon of North Dome, another granite monolith, which towers 3600 feet above the valley North Dome is nearly as high as the more famous El Capitan of Yosemite. Soon after the paths converge, the Zumwalt Meadow Trail branches north to a bridged crossing of the river and onward to the parking lot.

Stay on the River Trail and proceed downstream toward Roaring River Falls, through more mixed forest and past another boulder field. The trail gently declines to another junction, at 2.4 miles, with the Roaring River Trail. Before turning right toward the parking lot, take the stroll up to the viewpoint to see the falls (see Trip 21).

TRIP **23**

Zumwalt Meadow Nature Trail

E ⟳ DH

DISTANCE: 1.5 miles

ELEVATION: 5000/5050, +100'/-100'

SEASON: May to November

USE: Heavy

MAPS: *Cedar Grove*
Zumwalt Meadow Nature
Trail, SNHA

South Fork Kings River from Zumwalt Meadow Trail bridge

INTRODUCTION: The easy 1.5-mile loop around Zumwalt Meadow provides a leisurely way to get acquainted with the ecology of Kings Canyon. An inexpensive pamphlet filled with interesting tidbits about the natural history of the immediate area can be purchased at the trailhead. The short path offers plenty of fine scenery as well, with views of the picturesque meadows, the river, and the surrounding cliffs and spires, including the granite monoliths of Grand Sentinel and North Dome.

DIRECTIONS TO THE TRAILHEAD: Drive on Highway 180 into Kings Canyon and proceed to the Zumwalt Meadow parking lot, 4.25 miles east of Cedar Grove.

DESCRIPTION: Your first stop along the Zumwalt Meadow Nature Trail should be

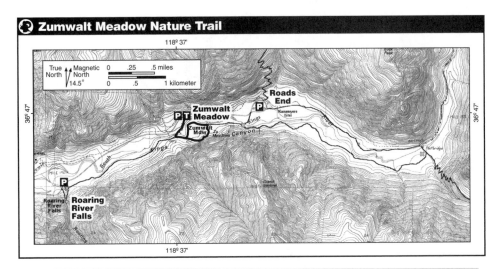

Zumwalt Meadow Nature Trail

the trailhead signboard, where you can purchase a pamphlet containing a map and detailed information corresponding to the numbered posts along the self-guiding trail. From here, follow the wide path toward a suspension bridge over the South Fork Kings River. Along the way and from the bridge, You have fine views of the meadow across the river and of Grand Sentinel rising sharply above the floor of the canyon.

Once across the bridge, you encounter a junction with the River Trail and turn right, proceeding upstream through cool forest, soon coming to the Zumwalt Meadow Nature Trail junction. Proceed straight ahead toward the meadow, leaving the forest canopy behind and making a brief climb through an exposed section of talus above the meadow. Form this slightly higher vantage point, you have a nice view across Zumwalt Meadow to the river and canyon wall beyond. You turn left at the next junction and follow the edge of the grassy meadow around to the riverbank. Wander along the winding river across a section of boardwalk and close the loop at the Nature Trail junction. Retrace your steps across the bridge and back to the trailhead.

CEDAR GROVE TRAILHEADS

TRIP 24

Kanawyer Loop Trail

E ↻ DH

DISTANCE: 4.7 miles

ELEVATION: 5045/5175, +265'/-265'

SEASON: May to November

USE: Heavy

MAPS: *The Sphinx*
Cedar Grove, SNHA

INTRODUCTION: Roads End is a very popular trailhead for an army of recreationists bound for the heart of the southern Sierra. Chances are you will share the first half of this loop with plenty of backpackers, dayhikers, and equestrians headed for popular destinations via the Paradise Valley and Bubbs Creek trails. However, on the second half of the journey the troops drop off considerably, making quiet solitude in the upper end of Kings Canyon a real possibility. The loop is an easy stroll up the nearly level valley floor, making this a route well-suited for just about anyone. Be prepared for hot temperatures at this elevation,

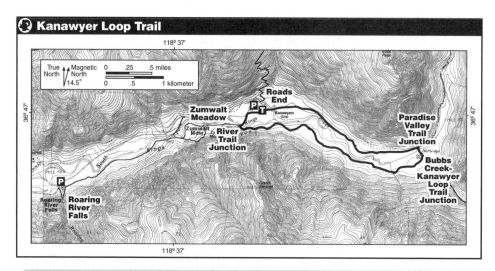

remembering that relief is never too far away with a refreshing dip in the chilly waters of the river.

DIRECTIONS TO THE TRAILHEAD: Drive on Highway 180 into Kings Canyon and to the day-use parking area at Roads End, 5.0 miles past the turnoff to Cedar Grove.

DIRECTIONS: The well-signed trail begins at the east edge of the paved turnaround, near the wilderness permit station. Follow the wide, sandy, gently ascending trail, which parallels the South Fork Kings River through a mixed forest of incense cedars, ponderosa pines, black oaks, sugar pines, and white firs. You quickly cross Copper Creek on a wood bridge. Up the trail, the forest cover thins somewhat, allowing views of the impressive granite walls of the canyon, which some compare favorably to the more famous walls of Yosemite Valley. Soon you enter a cool forest of ponderosa pines, sugar pines, white firs, and alders, and come to a signed Y-junction, 1.9 miles from the trailhead, with the Paradise Valley Trail.

Head right (south) from the junction and immediately cross a bridge over the South Fork Kings River, just downstream from its confluence with Bubbs Creek. Soon you encounter another trail junction, this one of the Bubbs Creek and Kanawyer Loop trails. Turn right (southwest), seeing more evidence of a recent fire. Cross Avalanche Creek via a pair of logs and continue on mild trail through thick forest. You pass a small meadow and eventually draw closer to the river. On occasion, the forest parts enough to allow grand views of the canyon walls. A short climb through a boulder field leads to a junction with the River Trail (see Trip 22) near a bridge across the South Fork. Turn right, cross the bridge, and make a mild ascent through thick forest and lush ground cover back to the parking lot.

TRIP **25**

Sphinx Creek

MS ✒ DH/BP

DISTANCE: 6.2 miles one way

ELEVATION: 5045/8575, +3745'/-215'

SEASON: Mid-June to November

USE: Moderate

MAP: *The Sphinx*

TRAIL LOG:

3.5 Sphinx Creek Camp
6.2 Upper Sphinx Creek Camp

INTRODUCTION: The stiff climb from the floor of Kings Canyon to Sphinx Creek may deter the casual hiker or backpacker, but the wonderful scenery is a just reward for those in good enough shape to survive the ascent. Most travelers who begin their adventures from Roads End are bound for places other than Sphinx Creek, which makes this trip even more attractive to those looking for an escape from the customary weekend crowds. Cross-country enthusiasts will enjoy the 2- to 3-mile off-trail route to the scenic Sphinx Lakes. Plan on an early start, as the low elevation and lack of shade make this trail a cooker in the afternoon sun.

DIRECTIONS TO THE TRAILHEAD: Drive on Highway 180 into Kings Canyon and to the day-use or overnight parking areas at Roads End, 5.0 miles past the turnoff to Cedar Grove.

DESCRIPTION: The well-signed trail begins at the east edge of the paved turnaround, near the wilderness permit station. Follow the wide, sandy, gently ascending trail, which parallels the South Fork Kings River through a mixed forest. You quickly cross Copper Creek on a wood bridge. Up the trail, the forest cover thins, allowing views of the impressive granite walls of the canyon. Soon you enter a cool forest of ponderosa pines, sugar pines, white firs, and alders, and come to a signed Y-junction, 1.9 miles from the trailhead, with the Paradise Valley Trail.

Head right (south) from the junction and immediately cross a bridge over the South Fork Kings River, just downstream from its confluence with Bubbs Creek. Soon you encounter another trail junction, this one the intersection of the Bubbs Creek and Kanawyer Loop trails. Turn up the Bubbs Creek Trail and follow a series of short, wooden bridges across multiple branches of Bubbs Creek.

A moderate climb leads to the first of many switchbacks that lead you away from the floor of the canyon and up the Bubbs Creek drainage. Through gaps in the scrub-

by forest, you have excellent views of Kings Canyon, the rock pinnacle known as The Sphinx, and, in early season, a spectacular cascade on Bubbs Creek. You take a break from the switchbacks as the trail ascends the east side of the canyon, well above the level of the creek. As you continue the moderate climb, you reach an area where conifers cover the slopes. At 3.5 miles, you reach Sphinx Creek Camp (6280'±) and a junction of the Bubbs Creek and Sphinx Creek trails. Excellent campsites with bear boxes, the first legal camping since the trailhead, are on both sides of Bubbs Creek. A pit toilet is on the creek's north side.

From the junction, cross Bubbs Creek on a log-and-plank bridge to the south bank. More switchbacks await as you begin the stiff climb of the Sphinx Creek canyon, where widely scattered conifers offer little shade. Higher up the drainage, white firs

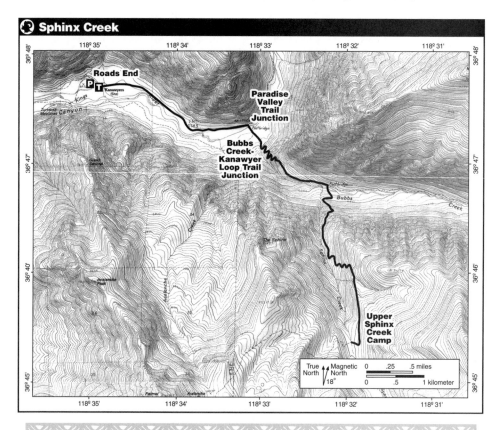

eventually provide some respite from the summer sun, but the moderate to moderately steep climb continues unabated. Good views of the mountainous terrain provide momentary relief from the seemingly interminable toil. You ascend higher above Sphinx Creek and finally reach a point, near the 5.5-mile mark, where the grade eases. A half-mile of gentle trail leads to a short descent that drops you to a ford of the creek. On the opposite side, across the creek, a lush forest floor carpeted with grasses and wildflowers holds the scattered campsites of Upper Sphinx Creek Camp.

The Sphinx Creek Trail continues its climb toward Avalanche Pass and the backcountry beyond, as described in Trip 26.

Long ago, a path followed alongside Sphinx Creek to Sphinx Lakes. The path was never a maintained trail, but a moderately difficult cross-country route still follows traces of the old trail up a valley to the series of lakes. The lakes are quite attrac-

tive, tucked beneath Sphinx Ridge at about 10,500 feet. They offer scenic campsites and good fishing. From the lakes, class-2 routes lead to the summits of Mt. Brewer and Cross Mtn.

R **PERMITS:** Wilderness permit required for overnight stays (quota: 25 per day).

CAMPFIRES: Not permitted above 10,400 feet.

CAMPING: Prohibited for first 3.5 miles to Sphinx Creek Camp.

Kings Canyon from the Bubbs Creek Trail

CEDAR GROVE TRAILHEADS

TRIP **26**

Circle of Solitude: Great Western and Kings-Kern Divides Loop

Ⓜ️Ⓢ ◯ BPx

DISTANCE: 68 miles

ELEVATION: 5045/10,040/7420/12,000/ 8080/13,180/+18,700'/ -18,700'

SEASON: Mid-July to early October

USE: Light

MAPS: *The Sphinx, Sphinx Lakes, Triple Divide Peak, Mt. Kaweah, Mt. Brewer, Mt. Williamson, Mt. Clarence King*

TRAIL LOG:

6.2	Sphinx Creek
8.5	Avalanche Pass
14.3	Roaring River R.S.
18.5	Cement Table Meadow
20.5	Upper ford-Roaring River
23.0	Colby Lake
24.6	Colby Pass
32.1	High Sierra Trail Jct./ Junction Meadow
40.7	Lake South America Jct.
48.5	Forester Pass
56.0	Bubbs Creek Trail Jct.
58.5	Junction Meadow

INTRODUCTION: A treasure trove of scenic wonders awaits backpackers on this extended loop through the heart of the Kings Canyon and Sequoia national parks backcountry. Wildflower-filled meadows, serene forests, scenic alpine lakes, glacier-carved canyons, and dramatic peaks are here in abundance. Beginning near 5000 feet at Roads End, above Cedar Grove, the

route eventually traverses three high passes before returning to the trailhead: Avalanche (10,040'), Colby (12,000'), and Forester (13,160'). Such a wide range in elevation assures backpackers of a wide diversity, from foothill woodland to alpine environments, and just about everything in between.

Much of the route passes through some of the most-scenic and least-visited backcountry in the parks. Once past the Sphinx Creek junction, secluded trails prevail until you intersect the heavily traveled John Muir and Bubbs Creek trails. So remote are the Sphinx Creek, Cloud Canyon, Kern-Kaweah, and upper Kern Canyon regions that this route has been dubbed the Circle of Solitude.

The vast elevation changes and the primitive condition of some stretches of trail reserve this route for seasoned backpackers in good shape. You may wish to explore the possibility of an off-trail route over Harrison Pass (class 2), bypassing the well-used trail over Forester Pass to visit the secluded lakes and tarns of East Creek canyon. Such a course complies more favorably with the secluded atmosphere of the loop, but requires a much higher degree of skill and experience than returning via the straightforward path of the Muir and Bubbs Creek trails. Both exits are provided at the end of this description. To extend the journey, a cornucopia of diversions awaits the traveler with a sense of adventure and the extra time to enjoy them.

DIRECTIONS TO THE TRAILHEAD: Drive on Highway 180 into Kings Canyon and to the overnight parking lot at Roads End, 5.0 miles east of the turnoff to Cedar Grove.

DIRECTIONS: The well-signed trail begins at the east edge of the paved turnaround, near the wilderness permit station. Follow the wide trail, which parallels the South Fork Kings River through a mixed forest. You quickly cross Copper Creek on a wood bridge. Up the trail, the forest cover thins, allowing views of the granite walls of the canyon. Soon you enter a cool forest of ponderosa pines, sugar pines, white firs, and alders, and come to a signed Y-junction with the Paradise Valley Trail, 1.9 miles from the trailhead.

Head right (south) from the junction and immediately cross a bridge over the South Fork Kings River, just downstream from its confluence with Bubbs Creek. Soon you encounter another trail junction, where the Bubbs Creek and Kanawyer Loop trails meet. Turn up the Bubbs Creek Trail and follow a series of short, wooden bridges across multiple branches of Bubbs Creek.

A moderate climb leads to the first of many switchbacks that lead you away from the floor of the canyon and up the Bubbs Creek drainage. Through gaps in the scrubby forest, you have excellent views of Kings Canyon, the rock pinnacle known as The Sphinx, and, in early season, a spectacular cascade on Bubbs Creek. You take a break from the switchbacks as the trail ascends the east side of the canyon. As you continue the moderate climb, you reach an area where conifers cover the slopes. At 3.5 miles, you reach Sphinx Creek Camp

(6280'±) and a junction of the Bubbs Creek and Sphinx Creek trails. Excellent campsites with bear boxes are on both sides of Bubbs Creek.

From the junction, cross Bubbs Creek on a log-and-plank bridge to the south bank. Switchbacks begin the stiff climb of the Sphinx Creek canyon, where there's little shade. Higher up the drainage, white firs eventually provide some respite from the summer sun. Good views of the mountainous terrain provide momentary relief from the long climb. High above Sphinx Creek, near the 5.5-mile mark, the grade eases. A half-mile of gentle trail leads to a short descent that drops you to a ford of the creek. Across the creek you will find the scattered campsites of Upper Sphinx Creek  Camp.

Leave the verdant creekside refuge and climb over a series of forested ridges with minor stream gullies between them. Western white pines, red firs, and lodgepole pines shade the trail as you make an extended moderate ascent toward Avalanche Pass. Through occasional gaps in the forest you have nice views of Palmer

The Whaleback above Big Wet Meadow, from the Colby Pass Trail

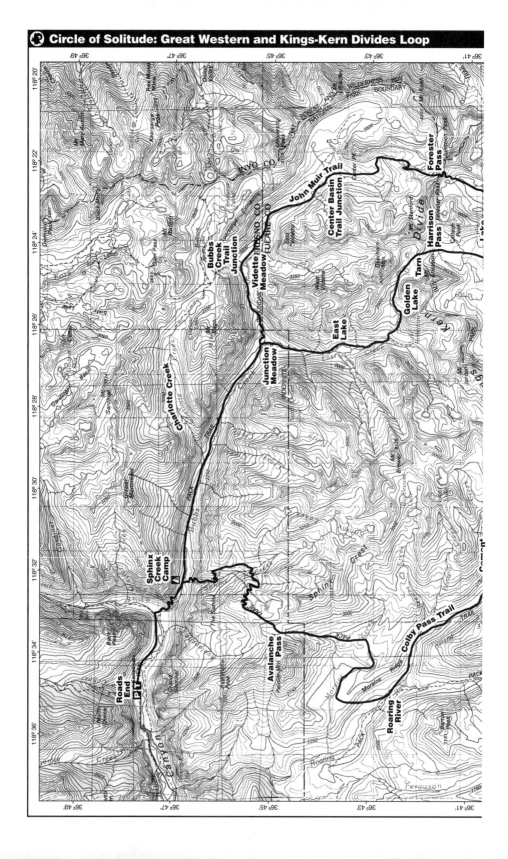

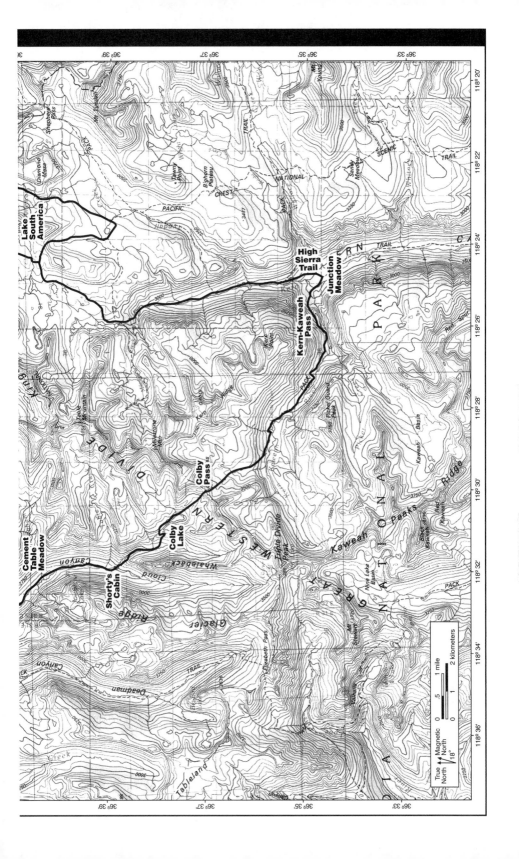

Mtn. At 8.6 miles from Roads End, you reach indistinctive Avalanche Pass (10,100'±), where foxtail pines obscure any possible views.

You descend from the pass via an occasional switchback, with views of Glacier Ridge and the Silliman Crest across willow-filled clearings, to a nascent tributary of Moraine Creek. Through scattered lodgepoles, aspens, and junipers, you head down, alongside the cavorting tributary, amid lush pockets of foliage and wildflowers, including larkspur, paintbrush, penstemon, gentian, pennyroyal, daisy, leopard lily, and Bigelow sneezeweed. Along the way, you step across numerous tiny rivulets bordered by narrow swaths of similarly verdant flora. Leave the tributary behind and continue the southbound descent of a forested hillside, interrupted by a pocket meadow, to the V-shaped canyon of Moraine Creek. You veer southwest and proceed down the canyon, passing a solitary campsite near the creek. The trail bends around the nose of the hill and leads you to a crossing of vigorous Moraine Creek, 12 miles from the trailhead. A number of fallen logs assist you across.

Paralleling Moraine Ridge, follow the trail northwest through scattered pines and firs, seeing evidence of a former fire along the way. Eventually you climb up and over the broad crest of Moraine Ridge, from where you have a fine view of Roaring River and Deadman Canyon. A steep, zigzagging descent on rocky trail amid scrubby manzanita and widely scattered Jeffrey pine leads to a long, descending traverse across the hillside toward the Roaring River.

Approaching the river, you pass a corral followed by campsites, and then come to a signed three-way junction at 14.3 miles. Your route, the Colby Pass Trail, continues up the east side of the river, while the other path heads over a bridge to the Roaring River Ranger Station (7445'±), more campsites and another three-way junction, this one with trails to Deadman Canyon and Sugarloaf Valley (see Trip 8).

From the junction, follow the gently ascending Colby Pass Trail along the east side of tumbling Roaring River, through scattered Jeffrey pine. A more moderate climb ensues, passing above a patch of meadow, through a gap in a drift fence, and into a light forest of lodgepole pines and red firs. You boulderhop Brewer Creek and 0.5 mile farther cross the twin channels of Barton Creek. Forested stands alternate with lush pockets of foliage for the next couple of miles. You climb mildly toward Cement Table Meadow (8495'±), an expansive clearing where the Roaring River becomes a tame, meandering brook weaving sinuously through grasses and an array of flowers, including lupine, leopard lily, daisy, delphinium, shooting star, buttercup, columbine, paintbrush, and monkey flower. Just past a three-pole gate, you cross broad Cunningham Creek at 18.6 miles and immediately encounter campsites with a hitching post nearby. Farther up the meadow, you pass additional campsites.

Beyond Cement Table Meadow, the trail starts to climb again, passing through a mixture of lodgepole pines, aspens, and lush clearings. Emerging from an extensive aspen grove, you encounter an absolutely gorgeous view across the green expanse of Big Wet Meadow to a statuesque formation named Whaleback. You circle around the south fringe of Big Wet Meadow beneath pines, mesmerized by the incredible scenery of the upper canyon. At the far end of the meadow, a couple of campsites nestle beneath lodgepole pines near a seasonal stream.

Ahead, a somewhat confusing stretch of trail (shown incorrectly on the *Sphinx Lake* quad) leads down to a ford of substantial Roaring River near its confluence with Table Creek. After the crossing, you climb moderately steeply up the hillside, passing a shaded campsite, to where the grade eases and the path bends back toward the river. Several yards off the trail is Shorty's Cabin, a rustic structure built by Shorty Lovelace (1886–1963), a trapper who established a line of shelters for use during his winter trapping expeditions in the southern Sierra. (See Sidebar on page 114.)

Continuing, you step across a wood platform above a spring-fed pool and come to the upper ford of the river, 6.2 miles from Roaring River Ranger Station. Spacious campsites are scattered beneath pines near the ford. One campsite, "Grand Palace Hotel," is named for a sheepherder's carving on a nearby pine that refers to the plush San Francisco hotel. At one time, a trail followed the west side of the river farther up Cloud Canyon, but the path has long been abandoned (see Options, below).

You leave the relatively mellow trail that goes through Cloud Canyon, as a much steeper ascent attacks the northern spine of Whaleback. Numerous switchbacks take you across the spine, above a tributary stream, and up a side canyon. About 0.75 mile from the upper ford of Roaring River, you boulderhop a creek and head upstream through open, rocky terrain broken by patches of grasses, wildflowers, heather, clumps of willow, and an occasional dwarf lodgepole pine. You continue the climb up the canyon, recrossing the creek numerous times. Views ahead of the Great Western Divide and behind of Cloud Canyon improve with each passing step. Eventually, you veer away from the stream to climb directly up the east wall of the canyon, and then follow an ascending traverse to a crossing of Colby Lake's outlet. A short stroll along the stream leads to the north shore of Colby Lake (10,584'), 8.75 miles from Roaring River Ranger Station. A few campsites are at this end of the lake, squeezed onto small pockets of soil between acres of rocky shoreline. If you don't mind sleeping on granite slabs, there is a plethora of camping options. The deep lake is a scenic gem, cradled by a large cirque beneath the craggy crest of the Great Western Divide. Anglers will drool over the sizable brook and rainbow trout gliding through the crystal-clear water.

The trail takes you above the east shore of the lake to a willow-lined inlet, where it begins a serious ascent toward Colby Pass. Switchbacks lead over rocky slopes to a ravine, which you ascend steeply to a cirque. A final zigzagging climb up a narrow chute leaves you winded at Colby Pass (12,000'), 10.3 miles from Roaring River Ranger Station and 24.6 miles from Roads End. The view is sublime, especially of the multihued Kaweah Peaks.

From the pass, you wind down a sandy hillside past a rocky tarn, and descend into a series of bowls, stepping over sprightly rivulets along the way. Excellent views of the Kern-Kaweah watershed and the Kaweah Peaks Ridge adorn the descent. Eventually, scattered lodgepole pines reappear as you stroll downhill across a verdant meadow. A steeper descent over sandy soil and rock leads to the Kern-Kaweah canyon.

The grade mercifully eases as you wander amid lush ground cover beneath scattered-to-light timber. The mellow nature of the trail is short-lived, as the path begins a steeper decline next to the tumbling Kern-Kaweah River, which races downstream through a series of cataracts. In due course, the grade eases once again as you approach expansive Gallats Lake, which in all but early season will resemble more of a wet meadow with a meandering brook than a bona fide lake. A couple of primitive campsites can be found along the fringe of the lake/meadow, with tiny contributing streams nearby for water.

Leaving the broad clearing holding Gallats Lake behind, the trail resumes a more moderate descent over granite slabs. The Kern-Kaweah River charmingly cascades through rock clefts and slithers across a number of slabs as well. You pass through a couple of avalanche swaths in a scattered-to-light lodgepole forest. The trail is sunk in a deep granite canyon sandwiched between Kern Point and Picket Guard Peak. As the river starts to meander again, you soon approach small, meadow-rimmed Rockslide Lake and stroll through a plethora of young aspen. Peaks of the Great Western Divide start to appear above the surrounding hills. Just beyond Rockslide

SHORTY LOVELACE — MOUNTAIN MAN

In the human history of Kings Canyon National Park, one colorful character stands out. Five-foot, four-inch Joseph Walter "Shorty" Lovelace lived the life of a modern-day mountain man.

He was born in 1886 near Three Rivers, Calif. Shorty and his four brothers grew up camping and exploring the local mountains. Their father taught them how to hunt and trap, skills Shorty would employ later in life.

Shorty Lovelace had one personal demon that plagued him throughout his life. His fondness for alcohol helped contribute to a ruined marriage and failed business dealings. His love of the mountains, developed in childhood, proved to be his salvation. While in the mountains he lost his desire to drink and remained sober. Using the skills taught to him as a boy, he returned to the Sierra and began his life as a fur trapper.

Around 1920 Shorty established a base-of-operations cabin in Crowley Canyon, in the mountains northeast of Visalia. From this location he pushed farther eastward into the Sierra. He established traplines in the rugged wilderness of what would one day become Kings Canyon National Park.

Along these traplines he constructed a series of miniature cabins. All were built in accordance with his 5-foot, 4-inch frame. He would seek out material at each cabin site. He used the smaller logs of downed trees, generally no larger than 12 inches in diameter. The smaller logs were easier to handle by himself. A fireplace of rocks was built on one end of the cabin, a wood-lined bed padded the floor at the opposite end. Shelves were built as needed. A door made of wood shakes, hung on leather hinges, helped keep out the elements. The cabins were very small and cramped, not large enough for the average person to stand upright in. They did, however, serve as secure one-person shelters against the fierce Sierra winters.

Beaver and otter were not to be found in Shorty's trapping region. He had to rely on the pelts of other animals for his income, mainly fishers, martens, and wolverines.

David Disbrow

One of Shorty's cabins

Shorty's income from these pelts varied season to season. A good winter of trapping could earn him $2000 or more. After cashing in his winter haul, Shorty would return to civilization and go on a drinking binge. During the subsequent drunken stupor he oftentimes was mugged and robbed. He quickly learned to turn his finances over to one of his brothers. The brother would then give Shorty a small drinking allowance. The majority of the cash would go where it was needed, to help Shorty resupply for another winter in the Sierra.

From 1920 to 1940 Shorty Lovelace weathered the harsh winters alone, working his traplines. Travel was by wooden skis. Freezing cold, treacherous ice, threat of avalanches — Shorty survived all the environmental fury nature could cast his way. Though the exact number of cabins he built may not be known, one estimate puts the total at 36 shelters.

In March of 1940 an act of Congress created Kings Canyon National Park. The park service notified Shorty trapping was an

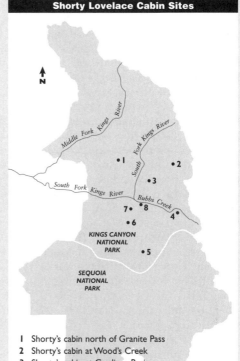

Shorty Lovelace Cabin Sites

1 Shorty's cabin north of Granite Pass
2 Shorty's cabin at Wood's Creek
3 Shorty's cabin at Gardiner Basin
4 Shorty's cabin at Vidette Meadow
5 Shorty's cabin in Cloud Canyon
6 Shorty's cabin in Moraine Meadow
7 Cabin on tributary of Sphinx Creek
8 The "Boulder" cabin site on Bubbs Creek

activity no longer allowed. Forced out of his old trapping grounds, Shorty headed to the region of the North Fork of the Kings River. By the mid-1940s he had established new traplines and built more miniature cabins. He continued to trap into the 1950s, living the life of a mountain man in a modern era. In the summer of 1961 he revisited one of his old trapping haunts, camping in the Roaring River area of Kings Canyon National Park. He died two years later, at the age of 77.

The present-day backcountry traveler can still see some of Shorty's old cabins. Three are easily accessible by well-established trails. One stands at Woods Creek Crossing and another at Vidette Meadow on the John Muir Trail; another is in Cloud Canyon on the scenic trail to Colby Pass. Two of these cabins, at Vidette Meadow and Cloud Canyon, are listed on the National Register of Historic Places, saved so future generations can enjoy the historic value of a bygone era and visit a piece of the human history of Kings Canyon National Park.

—David Disbrow

A graphic artist by profession, David Disbrow has backpacked extensively throughout John Muir's Range of Light since 1978. He currently resides in Reno, Nevada with his wife, Jenny, and daughters, Madeline and Catherine.

Lake, a few good campsites nestle beneath lodgepole pines alongside the river.

More arid vegetation of sagebrush and manzanita greets you as the canyon begins to narrow, forcing the trail to make an angling ascent across a hillside and up a series of tight, steep switchbacks out of a hanging valley to a narrow gap known as Kern-Kaweah Pass. You drop from the pass into a narrow ravine and wind down rocky trail between tall cliffs to a shrub-covered hillside. A deteriorating tread leads through sagebrush, currant, chinquapin, manzanita, willows, and assorted wildflowers to a set of switchbacks descending toward Junction Meadow. Reaching the floor of the Kern River canyon, you amble over to multiple fords of the river and tributaries. The main ford of the river can be quite difficult in early season. Through thickening forest of pines and cedars, you continue the stroll to the High Sierra Trail at Junction Meadow (8080'±), 7.5 miles from Colby Pass and 17.8 miles from Roaring River Ranger Station. A short distance south on the High Sierra Trail are some good campsites with a bear box, shaded by pines and next to a small stream near Junction Meadow.

From the junction, turn left (north) and climb moderately on the High Sierra Trail, through Jeffrey, ponderosa, and western white pines to a clearing, where you can hear the thundering roar of the Kern River and have excellent views of the Kern-Kaweah cleft. More climbing takes you up the canyon through light forest of pines and aspens, eventually offering a fine vista of the U-shaped Kern Trench. Soon you reach a junction, 1.1 mile from Junction Meadow, where the High Sierra Trail turns east, but your trail continues up the Kern River canyon.

Back into pines, you continue north, passing a number of good campsites on benches overlooking the river. On a mild-to-moderate ascent, you follow the course of the river through the trees, passing more campsites, to the ford of Tyndall Creek, which may be difficult in early season. At 3.0 miles from Junction Meadow, a small

cairn is all that marks a junction with a trail that follows Tyndall Creek and eventually connects to the John Muir Trail.

Continuing up the Kern Trench, you pass additional campsites and then climb more steeply up above a picturesque waterfall. The grade temporarily eases above the fall, but soon intensifies as the trail climbs to match the gradient of the cascading river. In and out of forest cover, you proceed upstream to a flower-carpeted glade, where columbine, aster, paintbrush, and groundsel add splashes of color. You step across a tiny stream and start to climb steeply up a series of short switchbacks to a crossing of a significant creek (campsites) that drains several unnamed tarns above. (The *Mt. Brewer* quad incorrectly shows the trail here crossing the Kern River.) Past the creek, the climb resumes, scaling a hillside covered with granite slabs, and then taking you up and over the lip of the upper Kern Plateau. The grade eventually eases as you ascend mildly over slabs and through scattered pines, again alongside the river. Just before a large tarn at the base of steep cliffs, you pass an unmarked route to Milestone Basin (see Options, below). Campsites on the tarn's south shore near its outlet offer good views. East of the tarn, you encounter a marked junction with another trail connecting to the JMT, 5.6 miles from Junction Meadow.

On sandy trail, you proceed upstream to improving views of the upper Kern River basin and the surrounding peaks, passing numerous picturesque tarns and some equally scenic meadows along the way. Sections of the trail may be hard to follow through here, so pay close attention to the route description. A more exquisite and remote basin in the Sierra is hard to imagine, as the upper Kern basin has it all, including seemingly limitless possibilities for off-trail hideaways. You mildly ascend slabs of granite through widely scattered whitebark and lodgepole pines, and pockets of vegetation. Steeper climbing over rock ribs, outcroppings, and gullies leads you to a signed junction with the lateral to

Lake South America, 8.6 miles from Junction Meadow.

Turn north from the junction and stroll to the far edge of a small tarn before dropping sharply to the south shore of austere Lake South America (11,945'±). Flanked by an amphitheater of peaks, including Mt. Genevra, Mt. Ericsson, and Caltech Peak, the lonely lake offers incredible scenery. A few campsites are scattered around the windswept shore in pockets of soil, apparently more than enough to satisfy the small number of backpackers willing to venture off the beaten track. Golden trout will test the skill of anglers.

From Lake South America, backpackers have two options for returning to Roads End. Experienced knapsackers can accept the challenge of the mostly easy off-trail route over Harrison Pass, but must face the challenge of a difficult class 2 descent down the north side of the pass. Those wishing to stick to maintained trail can follow the lengthier route to the JMT over Forester Pass and down the Bubbs Creek Trail.

FORESTER PASS ROUTE: From the junction with the lateral to Lake South America, fol-low the trail southeast up and over a low ridge to a long meadow basin with a pair of tarns at each end. Gently descending trail leads you across the lengthy clearing, where a herd of deer is frequently seen grazing in the lush meadow of this pastoral and quiet plain. At the far end of the valley, a short, mildly rising climb is followed by a similar descent leading to a T-junction 2.25 miles from the Lake South America junction. Turn left (east) and descend through open terrain with extraordinary views of the upper Tyndall Creek basin and peaks of the Sierra crest. You pass a tarn that has excellent campsites and meet the John Muir Trail, 3.2 miles from the Lake South America junction.

Turn left (north) onto the JMT and proceed on a mild-to-moderate climb above timberline through open terrain, which offers excellent views of the upper Tyndall Creek basin. You pass lovely tarns and step across trickling streams along the way to the base of the headwall below Forester Pass. As with many of the High Sierra passes, a viable route over the wall ahead seems unlikely until you begin the switchbacking

Remote Lake South America near the headwaters of the Kern River

climb up the face. The trail is something of an engineering marvel, literally blasted and cut out of the vertical rock wall—sections of the climb are definitely not for acrophobes. You finally reach a narrow gap in the Kings-Kern Divide at Forester Pass (13,160'), on the boundary between Sequoia and Kings Canyon national parks, 16.5 miles from the High Sierra Trail junction at Junction Meadow. The expansive views from the pass of myriad peaks to the north and south are amazing.

After the precipitous terrain on the south side of the pass, the descent of the north side is a piece of cake, on smooth, sandy trail that switchbacks down to the top of a rock rib above a tarn in the head of a canyon. You follow the path to the end of the rib, enjoying the excellent views along the way, then make an angling descent to a crossing of Bubbs Creek just below the tarn. From the crossing, you have a grand alpine view of the tarn backdropped by Junction Peak. You continue the winding, rocky descent, fording the creek several more times and following its course, which bends west and descends to more hospitable terrain. In a grove of pines, just beyond the NO FIRES sign, you pass a couple of poor campsites, tiered down the steep slope. More switchbacks lead you into a light forest of scattered lodgepole and whitebark pines, past small pockets of verdant, wildflower-dotted meadows, and through clumps of willow to a ford of Center Basin Creek. Past the ford, you encounter campsites with a bear box and the unsigned junction with the Center Basin Trail (10,675'±), 4.5 miles from Forester Pass. A side trip to Golden Bear Lake up the Center Basin Trail is well worth the extra time and effort.

In and out of scattered-to-light lodgepole forest, you continue the descent on the JMT, following the tumbling course of Bubbs Creek, which is sandwiched between the towering pinnacle of East Vidette to the west and the rugged spine of the Kearsarge Pinnacles to the east. Along the way, you hop across a number of tributary streams.

Eventually, you pass through a gap in a wire fence to reach Upper Vidette Meadow and a number of overused campsites under pines next to the creek. Beyond the meadow, you pass an unsigned trail that leads to a large packer's camp alongside the stream. Ahead are the ever-popular Vidette Meadow campsites (bear boxes), which cater to JMT through-hikers and backpackers bound for Rae Lakes. After a pair of stream crossings, you come to a three-way junction with the Bubbs Creek Trail (9530'±), 7.7 miles from Forester Pass.

Following signed directions for Cedar Grove, you turn away from the JMT and head west on the Bubbs Creek Trail, making a short descent to the north edge of expansive Lower Vidette Meadow. Overnighters will find excellent campsites (bear box) nestled beneath lodgepole pines along the meadow's fringe. Leaving the gentle grade of the meadows behind, you begin a more pronounced descent, following the now tumbling creek as it plunges down the gorge. Soon you break out into the open momentarily, where a large hump of granite provides an excellent vantage point from which to survey the surrounding landscape. Head back into the trees and continue down the canyon, stepping over numerous lushly lined freshets along the way. Periodic switchbacks and occasional views of the dramatic topography above the gorge of East Creek, including rugged Mt. Brewer, North Guard, and Mt. Farquhar, mark the protracted descent. Farther down the canyon, picturesque waterfalls and cascades on Bubbs Creek provide additional visual treats. The stiff descent eventually eases as you reach the grassy, fern-filled, and wildflower-covered clearing of Junction Meadow (8190'±). You stroll over to a signed three-way junction with a trail heading south along East Creek to East Lake and Lake Reflection (see Trip 27), 2.3 miles from the JMT. Those seeking overnight accommodations will find campsites along this trail on either side of the ford of Bubbs Creek. Additional campsites are farther along the Bubbs

Creek Trail, past the horse camp near the west edge of the meadow.

Past Junction Meadow, the moderate descent resumes as you proceed down Bubbs Creek canyon. You stroll alongside the turbulent creek through a moderate forest composed mainly of white firs. After nearly 2.0 miles of steady descent, Bubbs Creek mellows, and you hike gently graded trail through a grove of aspens and ferns on the way to a log crossing of Charlotte Creek. Nearby, a short path leads to fair campsites near Bubbs Creek, where fishing is reported good for rainbow, brook, and brown trout.

Gentle trail continues for a little while beyond Charlotte Creek, as you hop across a trio of streams and walk through shoulder-high ferns, before Bubbs Creek returns to its tumultuous course down the gorge. A steady, moderate descent follows the course of the tumbling stream for the next several miles. Proceeding farther down the canyon, the moderate fir forest gives way to a lighter cover of trees, mostly Jeffrey pines, with a smattering of firs, incense cedars, and black oaks. At 8.25 miles from the JMT, you reach Sphinx Creek Camp and the junction with the Sphinx Creek Trail, closing the loop. From there, retrace your steps 3.5 miles back to Roads End.

HARRISON PASS ROUTE: Beyond Lake South America, the cross-country route through the extreme upper basin of the Kern River is relatively straightforward. Ducks mark the course, which is indistinct despite its appearance on the *Mt. Brewer* quad as a bona fide trail. Follow the west shore of Lake South America and then head directly north up a broad valley, which is open and gently rising. Near the head of the valley, a boot-beaten path becomes more evident. This trail climbs steeply up the headwall to cross the crest at Harrison Pass (12,720'±), which is well east of the actual low point of the saddle. A partially obscured view to the north includes Mt. Goddard and the Palisades. A better vista to the south includes the hulk of Mt.

Guyot, the Kaweah Peaks Ridge, and Milestone Mtn.

The north side of the pass is the crux of the route, as steep and loose rock make the route difficult and potentially dangerous. In some years, ice or snow may cover the precipitous slope well into summer, further complicating the descent. Depending on the conditions and the experience of the party, rope and ice axes may be needed. Cautiously descend a chute to less difficult terrain and then angle toward the first tarn in the basin below. Cross the outlet and bend west across the stream between the next two lakes. Climb over a knoll, drop down alongside the outlet below the third lake, and then follow the stream into trees and on to a meadow. Near the meadow, you cross the creek to the north bank and continue down a canyon, following occasional ducks and blazes over a low rise and down to charming campsites at Golden Lake (10,690'±). Beyond the lake, the route follows the course of its outlet stream to traces of a dusty and rocky old trail that eventually switchbacks down a hillside to a junction with an unmaintained section of the East Lake Trail.

From the junction, you can head south along the creek and gently ascend through pockets of willow past a lakelet to the shore of wind-swept Lake Reflection (10,300'±), where campsites are scattered around the far shore. Turning north from the junction, descend the East Creek canyon through scattered stands of lodgepole and foxtail pines.

Just after stepping across a side stream, you reach the shore of grass-rimmed East Lake 9470'±), sandwiched between towering granite peaks. After the rocky terrain of the past few miles, the more pastoral surroundings are a welcome change. Good campsites line the south and north shore and, unlike many subalpine lakes in the parks, campfires are permitted.

Leaving East Lake, continue downstream, on a gentle to moderate descent. Beyond the crossing of a fern-lined tributary stream, the grade becomes steeper as the trail switchbacks down the east wall of the canyon through dense pine forest. Follow the course of vigorous East Creek to a ford, 1.4 miles from the lake. Continue the stiff descent along the west bank, as the switchbacking trail zigzags down the canyon through a light forest, composed of red firs, western white pines, lodgepole pines, and aspens. Reaching the floor of Bubbs Creek canyon, you pass some secluded campsites and come to a ford of the creek, which may be difficult in early season. Beyond the creek, stroll through the lush foliage of Junction Meadow (8190'±) to a junction with the Bubbs Creek Trail, 1.9 miles from East Lake.

From the junction, turn northwest and follow the Bubbs Creek Trail for 4.2 miles to Sphinx Creek Camp and then retrace your steps another 3.5 miles to Roads End.

⊙ So many options are available along this loop that the only limit is your own creativity. The first of many alternatives to consider is the off-trail route to Sphinx Lakes, mentioned in Trip 25.

⊙ Where the Colby Pass Trail crosses Roaring River to climb toward Colby Lake, an abandoned trail, once referred to as the Coppermine Trail, continues up Cloud Canyon. Traces of the trail can still be seen in blazes, ducks, or sections of old tread, but the unmaintained path is now considered a cross-country route. Proceed upstream to the head of the canyon, where you can veer southeast to Glacier Lake, or west over Glacier Ridge at Coppermine Pass (11,960'±), about 0.3 mile north of Peak 12345. From the pass, a westward traverse leads above the abandoned Oakland mine, to Elizabeth Pass Trail. From upper Cloud Canyon, Lion Lake Pass (11,600'±) provides access to Lion Lake, and Triple Divide Pass (12,200'±) provides a high route to the upper Kern-Kaweah country. Both passes are class 2.

⊙ Milestone Bowl can be reached via a cross-country jaunt that leaves the main trail approximately 1.0 mile southeast of Colby Pass. From upper Milestone Bowl, a route over 12,960'±. Milestone Pass (class 2), which is 0.2 mile southeast of Milestone Peak, allows a connection through Milestone Basin—via another abandoned trail down Milestone Creek—to the Kern River Trail. You meet the Kern River Trail approximately 200 yards south of an unnamed tarn (10,635'±), and just west of a junction with a connector to the JMT.

⊙ The upper Kern basin offers plenty of nooks for off-trail explorations. Three alternative crossings of the Kern-Kaweah Divide are Lucys Foot Pass (12,400'±), Ericson Pass (12,560'±), and Millys Foot Pass (12,240'±). All three are rated class 2.

⊙ Visitors to upper Cloud Canyon can climb Triple Divide Peak by a variety of class 2 and class 3 routes. From Milestone Bowl, Milestone Mtn. is class 2 from the south. From the Milestone Creek area, the east side of Milestone Mtn. is class 3, and the east ridge of Midway Mtn. is class 2. Peaks along the Great Western and Kings-Kern divides offer numerous intermediate climbs.

Ⓡ **PERMITS:** Wilderness permit required for overnight stays (quota: 25 per day).

CAMPFIRES: Not permitted above 10,400 feet.

CAMPING: Prohibited for first 3.5 miles to Sphinx Creek Camp.

Cascade on the Upper Kern River

CEDAR GROVE TRAILHEADS

TRIP **27**

East Lake and Lake Reflection

Ⓜ ↗ BP

DISTANCE: 11.6 miles one way to East Lake; +1.9 miles one way to Lake Reflection

ELEVATION: 5045/9475, +4665'/-230'
5045/10,300, +5420'/-410'

SEASON: July to mid-October

USE: Light

MAPS: *The Sphinx, Mt. Clarence King, Mt. Brewer*

TRAIL LOG:

3.5 Sphinx Creek Camp
6.7 Charlotte Creek
9.7 Junction Meadow
11.6 East Lake
13.5 Lake Reflection

INTRODUCTION: Of the 25 backpackers permitted to leave Roads End on the Bubbs Creek Trail each day, most are bound for the popular Rae Lakes Loop, neglecting the incredible scenery up the nearly forgotten side canyon of East Creek. While most of the loopers spend from four to five days completing their circuit, the same time could easily be spent enjoying the serene waters of East Lake and Lake Reflection, and exploring the nooks and crannies of East Creek's upper basin. From a stunningly picturesque base camp, mountaineers have a bounty of impressive summits to scale. Even anglers will be tempted up the canyon by the rumors of good-sized trout. Whatever their motivation, backpackers who make this trek will be rewarded by incomparable alpine scenery.

DIRECTIONS TO THE TRAILHEAD: Drive on Highway 180 to Kings Canyon and to the overnight parking area at Roads End, 5.0 miles past the turnoff to Cedar Grove.

DESCRIPTION: The well-signed trail begins at the east edge of the paved turnaround, near the wilderness permit station. Follow the wide trail, which parallels the South Fork Kings River through a mixed forest. You quickly cross Copper Creek on a wood bridge. Up the trail, the forest cover thins, allowing views of the granite walls of the canyon. Soon you enter a cool forest of ponderosa pines, sugar pines, white firs, and alders, and come to a signed Y-junction with the Paradise Valley Trail, 1.9 miles from the trailhead.

Head right (south) from the junction and immediately cross a bridge over the South Fork Kings River, just downstream from its confluence with Bubbs Creek. Soon you encounter another trail junction, where the Bubbs Creek and Kanawyer Loop trails meet. Turn up the Bubbs Creek Trail and follow a series of short, wooden bridges across multiple branches of Bubbs Creek.

A moderate climb leads to the first of many switchbacks that lead you away from the floor of the canyon and up the Bubbs Creek drainage. Through gaps in the scrubby forest, you have excellent views of Kings Canyon, the rock pinnacle known as The Sphinx, and, in early season, a spectacular cascade on Bubbs Creek. You take a break from the switchbacks as the trail ascends the east side of the canyon. As you continue the moderate climb, you reach an area where conifers cover the slopes. At 3.5 miles, you reach Sphinx Creek Camp (6280'±) and a junction of the Bubbs Creek and Sphinx Creek trails. Excellent campsites with bear boxes are on both sides of Bubbs Creek.

From Sphinx Creek Camp, you proceed east on the Bubbs Creek Trail, in and out of a mixed forest of black oaks, Jeffrey and ponderosa pines, white firs, and cedars. Shrubs and ferns make up the understory. Well past a trio of tiny brooks, you ford Charlotte Creek and then encounter a path,

6.7 miles from the trailhead, that leads to pleasant, tree-shaded campsites near the bank of Bubbs Creek, where fishing is reportedly fair for brown, brook, rainbow, and golden-rainbow trout.

Alternating stretches of lush foliage and dry slopes greet you for the next couple of miles as you make a steady ascent beyond Charlotte Creek. Through clearings, Mt. Bago looms above the north side of steep-walled Bubbs Creek canyon. You reach campsites, stroll through a gap in a drift fence, and pass a horse camp before encountering verdant Junction Meadow (8190'±), carpeted with lush grasses, wildflowers, and ferns. At 9.7 miles, near the east edge of the meadow, is the signed junction with the East Creek Trail, where you turn right.

Follow the trail south through the dense foliage of the meadow to a ford of Bubbs Creek (may be difficult in early season). On the far side of the creek are secluded campsites. You begin a steep climb up the canyon of East Creek via switchbacks, through a light covering of lodgepole and western white pines, red firs, and aspens. Views of the surrounding terrain improve with the gain in elevation. About 0.5 mile from Bubbs Creek, you ford East Creek and continue the climb along the east bank of the vigorous creek. The grade increases as you enter a thick pine forest, and begin switchbacking up the east wall of the canyon, until the grade eases beyond a fern-lined tributary draining an unnamed tarn. Moderate ascent for 0.5 mile leads to easy trail prior to your arrival at the north shore of picturesque East Lake (9470'±), 11.6 miles from Roads End.

Sandwiched between towering granite peaks, the grass-rimmed lake is a pleasant sight. Good campsites can be found on the south and north shores. Unlike at many

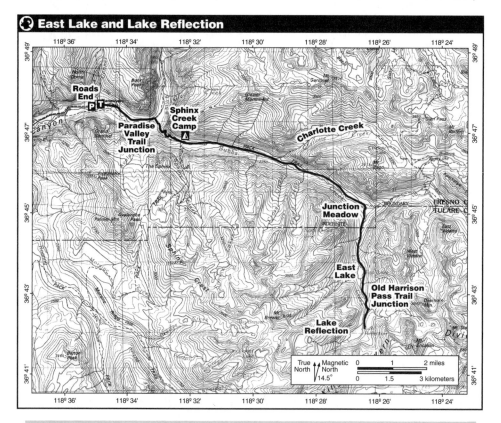

East Lake and Lake Reflection

subalpine lakes in the parks, campfires are permitted at East Lake.

Follow the trail around the east side of the lake, step across an inlet from a side canyon, and then begin climbing through scattered stands of lodgepole and foxtail pines. Approximately 1.0 mile from the south end of the lake, near a talus slide, the abandoned trail to Harrison Pass ascends eastward (see Options). After negotiating the talus slide, you pass some campsites along the creek and then gently ascend through pockets of meadow and willow. Just beyond a tarn, you come to the shore of wind-swept Lake Reflection (10,300'±). Campsites are scattered around the south shore. Anglers will delight in fishing for good-sized golden and rainbow trout.

O A bounty of cross-country routes offers a variety of choices for further wanderings. Unless otherwise noted, all passes are rated class 2.

- Two routes connect East Creek to South Guard Lake. The Brewer Pass route follows Ouzel Creek from East Lake to the pass (12,640'±), 0.5 mile southeast of Mt. Brewer. You then drop to South Guard Lake. From Lake Reflection, a class 1 route following an old trail heads over Longley Pass (12,400'±) to South Guard Lake.

- The Thunder Pass route proceeds from Lake Reflection along its easternmost inlet stream, past a series of tarns, and up a snowfield (ice axe) to the pass (12,660'±), 0.25 mile east of Thunder Mtn. From the pass, you descend easier terrain to the upper Kern basin.

- The Harrison Pass route is a relatively well-known off-trail route from East Lake over the Kings-Kern Divide to Lake South America (see Trip 26). Additional routes across the divide to the upper Kern basin include Millys Foot (12,240'±), Lucys Foot (12,400'±), Ericsson (12,560'±) (class 2–3) and Andys Foot (13,600'±) passes. Andys Foot pass may require the use of an ice axe.

- The Deerhorn Saddle route leaves the Harrison Pass route and climbs over the saddle (12,560'±), 0.4 mile southeast of Deerhorn Mtn., providing access to upper Vidette Creek.

- A bevy of peaks accessible from the East Creek canyon will tantalize mountaineers. Intermediate routes (class 2–3) can be found on North Guard, Mt. Brewer, South Guard, Thunder Mtn., Mt. Jordan, Mt. Genevra, Mt. Ericson, Gregorys Monument, Mt. Stanford, The Minster, and Deerhorn Mtn. More challenging routes can be found on many of the same peaks.

R **PERMITS:** Wilderness permit required for overnight stays (quota: 25 per day).

CAMPFIRES: Not permitted above 10,000 feet.

TRIP **28**

Charlotte Lake

M ⟋ BP

DISTANCE: 14.5 miles one way

ELEVATION: 5045/10,774, +5890'/-535'

SEASON: Mid-July to mid-October

USE: Heavy

MAPS: *The Sphinx,*
Mt. Clarence King

TRAIL LOG:

9.7 Junction Meadow
12.1 John Muir Trail Jct.
13.5 Charlotte Lake Trail Jct.

INTRODUCTION: Charlotte Lake offers a pleasant atmosphere for overnight stays in the heart of the Kings Canyon backcountry. However, due to the popularity of the region, backpackers can only enjoy camping at the lake for a single evening, as the Park Service has instituted a one-night limit. The lake is not only a fine destination in its own right, but JMT through-hikers and groups bound for the Rae Lakes will often overnight there as well, adding to the pressure on the area. Due to the distance and the moderate climb from the Roads End trailhead, most parties will opt for a campsite at Sphinx Creek, Junction Meadow, or Lower Vidette Meadow for the first night. Knapsackers possessing the extra time and inclination may follow the old trail route from Charlotte Lake to isolated Gardiner Basin (see Options, below).

DIRECTIONS TO THE TRAILHEAD: Drive on Highway 180 into Kings Canyon and to the overnight parking lot at Roads End, 5.0 miles past the turnoff to Cedar Grove.

DESCRIPTION: The well-signed trail begins at the east edge of the paved turnaround, near the wilderness permit station. Follow the wide trail, which parallels the South Fork Kings River through a mixed forest. You quickly cross Copper Creek on a wood bridge. Up the trail, the forest cover thins, allowing views of the granite walls of the canyon. Soon you enter a cool forest of ponderosa pines, sugar pines, white firs, and alders, and come to a signed Y-junction with the Paradise Valley Trail, 1.9 miles from the trailhead.

Head right (south) from the junction and immediately cross a bridge over the South Fork Kings River, just downstream from its confluence with Bubbs Creek. Soon you encounter another trail junction, where the Bubbs Creek and Kanawyer Loop trails meet. Turn up the Bubbs Creek Trail and follow a series of short, wooden bridges across multiple branches of Bubbs Creek.

A moderate climb leads to the first of many switchbacks that lead you away from the floor of the canyon and up the Bubbs Creek drainage. Through gaps in the scrubby forest, you have excellent views of Kings Canyon, the rock pinnacle known as The Sphinx, and, in early season, a spectacular cascade on Bubbs Creek. You take a break from the switchbacks as the trail ascends the east side of the canyon. As you continue the moderate climb, you reach an area where conifers cover the slopes. At 3.5 miles, you reach Sphinx Creek Camp (6280'±) and a junction of the Bubbs Creek and Sphinx Creek trails. Excellent campsites with bear boxes are on both sides of Bubbs Creek.

From Sphinx Creek Camp, you proceed east on the Bubbs Creek Trail, in and out of a mixed forest. Well past a trio of tiny brooks, you ford Charlotte Creek and then encounter a path, 6.7 miles from the trailhead, that leads to pleasant, tree-shaded campsites quite near the bank of Bubbs Creek, where fishing is reported to be fair for brown, brook, rainbow, and golden-rainbow trout.

Alternating stretches of lush foliage and dry slopes greet you for the next couple of

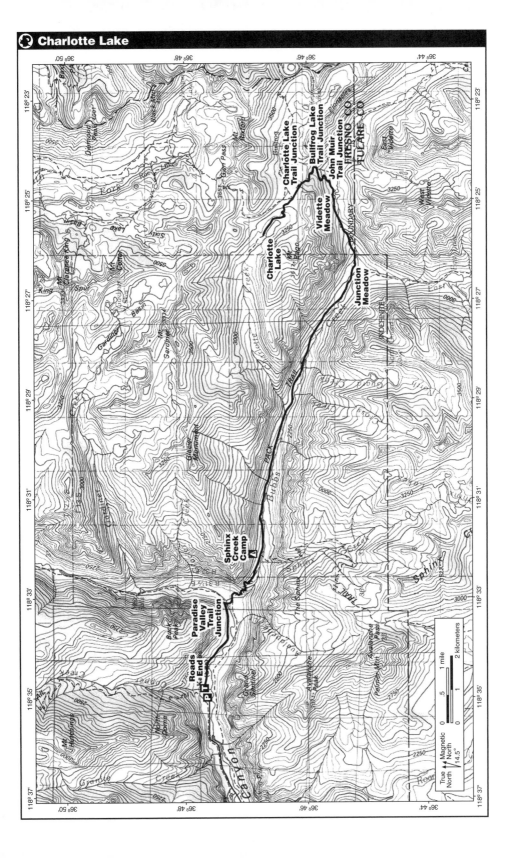

miles as you make a steady ascent beyond Charlotte Creek. Through clearings, Mt. Bago looms above the north side of steep-walled Bubbs Creek canyon. You reach campsites, stroll through a gap in a drift fence, and pass a horse camp. At 9.7 miles from the trailhead, you come to Junction Meadow (8190'±), carpeted with lush grasses, wildflowers, and ferns.

A short section of easy trail leads east from the junction, as you continue upstream on the Bubbs Creek Trail. Steeper climbing up switchbacks follows, taking you through alternating sections of forest and open terrain. On the way, a picturesque stretch of Bubbs Creek, where it cascades over sloping slabs in dramatic fashion, provides an excellent rest stop. Farther on, openings in the forest grant fine views of the canyon walls and the towering peaks above. The grade of the ascent eventually eases, and soon you stroll alongside the verdant expanse of Lower Vidette Meadow. Serene campsites near the meadow's fringe will tempt backpackers to linger overnight. Just beyond the meadow, in a stand of

conifers, you reach a signed three-way junction with the John Muir Trail, 12.1 miles from Roads End.

Turn north on the JMT and make a moderate, switchbacking climb up the north wall of Bubbs Creek canyon. Views of the Kearsarge Pinnacles to your right are quite dramatic, but don't neglect the views behind you of the Videttes and Deerhorn Mtn. After a pair of crossings over Bullfrog Lake's outlet, you come to a three-way junction of the JMT and the Bullfrog Lake Trail. (The lake is quite picturesque but has been closed to camping for several decades due to severe overuse). A series of short switchbacks lead over a lightly forested rise to a broad, sandy flat and a signed, four-way junction, 1.5 miles from the Bubbs Creek Trail. The Kearsarge Pass Trail heads northeast from the junction and the JMT continues north. (This 0.2-mile section of the JMT is not shown on the *Mt. Clarence King* quad). The Charlotte Lake Trail goes northwest to Charlotte Lake.

Following signs, you turn left (northwest) and wind down through light pine

Camp near Charlotte Lake

forest to the northeast shore of Charlotte Lake (10,385'±), 0.8 mile from the junction. Plenty of campsites are scattered beneath pines above the north shoreline, with a small ranger cabin and outhouse near the shoreline's mid-point and a bear box farther northwest. The serene lake is cradled in a deep bowl between forested hills. Brilliant sunsets are often displayed through the V-shaped notch of plunging Charlotte Creek. Fishing is fair for rainbow and brook trout.

O An abandoned trail (shown on the Mt. Clarence King quad) leaves Charlotte Lake and climbs above Charlotte Creek northwest to Gardiner Pass (11,200'±). The route then descends to Gardiner Creek and follows the drainage upstream to remote Gardiner Basin. From there, Sixty Lake Col provides the means for a potential loop through Sixty Lake Basin to the JMT at Rae Lakes. The east side of Mt. Bago is an easy climb southwest from Charlotte Lake.

R **PERMITS:** Wilderness permit required for overnight stays (quota: 25 per day).

CAMPING: One-night limit; bear canisters required.

CAMPFIRES: Not permitted above 10,000 feet.

CEDAR GROVE TRAILHEADS

TRIP **29**

Deer Cove Trail

Ⓜ ╱ DH

DISTANCE: 3.4 miles one way to Deer Cove Saddle

ELEVATION: 4425/6525, +2720'/-620'

SEASON: May to November

USE: Light

MAP: *Cedar Grove*

INTRODUCTION: The nearly forgotten Deer Cove Trail, in the Monarch Wilderness, offers hikers an opportunity to escape the crowds on a short ascent to a vantage point offering pleasant views of the Monarch Divide and Kings Canyon. The relatively low elevation and south-facing hillsides combine to make this a good early- or late-season trip. Summer hikers will appreciate an early start as the best bet to beat the heat. Although a network of trails penetrates deep into the Monarch Wilderness, allowing adventurous souls access to seldom-seen territory, these paths receive little maintenance. During autumn, visitors should be aware that hunting is allowed in the Monarch Wilderness, which lies outside of the park boundary.

DIRECTIONS TO THE TRAILHEAD: Drive on Highway 180 into Kings Canyon. The Deer Cove trailhead is on the north side of the road, approximately 31.5 miles beyond the Y-intersection with Generals Highway and 0.9 mile west of the Kings Canyon National Park boundary.

DESCRIPTION: The trail leaves the dusty parking area and heads uphill through mixed forest of Jeffrey pine, white fir, and black oak, with ground cover principally of manzanita. Soon it crosses into the signed Monarch Wilderness. The forest cover

Deer Cove Trail

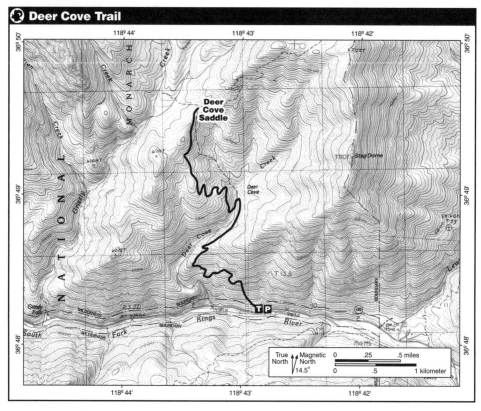

becomes scattered where you make a moderate-to-moderately steep diagonal climb of a south-facing hillside to the lip of Deer Cove canyon. A seemingly interminable series of switchbacks takes you up the slope well above a creek. Eventually, you enter thicker forest and make a short descent to a crossing of Deer Cove Creek, 1.75 miles from the trailhead.

Once across the creek, you climb out of dense forest and head southwest up the slope (the trail heading north from the creek as shown on the *Cedar Grove* quad is no longer passable). After a short while, you veer north and then west, following more switchbacks up the lightly forested hillside. Through gaps in the trees, you have alternating views of the peaks of the Monarch Divide to the north, and of the gorge of Kings Canyon and its neighboring summits to the east. A long ascending traverse across the slope brings you to Deer

Cove Saddle and a trail junction, 3.4 miles from the highway.

From the saddle, you can make a short descent to primitive campsites near Grizzly Creek, or continue on the Deer Cove Trail to Wildman Meadow.

TRIP **30**

Cedar Grove Overlook

(MS) ⟋ DH

DISTANCE: 2.4 miles one way

ELEVATION: 4675/6085, +1525/-115

SEASON: May to November

USE: Light

MAP: *Cedar Grove*

INTRODUCTION: One of the most scenic chasms in the Sierra, Kings Canyon is also one of the deepest gorges in North America, reaching a depth of 8,000 feet just outside the Park boundary as measured from the summit of Spanish Mtn. Consequently, in order to gain the extraordinary views from its rim, hikers must surmount the steep walls of Kings Canyon via one of a handful of correspondingly steep trails.

The trail to the Cedar Grove Overlook is no exception, gaining more than 1500 feet in nearly 2.5 miles. However, the effort is well rewarded, because successful summiteers are blessed with expansive views of Kings Canyon and the Monarch Divide. The ascent can become a scorching affair during the afternoon, thanks to the relatively low starting elevation coupled with a route up the exposed south-facing canyon wall. An early morning start will avoid climbing during the hottest part of the day. Unfortunately for photographers, the best light occurs late in the afternoon, when the sun is to the west.

DIRECTIONS TO THE TRAILHEAD: Drive on Highway 180 to the signed turnoff to Cedar Grove Village, 34 miles beyond the Y-intersection with Generals Highway. Follow signs toward the pack station, making a right turn 0.5 mile from the highway. Immediately past the turn, find a small parking area on your left at the Hotel Creek trailhead.

DESCRIPTION: You climb moderately steeply on the Hotel Creek Trail up a hillside to a junction with the trail from the pack station. Continue the ascent up the main trail through a mixed forest of oak, pine, and fir, now hearing the roar of Hotel Creek. You soon reach a trail spur, heading down to the stream, a convenient place to filter water if necessary. The main trail veers away from Hotel Creek to begin a series of switchbacks climbing up the hillside west of the stream. Initially, you climb

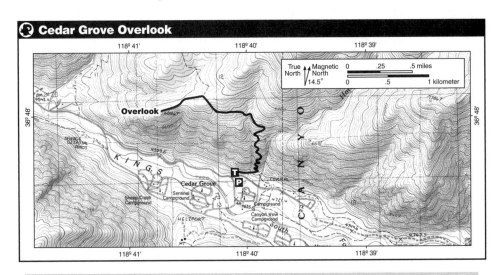

the north wall of Kings Canyon through scattered oak and pine, but after 0.5 mile you leave the trees behind, as they give way to chaparral for the remainder of the ascent. The switchbacks eventually end as you head west, away from Hotel Creek on a mild grade, a welcome change after the long climb up the north wall of the canyon. Beyond the crossing of a seasonal stream, a moderate climb resumes for 0.5 mile until you reach a signed trail junction, 1.9 miles from the trailhead. Here the Hotel Creek Trail veers right and the trail to the overlook heads left.

Turn left (west) at the junction and gently descend through scattered pine with views to the north, of the Monarch Divide. After 0.25 mile, you reach the low spot on a ridge, and then begin a mild, short climb toward Cedar Grove Overlook, a knob of granite near the end of the ridge. From this aerie, you gaze straight down to Cedar Grove, 1500 feet below. Your bird's-eye view of the South Fork Kings River is expansive, from the western foothills to beyond its confluence with Bubbs Creek. To the north, the peaks of the Monarch Divide beckon you toward further adventures. See Trip 31 for extending your journey on the Hotel and Lewis Creeks Loop.

TRIP 31

Hotel and Lewis Creeks Loop

M ↻/↗ DH

DISTANCE: 6.4 miles without shuttle; 5.0 miles with shuttle

ELEVATION: 4675/6225/4575, +1920'/-2035'

SEASON: May to November

USE: Light

MAP: *Cedar Grove*

INTRODUCTION: This loop trip offers hikers an opportunity to sample the transition zones between the riparian woodland community adjacent to the South Fork Kings River, the foothill woodland and chaparral communities of the lower slopes of Kings Canyon, and the mixed coniferous forest above. In addition, you have the opportunity to see forest succession at work in the upper part of the loop, where a series of forest fires have swept through the area. Throw in some great views of the Monarch Divide, and the possibility of a short extension to the fine vista from the Cedar Grove Overlook (see Trip 30), and you have the makings of a fine adventure.

Although not a major consideration, a car shuttle will save almost 1.5 miles of uninteresting hiking between the Hotel and Lewis creeks trailheads. Also, since this trip climbs the south-facing wall of Kings Canyon, try to arrange an early start to beat the heat.

DIRECTIONS TO THE TRAILHEAD: Drive on Highway 180 to the signed turnoff to Cedar Grove Village, 34 miles beyond the Y-intersection with Generals Highway. Follow signs toward the pack station, making a right turn 0.5 mile from the highway. Immediately past the turn, find a small parking area on your left at the Hotel Creek trailhead.

If you're planning on using a car shuttle, leave a car or arrange a pickup at the Lewis Creek trailhead. Find the trailhead on the north shoulder of Highway 180, 0.4 mile east of the Park boundary and 1.3 miles west of the Cedar Grove turnoff.

DESCRIPTION: Climb the Hotel Creek Trail up a hillside to a junction with the trail from the pack station. Continue the ascent up the main trail through a mixed forest of oak, pine, and fir, now hearing the roar of Hotel Creek. You soon reach a trail spur, heading down to the stream, a convenient place to filter water if necessary. The main trail veers away from Hotel Creek to begin a series of switchbacks climbing up the hillside west of the stream. Climb the north wall of Kings Canyon through scattered oak and pine, which after 0.5 mile give way

to chaparral for the remainder of the ascent. The switchbacks eventually end as you head west, away from Hotel Creek on a mild grade, a welcome change after the long climb up the north wall of the canyon. Beyond the crossing of a seasonal stream, a moderate climb resumes for 0.5 mile until you reach a signed trail junction, 1.9 miles from the trailhead.

From the junction, you make a mild descent through a forest of scattered Jeffrey pine that was previously burned and is now carpeted with mountain misery. Paintbrush and lupine brighten up the area in season. After crossing a pair of seasonal drainages, you start to climb moderately toward the high point of the trip at the top of a ridge. Along the way, you have good views northwest to the Monarch Divide. Beyond the ridge top, you begin the long descent back to Kings Canyon. Passing through light forest and paralleling an unnamed tributary of

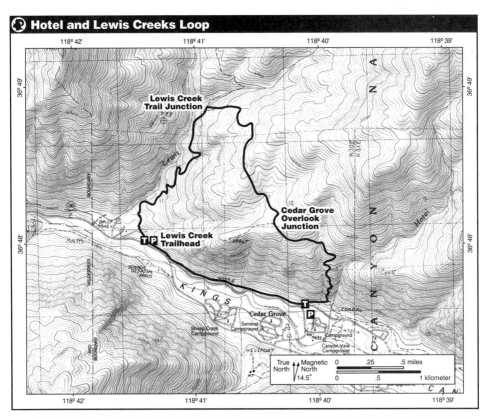

Lewis Creek, you reach a signed junction with the Lewis Creek Trail at 3.25 miles. Here you turn left.

Heading downhill from the junction, you pass through more Jeffrey pines in various stages of succession following periodic fires that are common in this area. High above Lewis Creek, you follow numerous switchbacks down its canyon, alternating between brief periods of light shade from a mixed forest of ponderosa pines, black oaks, and incense cedars, and sunny stretches on exposed slopes covered with chaparral. You reach the Lewis Creek trailhead at 5.0 miles from your starting point.

If you don't have the benefit of a car shuttle, you must walk a little-used trail from the Lewis Creek trailhead that heads southeast and parallels the road to the Hotel Creek trailhead. The 1.4-mile trail seems to undulate needlessly across the hillside above the level access road, but it provides a straightforward return to your starting point.

CEDAR GROVE TRAILHEADS

TRIP 32

East Kennedy Lake

M ↗ BP

DISTANCE: 11.0 miles one way

ELEVATION: 4575/10,800/10,160, +7280'/-1690'

SEASON: July to late October

USE: Light

MAPS: *Cedar Grove, Slide Bluffs*

TRAIL LOG:

6.2	Frypan Meadow
10.1	Kennedy Pass
11.0	East Kennedy Lake

INTRODUCTION: Any route across the Monarch Divide, which separates the yawning gorges of the South and the Middle forks of the Kings River, requires a significant change in elevation. The Lewis Creek Trail is no exception, demanding that backpackers surmount a stiff 6225-foot, 10-mile climb to Kennedy Pass. The south-facing trail starts low, climbs steeply, and is exposed for much of the way, so even with an early start the route can be a scorcher. Despite these drawbacks, the scenery is superb, and adventurous souls willing to undertake such a journey will be able to appreciate beauty sans crowds. This trail sees far fewer users than other trails emanating from Kings Canyon.

East Kennedy Lake is an alpine gem, sure to please the most discriminating camper. West Kennedy Lake is easily accessible, and a straightforward cross-country route between East Kennedy Lake and Granite Pass will tempt knapsackers in search of a semi-loop trip.

DIRECTIONS TO THE TRAILHEAD: You'll find the Lewis Creek trailhead on the north

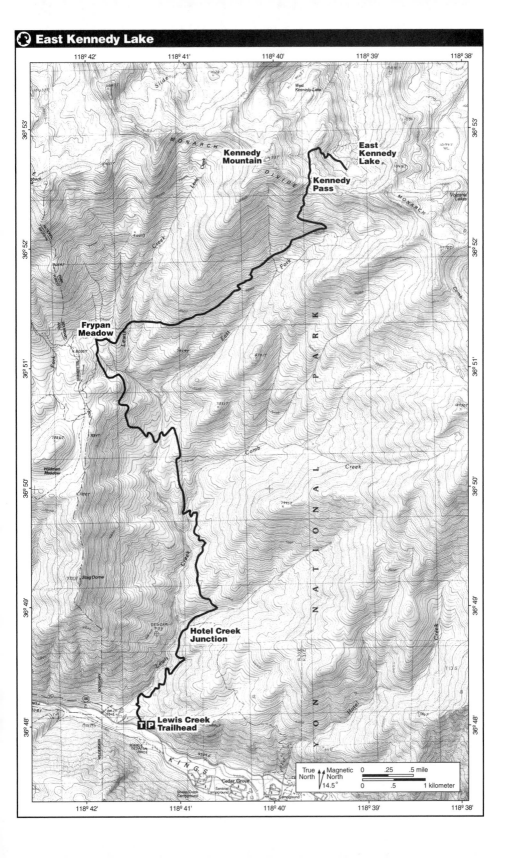

East
Kennedy
Lake

Kennedy
Mountain

Kennedy
Pass

Frypan
Meadow

Hotel Creek
Junction

Lewis Creek
Trailhead

True North	Magnetic North	0	.25	.5 mile
	14.5°	0	.5	1 kilometer

shoulder of Highway 180, 0.4 mile east of the Park boundary and 1.3 miles west of the Cedar Grove turnoff.

DESCRIPTION: Take the Lewis Creek Trail, which climbs numerous switchbacks up through the creek's canyon. You pass through mixed forest, arriving at a junction with the Hotel creek Trail, 1.75 miles from the trailhead.

From the junction, you drop into the canyon of a Lewis Creek tributary and follow it northeast to a crossing. A stretch of uneven climbing soon brings you well above Lewis Creek once more, where patches of canyon live oak offer intermittent shade. At 3.5 miles, you drop down to a handful of campsites at the crossing of Comb Creek. The ascent continues to where mountain misery, manzanita, and the charred trunks of scattered Jeffrey pines cover the once fire-swept slope. You cross Lewis Creek at 4.6 miles and climb steadily up a hillside, away from the creek temporarily. Through scattered-to-light forest, you arrive at a signed three-way junction 6.2 miles from the trailhead, where an infrequently used path heads south to Wildman Meadow. After a 0.1-mile stretch of gently graded trail, you draw near to a branch of Lewis Creek and encounter the lush flora of Frypan Meadow (7850'±). A pair of campsites with a bear box nestle beneath towering white firs. Near the far edge of the meadow is a junction with an overgrown and unimproved trail to Grizzly Lake.

Away from Frypan Meadow, you proceed through dense timber, stepping over multiple branches of Lewis Creek before switchbacks take you out of the trees near the beginning of a long, ascending traverse across the southeast-facing slope of Kennedy Mtn. The mostly open hillside is covered with young aspens, wildflowers, and shrubs, well watered by a number of seeps that ooze down the hillside. The combination of verdant foliage and expansive views of the Great Western and Kings-Kaweah divides produces exquisite scenery,

as picturesque as any in the Sierra. After fighting your way through the trailside brush, you cross a willow-and-flower-lined tributary of the East Fork Lewis Creek and begin a series of switchbacks that climb toward the pass through scattered lodgepole and whitebark pines. At 10.1 miles, you stand atop Kennedy Pass (10,900'), between two of the deepest canyons in North America, the Middle and South Forks of the Kings River. The incredible view from here includes an array of Sierra summits. A sprinkling of tarns just below the north side of the pass offer airy campsites.

From the pass, the trail zigzags down sandy slopes amid boulders and rocks to a shallow, steep gully. The inordinately steep trail is quite indistinct in parts, rough in others, and badly needs maintenance. Descend the gully to more tight switchbacks, which lead you down to an elevation of about 10,100 feet, approximately 0.6 mile from the pass. To reach East Kennedy Lake, leave the trail here to head around the north side of a small tarn northeast of the pass, climb over a rise, and arrive above the west shore of East Kennedy Lake (10,160'±).

Alpine in nature, East Kennedy Lake casts a foreboding presence, backdropped by the cirque's huge vertical wall rising from the surface of the lake straight up to the crest of the Monarch Divide. Surrounded by steep cliffs, the shoreline is nearly inaccessible, but exposed campsites can be found above the west shore on tiny pockets of sand. The view to the north down Kennedy Canyon and over the deep gorge of the Middle Fork is breathtaking.

ROBERT KENNEDY

The lakes, pass, and canyon were all named for Robert Kennedy—not the former presidential candidate and brother of the slain president, but a sheep rancher from Fresno.

○ The Kennedy Pass Trail can be followed downstream to a short, off-trail romp up the West Fork of Kennedy Creek to seldom-visited West Kennedy Lake. Farther down the canyon, the tread deteriorates even more, but some parties still follow the old trail over Dead Pine Ridge to Volcanic Lakes, although a much more direct cross-country route is described below.

○ Access to Volcanic Lakes is straightforward for experienced cross-country hikers. Follow the rocky terrain around the north side of East Kennedy Lake to a grassy gully above its east shore. Climb the steep gully northeast to an obvious saddle (10,900'±). From the saddle, you have an excellent view down a grassy gully on the east side of the saddle to Lake 10199. After descending steep talus below the saddle, better footing leads to the floor of the basin, from where you can explore the rest of the Volcanic Lakes.

○ An off-trail route continues to Granite Pass for those interested in returning to Kings Canyon via the Copper Creek Trail (shuttle required). From the northern tip of Lake 10199, follow the inlet upstream and cross the creek below the second highest lake (10,325'±) in the chain. Curve around to the south and pass between Lake 10288 and Lake 10284 to a grassy gully that ascends the east side of the basin to the top of the ridge above. Once atop the ridge, follow easy terrain over to Granite Pass and the Copper Creek Trail.

○ The ascent of Kennedy Mtn. (11,433') from Kennedy Pass is rated class 1–2. Kennedy Mtn. is about 0.5 mile northwest of the pass.

R **PERMITS:** Wilderness permit required for overnight use (quota: 25 per day).

CAMPFIRES: Not permitted above 10,000 feet.

CEDAR GROVE TRAILHEADS

TRIP 33

Copper Creek Trail to Granite Basin

S ⤢ BP

DISTANCE: 9.5 miles one way

ELEVATION: 5045/10,347/10,093, 5735'/-685'

SEASON: July to mid-October

USE: Light to moderate

MAP: *The Sphinx*

TRAIL LOG:

4.0	Lower Tent Meadows
9.0	Granite Lake Jct.

INTRODUCTION: Granite Basin is a gently sloping bowl filled with scenic tarns and flower-bedecked meadows. However, the route to the basin is steep and usually hot during normal summer weather. Backpackers who don't mind the steady ascent can recuperate along the restful, pine-dotted shores of Granite Lake or beside a bevy of unnamed tarns scattered throughout the picturesque basin. Anglers will find the basin's streams and lakes a fitting challenge for a potentially ample reward.

Backpackers who don't want to make the entire 9.5-mile climb to Granite Lake in one day must be satisfied with campsites at Lower Tent Meadow, as there are no decent camping opportunities between there and the basin. Don't expect a typical meadow at either Lower or Upper Tent meadows, since neither offers anything close to flat, grassy terrain. Both are moderately sloped and choked with brush.

DIRECTIONS TO THE TRAILHEAD: Drive on Highway 180 into Kings Canyon and to the

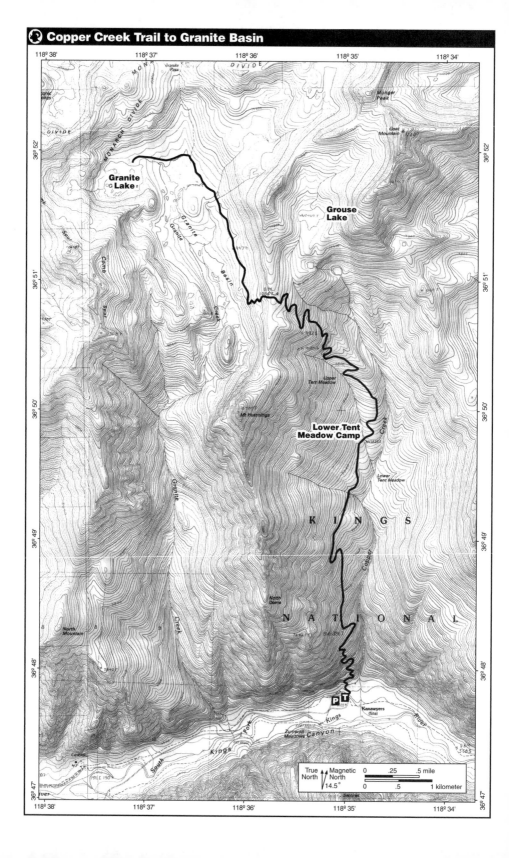

overnight parking lot at Roads End, 5.0 miles past the turnoff to Cedar Grove.

DESCRIPTION: From the north side of the overnight parking lot, you follow a sandy trail that switchbacks up a mostly open hillside through scattered Jeffrey pines and canyon live oaks. While granting insufficient shade, the sparse vegetation allows fine views of the Grand Sentinel. More switchbacks now take you high up the Copper Creek drainage and into partial shade from a light forest of sugar pines, incense cedars, Jeffrey pines, and white firs. More switchbacks lead past tiny brooks, over a tributary of Copper Creek, and across a sloping, manzanita-filled clearing. Soon you encounter a larger, aspen-and-brush-covered clearing with a small campsite. Pass through the clearing, step over a couple of rivulets, and reenter forest as you climb to the next creek crossing. Immediately past the creek, you come to Lower Tent Meadows camp (7825'), 4.0 miles from the trailhead. Conifers cast shade on five designated campsites with a bear box.

You climb moderately away from the camp, ascending through more brush-filled burns and across an avalanche-swept slope. A long, steady climb on switchbacks leads you back into a light covering of red firs. Farther on, western white pines and then lodgepole pines shade the trail. Near the 7-mile mark you cross a moraine at the edge of Granite Basin. From this vantage point, there are fine views through the trees of the basin below and of Mt. Clarence King and of Mt. Gardiner.

A short, winding descent leads through a gap in a drift fence and down toward the basin, which is filled with delightful tarns and irregular-shaped meadows. The trail avoids the basin in favor of an undulating traverse across the lodgepole pine-dotted hillside above. Parties interested in campsites near the tarns must leave the trail and journey cross-country. Just beyond the large meadow at the north end of the basin, in a pocket of willows, you reach a signed junction with a lateral to Granite Lake, 9.0 miles from the trailhead.

Granite Basin from Granite Pass

Turning left (west), you follow the trail over a stream and past a couple of seldom-used campsites on a mild ascent toward the lake. Step across the seasonal inlet and come to campsites along the north shore of Granite Lake (10,093'), 0.5 mile from the junction. Island-dotted Granite Lake nestles in a rocky basin below cliffs of the Monarch Divide. Sparse pines offer little shelter for the smattering of campsites scattered around the shore. Anglers can test their skill on fair-sized brook trout.

O For a description of the Copper Creek Trail beyond the junction to Granite Lake, see Trip 34.

O Cross-country enthusiasts can access Grouse Lake from the Copper Creek Trail by following a part of Roper's Sierra High Route, a 195-mile, mostly off-trail route that closely follows the Sierra crest between Cedar Grove and Twin Lakes. Leave the trail near the crest of the moraine above Granite Basin and traverse north through scattered lodgepole pines for 0.5 mile to the meadow bordering the outlet. From there, make the easy climb up to the lake.

R **PERMITS:** Wilderness permit required for overnight stays (quota: 25 per day).
CAMPFIRES: Not permitted in Granite Basin.

CEDAR GROVE TRAILHEADS

TRIP **34**

State and Horseshoe Lakes

Ⓜ ↗ BPx

DISTANCE: 18 miles one way
ELEVATION: 5045/10,515, +7735'/-2275'
SEASON: Mid-July to mid-October
USE: Light
MAPS: *The Sphinx, Marion Peak*

TRAIL LOG:
9.0   Glacier Lake Jct.
12.25   Kennedy Pass Trail Jct.
15.9   Lower State Lake
18.0   Horseshoe Lakes

INTRODUCTION: The trip to Granite Basin and Granite Lake, as described in Trip 33, is a worthy goal for weekend backpackers in search of great scenery. This extension to State and Horseshoe lakes offers those with more time the opportunity to add a visit to a pair of pleasant lake basins that see relatively few visitors. After the initial stiff climb from Roads End to Granite Basin, the terrain mellows considerably. Anglers will enjoy a wide variety of lakes that see little pressure. Cross-country types with time on their hands may be overwhelmed by the number of possible trip extensions through the alpine terrain northeast of Horseshoe Lakes.

DIRECTIONS TO THE TRAILHEAD: Drive on Highway 180 into Kings Canyon and to the overnight parking lot at Roads End, 5.0 miles past the turnoff to Cedar Grove.

DESCRIPTION: From the north side of the overnight parking lot, you follow a sandy trail that switchbacks up a mostly open hillside through scattered Jeffrey pines and canyon live oaks. More switchbacks take you high up the Copper Creek drainage

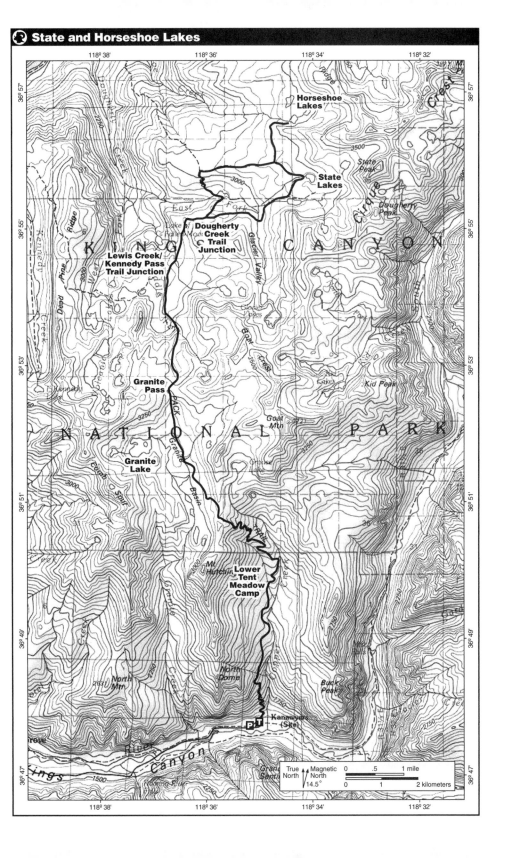

and into partial shade from a light forest, then on past tiny brooks, over a tributary of Copper Creek, and across a sloping, manzanita-filled clearing. Soon you encounter a larger, aspen-and-brush-covered clearing with a small campsite. Pass through the clearing, step over a couple of rivulets, and reenter forest as you climb to the next creek crossing. Immediately past the creek, you come to Lower Tent Meadows camp (7825'), 4.0 miles from the trailhead. Conifers shade five designated campsites with a bear box.

You climb moderately away from the camp, ascending through more brush-filled burns and across an avalanche-swept slope. A long, steady climb on switchbacks leads you back into a light covering of red firs. Farther on, western white pines and then lodgepole pines shade the trail. Near the 7-mile mark you cross a moraine at the edge of Granite Basin. From this vantage point, there are fine views through the trees of the basin below and of Mt. Clarence King and of Mt. Gardiner.

A short, winding descent leads through a gap in a drift fence and down toward the basin, which is filled with delightful tarns and irregular-shaped meadows. The trail makes an undulating traverse across the lodgepole pine-dotted hillside above. Just beyond the large meadow at the north end of the basin, in a pocket of willows, you reach a signed junction with a lateral to Granite Lake, 9.0 miles from the trailhead.

From the junction, you break out of light forest and make a steep, rocky climb toward Granite Pass. After 0.6 mile of climbing, you surmount Granite Pass (10,673'), from where there are good views.

From the pass, a zigzagging path leads down past a series of meadow-covered benches rimmed by granite walls. The trail nears Middle Fork Dougherty Creek several times along this descent. After a pair of drift fences, you continue to wind downstream through scattered lodgepole pines, stepping over the creek three times and climbing a ridge that affords a fine view down the Middle Fork's canyon. Soon, you follow mildly graded trail to a junction with the Lewis Creek/Kennedy Pass Trail, 12.25 miles from Roads End.

Early evening at State Lake

About 0.3 mile beyond the junction, you step across the creek flowing toward Lake of the Fallen Moon. Approximately 0.25 mile beyond the creek, an old trail heads west toward the lake, but the route is unmarked and obscure. Now a short, moderate climb leads to a traverse across a forested hillside, a brief descent to a pocket of lush meadow, and a junction 13.6 miles from the trailhead.

From here, the Dougherty Creek Trail continues northeast to Dougherty Meadow before veering northwest toward Simpson Meadow along the Middle Fork Kings River. You turn right (east), heading toward State Lakes. Proceeding through lodgepole pine forest, you pass a good-sized meadow carpeted with wildflowers, including tiger lily, aster, and shooting star, and climb to the crest of a rise. Drop from the rise to a crossing of the creek draining beautiful Glacier Valley, and then traverse to the crossing of a vigorous stream plummeting from lower State Lake. Beyond the creek, make a moderately steep climb up a hillside and over the lip of the lake basin to gently rising, flower-dotted terrain below the lake. At 15.9 miles, you stand at the northwest end of the lower State Lake (10,250'). Backdropped by the impressive cliffs of Cirque Crest, the lower lake offers a few lodgepole pine-shaded campsites along the north shore. Fishing is decent for good-sized rainbow and golden trout, Probably because the lake sees so few anglers. Off-trail types may enjoy the scramble to higher lakes nearer the crest.

A lightly used trail leads north from the lower lake on a mild-to-moderate 0.5 mile ascent through lodgepole pine, currant, and gooseberry to upper State Lake (10,450'±). This seldom-visited lake is not as desirable as its lower neighbor, offering only a nice view of State Peak and a couple of primitive campsites around the forest- and meadow-rimmed shore. Also, the shallow lake seems devoid of fish. Step across the outlet and stroll through boulder-strewn and lightly forested terrain on a moderately ascending trail past a small meadow to the crest of a

hill and a Y-junction, 16.6 miles from Roads End.

At this junction, a faint connecting trail leads west to the Dougherty Creek Trail, but you bend right (north) and make a quick descent to a meadow and a crossing of a flower-lined stream (neither the trail nor the stream appears on the *Marion Peak* quad). A mildly rising traverse follows, which leads across a dry, sandy slope dotted with lodgepole and western white pines. Approximately 0.75 mile from the junction, the trail rounds the nose of a moraine and veers northeast up the canyon of Horseshoe Creek, revealing impressive views of Windy Ridge and cliffs rimming the cirque basin ahead. You approach the creek through willows and wildflowers, boulderhop across it, and then continue upstream to Horseshoe Lakes.

The first Horseshoe Lake is small and shallow. A short walk on a use-trail leads to the second lake—a larger and deeper body of water—rimmed by morainal cliffs and green hills dotted with pines and boulders. From the northwest shore of the second lake, a short, off-trail jaunt leads northwest across gently rising terrain to the third lake (10,515'), which is large, deep, and surrounded by pines and boulders. Seldom-used campsites are plentiful between the second and third lakes, where good-sized rainbow trout will tantalize the angler.

Rather than backtrack from the Horseshoe Lakes junction past State Lakes, you have the option of making a loop back to the junction at 13.6 miles. Follow a very faint, little-used trail heading west on a mild, 1.3-mile descent to the Dougherty Creek Trail. From there, turn south and then southeast, and drop more steeply to a ford of the East Fork Dougherty Creek. Now make a short climb to the crest of a ridge, and then gradually descend to the trail junction at the close of the loop.

Backpackers can access the remote Middle Fork Kings River at Simpson Meadow by continuing northbound on the Dougherty Creek Trail. However, such a trip will necessitate a steep, 2300-foot, 2.75-mile descent and subsequent ascent for a return to Roads End.

O Experienced cross-country enthusiasts can access the exquisite Marion Lake and Lakes Basin region by continuing roughly northeast from Horseshoe Lakes on the Sierra High Route over Gray, White, and Red passes. From Lakes Basin, a bounty of extended loops may be created. One such loop descends Cartridge Creek from Marion Lake to the Middle Fork Trail, leads southwest to Simpson Meadow, and then returns via the Dougherty Creek Trail. Another possibility heads roughly northeast from Lakes Basin over either Vennacher Col (class 3) or Frozen Lake Pass (class 2–3). Then the route drops to the John Muir Trail, returning to Roads End via either the Bubbs Creek Trail or an off-trail route through Muro Blanco to the Paradise Valley Trail. A third alternative heads north from Lakes Basin over Dumbell Lakes and Cataract Creek passes (both class 2) to the JMT west of Palisade Lakes.

Both Dougherty and State peaks are class 2 climbs from State Lakes. The peaks are east of the lakes on Cirque Crest.

R **PERMITS:** Wilderness permit required for overnight stays (quota: 25 per day).

CAMPFIRES: Not permitted above 10,000 feet or in Granite Basin.

CEDAR GROVE TRAILHEADS

TRIP **35**

Mist Falls

Ⓜ ↗ DH

DISTANCE: 3.9 miles one way

ELEVATION: 5045/5810, +765/-0

SEASON: May to November

USE: Heavy

MAP: *The Sphinx*

INTRODUCTION: Anyone who comes to Kings Canyon should make the nearly 4-mile trek to Mist Falls, especially during the first part of the season when the falls are at full force. The first half of the trail is relatively flat, and the second half climbs at a fairly manageable rate, allowing both bona fide hikers and sightseers in modest shape the opportunity to see the majestic falls and possibly experience the driving spray at the base. The trail is popular not only with hikers, but also with backpackers as a highly coveted route heading to Paradise Valley and Rae Lakes. Consequently, don't expect a high degree of solitude.

DIRECTIONS TO THE TRAILHEAD: Drive on Highway 180 into Kings Canyon and to the day-use parking area at Roads End, 5.0 miles past Cedar Grove.

DESCRIPTION: The well-signed trail begins at the east edge of the paved turnaround, near the wilderness permit station. Follow the wide trail, which parallels the South Fork Kings River through a mixed forest. You quickly cross Copper Creek on a wood bridge. Up the trail, the forest cover thins, allowing views of the granite walls of the canyon. Soon you enter a cool forest of ponderosa pines, sugar pines, white firs, and alders, and come to a signed Y-junction with the Paradise Valley Trail, 1.9 miles from the trailhead.

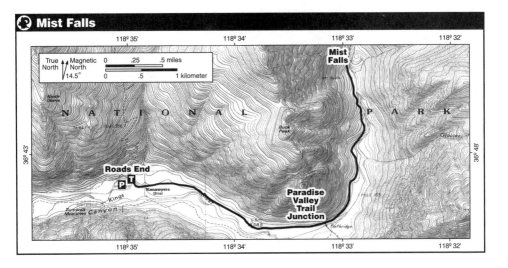

Mist Falls

Veer left at the junction and ascend through a mixed forest of alders, black oaks, canyon live oaks, incense cedars, white firs, and ponderosa pines. Sunny areas are carpeted with manzanita and mountain mahogany, while ferns and thimbleberries thrive in the damper soils. You follow the course of the South Fork Kings River past delightful pools and tumbling cascades, arcing around the base of Buck Peak, which plays hide and seek through gaps in the forest cover, as do The Sphinx and Avalanche Peak on the opposite side of the South Fork canyon. Ascending rock steps and slabs, you continue up the narrow chasm with periodic views of the dramatic canyon topography. After a long, forested stretch, you begin to hear the thundering roar of Mist Falls, and soon you reach a use-trail branching to the right. Follow this path, scrambling over large boulders, to a viewpoint near the base of the falls.

Aptly named Mist Falls tumbles over a precipitous cliff and smashes into the boulders and rocks near its base. A spray of mist catapults down the South Fork canyon, coating everything in its path. Even on summer days, characteristically hot, you can feel cool and moist near the falls, which may account for part of the trail's popularity. As with most Sierra waterfalls, Mist Falls is best appreciated in early summer, when peak snowmelt from the mountains above pours down the river, creating a raging torrent. By mid- to late summer, the falls become fairly tame.

CEDAR GROVE TRAILHEADS

TRIP **36**

Rae Lakes Loop

(MS) ↻ BPx

DISTANCE: 38.9 miles

ELEVATION: 5045/8495, +3870'/-400'

SEASON: Mid-July to mid-October

USE: Heavy

MAPS: *The Sphinx,*
Mt. Clarence King

TRAIL LOG:

5.8	Lower Paradise Valley
7.25	Middle Paradise Valley
8.4	Upper Paradise Valley
12.0	Castle Domes Meadow
13.5	John Muir Trail Jct./Woods Creek Crossing
17.25	Baxter Pass Trail/Dollar Lake
20.25	Sixty Lake Basin Trail Jct.
24.3	Charlotte Lake/Kearsarge Pass Trail Jct.
26.8	Bubbs Creek Trail Jct./Lower Vidette Meadow
29.25	Junction Meadow
35.25	Sphinx Creek Camp

INTRODUCTION: Many consider the Rae Lakes Loop the quintessential High Sierra trek. Certainly the route is among the most popular, as thousands of backpackers flock to the area every summer, routinely filling the daily quota for wilderness permits. The Rae Lakes area is blessed with subalpine scenery as fine as any in the Sierra, with crystalline lakes reflecting an array of glacier-sculpted domes and jagged peaks. Jaunts into the mountain splendor of the neighboring Sixty Lake Basin offer a dose of serenity, away from the crowded John Muir Trail.

Such popularity has resulted in certain consequences affecting travelers to the Rae Lakes area. Long ago, bears have figured out the counterbalance system of hanging food, and now all backpackers departing from Cedar Grove must carry bear-resistant containers, leaving the bear boxes available for John Muir Trail through-hikers. A one-night camping limit applies around the individual lakes, including not only the three Rae Lakes, but Arrowhead, Dollar, and Charlotte lakes as well.

DIRECTIONS TO THE TRAILHEAD: Drive on Highway 180 into Kings Canyon and to the overnight parking lot at Roads End, 5.0 miles past the turnoff to Cedar Grove.

DESCRIPTION: The well-signed trail begins at the east edge of the paved turnaround, near the wilderness permit station. Follow the wide trail, which parallels the South Fork Kings River through a mixed forest. You quickly cross Copper Creek on a wood bridge. Up the trail, the forest cover thins, allowing views of the granite walls of the canyon. Soon you enter a cool forest of ponderosa pines, sugar pines, white firs, and alders, and come to a signed Y-junction with the Paradise Valley Trail, 1.9 miles from the trailhead.

Veer left at the junction and ascend through a mixed forest. You follow the course of the South Fork Kings River past delightful pools and tumbling cascades, arcing around the base of Buck Peak, which plays hide and seek through gaps in the forest cover, as do The Sphinx and Avalanche Peak on the opposite side of the South Fork canyon. You continue up the narrow chasm with periodic views of the dramatic canyon topography. After a long stretch, you begin to hear the thundering roar of Mist Falls, and soon you reach a use-trail branching to the right. Follow this path, scrambling over large boulders, to a viewpoint near the base of the falls. As with most Sierra waterfalls, Mist Falls is best appreciated in early summer, when peak snowmelt from the mountains above pours down the river, creating a raging torrent.

From the Mist Falls area, continue upstream on a moderate climb following the course of the South Fork Kings River. Above the falls, the river is a picturesque sight, dancing vigorously over granite slabs before tumbling into a sculpted pool. You follow the well-used trail past large boulders and up rock-stepped switchbacks, with occasional views of the South Fork Kings River canyon and the towering peaks and ridges above. Just before the lip of Paradise Valley, the grade eases as you pass through a mixed forest of red firs, lodgepole and Jeffrey pines, pockets of aspen, and the occasional juniper. A tangle of driftwood chokes the slow-moving river and signals your arrival at the lower end of the valley. A short distance ahead, you encounter the camp at Lower Paradise Valley (6590'±), 5.8 miles from Roads End. The camp has designated sites, a pit toilet, and bear boxes.

You proceed on a gentle stroll alongside the sedate river through a mixed forest to Middle Paradise Valley camp (6670'±), 7.25 miles from the trailhead, where more designated sites and bear boxes are available for overnighters. You continue upstream on easy trail through alternating stands of mixed conifers and open areas with awesome views of the steep-walled South Fork canyon. A more moderate climb ensues, followed again by milder trail near a flower-filled meadow. At 8.4 miles, you reach the last of the valley camps at Upper Paradise Valley (6910'±). Here too, designated campsites and bear boxes are available for backpackers.

Immediately beyond the camp, a system of logs allows a straightforward crossing to the east side of the South Fork Kings River, upstream from its confluence with Woods Creek. The crossing may be difficult in early season. The first 0.5-mile is an easy climb away from Woods Creek, but then the trail draws nearer to the creek and begins more of a moderate climb up the steep-walled valley for the next couple of miles. Where avalanches have swept the slopes, you have good views of the granite walls and domes above. After crossing two side streams, you emerge into Castle Domes

Meadow (8160'), where campsites and a bear box can be found near its east end, 12.0 miles from the trailhead.

Beyond the meadow, the grade of ascent is mild as you head east toward a junction with the John Muir Trail (8495'). As you continue, lodgepole pine becomes the dominant conifer. At 13.5 miles, you reach a junction with the well-signed John Muir Trail. Just up the hillside, some 150 yards north of the junction, is an open-air pit toilet.

You turn right (south) and soon arrive at roaring Woods Creek (8505'±). Fortunately, a 1988 suspension bridge provides an alternative to the otherwise difficult ford necessitated by periodic washouts of previous bridges. Cross the lively bridge one person at a time, to arrive at the overused campsites on the south side of the creek. Shaded by pines, the sites have bear boxes and fire rings, but most of the firewood is usually gone by midsummer.

Beyond Woods Creek, you curve around the north end of King Spur and begin a moderate climb up the lightly forested canyon of the South Fork Woods Creek, through alternating stretches of red firs, lodgepole pines, and aspens. You also cross sagebrush-covered slopes and stroll through pockets of verdant foliage. The steady ascent continues well above the creek, leading you across a stream rushing down from Lake 3144 and up exposed, rocky terrain to a boggy meadow. Beyond the meadow, you pass through a gap in a drift fence, ascend over a rocky ridge, and come upon a pair of campsites near the crossing of the willow- and wildflower-lined stream that drains Sixty Lake Basin.

A mile-long ascent through diminishing forest cover brings you to a junction with the Baxter Pass Trail just north of Dollar Lake, 17.25 miles from the trailhead, where an old post is all that marks the unsigned junction. (Solitude-seekers will be rewarded by a 2.25-mile climb on the Baxter Pass Trail to fairly decent campsites at the largest Baxter Lake.) Although some poor campsites are ahead at Dollar Lake

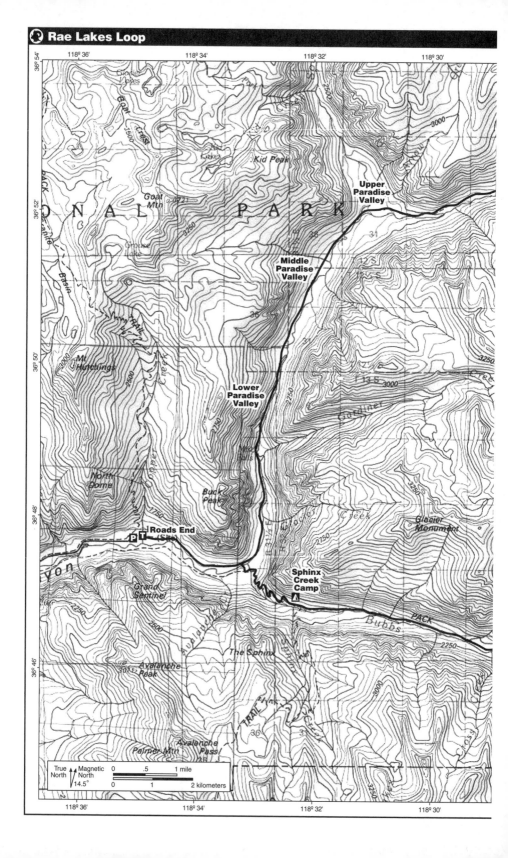

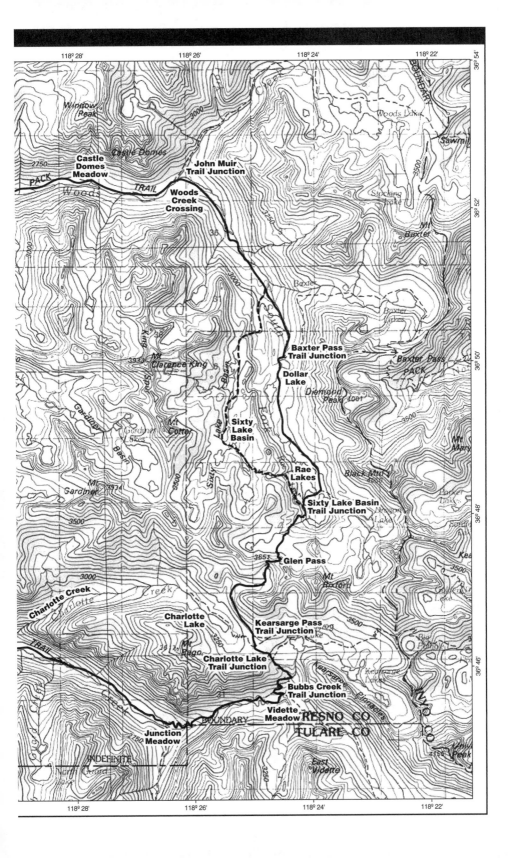

(10,220'±), overnighters are encouraged to find better sites at Arrowhead and Rae lakes farther along the trail. The one-night camping limit for Rae Lakes includes Dollar Lake.

Leaving Dollar Lake, you continue the ascent with ever-improving scenery blessing your progress. Good views of King Spur and Fin Dome propel you onward, past a small waterfall and across the creek to arrive above the shores of Arrowhead Lake (10,292'±), where a use-trail near the north end leads to campsites with a bear box.

After a short climb through widely scattered lodgepole pines and past an unnamed lake, you crest the lip of the Rae Lakes basin to encounter the first of the Rae Lakes (10,535'±). Campsites and bear boxes are found here and also at the middle lake (10,538'±), where a ranger cabin is tucked into the pines above the northeast shore. The gently ascending trail leads around the east side of the first and second lakes to the upper Rae Lake (10,541'±), where a use-trail heads east to more-secluded camping around Dragon Lake. The path then bends around the north shoreline of the upper lake, fords a stream, and comes to a junction with the Sixty Lake Basin Trail, 20.25 miles from the trailhead. The Rae Lakes basin is one of the most scenic areas in the Sierra. Views of monolithic Fin Dome, rugged King Spur, multi-hued Painted Lady, and rugged peaks of the Sierra crest are a fine complement to the sparkling, island-dotted lakes surrounded by glistening slabs of granite and pockets of verdant meadow. Fishing for brook and rainbow trout is reported to be good, despite the obvious pressure the lakes receive.

From the junction, you pass above the west shoreline of the upper lake and begin the climb toward Glen Pass, following switchbacks through diminishing vegetation to a tarn-filled bench in a rock-filled landscape. The winding ascent brings you to the crest of a ridge, which you follow a short distance to Glen Pass (11,978'), 22 miles from the trailhead. The view from the pass is rather scanty compared to many other High Sierra passes, but you do get a fine farewell glimpse of Rae Lakes.

Rae Lakes Basin from Glen Pass

You make a winding, rocky descent from the pass via switchbacks, passing a pair of greenish-colored, rockbound tarns on the way to a seasonal stream and a pair of poor campsites. The trail continues to descend beside more rocks and boulders until reaching more hospitable terrain, where the path veers southeast. The grade eases as you make a descending traverse across a lodgepole pine-covered hillside above Charlotte Lake. For brief moments through gaps in the pines, you enjoy views of the lake and Charlotte Dome farther down Charlotte Creek canyon. At 2.3 miles from the pass, you meet a connecting trail the to Kearsarge Pass Trail. Continuing south on the JMT, you break out of the forest to fine views of Mt. Bago, and stroll across a sandy flat to a four-way junction, 0.2 mile from the previous one. From here, the Kearsarge Pass Trail heads northeast and the Charlotte Lake Trail heads northwest 0.8 mile to the lake, where you will find excellent campsites (one-night limit) and a ranger cabin.

Remain on the JMT and climb east, away from the sandy flat over a low rise. Follow tight switchbacks downhill through dense forest to another junction, this one with the Bullfrog Lake Trail, which climbs northeast to picturesque Bullfrog Lake (no camping) and then east to Kearsarge Lakes (one-night limit). The descent continues, crossing the outlet from Bullfrog Lake twice, before you arrive at Lower Vidette Meadow and a junction with the Bubbs Creek Trail, 26.8 miles from the trailhead.

Following signed directions for Cedar Grove, you turn away from the JMT and head west on the Bubbs Creek Trail, making a short descent to the north edge of expansive Lower Vidette Meadow. Overnighters will find excellent campsites (bear box) nestled beneath lodgepole pines along the meadow's fringe. Leaving the gentle grade of the meadows behind, you begin a more pronounced descent, following the now tumbling creek as it plunges down the gorge. Soon you break out into the open momentarily, where a large hump of granite provides an excellent vantage point from which to survey the surrounding landscape.

Head back into the trees and continue down the canyon, stepping over numerous lushly lined freshets along the way. Periodic switchbacks and occasional views of the dramatic topography above the gorge of East Creek, including rugged Mt. Brewer, North Guard, and Mt. Farquhar, mark the protracted descent. The stiff descent eventually eases as you reach the grassy, fern-filled, and wildflower-covered clearing of Junction Meadow (8190'±). You stroll over to a signed three-way junction with a trail heading south along East Creek to East Lake and Lake Reflection (see Trip 27), 2.3 miles from the JMT. Those seeking overnight accommodations will find campsites along this trail on either side of the ford of Bubbs Creek. Additional campsites are farther along the Bubbs Creek Trail, past the horse camp near the west edge of the meadow.

Past Junction Meadow, the moderate descent resumes as you proceed down Bubbs Creek canyon. You stroll alongside the turbulent creek through a moderate forest composed mainly of white firs. After nearly 2 miles of steady descent, Bubbs Creek mellows, and you hike gently graded trail through a grove of aspens and ferns on the way to a log crossing of Charlotte Creek. Nearby, a short path leads to fair campsites near Bubbs Creek, where fishing is reported to be good for rainbow, brook, and brown trout.

Gentle trail continues for a little while beyond Charlotte Creek, as you hop across a trio of streams and walk through shoulder-high ferns, before Bubbs Creek returns to its tumultuous course down the gorge. A steady, moderate descent follows the course of the tumbling stream for the next several miles. At 8.25 miles from the JMT, you finally reach Sphinx Creek Camp and the junction with the Sphinx Creek Trail. From there, retrace your steps 3.5 miles back to Roads End.

No trip to the Rae Lakes would be complete without a side journey to Sixty Lake Basin. Although there is no access by maintained trail, the route through the basin has been so well-used over the years that there shouldn't be any complications following the beaten path. Once in the mostly open basin, cross-country travel between the lakes is easy and the convoluted terrain offers plenty of nooks and crannies to explore.

From the junction at the northwest corner of the upper Rae Lake, head south along the west shore of the middle lake, cross a marshy area, and climb northwest to the lip of a small basin overlooking a tarn below. The view of the Rae Lakes area during the ascent is superb. Drop around the north side of the tarn and make a short climb up to a saddle in the ridge that divides Rae Lakes and Sixty Lake basins. Mt. Clarence King and Mt. Cotter dominate the impressive vista to the northwest. A winding, rocky descent leads to the shore of an irregular-shaped lake (10,925'±), with campsites near its outlet.

Continuing northwest, you round a ridge and enter the heart of Sixty Lake Basin, approaching a sizable, island-dotted lake (10,795'±), 1.9 miles from the junction. The trail continues north from here, eventually deteriorating to a cross-country route that follows the basin's outlet stream back to the JMT, just south of Baxter Creek. You also have the option of returning to the JMT over Basin Notch, an easy route through a gap in a ridge about 1.0 mile north of Fin Dome. From Basin Notch, you descend to the west shore of Arrowhead Lake; the JMT passes along the lake's east shore.

Another off-trail route leaves the vicinity of Lake 10795 and heads along the west shore of Lake 10840. Near its inlet, leave the lake and climb southwest over talus and slabs to Sixty Lake Col (11,680'±), a saddle approximately 1.0 mile south of Mt. Cotter. The descent on the west side of the col (class 2), which leads into remote Gardiner Basin, is the most difficult section of this route. The old Gardiner Pass Trail, shown on the *Mt. Clarence King* quad, has long been abandoned and is now a difficult cross-country route.

A class 2 route up Painted Lady leaves the JMT and then heads east from the tarn-dotted bench just north of Glen Pass.

From Sixty Lake Basin, the west face of Fin Dome is rated class 3–4 and Mt. Cotter is class 2–3.

PERMITS: Wilderness permit required for overnight stays (quota: 25 per day).

CAMPING: One-night limit per lake at Dollar, Arrowhead, Charlotte, and Rae lakes.

CAMPFIRES: Not permitted above 10,000 feet.

The Citadel as seen from the Middle Fork Kings River

Introduction to Sierra National Forest

John Muir Wilderness forms a sizable buffer, lying as it does between the end of the access roads from the San Joaquin Valley and the western edge of Kings Canyon National Park. Most of the wilderness is heavily forested, interrupted only intermittently by meadows or lakes. Not until you approach the boundary of the Park do the high peaks so characteristic of the Sierra begin to emerge. The longer-than-weekend trips necessary to reach the heart of the backcountry, plus the typically long drive to trailheads, insure that backpackers who do visit can enjoy the area with a modicum of solitude.

Trail users who do invest the time to penetrate the forested wilderness will find magnificent scenery awaiting them in the western realm of Kings Canyon National Park. High, lake-dotted basins beneath the shadow of the craggy LeConte Divide and Kettle Ridge are a suitable reward for hiking the miles of tree-lined trail. The few trails in this area that cross into Kings Canyon National Park lead into impressive canyons. The two trips described in this section both offer extended routes into Goddard Canyon, a sublime, glacier-carved canyon in its own right, and the gateway to some of the grandest and most remote off-trail backcountry in the High Sierra.

ACCESS: *(Open all year to Huntington Lake, open beyond the lake May to October depending on snow conditions)* Sierra National Forest, adjacent to Kings Canyon National Park, is accessed eastbound from Fresno/Clovis on State Highway 168. Along the way you pass

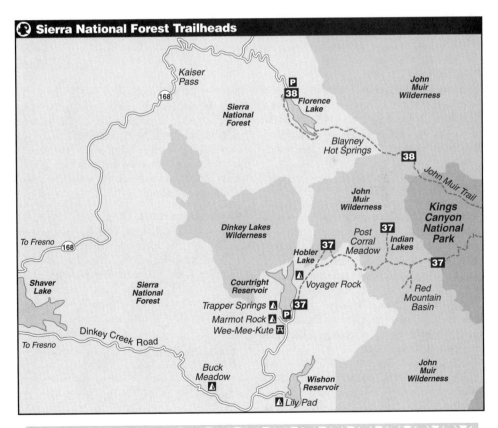

CAMPGROUNDS (only campgrounds near trailheads are listed)

Campground	Fee	Elevation	Season	Restrooms	Drinking Water	Bear Boxes	Phones
SAWMILL FLAT (SW of Wishon Res. on 11S12)	free*	6700'	May to October	Vault Toilets	No	No	No
LILY PAD (Wishon Res.)	$10	6500'	June to November	Vault Toilets	Yes	No	No
BUCK MEADOW (W. of Wishon Res.)	free*	6800'	June to November	Vault Toilets	No	No	No
MARMOT ROCK (Courtright Res.)	$10	8200'	June to November	Vault Toilets	Yes	No	No
TRAPPER SPRINGS (Courtright Res.)	$10	8200'	June to November	Vault Toilets	Yes	No	No
VOYAGER ROCK (4WD) (Courtright Res.)	free*	8200'	May to November	Vault Toilets	No	No	No
JACKASS MEADOW (Florence Lake)	$14	7200'	Late May to October	Vault Toilets	Yes	No	No
WARD LAKE (N. of Florence Lake)	free*	7300'	June to October	Vault Toilets	No	No	No
MONO HOT SPRINGS (N. of Florence Lake)	$14	6500'	Early June to Late September	Vault Toilets	Yes	No	No

*Subject to change

recreation and summer resorts at a series of artificial lakes— Shaver, Huntington, Florence, Courtright, and Wishon. The drives to the trailheads are long, occasionally over narrow and winding secondary roads.

AMENITIES: Since summer recreation is the primary economic stimulus for communities around the lakes, a wide variety of services is offered. The year-round community of Shaver Lake provides general stores, gasoline, lodging, and dining. Huntington Lake offers similar services during the summer and snowmobile-related amenities during the winter. Florence Lake has a small general store operating during the summer only. No services are offered at Courtright or Wishon Reservoirs.

Muir Trail Ranch, 4.0 miles from Florence Lake and inside the John Muir Wilderness, is a backcountry resort offering rustic accommodations: (209) 966-3195 or www.muirtrailranch.com. Very limited supplies are available to backpackers at the ranch, and through-hikers can make arrangements to have packages held for them. The ranch also operates the ferry service across Florence Lake, which saves hikers and backpackers 4.0 miles of trail along the lakeshore.

RANGER STATIONS: Wilderness permits may be obtained at the Pine Ridge Ranger Station on the west edge of the town of Shaver Lake. Backpackers heading for the Florence Lake trailhead may pick up permits at the High Sierra Ranger Station on the Kaiser Pass Road, 0.75 mile before the Florence Lake/Lake Edison junction.

TRIP **37**

Red Mountain Basin

Ⓜ ↗ BP / BPx

DISTANCE: 12 miles one way to Rae
Lake; 15 miles one way to
Hell-for-Sure Lake

ELEVATION: 7990/9890, +2840'/-1040'
7990/10,765, +4035'/-1375'

SEASON: Late June to mid-October

USE: Light

MAPS: *Courtright Reservoir,
Ward Mountain, Blackcap
Mountain, Mt. Henry*

TRAIL LOG:

3.5	Hobler Lake Jct.
7.0	Post Corral Creek Ford
11.5	Fleming Lake
11.75	Rae Lake/Indian Lakes Jct.
13.5	Meadow Brook Trail Jct.
13.75	Disappointment Lake
15.0	Hell-for-Sure Lake
15.25	Hell-for-Sure Pass

INTRODUCTION: Red Mountain Basin offers the type of scenery for which the High Sierra is famous. However, a fairly long journey through the montane forest belt is necessary before you can experience the classic mountain scenery beneath the rugged LeConte Divide. Aside from 3.0 miles of moderate ascent, most of the 15-mile journey to Hell-for-Sure Lake is over gently graded trail. A bounty of picturesque lakes, some near the trail and others requiring easy cross-country travel, make excellent base camps from which to explore the basin and surrounding terrain. A lightly used trail in combination with a wide assortment of lakes produces a reasonable expectation of solitude. Crossing the LeConte Divide at Hell-for-Sure Pass opens

the gateway for extended trips into Kings Canyon National Park.

DIRECTIONS TO THE TRAILHEAD: Drive on Highway 168 from Fresno/Clovis to the community of Shaver Lake and turn right onto Dinkey Creek Road. Approximately 12 miles from Shaver Lake, turn right onto McKinley Grove Road and travel another 14 miles to the Courtright/Wishon Y-junction. Bear left, following signs for Courtright Reservoir, and proceed 7.0 miles to a fork near the south end of the reservoir. The left-hand road leads to campgrounds on the reservoir's south and west shores, while the right-hand branch heads across the dam and above the southeast shore to the paved parking lot for the Maxson trailhead at the end of the road. Pit toilets are nearby but water is not available.

DESCRIPTION: From the parking lot, follow the hiking trail on a short, winding descent through light lodgepole pine forest, past the equestrian trail, and down to a jeep road at the bottom of a hill. Stroll north along the road for the next mile on a nearly level grade. Near Maxson Meadow, you encounter a signed junction. Bend right (northeast) on single-track trail across the meadow and head back into the trees. Mildly climbing, you follow the path paralleling and then crossing a creek near the 2-mile mark. Beyond the crossing, you enter the John Muir Wilderness, ascend a forested hillside to the crest of a rise, and come to a junction with the trail toward Hobler Lake, 3.5 miles from the trailhead.

⊡ **SIDE TRIP TO HOBLER LAKE:** A quick descent leads to the crossing of a small stream, followed by a mild, forested ascent to Hobler Lake (8995'±), 0.75 mile from the junction.

The placid lake is nearly surrounded by lodgepole pines and red firs, which shelter a smattering of campsites. Grassy meadows border the lake in the few areas too wet for conifers. Brook trout will entice anglers, and swimmers should find the temperate 〰 waters reasonably pleasant.

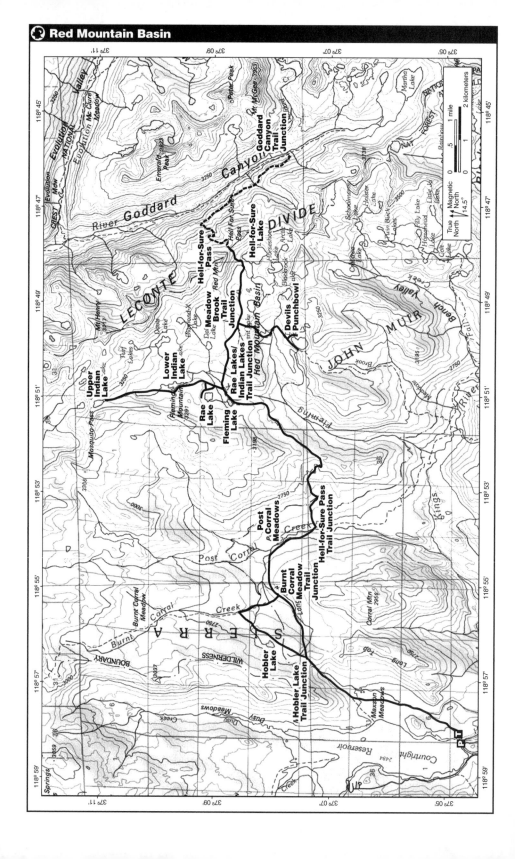

Rather than retrace your steps, you could follow the continuation of the trail northeast from the lake 1.0 mile to a junction, and then make a nearly mile-long descent on the Burnt Corral Meadow Trail back to the Blackcap Basin Trail at Long Meadow. **END OF SIDE TRIP**

From the Hobler Lake Trail junction, continue northeast on nearly level trail, until a mild descent amid lodgepole pines and red firs leads you to the fringe of Long Meadow (8535'). A gentle stroll through the meadow along Post Corral Creek provides enticing glimpses of the distant peaks and ridges to the east. In the midst of the meadow, you encounter a signed junction with the Burnt Corral Meadows Trail, 5.0 miles from the trailhead. Just beyond the junction, you ford the creek and head back into forest cover.

A mild descent brings you to Post Corral Meadow (8250'±), 6.3 miles from the trailhead, where a series of posts line the path and a use-trail branches northeast across the creek to the heart of the meadows and a leaseholder's cabin. As part of the Forest Service's multiple-use approach, cattle have been allowed to graze in this part of the wilderness, which is an effective deterrent to backpackers in search of campsites near the meadow. Overnighters need not despair, as better campsites are 0.25 mile down the trail near a crossing of Post Corral Creek.

Proceed downstream on a nearly level trail to a ford of Post Corral Creek (8201'), 7.0 miles from the trailhead. The broad channel is usually crossable without incident, but until late in the summer you should be prepared to get your feet wet. Campsites can be found on either side of the ford. A short distance beyond the creek, near a small meadow, you encounter a signed three-way junction with the Hell-for-Sure Pass Trail, where the Blackcap Basin Trail heads east.

Continue straight ahead from the junction, and following a sign marked RED MOUNTAIN BASIN, proceed on the Hell-for-

Sure Pass Trail. The gentle grade of the previous 7.0 miles is left behind as you begin a moderate climb up a ridge separating the Post Corral Creek and Fleming Creek drainages. Midway up the climb, the grade increases as you ascend over granite slabs that have been dynamited by the Forest Service to provide easier stock access. The 2-mile, moderately steep and sometimes winding climb ends at a saddle, from where you have limited views of the mountainous terrain ahead.

A brief descent from the saddle leads to a gentle 1.25-mile climb through lodgepole pine forest across the side of the canyon above Fleming Creek. Along the way, you cross a number of small, lushly lined seasonal streams. Switchbacks take you over a rise to easier trail alongside meadows dotted with scattered conifers. Just beyond a low hummock, oval-shaped Fleming Lake (9725'±) springs into view, 11.5 miles from the trailhead. After so many miles of forest, broken only by a handful of meadows, the subalpine lake offers a welcome change in scenery. An exposed shoreline of boggy meadows is complemented by views of the craggy Glacier Divide. Widely scattered pines shelter a few good campsites on the hummock. Anglers may test their skill on a sizable population of brook trout. Halfway along the lakeshore, you cross its outlet and pass an old campsite closed for restoration.

Following the course of Fleming Creek, you head northeast on the trail to impressive views of the Glacier Divide across an expansive meadow. In the middle of this meadow is a signed junction with the Rae Lake/Indian Lakes and Hell-for-Sure Pass trails, 11.75 miles from the trailhead. Continue straight, skirting the meadow, to an indistinct junction in a grove of trees. Follow the left-hand trail over a forested rise and down to the northeast shore of meadow-rimmed Rae Lake (9889'). Fine campsites nestle beneath scattered pines around the lake, with the best sites on the west and north sides. Brook trout will test the skill of anglers. Now named for a packer, Rae lake originally was called Wolverine

Lake, but the name disappeared about the same time as the namesake mammal which, while not extinct, is no longer found in the southern Sierra.

◎ SIDE TRIP TO INDIAN LAKES: From the indistinct junction with the lateral to Rae Lake, make a moderate climb up a forested hillside on the right-hand trail. As the grade eases, the trees start to thin, allowing improving views of the Glacier Divide across the huge meadow encircling Lower Indian Lake (10,045'). Approximately 0.75 mile from the Hell-for-Sure Pass junction, you draw alongside the narrow south finger of the lake. Although developed campsites are nonexistent, plenty of primitive campsites exist in this secluded setting. Fishing pressure on brook trout at both Indian lakes appears to be quite light.

Beyond the lower lake, a discernible path disappears, but the wide-open basin, sprinkled with boulders and compact granite slabs, is easily traversed in the absence of a bona fide trail. At the far end of the meadow, you step over a seasonal stream and make a short, moderately steep climb alongside a creek that pours down a narrow cleft in the hillside above. A final 0.5 mile ascent across the hillside brings you to the south shore of pristine Upper Indian Lake (10,255'±), perched at the very head of a canyon. Steep slopes nearly surround the lake, culminating in the 11,318-foot Zingheim Heights above the west shore. Mosquito Pass, just above the far shore, offers a glance down the canyon to the South Fork San Joaquin River.

The *Mt. Henry* quad indicates a shortcut between Rae Lake and Lower Indian Lake. Although the faint path does exist, the start of the trail near the northeast shore of Rae Lake is difficult to discern, marked only by some insignificant ducks. The path climbs up the hillside above the lake and connects with the Indian Lakes Trail approximately 0.25 mile south of the lower lake. Fortunately, the junction with the Indian Lakes Trail is much more distinct. **END OF SIDE TRIP**

Hell-for-Sure Lake near the Goddard Divide

From the Rae Lake/Indian Lakes junction, turn right (east) to follow the Hell-for-Sure Pass Trail across Fleming Creek and around the lower edge of a meadow. A moderate climb through light forest takes you past a junction with a lateral to seldom-visited Dale Lake. You continue the ascent through dwindling trees, boulder fields, and pocket meadows to the crest of a ridge. Entering Red Mountain Basin, you have a fine view of the LeConte Divide and the east ridge of Mt. Hutton. Beyond a stream crossing is a junction with the Meadow Brook Trail, 13.5 miles from the trailhead.

⊡ **SIDE TRIP TO DEVILS PUNCHBOWL:** From the Hell-for-Sure Pass Trail, head south on a mild descent through light pine forest past a small, meadow-rimmed pond. Eventually the descent becomes more pronounced as you round a hill and wind down to lush meadowlands at the crossing of a picturesque stream draining the lakes in the basin above. Beyond the creek, you stroll past more meadows until a moderately steep climb forces you to regain most of the lost elevation. At the top of the climb, you encounter a beautiful lake named Devils Punchbowl (10,098'), 1.5 miles from the junction.

Devils Punchbowl sits in a scenic basin carved out of a rocky cleft at the very edge of steep cliffs overlooking the canyon of Fleming Creek. The outlet pours out of the lake and immediately plummets dramatically down the face of those cliffs, bound for the diminutive Jigger Lakes, before adopting a less riotous path to a union with the main creek. A trip to the lake is incomplete without a view from the edge of the rim near the outlet, particularly in early season when the water flows at full force. An expansive western view provides a splendid opportunity to enjoy some magnificent sunsets. The lake itself is quite scenic as well, backdropped by rugged peaks and lined with a smattering of graceful pines. Excellent campsites are spread around the shoreline, and a sandy beach offers an excellent spot for sunbathing and swimming. Anglers may test their luck on rainbow and brook trout.

An alternative to retracing your steps is to follow the slightly longer route on the Meadow Brook Trail southwest for 6.5 miles to the North Fork Kings River. Turn right (northwest) at a junction with the Blackcap Basin Trail and go another 4.0 miles to the junction with the Hell-for-Sure Pass Trail near the ford of Post Corral Creek. Such a detour offers picturesque meadows, views along the upper part of the Meadow Brook Trail, and a scenic, mile-long stretch of the North Fork Kings River along the Blackcap Basin Trail. **END OF SIDE TRIP**

From the Meadow Brook Trail junction, go southeast, following ducks over granite slabs and past dwarf pines to an unmarked lateral to Disappointment Lake (10,342'). A short stroll down this trail takes you above the northwest shore of this scenic lake. Backdropped by Mt. Hutton and the LeConte Divide, Disappointment Lake is as attractive as any of the Sierra lakes, with alternating pockets of meadow and sandy beach on the near shore, and rolling granite slabs covering the far shore. Campsites with suberb views are sure to lure weary backpackers for at least a one-night stay.

Continuing on the Hell-for-Sure Pass Trail, you stroll along the sandy trail on a gentle grade with expansive views as your companion. You cross over a stream and pass some delightful tarns before starting a moderate, winding climb that leads up a

DISAPPOINTMENT LAKE

Hardly a disappointment to modern-day travelers, the lake received the name from some anglers unhappy with the fishing. Today, a healthy population of good-sized brook trout will satisfy most hikers bent on catching their dinner.

hillside composed of granite slabs. At the top of the climb, you come above Hell-for-Sure Lake (10,762'), 15 miles from the trailhead. Another spectacularly beautiful lake, Hell-for-Sure Lake is surrounded by polished granite slabs that glisten in the sunlight of a typically clear Sierra sky. Small pockets of meadow make a feeble attempt to break up the rocky basin, over-shadowed by the immediate presence of steep walls ascending toward the crest of the LeConte Divide, and by the craggy cliffs of the north face of Mt. Hutton. Developed campsites are few but enough to provide havens for the hearty souls who venture this far from the trailhead. Fishing is reportedly good for medium-sized brook trout. The name given to this lake seems as uninspired and misguided as the name of Disappointment Lake.

Beyond Hell-for-Sure Lake, the trail begins a steady climb alongside a lushly vegetated creek, as you head toward a cleft in the divide above. You wind around over and beside large boulders until you're standing atop Hell-for-Sure Pass (11,297'), merely 0.25 mile from the lake. The dra-matic view down into Goddard Canyon is a worthy reward for the short but steep ascent. Emerald Peak, Peter Peak, and Mt. McGee crown the ridge on the far side of the canyon.

From the pass, the descent drops nearly 1500 feet in 4.0 miles to a connection with the Goddard Canyon Trail, 2.75 miles north of Martha Lake (see Trip 38).

☐ Red Mountain Basin provides excellent opportunities for wandering to a number of scenic lakes not served by maintained trails. Cross-country enthusiasts with a modicum of experience should be able to easily navi-gate the open terrain.

☐ The Two Passes cross-country route is a class 2 connection between the basin and Bench Valley.

☐ Mountaineering is somewhat limited in and around the basin. From Hell-for-Sure Pass, Red Mtn., just northwest, is a short

class 1 climb. From the vicinity of Indian Lakes, both Zingheim Heights and Fleming Mtn. are straightforward ascents.

R **PERMITS:** Wilderness permit required for overnight stays (No quota).

CAMPFIRES: Permitted in areas west of the Park boundary.

TRIP **38**

Blayney Hot Springs, Goddard Canyon, and Martha Lake

Ⓜ ⟋ BPx

DISTANCE: 23 miles one way via trail (or 19 miles one way via ferry)

ELEVATION: 7350/11,005, +4830'/-1175'

SEASON: Mid-July to late September

USE: Moderate to Blayney Hot Springs; Light beyond Blayney Hot Springs

MAPS: *Florence Lake, Ward Mountain, Blackcap Mountain, Mt. Henry, Mt. Goddard*

TRAIL LOG:

3.5	S. Fork San Joaquin River
4	Ferry Landing Jct.
6.25	Lower Blayney CG
8	Blayney Hot Springs Jct.
9.5	John Muir Trail Jct.
11.75	Piute Pass Trail Jct.
13.25	Aspen Meadow
15.25	Goddard Canyon Trail Jct.
16	Franklin Meadow
20.25	Hell-for-Sure Pass Jct.
23	Martha Lake

INTRODUCTION: This multi-day trip visits the remote northwestern corner of Kings Canyon National Park. Although during the first part of this journey you may see a number of recreationists on their way to Muir Trail Ranch, a healthy dose of solitude should be expected once you reach Goddard Canyon. Solitude is not the only benefit of this trip, as the scenery along the South Fork San Joaquin River is superb. A succession of thrilling cataracts, cascades, and waterfalls greets you along the length of the trail as you trace the route of the river from Florence Lake to its headwaters. Anglers will find the South Fork offers excellent fishing opportunities. The journey up the river reaches a splendid crescendo at Martha Lake, a large alpine lake cradled in a rocky basin and backdropped by craggy peaks and ridges. Along the way, beautiful meadows, peaceful forest grottos, and an opportunity to soak in a natural hot spring are additional treats. A number of shaded, riverside campgrounds provide pleasant havens for backpackers.

The first obstacle to overcome is the drive to the trailhead. The route over Kaiser Pass on a narrow, single-lane road is time consuming—plan on an hour from Huntington Lake. Once you get to Florence Lake, you have the option of hiking the 4.0 miles around the lake or boating across the lake via the ferry service (see comments below).

The 4.0 miles of trail east of Florence Lake parallel and sometimes share the route of a jeep road used by Muir Trail Ranch to transport guests to their backcountry resort. The ranch is a hubbub of activity at times, providing anglers, equestrians, and hikers a base camp from which to explore the nearby trails. Backpackers attempting the John Muir and Pacific Crest trails also use the ranch as a mail drop.

Blayney Hot Springs, just past the ranch, is a popular spot for backpackers wishing to soak their weary bodies in soothing springs. However, in order to reach the springs, the South Fork San Joaquin River must be forded, which can be dangerous in early season. Do not attempt this ford when the river is high! Once the ranch and hot springs are left behind, the activity along the trail diminishes considerably.

DIRECTIONS TO THE TRAILHEAD: Drive on Highway 168 from Fresno and Clovis, heading east through Prather (wilderness permits available) and past Shaver Lake.

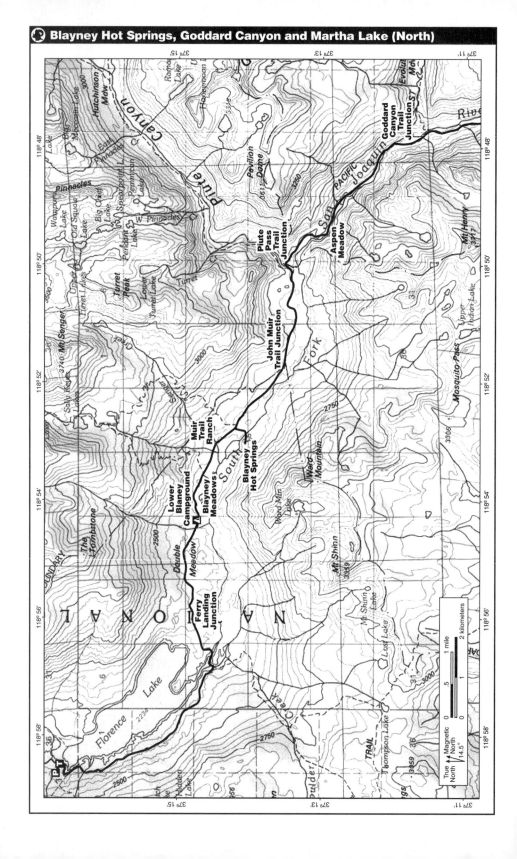

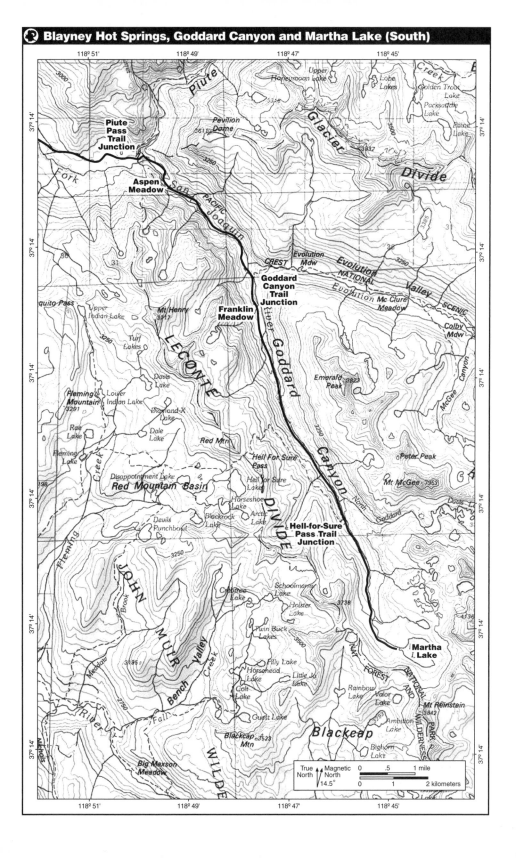

Just before Huntington Lake, turn right at a sign marked FLORENCE LAKE and continue for 5.5 miles on the two-lane, paved road to where the road abruptly narrows. From this point on, you will experience slow going as you follow the now narrow, winding road on a steep climb to Kaiser Pass, and then down to the High Sierra Ranger Station (wilderness permits available), 15 miles from Highway 168. You encounter the Florence Lake/Lake Edison Y-junction 0.75 mile from the ranger station, and continue straight ahead, following another sign marked FLORENCE LAKE. Pass Ward Lake Campground and continue to the trailhead at Florence Lake, 21 miles from Highway 168.

DESCRIPTION: From Florence Lake, you have two options to begin your journey:

FOUR-MILE HIKE: From the parking lot, follow a paved service road on a curving descent through the picnic area toward the lakeshore. At the bottom of the descent, follow the service road along the west shore of the lake to the beginning of a single-track trail near a sign marked BLAYNEY MEADOWS 8. A series of steps takes you away from the road and quickly into the John Muir Wilderness. Now you proceed on gently graded trail across a rolling hillside through a light, mixed forest of Jeffrey pines, ponderosa pines, white firs, junipers, and aspens. Occasionally, the forest cover thins enough to allow views across the lake of the dam and the granite walls above the far shore, as well as of Mt. Shinn and Ward Mtn. southeast of the lake. You reach a junction, 2 miles from the trailhead, where the Burnt Corral Meadows Trail heads south to Thompson and Lost lakes.

You continue straight ahead from the junction, traveling above the southwest arm of Florence Lake for about a mile to a signed junction with a connecting trail to the Burnt Corral Meadows Trail. You head downhill to a bridge over a tributary stream, which in the summer of 2000 was partially damaged and noticeably listing downstream. A short, nearly level stroll leads quickly to another, more substantial bridge across the South Fork San Joaquin River, 3.5 miles from the trailhead. Fine campsites nestled beneath lodgepole pines are spread along both banks of the river, and a pit toilet is up the hillside above the river's far side.

Turn upstream and briefly follow the course of the river, until a moderate, 0.5-mile climb leads up over sloping slabs and humps of granite to a signed junction with the lateral to the ferry dock, 4.0 miles from the trailhead.

FERRY SERVICE OPTION: Rather than backpack the 4.0 miles around the lake, you can rest your legs while enjoying the ferry ride across Florence Lake. Between late May and late September, subject to weather closures, the ferry typically makes five runs per day, between 8:30 A.M. and 4:30 P.M. On Saturdays, and on other days as needed, additional runs are made to accommodate increased traffic. A per-passenger fee of $8 one way and $15 round trip includes transport of your backpack. (Kids under 12 and llamas are half price; dogs and goats are $2 round trip/$1 one way). Purchase tickets at the store above the parking lot and catch the boat at the dock below. Advanced reservations are necessary only for a group of 30 or more.

On the return trip, a radio phone is available near the landing at the south end of the lake for use in contacting the ferry for pickup. Usually, five daily trips are made between 9 A.M. and 5 P.M., but extra runs may be added if needed. If necessary, your decision to ride across the lake can be made on the fly. Once across the lake, simply pay for your ticket at the store. For more information, visit www.muirtrail-ranch.com/FL-Ferry.html, or write to Muir Trail Ranch, PO Box 176, Lakeshore, CA 93634-0176 (June–September) or PO Box 269, Ahwahnee, CA 93601-0269 (October –May).

To reach the junction between the trail to the ferry landing and the trail around Florence Lake, climb from the dock uphill over bare granite slopes about 0.5 mile, following ducks and short patches of trail, to the well-marked junction. Current information about the ferry service is usually posted near the junction.

NOTE: all mileages in the trip description are from the trailhead parking area at Florence Lake. If you use the ferry service, in the following trip description deduct 4.0 miles from the total mileages.

Keen eyes will detect a primitive jeep road beyond the southeast end of Florence Lake. Muir Trail Ranch utilizes an army personnel carrier to transport its guests along this road, which parallels and occasionally coincides with sections of the hiking trail beyond the lake. Such activity would seem incompatible with the concept of wilderness, but the family-owned operation has been in business for over 50 years, and thus was grandfathered into the 1964 Wilderness Act.

From the ferry landing junction with the trail around Florence Lake, 4.0 miles from the parking lot trailhead, you climb over granite slabs and up dry gullies for a mile to the edge of pastoral Double Meadow (7795'±). The trail soon veers away, skirting the meadow through a light forest. Nearing the far end of the meadow, you step across a seasonal stream lined with grasses and wildflowers, and catch a final glimpse of the meadow before a mild, forested descent leads to a crossing of Alder Creek, 6.0 miles from the trailhead. Sheltered campsites can be found near the far bank. A short distance beyond Alder Creek, you pass a lateral that leads to fine campsites near the South Fork San Joaquin River at Lower Blayney Campground (7625'±). Past this junction, you encounter a splendid view of the broad expanse of Blayney Meadows, but the path quickly veers away from the meadows in favor of a route through the trees.

Approximately 6.5 miles from the trailhead, you pass through a gate at the fenced boundary of the private Muir Trail Ranch. Beyond the gate the backpacker's route around the ranch may be difficult to discern amongst the maze of dusty stock trails

and the churned-up jeep road. Farther down the road, pay close attention for a makeshift sign marked SELDEN PASS, KINGS CANYON PARK and PUBLIC HOT SPRINGS to the left, and MTR to the right. At this point, leave the dusty road, which continues toward the ranch, and veer to your left onto a single-track trail.

Despite the apparent intrusion of a resort in the backcountry, Muir Trail Ranch is hiker-friendly. The owners not only offer inexpensive ferry rides across Florence Lake, for a small fee they will hold packages and mail for PCT/JMT through-hikers. On the rare occasion when the ranch is not full (usually early June only), backpackers can purchase an overnight package complete with three meals. However, single meals are not available to non-guests. For more information, check the ranch Web site, or send a self-addressed, stamped envelope to the address given on page 162.

You head away from the road through open terrain and light forest on gently graded trail to the crossings of Sallie Keyes and Senger creeks. A moderate climb up a hillside leads to a lightly forested traverse that takes you to a chain gate. Once through the gate, you continue across the open hillside with the rhythmic sound of a pelton wheel generating electricity for the ranch as your companion. From an open knoll, you have a nice view of the surrounding terrain before dropping to a signed, Y-junction with a lateral leading to Muir Trail Ranch and Blayney Hot Springs.

⊡ **SIDE TRIP TO BLAYNEY HOT SPRINGS:** Just 50 feet from the Y-junction, you reach another junction with a path on your left to Muir Trail Ranch. Continue straight at the junction, following a sign marked HOT SPRINGS, and proceed down the hillside through lush vegetation and past numerous overused campsites (some of which may be closed for restoration). Reach the north bank of the South Fork San Joaquin River and follow a path upstream for a short distance to a ford of the wide river. Proceed across the river with caution, particularly in early season when the ford may be too dangerous to even attempt. The riverbed is quite slippery, so you may want to pack along a pair of sandals or old tennis shoes for the crossing. On the far side are more campsites and a use-trail that crosses Shooting Star Meadow to the hot springs. Beyond a patch of willows is Warm Lake, well-suited for a refreshing swim after a lengthy soak in the springs. The area surrounding the lake and springs is quite fragile, so take care to minimize your environmental impact. **END OF SIDE TRIP**

From the junction with the trail to Blayney Hot Springs, head southeast on a mild climb through light forest. Soon you encounter a well-signed junction with a trail on your left that provides a steep connection to the John Muir Trail en route to Selden Pass. Following signed directions for Kings Canyon National Park and Piute Pass, veer right at the junction and proceed upstream as the trail continues to parallel South Fork San Joaquin River. Before long, pass an unmarked use-trail branching down toward the river through a stand of aspen. You continue on easy trail amid a scattered forest of aspens, lodgepole pines, and Jeffrey pines, passing a stagnant pond on the way. An extensive camping area appears below the trail on a forested bench above the South Fork, just before you reach a junction with the John Muir Trail (7890), 9.5 miles from the trailhead.

Proceeding straight, now on the John Muir Trail, you follow the course of the river through a mixture of granite and conifers. You have fine views of South Fork canyon as you curve around for the next couple of miles, heading toward the confluence of Piute Creek with the South Fork San Joaquin River. At 11.75 miles from the trailhead, just before a steel bridge spanning the tumultuous creek, you reach a junction with the Piute Pass Trail (8050') (see Trip 60).

On the far side of the bridge, you enter Kings Canyon National Park, and as you

stroll along the path through chaparral and widely scattered Jeffrey pines, you encounter a number of fine campsites spread around a flat. You proceed upstream on a mild, exposed climb, rounding John Muir Rock and drawing near the tumbling river where it flows through a narrow channel of dark rock. About 1.5 miles from the previous junction, you enter the cool forested glade of aspens and pines, misnamed Aspen Meadow (8250'±). While there is no longer a meadow here, there are a few sheltered campsites offering refuge to tired hikers.

Beyond Aspen Meadow, you leave the shade behind and follow the course of the river on a mild, mile-long climb up another narrow, exposed section of a canyon. At 14.25 miles, you cross a steel bridge over the South Fork to a small, forested flat, where a use-trail leads quickly downstream to campsites. Now traveling on the south bank of the river, you pass through a gate near more campsites, then proceed through lush wildflower gardens to a boulderhop over a vigorous stream that drains several tarns below the LeConte Divide. Beneath the shade of aspens, lodgepole pines, and junipers, you pass campsites and come to the signed Goddard Canyon Trail junction (8445'±), 15.25 miles from the trailhead. Here, the JMT goes left, crosses another steel bridge over the South Fork and climbs toward Evolution Valley. Good campsites are a short way up the Goddard Canyon Trail and also across the river.

From the junction, you continue straight ahead as you climb moderately on the Goddard Canyon Trail, through a light covering of lodgepole pines, with the sound of the churning South Fork coming from your left. Approximately 0.5 mile from the junction, you enter Franklin Meadow (8700'±), where picturesque, wildflower-laden grassland is dotted with tall aspens and occasional lodgepole pines. In the middle and near the far end of the meadow, you step across streams draining unnamed tarns near the LeConte Divide. Primitive campsites can be found just above the river toward the south end of the meadow.

Beyond Franklin Meadow, you follow the trail away from the river for a while on a mild-to-moderate climb through more scattered lodgepole pines. Soon the canyon narrows and the path is forced up the hillside above the river. In the midst of this ascending traverse, you pass above campsites nestled on a narrow bench overlooking the river. Soon you encounter a lush hillside carpeted with willows, aspens, and wildflowers, including paintbrush, clover, coneflower, columbine, and heather, all well watered by a series of rivulets that you step over as you continue up the path. On the far side of the South Fork is Pig Chute, where a seasonal stream pours down a narrow cleft in the rock beside a rocky, knife-edged protrusion. Farther up the trail, a spectacular waterfall spills dramatically into an emerald pool.

For the next 1.5 miles, you proceed upstream with splendid views across Goddard Canyon of the cascading river plunging down its narrow, deep, and rocky cleft. Along the way, you pass two more waterfalls as scenic as any in the High Sierra, and cross a number of flower-lined side streams spilling across the trail.

Near the confluence with North Goddard Creek, the canyon widens temporarily, allowing the river to adopt a more leisurely pace. You stroll through meadowlands with a fine view of both river canyons separated by a low rock dome. A short, moderate climb leads to an unsigned junction with the Hell-for-Sure Pass Trail (9865'±), 20.25 miles from the trailhead (see Trip 37). At the time of research, a cairn with a stick poking out was all that marked the somewhat indistinct junction. A few primitive campsites shaded by a grove of trees can be found a short distance beyond the junction, near a creek crossing.

Upper Goddard Canyon spreads out before you in subalpine splendor as you ascend the lush meadowlands, unbroken except for an occasional stunted pine or small clump of willow. Pockets of lupine and heather gracefully accent the deep-green meadow grass as you gaze toward the

A tranquil meadow in remote Goddard Canyon

mighty hulks of Mt. Goddard and Mt. Reinstein. The path becomes indistinct in the upper canyon, but the route is evident if you follow the course of the South Fork upstream toward its birthplace beneath the LeConte and Goddard divides. A plethora of wildflowers carpets the upper slopes of the canyon, including daisies, shooting stars, and paintbrush. After you cross the outlet from Lake Confusion, you start the moderately steep, cross-country ascent over grassy benches and granite slabs. Once over the lip of a basin, easy hiking leads to the west shore of Martha Lake (11,004'), 23 miles from the trailhead.

Martha is an austere, rockbound lake where only a few pocket meadows soften the otherwise barren shoreline. Situated above timberline near the convergence of three divides—Goddard, LeConte, and White—the lake is truly alpine in nature. The dark, rugged flanks of Mt. Goddard (13,368') tower 2500 feet over the lake to the northeast, while Mt. Reinstein (12,604') provides a fine backdrop to the south. Developed campsites are virtually nonexistent, but resourceful backpackers should be able to find spots suitable for pitching a tent somewhere around the lake. Anglers can ply the waters in search of rainbow and golden trout.

O For cross-country enthusiasts, Martha Lake is the western gateway into one of the High Sierra's most spectacular regions. Directly east lies the mysterious realm of Ionian Basin, a trip through which is considered a classic by Sierra standards. By traversing the basin and connecting with the JMT near Muir Pass, a fine loop can be followed through Evolution Basin and Evolution Valley to the JMT/Goddard Canyon junction (see Options, Trip 62).

O Southwest of Martha Lake, Valor Pass (11,760') offers a class 2–3 route across the LeConte Divide to Blackcap Basin. Southeast of Martha Lake, and 0.2 mile northeast of Mt. Reinstein, is Reinstein Pass (11,880'), providing a class 2 route to the Goddard Creek drainage.

O Two moderately difficult cross-country routes cross the LeConte Divide from Goddard Canyon, approximately one mile below Martha Lake. The first is a class 2 route that makes a tedious climb up talus to Lake Confusion (11,365'±), over LeConte Divide at Confusion Pass (11,370'±) and down into Blackcap Basin. Halfway between Goddard Canyon and Lake Confusion, the second route, also class 2, climbs west over talus-filled slopes toward a crossing of the LeConte Divide at Gunsight Pass (11,635'±) and down to Bench Valley.

O From Martha Lake, the southeast ridge of Mt. Goddard is class 2–3 and the northeast ridge of Mt. Reinstein is class 3.

R **PERMITS:** Wilderness permit required for overnight stays (No quota).

CAMPFIRES: Not permitted above 10,000 feet.

Sunset at Charlotte Lake

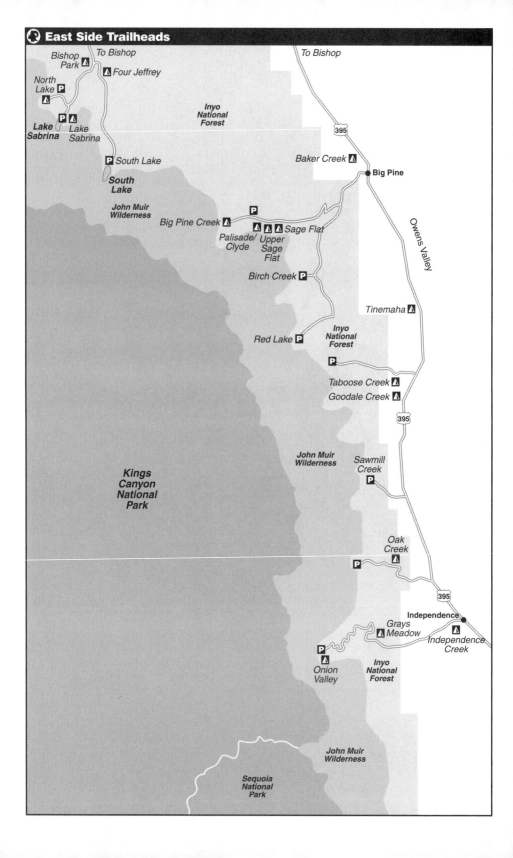

East Side Trailheads

CHAPTER 5

East Side Trips

In contrast to the gradually rising terrain on the west side of the Sierra Nevada, the east side rapidly catapults itself from the floor of Owens Valley, sharply upward toward the crest of the range. This massive wall of mountains can look like an impenetrable barrier to a wee, small individual staring upward thousands of feet from the western lip of the Great Basin to the spine of the Sierra. East side trails assume one of two approaches, either abandoning all hope of crossing the range to follow raucous streams up the steep cleft of a dead-end canyon, or attacking the towering east face of the Sierra on a steep, protracted climb toward a handful of high passes where the crest dips to around 11,000 or 12,000 feet. No easy approach to the backcountry will be found from this side; the principal reward of an eastern approach is the shorter distance required for access into the alpine heights of the High Sierra.

The high and rugged terrain on King Canyon National Park's east boundary has limited the number of trailheads to just five (six if you include Piute Pass, just north of the park). Consequently, wilderness permit quotas tend to fill up very quickly. Groups or individuals without advanced reservations should try to begin their trip on a weekday rather than a weekend to allow themselves a better shot at securing a wilderness permit.

Middle Palisade and Disappointment Peak, South Fork Big Pine Creek Trail

Introduction to the Mt. Whitney Ranger District

The eastern escarpment of the Sierra spanning the Mt. Whitney Ranger District contains some of the region's most noteworthy scenery. The majestic east face of the Mt. Whitney group towers above the Lone Pine community 10,000 feet below. A plethora of Hollywood movies have been filmed in and around the Alabama Hills near Mt. Whitney's base. Although this terrain is quite impressive when viewed from the window of a car or on the silver screen, the real splendor of the Mt. Whitney area is available only to those who venture into the backcountry via trail. Certainly the centerpiece of interest for the majority of trail users within the district is Mt. Whitney. Hundreds of hikers and backpackers leave Whitney Portal each day bound for the summit of the highest peak in the lower 48. However, by concentrating only on the peak itself and ignoring the vast remaining terrain, the majority of travelers to the area are missing out on some of the most impressive mountain scenery in the High Sierra.

Discounting the relatively gentle Cottonwood and New Army passes at Sequoia National Park's extreme southern end, the nearly impenetrable wall of the Sierra crest within the Whitney district remains untarnished by any road, and is successfully surmounted by only six trails —Mt. Whitney, Shepherd Pass, Kearsarge Pass, Baxter Pass, Sawmill Pass, and Taboose Pass. Three of these trails, Baxter, Sawmill, and Taboose, are unmaintained. The Mt. Whitney Trail, which has the highest demand for permits in the Sierra, and the Shepherd Pass Trail, which is a very difficult climb starting in Owens Valley, lie outside the scope of this book (see *Sequoia National Park: A Complete Hiker's Guide*). This leaves the Kearsarge Pass Trail as the most viable alternative for backpackers seeking the least difficult way in the nearly 60 miles between New Army and Bishop passes to cross the rugged Sierra crest. A relatively moderate climb compared to the other trails, the 4.5-mile ascent from 9185-foot Onion Valley on up to 11,823-foot Kearsarge Pass is also the eastern gateway to the John Muir Trail and the highly coveted Rae Lakes region, which makes this route very popular with backpackers and equestrians alike.

This region is filled with myriad peaks, majestic canyons, wildflower-filled meadows, beautiful subalpine and alpine lakes, rushing streams, and gorgeous vistas that even the most jaded wilderness traveler will enjoy. The 13,000- to 14,000-foot peaks along the Sierra crest lure not only backpackers, but mountaineers, technical climbers, and cross-country enthusiasts from all over the globe.

ACCESS: The north-south thoroughfare of U.S. 395 is the principal access route for all east side trips. Secondary roads branch off the highway toward the trailheads.

AMENITIES: The small towns of Lone Pine and Independence provide basic services, including motels, cafes, general stores, and gas stations, to travelers on U.S. 395 and recreationists visiting the eastern Sierra. A very limited selection of outdoor equipment is available, consisting mainly of fishing and camping supplies.

SHUTTLE SERVICE: The following companies offer a trailhead shuttle service: Inyo-Mono Dial-A-Ride (800) 922-1930 or (760) 872-1901, Kountry Korners (877) 656-0756 or (760) 872-3951, and Sierra Express (760) 924-8294.

BUS SERVICE: Greyhound makes stops in both Lone Pine and Independence.

OUTFITTERS: The following pack stations operate trips into this region:

Mt. Whitney Pack Trains
PO Box 248
Bishop, CA 93515
(760) 872-8331
www.rockcreekpackstation.com

Sequoia Kings Pack Trains
PO Box 209
Independence, CA 93526
(760) 387-2797 or (800) 962-0775
www.sequoiakingspacktrains.com

Cottonwood Pack Station
Star Route 1, Box 81-A
Independence, CA 93526
(760) 878-2015

RANGER STATION: The Inyo National Forest Mt. Whitney Ranger Station is located in Lone Pine, on U.S. 395, south of the junction with the Whitney Portal Road. Reserved or walk-in wilderness permits may be picked up during normal office hours, and bear canisters may be purchased or rented. A broad selection of books and maps is also for sale.

WILDERNESS PERMITS: Quotas are in effect between May 1st and November 1st. While 60 percent of the quota is available by advanced reservation, the remaining 40 percent is available on a first-come, first-served basis (no fee). A non-refundable, $5 per-person fee is required for each member of your party for advance reservations. Reservations may be made up to six months before your trip. For wilderness permits, you can call the reservation line at (760) 873-2483. You may also send your

Campgrounds

Campground	Fee	Elevation	Season	Restrooms	Running Water	Bear Boxes	Phone
COTTONWOOD PASS (walk-in)	$6	10,000'	Late-May to mid-October	Vault Toilets	Yes	Yes	Yes
GOLDEN TROUT (walk-in)	$6	10000'	Late-May to mid-October	Vault Toilets	Yes	Yes	Yes
TUTTLE CREEK (BLM)	free	4000'	March to November	Vault Toilets	No	No	No
PORTAGEE JOE (Inyo Co.)	$10	3800'	Open All Year	Vault Toilets	Yes	No	Yes
LONE PINE	$12	6000'	Late April to mid-October	Pit Toilets	Yes	No	No
WHITNEY PORTAL	$14	8000'	Late-May to mid-October	Flush Toilets	Yes	Yes	Yes
WHITNEY TRAILHEAD (walk-in, 1-night limit)	$6	8300'	Late-May to mid-October	Flush Toilets	Yes	Yes	Yes
INDEPENDENCE CREEK (Inyo Co.)	$10	3800'	Open All Year	Flush Toilets	Yes	No	No
LOWER GRAYS MEADOW	$11	5200'	Mid-March to mid-October	Vault Toilets	Yes	No	Yes
UPPER GRAYS MEADOW	$11	5900'	Late May to November	Vault Toilets	Yes	No	No
ONION VALLEY	$11	9200'	Early June to early October	Vault Toilets	Yes	Yes	No
OAK CREEK	$11	5000'	Open All Year	Vault Toilets	Yes	No	No

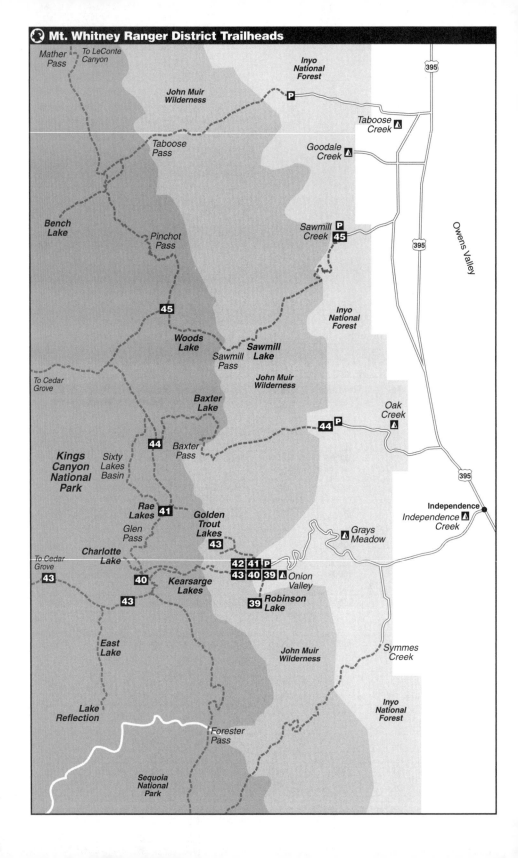

Mt. Whitney Ranger District Trailheads

application and fee information by fax at (760) 873-2484 or by regular mail to:

Inyo National Forest
Wilderness Permit Office
873 North Main Street
Bishop, CA 93514

Advanced reservations may be picked up at the ranger station the day before departure.

For more information, visit the website at www.fs.fed.us/r5/inyo.

MT. WHITNEY ZONE PERMITS: Different rules apply for permits to use the Mt. Whitney Trail. Both dayhikers and backpackers must have a valid permit. See Sequoia National Park, A Complete Hiker's Guide for specific information.

GOOD TO KNOW BEFORE YOU GO:
1. The Onion Valley and Whitney Portal areas are notorious for bear activity, and space in bear lockers is at a premium. As at all trailheads, don't leave any food or scented items in your vehicle while parked overnight. The authorities require backpackers on the Kearsarge Pass Trail and the Mt. Whitney Trail to carry bear canisters.

ONION VALLEY TRAILHEAD

TRIP **39**

Robinson Lake

Ⓜ ↗ DH / BP

DISTANCE: 1.5 miles one way

ELEVATION: 9185/10,535, +1335'/-5'

SEASON: Mid-July to early October

USE: Light

MAP: *Kearsarge Peak*

INTRODUCTION: A short hike leading to splendid alpine scenery is generally the recipe for severe overuse. However, such is not the case with Robinson Lake. Perhaps the majority of hikers and backpackers dismiss the area as unworthy, lying as it does outside of the John Muir Wilderness. Nothing could be further from the truth; the lake is quite scenic, cradled in a dramatic glacial cirque topped with craggy pinnacles. The 1.5-mile climb is steep in parts, but short enough for a pleasant hike or an easy overnight backpack.

DIRECTIONS TO THE TRAILHEAD: In the town of Independence, leave U.S. 395 by

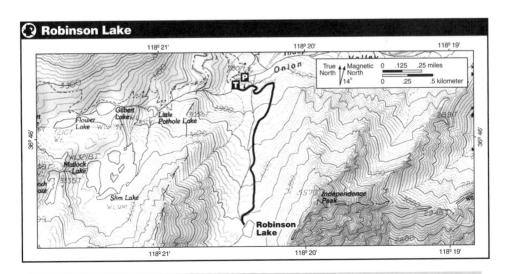

The sparkling blue waters of Robinson Lake

turning west on Market Street, following signs for Onion Valley. Travel 12.5 miles along the steep, winding Onion Valley road to the parking area at Onion Valley. A campground, restrooms, and running water are available near the trailhead. Do not leave food overnight in vehicles, as Onion Valley is a favorite haunt of bears.

DESCRIPTION: A small sign directs you from the parking area to the Onion Valley Campground. Find the signed trailhead near campsite No. 8 and follow the stone path, which sometimes doubles as a seasonal stream, to sandy trail above. Through aspen, whitebark pines, and foxtail pines, you follow the trail on switchbacks up a steep hillside. The moderately steep climb continues to a small, sloping basin where scattered timber reveals that avalanches have swept through here previously. Leave this area on a more moderate climb that eventually brings you near the banks of Robinson Creek. As you proceed up the creek canyon, the grade of the trail increases again where a large field of willows covers the drainage. Above the willows, you climb beside and then across a small

stream, wind through a field of large boulders, and then crest the lip of the Robinson Lake basin. The grade eases as you head through an open area of rock, sand, and dwarf pines to the north shore of Robinson Lake (10,535').

Nestled in a steep, horseshoe-shaped, glacial-scoured basin, sapphire-blue Robinson Lake radiates a bold alpine presence. Steep granite walls and talus slopes rise up from the lakeshore toward the summits of Independence and University peaks. Foxtail pines above the west shore shade a number of pleasant campsites. Rainbow and brook trout will tempt the angler.

Robinson Lake represents the end of the line for the average hiker. Mountaineers can accept the challenge of a difficult, class 2 cross-country route over University Pass to Center Basin, or a similarly rated climb of 13,632-foot University Peak.

PERMITS: None.
CAMPFIRES: Not permitted.

ONION VALLEY TRAILHEAD

TRIP 40

Kearsarge and Bullfrog Lakes

Ⓜ ↗ DH/BP

DISTANCE: 5.25 miles to Kearsarge Lakes; .25 miles to Bullfrog Lake

ELEVATION: 9185/11,823/10,895, +2685'/-1415'

SEASON: Mid-July to early October

USE: Heavy

MAPS: *Kearsarge Peak, Mt. Clarence King*

TRAIL LOG:

2.0   Gilbert Lake
2.25   Flower Lake
4.5   Kearsarge Pass
4.75   Bullfrog Lake Trail Jct.
5.25   Kearsarge Lakes
6.25   Bullfrog Lake
7.4   JMT Jct.

INTRODUCTION: Kearsarge Pass provides one of the least difficult eastern gateways

into the High Sierra. Consequently, the trail over the pass is heavily used, while more difficult, infrequently maintained or unmaintained trails nearby, such as Sawmill Pass, Baxter Pass, and Shepherd Pass, see relatively little use. The trail to Kearsarge Pass still requires an elevation gain of over 2500 feet in 4.5 miles at reasonably high altitudes, but the climb is short by eastern Sierra standards and is rarely at more than a moderate grade.

Ease alone is not what makes the Kearsarge Pass Trail so popular with scores of backpackers. Stunning terrain composed of serrated peaks, subalpine lakes, flower-filled meadows, and rushing streams is the real lure of this portion of the Kings Canyon backcountry. In addition, short connections to the John Muir and Bubbs Creek trails provides a bounty of options for extended trips through some of the High Sierra's grandest scenery, thus making this trail even more popular.

Unfortunately, severe overuse of this relatively easy Sierra crest crossing has resulted in a camping ban at Bullfrog Lake and a one-night limit at Kearsarge Lakes.

DIRECTIONS TO THE TRAILHEAD: In the town of Independence, leave U.S. 395 by turning west on Market Street, following signs for Onion Valley. Travel 12.5 miles

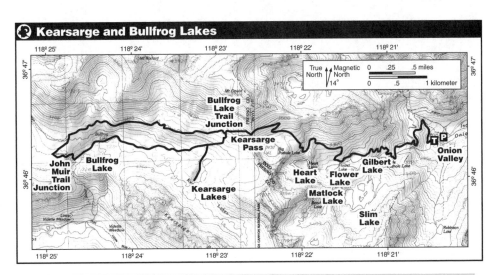

Kearsarge and Bullfrog Lakes

along the steep, winding Onion Valley road to the parking area at Onion Valley.

DESCRIPTION: Locate the signed trailhead near a concrete-block restroom; running water is usually available nearby during the summer months. From the trailhead you climb moderately on single-track Kearsarge Pass Trail across a sagebrush-covered slope, soon reaching the first of many switchbacks. Nearing the drainage of Golden Trout Creek, you encounter an unsigned junction with a short connecting path to the Golden Trout Lakes Trail (see Trip 43). After a switchback, the Kearsarge Pass Trail leads you through manzanita, mountain mahogany, and widely scattered red fir and limber pine to the Independence Creek drainage. After you cross into the John Muir Wilderness, more switchbacks zigzag across a hillside as you play a game of hide and seek with the creek. At one point access to the wildflower-lined creek is handy enough for a thirst-slaking break.

Along the way up the hillside, there are fine views down the creek canyon and across Owens Valley to the Inyo Mountains. To the south, University Peak looms above. A more gentle set of switchbacks leads to Little Pothole Lake (10,035'), 1.3 miles from the trailhead. The willow-lined lake is attractively placed in a small, half-moon-shaped basin, where waterfalls pour down cliffs and flow briefly through patches of willows into the lake. A few overused campsites can be found around the shore beneath foxtail pines.

More switchbacks take you away from Little Pothole Lake and up the canyon. After a long talus slope, you come alongside willow-lined Independence Creek again and soon reach Gilbert Lake (10,417'), 2 miles from the trailhead. Gilbert is an oval lake with a pleasant backdrop of craggy peaks. Grassy meadows dotted with clumps of willows provide easy shoreline access for anglers. Fishing is reported to be good in early season for brook and brown trout, but the relatively easy access means that the lake may be fished out by midseason. However, hikers will find the lake well-suited for swimming.

Kearsarge Lakes and Pinnacles

Plenty of overused campsites lie around the lakeshore.

The Kearsarge Pass Trail follows an easy course along the north side of Gilbert Lake before the climbing resumes. Through light pine forest you follow Independence Creek 0.25 mile to Flower Lake (10,531'), 2.25 miles from the trailhead. A short side trail leads down to the forested shoreline and nice campsites. Brook trout inhabit these waters, but like at the previous lake, easy access probably diminishes the quality of the fishing by mid-season.

Near the north end of Flower Lake, switchbacks start again and the trail veers roughly northeast to attack the headwall of the canyon. Through scattered whitebark and foxtail pines you zigzag up the head-wall to an overlook of Heart Lake. More switchbacks take you through diminishing timber and rockier terrain to another over-look, 3.5 miles from the trailhead, this one of photogenic Big Pothole Lake (11,256'). Despite the name, given by Joseph N. LeConte, the lake is both deep and scenic. Set in a horseshoe-shaped cirque beneath the very crest of the Sierra, the deep-blue, oval lake possesses an austere beauty. A short cross-country ramble is necessary to reach the lake from the trail. Although there is no permanent inlet or outlet, the lake is reported to have a small population of brook trout. A few exposed campsites are scattered around the shore.

Now the trail crosses stark, shale-like terrain via some long-legged switchbacks as you head toward Kearsarge Pass. A smat-tering of gnarled, dwarf whitebark pines defy the elements by clinging desperately to small pockets of soil, looking more like wind-blasted shrubs than trees. The moder-ate upward traverse culminates in a sweep-ing vista at Kearsarge Pass (11,823'), 4.5 miles from the trailhead. Directly below lie Kearsarge Lakes and Bullfrog Lake, shim-mering in the Sierra sun. Above the lakes are the rugged Kearsarge Pinnacles, and beyond is the serrated crest of the Kings-Kern Divide. The high peak directly west is Mt. Bago. A number of signs greet you at

TREAD LIGHTLY

Originally, the main trail from Kearsarge Pass followed the older route now known as the Bullfrog Lake Trail. The current Kearsarge Pass Trail was constructed in more recent times in response to the tremendous-ly destructive impact that overuse had created at Bullfrog Lake and, to a lesser extent, at Kearsarge Lakes. The relocation of the trail out of the basin, coupled with a camping ban at Bullfrog Lake and a one-night limit at Kearsarge Lakes, has sufficiently dis-couraged the hordes of backpackers who previously visited these areas. While in this region, you must be ultra-sensitive to the environment by observing all minimum-impact techniques and regulations.

the pass, marking the entrance to Kings Canyon National Park.

A moderately steep descent from the pass takes you high above the lake basin and quickly down toward more hospitable terrain. Near timberline, you reach the signed junction with the Bullfrog Lake Trail, 4.75 miles from the trailhead, and head south toward Kearsarge Lakes.

Now on the Bullfrog Lake Trail, you follow switchbacks, crossing several sea-sonal streams, on a descent toward Kearsarge Lakes. Approximately 0.3 mile from the junction, a fainter use-trail branches south from the main trail toward the northernmost lakes. This use-trail leads you south across the granite basin through widely scattered clumps of whitebark pine and past a pair of delightful tarns to the largest of the Kearsarge Lakes (10,895'). Tucked beneath the wall of the serrated Kearsarge Pinnacles, the lakes are quite pic-turesque. Use-trails lead to plentiful camp-sites and an assortment of bear boxes for storing your food and scented items. Anglers should find that the rainbow trout present a sufficient challenge to their skills.

Back at the use-trail's junction with the Bullfrog Lake Trail, you head west through stunted pines and pockets of meadows on a moderate descent, stepping across numerous seasonal streams along the way. Soon you near the main creek and proceed through delightful open meadowlands to Bullfrog Lake (10,610'), 6.25 miles from the trailhead.

Near the shore of the blue-green lake you realize why this area was such a popular destination for backpackers — the meadow-rimmed lake rivals any other lake in the Sierra for picturesque scenery. Across the deep trench of Bubbs Creek, the pyramidal summit of East Vidette rises sharply into the Sierra sky, providing dramatic counterpoint to the usually placid waters of the lake. Above the shoreline, clumps of pine shelter campsites graced with splendid views — but these sites are now closed, in an attempt to let the land recover from the damage caused by years of overuse. Obey the signs restricting travel across sensitive meadow areas. Nowadays, visitors enjoy the surroundings for only limited periods, because they must find overnight accommodations elsewhere.

The trail passes gently along the north shore of Bullfrog Lake and then continues a moderate descent toward the John Muir Trail. The grade eases momentarily as you pass a pair of meadow-rimmed ponds, but soon returns to moderate as you travel through scattered lodgepole pine forest to the well-signed John Muir Trail junction, 7.4 miles from the Onion Valley trailhead.

From the junction, turn right (west) and climb on the JMT for 0.3 mile to sandy flat and a four-way junction with the Charlotte Lake and Kearsarge Pass trails. From here, a 0.75-mile descent leads west and then northwest to Charlotte Lake (see Trip 41), providing a potential one-night destination for backpackers. To return to the Onion Valley trailhead, leave the JMT at the four-way junction and go northeast on the Kearsarge Pass Trail. Soon you encounter a Y-junction with a connecting trail to the JMT that provides a shortcut from the Kearsarge Pass Trail to the Rae Lakes. Bear right (east) at the junction and travel 2 miles to the junction with the Bullfrog Lake Trail, thereby closing the loop. Along the way you have fine views of Bullfrog Lake and Kearsarge Lakes in the basin below the trail. From the junction, retrace your steps over Kearsarge Pass and down to Onion Valley.

⊡ A straightforward cross-country route from Gilbert Lake and a faint use-trail from Flower Lake leads across the low spur to their south into the forested cirque basin of Slim (10,545') and Matlock (10,558') lakes. Hidden in the shadow of University Peak, these lakes provide anglers with a better opportunity to fish for brook and rainbow trout than the more popular lakes along the Kearsarge Pass Trail. Backpackers will appreciate the lesser-used campsites as well. Even less visited is Bench Lake (10,889'), a short but steep jaunt from the lower lakes.

⊡ If you wish to visit Heart Lake, follow a faint path west from Flower Lake up a creek to the lake's east shore. Although just 0.1 mile from the Kearsarge Pass Trail, the lake is seldom visited, as there is no direct access from the trail. Fine campsites amid whitebark pines occur at the east end of the lake and fishing is reported to be decent for rainbow and brook trout.

⊡ An ascent of Mt. Gould (13,005') north from Kearsarge Pass is a relatively easy and popular climb for those who don't mind scrambling up talus. So popular is this route that more than one use-trail has been created across the lower slopes of the peak.

⊞ **PERMITS:** Wilderness permit required for overnight stays (quota: 60 per day, only 24 of which may enter the Whitney Zone).

CAMPFIRES: No.

CAMPING: No camping at Bullfrog Lake; one-night limit at Kearsarge Lakes.

BEARS: Canisters required.

TRIP **41**

Charlotte Lake and Rae Lakes Basin

MS ✒ BPx

DISTANCE: 12 miles to Rae Lakes

ELEVATION: 9185/11,823/10,790/11,978/
10,541, +4050'/-2685'

SEASON: Mid-July to early October

USE: Heavy

MAPS: *Kearsarge Peak,*
Mt Clarence King

TRAIL LOG:

4.5	Kearsarge Pass
4.75	Bullfrog Lake Trail Jct
7.4	Kearsarge Pass Trail/JMT Jct.
9.3	Glen Pass
12.0	Rae Lakes/Sixty Lake Basin Jct.

INTRODUCTION: The Rae Lakes basin is arguably one of the prettiest alpine basins in the High Sierra. Certainly large numbers of backpackers must think so, as this area is one of the most heavily used and regulated jurisdictions outside of the Whitney Zone. You may camp for only one night in the Rae Lakes basin. Additionally, in such a popular area, bears have learned to overcome the best techniques of hanging food, so the Park Service insists that all backpackers entering the Park from Kearsarge Pass (and from Cedar Grove) use bear-proof canisters. The limited space in the bear-proof lockers at Rae Lakes should be left for John Muir Trail through-hikers.

Restrictions aside, the journey to Rae Lakes may represent the quintessential Sierra outing. You experience a wide range of environments along the way, including the arid eastern Sierra approach from Owens Valley, the above-timberline moon-

scape around Kearsarge Pass, the serene forest encircling Charlotte Lake, and the splendid alpine scenery of the Rae Lakes basin. Throw in wildflower-laden meadows, sparkling creeks, and splendid views, and you may indeed have the complete High Sierra experience. If you still find something lacking in this assortment of virtues, a touch of creative planning will allow you to experience even more of this majestic terrain, including visits to Sixty Lake and Gardiner basins.

Because getting to Rae Lakes from Onion Valley by trail involves crossing two major Sierra passes, Kearsarge and Glen, the average backpacker should view this trip as a multi-day outing. Besides, the surrounding terrain is spectacular enough to justify some extra time (see Options, below). A first night's camp can be established at either Kearsarge Lakes (see Trip 40), or at Charlotte Lake as described here.

DIRECTIONS TO THE TRAILHEAD: In the town of Independence, leave U.S. 395 by turning west on Market Street, following signs for Onion Valley. Travel 12.5 miles along the steep, winding Onion Valley road to the parking area at Onion Valley.

DESCRIPTION: Locate the signed trailhead near a concrete-block restroom; running water is usually available nearby during the summer months. From the trailhead you climb moderately on single-track Kearsarge Pass Trail across a sagebrush-covered slope, soon reaching the first of many switchbacks. Nearing the drainage of Golden Trout Creek, you encounter an unsigned junction with a short connecting path to the Golden Trout Lakes Trail (see Trip 43). After a switchback, the Kearsarge Pass Trail leads you to the Independence Creek drainage. After you cross into the John Muir Wilderness, more switchbacks zigzag across a hillside. At one point access to the wildflower-lined creek is handy enough for a thirst-slaking break.

Along the way up the hillside, there are fine views down the creek canyon and across the Owens Valley to the Inyo

Charlotte Lake and Rae Lakes Basin

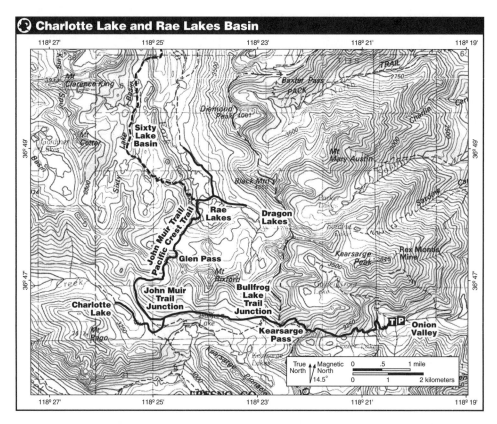

Mountains. To the south, University Peak looms above. A more gentle set of switchbacks leads to Little Pothole Lake (10,035'), 1.3 miles from the trailhead.

More switchbacks take you away from Little Pothole Lake and up the canyon. After a long talus slope, you come alongside willow-lined Independence Creek again and soon reach Gilbert Lake (10,417'), 2 miles from the trailhead. Fishing is reported to be good in early season for brook and brown trout, and dusty hikers will find the lake well-suited for swimming. Plenty of overused campsites lie around the lakeshore.

The Kearsarge Pass Trail follows an easy course along the north side of Gilbert Lake before the climbing resumes. Through light pine forest you follow Independence Creek 0.25 mile to Flower Lake (10,531'), 2.25 miles from the trailhead. A short side

trail leads down to the forested shoreline and nice campsites.

Near the north end of Flower Lake, switchbacks start again and the trail veers roughly northeast to attack the headwall of the canyon. You zigzag up the headwall to an overlook of Heart Lake. More switchbacks take you through diminishing timber and rockier terrain to another overlook, 3.5 miles from the trailhead, this one of photogenic Big Pothole Lake (11,256'). A short cross-country ramble is necessary to reach the lake from the trail.

Now the trail crosses stark, shale-like terrain via some long-legged switchbacks as you head toward Kearsarge Pass. A smattering of gnarled, dwarf whitebark pines defy the elements by clinging desperately to small pockets of soil. The moderate upward traverse culminates in a sweeping vista at Kearsarge Pass (11,823'), 4.5 miles from the trailhead.

From the junction, continue west on the Kearsarge Pass Trail, entering more hospitable terrain below timberline, where meadow grass, clumps of willow, and seasonal creeks soften the rocky slopes. Fine views of Kearsarge Lakes and Kearsarge Pinnacles are constant companions along the moderate descent. Farther down the trail, Bullfrog Lake makes a stunning appearance, framed by the spiked summits of East Vidette and West Vidette across the deep chasm of Bubbs Creek. To the south, you can also see Junction and Center peaks. Eventually the expansive vista diminishes a bit as a scattered-to-light forest of whitebark and foxtail pine appears. You continue onward to a signed Y-junction with a connecting trail to the John Muir Trail that provides a shortcut from the Kearsarge Pass Trail to the Rae Lakes. Unless you're headed to Charlotte Lake for the night, veer right and follow this connecting trail 0.2 mile westbound to the John Muir Trail.

☐ **SIDE TRIP TO CHARLOTTE LAKE:** To reach Charlotte Lake, continue on the Kearsarge Pass Trail heading south and then southwest. You begin in forest and eventually break out into the open as you cross a sandy flat to a four-way junction with the John Muir and Charlotte Lake trails, 0.3 mile from the previous junction. Head west and then northwest for 0.75 mile on a winding, forested descent to Charlotte Lake (10,370').

Charlotte is a delightful lake rimmed by scattered pines and nearly surrounded by high hills. At the northwest end of the lake, a splayed, V-shaped cleft allows the waters of the lake to tumble down Charlotte Creek and late in the day lets in the rosy glow from dramatic sunsets. As the only lake with decent campsites easily accessible from the JMT between Forester and Glen passes, Charlotte receives a fair share of overnighters (one-night limit). Sufficient campsites are spread along the northeast shore of the lake. The Park Service has a ranger cabin near the shore's midpoint, and there are bear boxes toward the lake's northwest end. Solitude seekers may find a few more secluded campsites scattered

The multicolored Painted Lady, rising above the Rae Lakes

around the area. Anglers will be tempted by rainbow and brook trout. **END OF SIDE TRIP**

Back at the Y-junction with the 0.2-mile connecting trail from the Kearsarge Pass Trail, you head northbound on the gently graded JMT with views of azure Charlotte Lake through the trees. Where the grade increases, the characteristic granite of Charlotte Dome comes briefly into view farther west down the canyon of Charlotte Creek. Proceeding up the JMT, you soon begin to encounter the rocks and boulders that will be your nearly constant companions until you reach more hospitable terrain near the Rae Lakes. As the trail bends east, you make a short descent, but the climbing soon resumes as you bend back around to the north. A couple of marginal campsites appear near a seasonal stream, sites even less desirable in late season when the creek is dry. You wind around through the rocky terrain a bit more steeply via some switchbacks, passing a pair of greenish-colored tarns on the way.

Gazing toward Glen Pass, your mind remains steadfast in the knowledge that a trail as significant as the JMT must certainly cross the formidable crest in front of you, but your eyes convince you that the ridge ahead is totally impassable. More switchbacks and more climbing eventually lead up the rock headwall to Glen Pass (11,978'), 9.3 miles from the trailhead. The view from the pass is not as remarkable as from many in the High Sierra, but some of the Rae Lakes can be seen in the seemingly barren basin below.

You follow the crest of the ridge momentarily before heading down from the pass on a winding, rocky descent that can seem interminable. The grade of descent eases a bit as you cross a tarn-filled granite bench, but you soon find yourself on a switchbacking descent once again. Eventually signs of life begin to appear on the banks of trickling little streams, where wildflowers, sedges, grasses, and small shrubs grab tenuous holds in small pockets of soil. Scattered pines give further evidence

of more temperate surroundings as you continue to descend. More switchbacks lead across more tiny creeks and finally down to the shoreline of the southernmost of the Rae Lakes (10,541').

The JMT continues along the northwest side of the upper lake toward the isthmus separating it from the middle lake. Just before this isthmus, you encounter a less frequently used spur trail to Sixty Lake Basin (see Options, Trip 36), 12 miles from the trailhead, near a small signboard where current camping regulations are posted. Beyond the junction, the JMT follows the eastern shoreline of the middle and lower lakes, where you have fine views of Fin Dome and King Spur beyond.

The Rae Lakes basin is characterized by beautiful aquamarine lakes dotted with tiny islands, by shorelines of rolling granite slabs interspersed with pockets of green meadow and scattered pine forest, and by a border of steep cliffs and picturesque peaks. These include the exfoliated Fin Dome and the multicolored Painted Lady. Exquisite views in this scenery-rich basin appear in every direction. Campsites with bear boxes can be found around the middle and lower lakes—don't even consider hanging your food in this area, as these bears have long been hip to that trick. Remember that there is a one-night camping limit in the Rae Lakes basin. Despite the region's popularity, fishing is reportedly quite good for brook and rainbow trout. A ranger cabin is located above the northeast shore of the middle lake.

⊡ Options for further wanderings around the Rae Lakes are numerous, but you are restricted by the one-night camping limit that prevents the establishment of a base camp within the basin. However, camping for more than one night is possible nearby at Dragon Lake and in the Sixty Lake Basin. (For excursions on the infrequently maintained trail to Sixty Lake Basin and over to Gardiner Basin via a straightforward cross-country route, see the description in Trip 36.)

O Dragon Lake is just over 0.5 mile east of the JMT and is easily accessed by a use-trail. Backpackers will find a few campsites around the lake. Experienced cross-country enthusiasts can avoid hiking the trail back to Onion Valley by crossing the Sierra crest at Dragon Pass (12,800'), also known as Gould Pass, halfway between Dragon Peak and Mt. Gould. This class 2 route involves a seemingly interminable boulderhop and scramble over loose rock south from Dragon Lake to the easternmost of three unnamed lakes, and then up more talus to the steep chute below the pass. Once up the chute and across the crest, you encounter more boulders and talus on the descent until you can follow the unmaintained trail from Golden Trout Lake back to the trail-head (see Trip 43). An alternate route of equal difficulty exists from Dragon Pass heading around the west side of Mt. Gould to the trail at Kearsarge Pass.

O Peak baggers are at a bit of a disadvantage in this area because climbs of most of the nearby mountains are technical in nature. Painted Lady is perhaps the easiest ascent, rated as class 2 from the JMT. Leave the trail on the granite bench below Glen Pass and climb the peak's west face to the summit.

R **PERMITS:** Wilderness permit required for overnight stays (quota: 60 per day, only 24 of which may enter the Whitney Zone).

CAMPFIRES: Not permitted.

CAMPING: One-night limit at Charlotte Lake and in the Rae Lakes basin.

BEARS: Canisters required.

ONION VALLEY TRAILHEAD

TRIP **42**

Trans-Sierra Trek: Onion Valley to Cedar Grove

(MS) ↗ DH/BP

DISTANCE: 20.5 miles one way

ELEVATION: 9185/11,823/5045, +2845'/-4140'

SEASON: Mid-July to mid-October

USE: Heavy

MAPS: *Kearsarge Peak, Mt. Clarence King, The Sphinx*

TRAIL LOG:

2.0	Gilbert Lake
4.5	Kearsarge Pass
4.75	Bullfrog Lake Trail Jct.
7.4	John Muir Trail Jct.
8.8	Bubbs Creek Trail Jct.
11.0	Junction Meadow/East Lake Trail Jct.
17.0	Sphinx Creek Camp
20.5	Roads End

INTRODUCTION: This route provides the least difficult way to traverse the High Sierra on foot. However, the trip is not easy: the long drive to set up a car shuttle between the Onion Valley and Cedar Grove trailheads may take as much time as the hike itself. The first order of business is deciding whether to attempt the trip as a one-day hike or an overnight backpack. The main advantage of a dayhike is not having to carry a heavy pack. But the 21-mile distance requires that dayhikers get a very early start and maintain a fast pace to avoid finishing the trip in the dark. Backpackers, burdened with a heavier pack, will require more time to complete the journey, but may have extra hours to

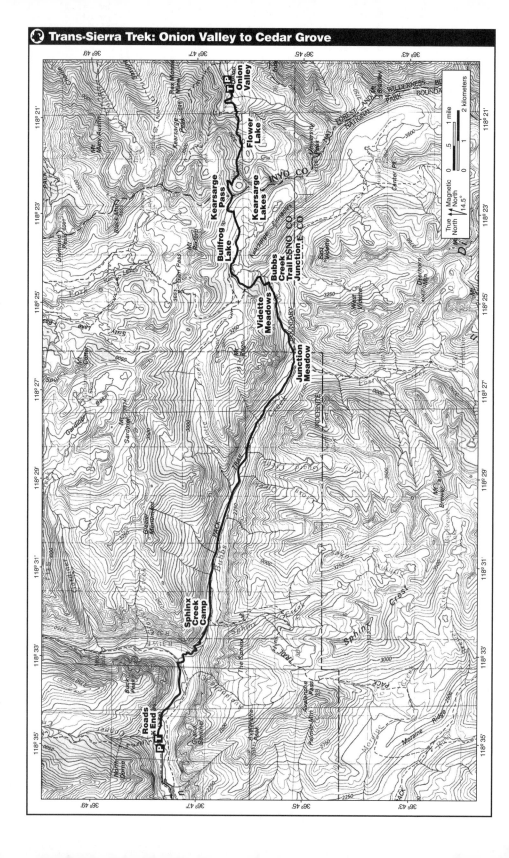

appreciate the scenery along the way. Dayhikers have the additional blessing of not having to obtain one of the limited number of wilderness permits.

Whichever way is chosen to approach this trip, dayhikers and backpackers alike will be treated to a sampling of great scenery and a wide variation of plant communities over the 21-mile course. Starting at Onion Valley in a typical eastside environment, you climb through subalpine and alpine zones to the crest of the route at Kearsarge Pass, passing a lovely set of lakes in the Independence Creek canyon along the way. From the pass, a nearly 6800-foot descent leads you from the alpine to the dramatic subalpine realms of Kearsarge and Bullfrog lakes, and then down into the lodgepole pine, red fir, and mixed-coniferous forests along Bubbs Creek. Intermixed with these forests are pockets of lovely flower-filled meadows. Great scenery and variety make this trip an experience to treasure.

DIRECTIONS TO THE TRAILHEAD: Plan on taking several hours to travel between the Roads End and Onion Valley trailheads. The two shortest paved routes from the west side of Kings Canyon east across the Sierra are both to the south of Kings Canyon and Sequoia national parks. One route heads east from Porterville on Highway 190 to Camp Nelson, follows a network of national forest and county roads over the range at Sherman Pass, and then descends past Kennedy Meadows to U.S. 395 just north of Indian Wells. The second option follows Highway 155 to Highway 178 near Lake Isabella, and then over Walker Pass to a junction with U.S. 395 in the tiny community of Freeman.

Whichever way you elect to traverse the Sierra, once you're on the east side you will head north on U.S. 395 to a junction with the Onion Valley Road, in the town of Independence. (Although about 100 miles longer, a northern alternative, on Highway 120 through Yosemite National Park over Tioga Pass to U.S. 395 and then south to Independence, is also possible.)

BEGIN: In the town of Independence, leave U.S. 395 by turning west on Market Street, following signs for Onion Valley. Travel 12.5 miles along the steep, winding Onion Valley road to the parking area at Onion Valley.

END: Drive on Highway 180 into Kings Canyon and to the day-use parking area at Roads End, 5.0 miles from the turnoff to Cedar Grove.

DESCRIPTION: Locate the signed trailhead near a concrete-block restroom; running water is usually available nearby during the summer months. From the trailhead you climb moderately on single-track Kearsarge Pass Trail across a sagebrush-covered slope, soon reaching the first of many switchbacks. Nearing the drainage of Golden Trout Creek, you encounter an unsigned junction with a short connecting path to the Golden Trout Lakes Trail (see Trip 43). After a switchback, the Kearsarge Pass Trail leads you through manzanita, mountain mahogany, and widely scattered red fir and limber pine to the Independence Creek drainage. After you cross into the John Muir Wilderness, more switchbacks zigzag across a hillside as you play a game of hide and seek with the creek. At one point access to the wildflower-lined creek is handy enough for a thirst-slaking break.

Along the way up the hillside, there are fine views down the creek canyon and across the Owens Valley to the Inyo Mountains. To the south, University Peak looms above. A more gentle set of switchbacks leads to Little Pothole Lake (10,035'), 1.3 miles from the trailhead. The willow-lined lake is attractively placed in a small, half-moon-shaped basin, where waterfalls pour down cliffs and flow briefly through patches of willows into the lake. A few overused campsites can be found around the shore beneath foxtail pines.

More switchbacks take you away from Little Pothole Lake and up the canyon. After a long talus slope, you will come alongside willow-lined Independence Creek again and soon reach Gilbert Lake (10,417'), 2 miles from the trailhead. Gilbert is an oval lake with a pleasant backdrop of craggy peaks. Grassy meadows dotted with clumps of willows provide easy shoreline access for anglers. Fishing is reported to be good in early season for brook and brown trout, but the relatively easy access means that the lake may be fished out by midseason. However, hikers will find the lake well-suited for swimming. Plenty of overused campsites lie around the lakeshore.

The Kearsarge Pass Trail follows an easy course along the north side of Gilbert Lake before the climbing resumes. Through light pine forest you follow Independence Creek 0.25 mile to Flower Lake (10,531'), 2.25 miles from the trailhead. A short side trail leads down to the forested shoreline and nice campsites.

Near the north end of Flower Lake, switchbacks start again and the trail veers roughly northeast to the headwall of the canyon. You zigzag up the headwall to an overlook of Heart Lake, and more switchbacks take you through diminishing timber and rockier terrain to another overlook, 3.5 miles from the trailhead, this one of photogenic Big Pothole Lake (11,256'). A short cross-country ramble is necessary to reach the lake from the trail. A few exposed campsites are scattered around the shore.

Now the trail crosses stark, shale-like terrain via some long-legged switchbacks as you head toward Kearsarge Pass. The moderate upward traverse culminates in a sweeping vista at Kearsarge Pass (11,823'), 4.5 miles from the trailhead. Directly below lie Kearsarge Lakes and Bullfrog Lake, shimmering in the Sierra sun. Above the lakes are the rugged Kearsarge Pinnacles, and beyond is the serrated crest of the Kings-Kern Divide. The high peak directly west is Mt. Bago. A number of signs greet you at the pass, marking the entrance to Kings Canyon National Park.

Sign at Kearsarge Pass

A moderately steep descent from the pass takes you high above the lake basin and quickly down toward more hospitable terrain. Near timberline, you reach the signed junction with the Bullfrog Lake Trail, 4.75 miles from the trailhead, and head south toward Kearsarge Lakes.

Now on the Bullfrog Lake Trail, you follow switchbacks, crossing several seasonal streams, on a descent toward Kearsarge Lakes. Approximately 0.3 mile from the junction, a fainter use-trail branches south from the main trail toward the northernmost lakes. This use-trail leads you south across the granite basin through widely scattered clumps of whitebark pine and past a pair of delightful tarns to the largest of the Kearsarge Lakes (10,895'). Use-trails lead to plentiful campsites and an assortment of bear boxes.

Back at the use-trail's junction with the Bullfrog Lake Trail, you head west through stunted pines and pockets of meadows on a moderate descent, stepping across numerous seasonal streams along the way. Soon you near the main creek and proceed through open meadowlands to Bullfrog Lake (10,610'), 6.25 miles from the trailhead.

Near the shore of the blue-green lake you realize why this area was such a popular destination for backpackers—the meadow-rimmed lake rivals any other lake in the Sierra for picturesque scenery. Above the shoreline, clumps of pine shelter campsites graced with splendid views—but these sites are now closed, in an attempt to let the land recover from the damage caused by years of overuse. Obey the signs restricting travel across sensitive meadow areas.

The trail passes gently along the north shore of Bullfrog Lake and then continues a moderate descent toward the John Muir Trail. The grade eases momentarily, but soon returns to moderate as you travel through scattered lodgepole pine forest to the well-signed John Muir Trail junction, 7.4 miles from the Onion Valley trailhead.

Turn south on the JMT and follow descending trail toward Bubbs Creek. After a pair of crossings over Bullfrog Lake's outlet, you follow a steeper switchbacking descent down the wall of the canyon to Lower Vidette Meadow and a junction with the Bubbs Creek Trail, 1.3 miles from the Bullfrog Lake junction.

Following signed directions for Cedar Grove, you turn away from the JMT and head west on the Bubbs Creek Trail, making a short descent to the north edge of expansive Lower Vidette Meadow. Overnighters will find excellent campsites (bear box) nestled beneath lodgepole pines along the meadow's fringe. Leaving the gentle grade of the meadows behind, you begin a more pronounced descent, following the now tumbling creek as it plunges down the gorge. Soon you break out into the open momentarily, where a large hump of granite provides an excellent vantage point from which to survey the surrounding landscape. Head back into the trees and continue down the canyon, stepping over numerous lushly-lined freshets along the way. Periodic switchbacks and occasional views of the dramatic topography above the gorge of East Creek, including rugged Mt. Brewer, North Guard, and Mt. Farquhar, mark the protracted descent. Farther down the canyon, picturesque waterfalls and cascades on Bubbs Creek provide additional visual treats.

The stiff descent eventually eases as you reach the grassy, fern-filled, and wildflower-covered clearing of Junction Meadow (8190'±). You stroll over to a signed 3-way junction with a trail heading south along East Creek to East Lake and Lake Reflection (see Trip 27), 2.3 miles from the JMT. Those seeking overnight accommodations will find campsites along this trail on either side of the ford of Bubbs Creek. Additional campsites are farther along the Bubbs Creek Trail, past the horse camp near the west edge of the meadow.

Past Junction Meadow, the moderate descent resumes as you proceed down Bubbs Creek canyon. You stroll alongside the turbulent creek through a moderate forest composed mainly of white firs. After nearly 2 miles of steady descent, Bubbs Creek mellows, and you hike gently-graded trail through a grove of aspens and ferns on the way to a log crossing of Charlotte Creek. Nearby, a short path leads to fair campsites near Bubbs Creek, where fishing is reported to be good for rainbow, brook, and brown trout.

Gentle trail continues for a little while beyond Charlotte Creek, as you hop across a trio of streams and walk through shoulder-high ferns, before Bubbs Creek returns to its tumultuous course down the gorge. A steady, moderate descent follows the course of the tumbling stream for the next several miles. As you proceed farther down the canyon, the moderate fir forest gives way to a lighter cover of trees, mostly Jeffrey pines, with a smattering of firs, incense cedars, and black oaks. At 8.25 miles from the JMT, you reach Sphinx Creek Camp and a three-way junction with the Sphinx Creek Trail. Excellent campsites with bear boxes on either side of a log-and-plank bridge across Bubbs Creek will lure overnighters. A pit toilet is located on the north side of the creek.

Away from Sphinx Creek Camp the descent resumes across the east side of the canyon, as you stroll through thickening conifers well above the level of the creek. Soon, switchbacks descend the steep wall of the canyon of South Fork Kings River. During the descent, gaps in the scrubby forest allow views of Kings Canyon below and The Sphinx above. Early season travelers have the added bonus of glimpses of a spectacular cascade plunging across the granite wall of the canyon. The switchbacks eventually end at the floor of the canyon, near the first junction with the Kanawyer Loop Trail. Continue northwest and stroll across a series of short wooden bridges across branches of braided Bubbs Creek to a junction with the Kanawyer Loop and Paradise Valley trails.

From the junction, turn west and follow a very gently descending trail along South Fork Kings River through a mixed forest of incense cedars, ponderosa pines, black oaks, sugar pines, and white firs. Just past a short bridge over Copper Creek, you reach the Roads End trailhead, 3.5 miles from Sphinx Creek Camp.

O See Trips 27, 28 and 40.

R **PERMITS:** Wilderness permit required for overnight stays (quota: 60 per day).

CAMPFIRES: Permitted only along Bubbs Creek.

CAMPING: No camping at Bullfrog Lake; one-night limits at Kearsarge and Charlotte lakes.

BEARS: Canisters required.

TRIP **43**

Golden Trout Lakes

Ⓜ ↗ DH/BP

DISTANCE: 2.5 miles to Golden Trout Lake; + 1.0 mile to other lakes

ELEVATION: 9185/11,390, +2295'/-80'

SEASON: Mid-July to early October

USE: Light

MAP: *Kearsarge Peak*

INTRODUCTION: The Golden Trout Lakes provide a fine destination for either a pleasant dayhike or an easy overnight backpack.

The lakes are cradled in talus-filled cirques just below the Sierra crest in the shadow of Mt. Gould and Dragon Peak. Few trails allow hikers into such an austere alpine setting so quickly.

Although the Kearsarge Pass Trail in the next canyon south is one of the most popular eastern Sierra trails, relatively few hikers find their way up the unmaintained Golden Trout Lakes Trail. If ever a trail deserved adoption by some civic-minded hiking club, it is this one, although perhaps the lack of maintenance is enough of a deterrent to keep the number of hikers at a manageable level. Despite the condition of the trail, the route to the lakes is straightforward, and the impressive scenery more than compensates for any rough stretches.

DIRECTIONS TO THE TRAILHEAD: In the town of Independence, leave U.S. 395 by turning west on Market Street, following

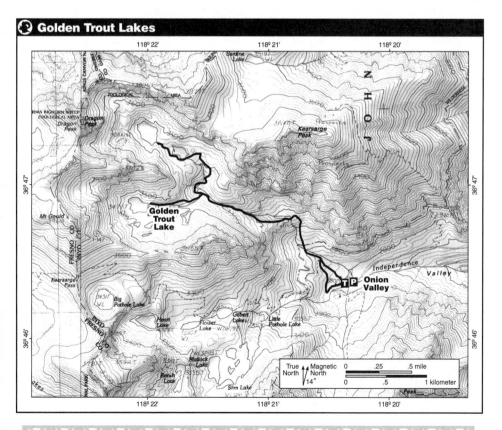

Golden Trout Lakes

signs for Onion Valley. Travel 12.5 miles along the steep, winding Onion Valley road to the parking area at Onion Valley.

DESCRIPTION: You have two options for beginning your trip to the Golden Trout Lakes, neither possessing tremendous advantages or disadvantages over the other. The first follows the Kearsarge Pass Trail for 0.25 mile to an unsigned junction with a short spur trail connecting to the Golden Trout Lakes Trail. The second option is to hike from the lower parking area up the access road toward the pack station. A short way up the road, follow another road branching to your left that passes the snow-survey shelter, an A-frame structure, and a wooden shack. Soon this rocky road shrinks to a single-track trail and meets the connector from the Kearsarge Pass Trail mentioned above, approximately 350 yards from the parking area.

From the junction with the connector trail, proceed up the canyon through open pinyon-pine-and-sagebrush terrain with views of Golden Trout Fall. Soon riparian vegetation appears where the trail follows alongside a stretch of Golden Trout Creek. You eventually cross the creek, quickly entering the John Muir Wilderness and the no-fire zone. Follow the trail as it makes a winding climb through loose rock up a hillside to get above a waterfall. Once above the fall, you pass through a flower-lined gully and cross back over the creek. From there, the path becomes faint and hard to follow in places, particularly in areas of boulders and talus, but route is obvious, heading upstream through a narrow canyon. The established alignment of the trail fords the creek and quickly crosses back again, but the trail is so faint that these crossings are easily missed. Eventually you encounter less steep terrain in a lush meadow near where the creek forks into two branches. Campsites are nearby on a low rise.

To reach Golden Trout Lake, cross the left-hand branch of the creek and head west along the north bank through gnarled whitebark pines and a few foxtail pines. Once again, the trail is sketchy but the route is obvious. Continue up the creek to Golden Trout Lake (11,388'). A few matted

One of the Golden Trout Lakes near Onion Valley

shrubs and widely scattered dwarf white-bark pines meet you at the eastern shore, where the boulders and talus of the glacier-carved amphitheater border the lake. The apex of the amphitheater is 13,005-foot Mt. Gould. Backpackers may be tempted by a couple of nice campsites near the outlet, while anglers can test their skill on brook trout and the lake's namesake fish.

The *Kearsarge Peak* quad shows a trail following the right-hand branch of Golden Trout Creek to a pair of unnamed lakes east of Dragon Peak. Although this path has mostly disappeared over the years, the route is an easily managed cross-country trek. From where Golden Trout Creek forks, follow the right-hand branch around meadows, across the creek, and up the drainage to the first lake. The route to the upper lake is equally straightforward. Both lakes are quite scenic, nicely backdropped by the multi-hued rocks of Dragon Peak. A smattering of campsites can be found at either lake.

O A shortcut to Rae Lakes is available over Dragon Pass, just south of Dragon Peak, for experienced cross-country hikers (see Trip 41).

R **PERMITS:** Wilderness permit required for overnight stays (quota: 25 per day).
CAMPFIRES: Not permitted.

OAK CREEK TRAILHEAD

TRIP **44**

Baxter Pass Trail

S ↗ BP

DISTANCE: 11 miles one way to JMT

ELEVATION: 5990/12,245/10,210, +6650'/-2430'

SEASON: mid-July to mid-October

USE: Light

MAPS: *Kearsarge Peak, Mt. Clarence King*

INTRODUCTION: Only a small percentage of the backpacking population will find this trip enjoyable: loners in incredible shape with a penchant for masochism. The trail —if one can still refer to the unmaintained, overgrown, washed out, disappearing track as such—is a long, steep, hot, difficult, and generally nasty route that begins practically on the floor of Owens Valley. The route to Baxter Pass climbs 6,300 feet in a little over 6.0 miles, which simple arithmetic calculates as a 1,000-feet-per-mile ascent. The steep climb will be enjoyed by hearty back-packers in great shape, despite the deteriorating condition of the trail. This trip is not entirely bad news, however, as the Baxter Lakes are quite scenic and relatively deserted. However, accessing them from the John Muir Trail rather than the Oak Creek trailhead may be a preferable option.

DIRECTIONS TO THE TRAILHEAD: Leave U.S. 395 approximately 2.5 miles north of Independence, and turn west onto Fish Hatchery Road. Proceed on paved road 1.3 miles to a Y-junction and turn right, passing Oak Creek Campground on the way to the trailhead at the end of the road, 5.8 miles from the Y-junction.

DESCRIPTION: Follow an old roadbed from the oak-shaded campsite at the end of the

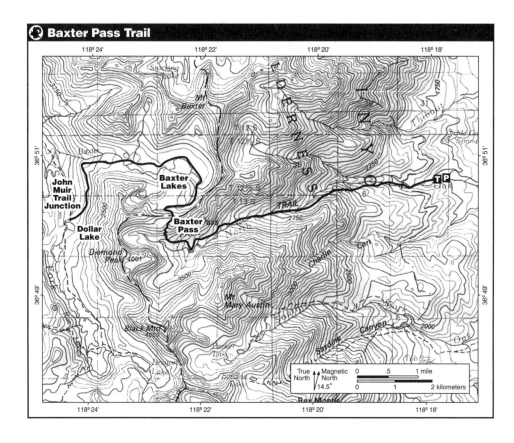

Baxter Pass Trail

road up the canyon of North Fork Oak Creek, through typical eastside terrain. Eventually the roadbed becomes a single-track trail, but much of the path may be washed out, overgrown with brush, and generally indistinguishable. You ford a tributary, then, near the 1-mile mark, ford the main channel of the creek. The zigzagging path takes you another 1.5 miles to the next ford, followed by a steady climb up the creek canyon to Summit Meadow, approximately 4.0 miles from the trailhead. About 1.0 mile beyond the meadow, the deteriorating path becomes rockier as you veer away from the creek and bend north toward the pass through a field of scree dotted with a smattering of stunted whitebark pines. Switchbacks lead to barren Baxter Pass (12,245'±) and the Kings Canyon National Park boundary, 6.25 miles from the trailhead. The good view

includes sections of the Sierra crest, and to the east, Owens Valley and the town of Independence.

A steep, rocky descent from the pass leads to mellower terrain once you reach the Baxter Lakes basin, where wildflowers and grasses lend a vibrant touch of life after the mostly barren terrain above. Seldom-used campsites are scattered around the shore of the upper lake (11,145'). Farther down, backpackers may find additional sites in small groves of whitebark pines near the lower string of lakes. You cross Baxter Creek and continue the descent west until the path bends south and drops more steeply toward Dollar Lake and South Fork Woods Creek. Along the descent, there are good views of King Spur, Fin Dome, and Dollar Lake. You reach an unsigned junction with the John Muir Trail directly north of Dollar Lake, 11 miles from the trailhead.

O If your party is hell-bent on visiting Rae Lakes and all the permits have been gobbled up for the Kearsarge Pass Trail, this could be an alternate route. There can't be a high demand for the 10-spots-per-day quota for the Baxter Pass Trail. In fact, it would be surprising to learn that 10 people per month backpack this trail the full 11 miles from the Owens Valley to the JMT.

R **PERMITS:** Wilderness permit required for overnight stays (quota: 10 per day).

BIGHORN SHEEP AREA: Dogs and domestic sheep prohibited.

CAMPFIRES: Not permitted in Kings Canyon National Park, but permitted east of the crest.

SAWMILL CREEK TRAILHEAD

TRIP 45

Sawmill Pass Trail

S ✗ BP

DISTANCE: 12.5 miles to JMT

ELEVATION: 4600/11,300/10,350, +7315'/-1560'

SEASON: Mid-July to mid-October

USE: Light

MAPS: *Aberdeen, Mt. Pinchot*

TRAIL LOG:

5.5	Sawmill Meadow
7.5	Sawmill Lake
9.3	Sawmill Pass
11.0	Woods Lake

INTRODUCTION: This is another one of those grueling eastside trails that will repel just about any clear-thinking backpacker. This one starts 1300 feet lower than the Baxter Pass Trail (Trip 44), only a few hundred feet above a sinkhole in the Owens Valley. There is absolutely no shade for the first 4.0 miles, and not much promise of more beyond that. This trail is also unmaintained by the Forest Service, but has deteriorated at a slower rate than its neighbor to the south—a definite bonus for the hearty few who attempt this route. Don't expect a well-defined path, however, as sections of the trail have virtually disappeared.

For those who can overcome the hellish beginning of this trail, the terrain eventually becomes quite attractive, culminating in a splendid alpine basin on the west side of Sawmill Pass. However, like Baxter Lakes, this charming area may be more easily accessed from the JMT. But, for those who appreciate fine country and few people, the Sawmill Pass Trail does have something to offer.

Sawmill Pass Trail

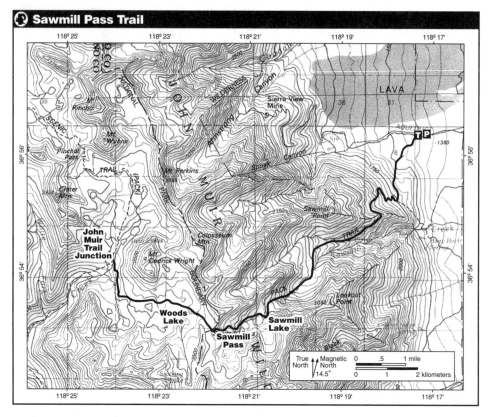

DIRECTIONS TO THE TRAILHEAD: Leave U.S. 395 approximately 17.5 miles south of Big Pine and turn west onto signed Black Springs Road. Proceed 0.8 mile to a T-junction with Tinemaha Road and turn right. After 1.2 miles, turn left onto Division Creek Road and proceed 1.5 miles to the end of pavement near the powerhouse. Continue on dirt road another 0.4 mile to the trailhead.

DESCRIPTION: The trail begins seemingly in the middle of nowhere, heading across a vast ocean of sagebrush toward distant Sawmill Creek canyon. Hikers and backpackers must overcome the first 4.0 miles of trail—a shadeless, waterless, rising traverse along the eastern base of the Sierra—just to reach the canyon. Along the way, you may be able to temper your heat-induced stupor with fixed gazes to the Big Pine volcanic field, where reddish cinder cones and black lava fields break up the sage-colored slopes.

Staggering into the canyon, you encounter a smattering of Jeffrey pines, white firs, and oaks which provide a mirage of shade as you approach the Hogsback. As the trail parallels this sloping ridge, you ford the north tributary of Sawmill Creek three times before crossing over the Hogsback, veering south toward Sawmill Creek canyon, and ascending to Sawmill Meadow (8415'±), 5.5 miles from the trailhead. A pine-covered bench just before the meadow offers a couple of marginal campsites, and a few more appear around the fringe of the meadow itself.

Away from the meadow, you begin a moderate climb up the trail, which follows the southwest-trending canyon. A steeper, zigzagging section of trail through Jeffrey pines and red firs leads to marshy Mule Lake (9735'±) at 6.9 miles. A rocky climb and a pair of creek crossings bring you to lovely Sawmill Lake (10,023'), 7.5 miles from the trailhead. Good campsites beneath foxtail pines will lure overnighters, and a healthy population of brown and rainbow trout will tempt any anglers in your party.

Leaving the lake behind, the winding trail heads for the pass through a diminishing forest of whitebark and foxtail pines, eventually passing timberline. A final climb leads to Sawmill Pass (11,347') and the boundary of Kings Canyon National Park, 9.3 miles from the trailhead.

Beyond the pass, stunning alpine scenery awaits the diligent backpacker. A gentle trail leads to a slightly more pronounced descent that drops you into a lovely alpine basin sprinkled with shimmering lakes and ponds. A smattering of whitebark pines dots a series of verdant, wildflower-carpeted meadows surrounding the lakes, beautiful enough to make you almost forget the previous 9.0 miles of torturous climbing. The obscure path becomes a route-finding challenge, but if you've survived this far, you probably possess the wherewithal to navigate your way through the convoluted basin. Woods Lake (10,710'±) is a short cross-country jaunt south from the trail, offering a few decent campsites and good fishing for rainbow trout. The faint trail continues west before arcing around the lower slopes of Mt. Cedric Wright and dropping to an unsigned connection with the John Muir Trail, marked only by a cairn and a stick.

O Both Mt. Cedric Wright and Colosseum Mtn. provide class 1 ascents from the trail.

R **PERMITS:** Wilderness permit required for overnight stays (quota: 13 per day).

BIGHORN SHEEP AREA: Dogs and domestic sheep prohibited.

CAMPFIRES: Not permitted in Kings Canyon National Park, but permitted east of the pass.

Introduction to the White Mountain Ranger District

Many hikers, backpackers, mountaineers, technical climbers, anglers, equestrians, and photographers have long known about the magnificent beauty in this part of the eastern Sierra. Towering peaks, glacial cirques, flower-bedecked meadows, shimmering alpine lakes, and deeply cleft canyons are all here in abundance. Whether they seek the airy summits of the Palisades or the depths of Evolution Valley, travelers to this part of the Sierra will find exquisite scenery. Some of the most remote and inaccessible backcountry in either of the two national parks or their adjoining wilderness areas is also found within this realm, providing an off-trail enthusiast's Mecca for extended trips into such remote destinations as the Enchanted Gorge and Palisade and Ionian basins. Bounded by the Glacier Divide on the north and the main Sierra crest to the east, the rugged terrain of this part of Kings Canyon National Park is the birthplace of two of the region's mightiest rivers, the South Fork San Joaquin and the Middle Fork Kings.

Such mountain splendor has attracted hordes of admirers over the years, and the demand for wilderness permits is high for areas within reach of weekend backpackers. Less difficult routes over the Sierra crest are also favored by backpackers, such as the Bishop Pass and Piute Pass trails. Advance planning or creative scheduling (starting a trip mid-week) is recommended for the more popular trailheads. Off-trail users with plenty of time will be able to escape the crowds via a number of rugged cross-country routes.

ACCESS: The north-south thoroughfare of U.S. 395 is the principal access route for all eastside trips. Secondary roads branch off toward the trailheads.

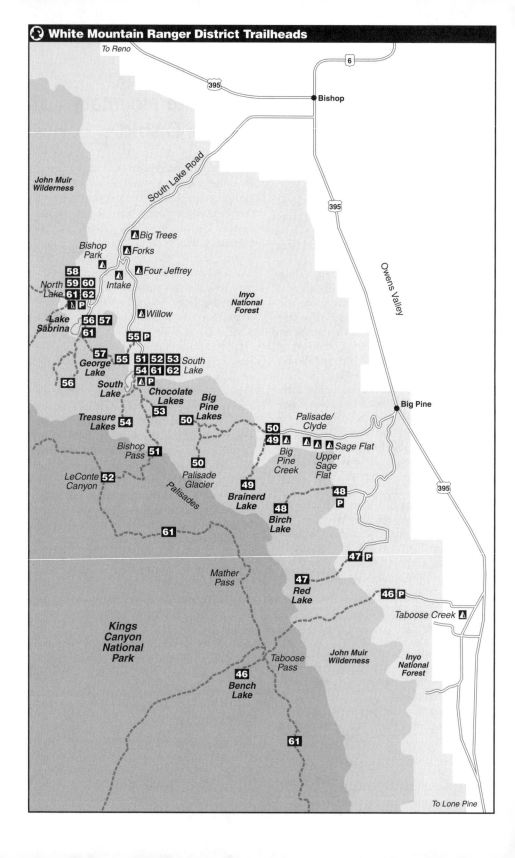

AMENITIES: What you can't find in the small berg of Big Pine you should be able to locate in the larger community of Bishop. Not only does Bishop provide a wide range of choices for the usual tourist-related amenities, but you'll also find stores that actually sell backpacking equipment.

LODGING: Big Pine offers a few small motels, and an extensive selection of motels is available in Bishop. In the mountains above Big Pine and Bishop, there are a number of seasonal resorts that offer food, lodging, and at least a limited range of merchandise.

Glacier Lodge is west of Big Pine near the end of the Glacier Lodge Road. Although the main lodge building burned down a number of years ago, the cabins and trailer park are still open, and the resort offers guided backcountry trips. Showers are available to the general public. Call (760) 938-2837, or visit the lodge web site (www.395.com/glacierlodge/) for more information .

Bishop Creek has a few more offerings, as follows:

Bishop Creek Lodge
2100 South Lake Road
Bishop, CA 93514
(760) 873-4484
www.bishopcreekresorts.com
(housekeeping cabins, restaurant/bar, general store)

Cardinal Village Resort *(open all year)*
Route 1, Box A3
Bishop, CA 93514
(760) 873-4789
(cabins, meeting room, cafe, general store)

Parcher's Resort
2100 South Lake Road
Bishop, CA 93514
(760) 873-4177
www.bishopcreekresorts.com
(housekeeping cabins, restaurant, RV sites)

BACKPACKING EQUIPMENT:

Wilson's Eastside Sports
206 N. Main Street
Bishop, CA 93514
(760) 873-7520

Allen Outdoor Products
200 S. Main Street
Bishop, CA 93514
(760) 873-5903

SHUTTLE SERVICE: The following companies offer trailhead shuttle service: Inyo-Mono Dial-A-Ride (800) 922-1930 or (760) 872-1901; Kountry Korners (877) 656-0756 or (760) 872-3951; and Sierra Express (760) 924-8294.

BUS SERVICE: Greyhound stops in both Big Pine and Bishop.

OUTFITTERS: The following pack stations operate trips into this region:

Bishop Pack Outfitters
247 Cataract Road
Bishop, CA 93514
(760) 873-8877

Rainbow Pack Station
600 S. Main Street
Bishop, CA 93514
(760) 873-8877

Glacier Pack Train
PO Box 321
Big Pine, CA 93513
(760) 938-2538

Rock Creek Pack Station
PO Box 248
Bishop, CA 93515
(760) 872-8331
(760) 935-4493 *(summer)*
www.rockcreekpackstation.com

Mt. Whitney Pack Trains
PO Box 248
Bishop, CA 93515
(760) 872-8331

CAMPGROUNDS

Campground	Fee	Elevation	Season	Restrooms	Running Water	Bear Boxes	Phone
GOODALE CREEK (BLM) 14 mi. S of Big Pine	free	3900'	Mid-April to November	Vault Toilets	No	No	No
TABOOSE CREEK (Inyo Co.) 13 mi. S of Big Pine	$10	3900'	All Year	Vault Toilets	Yes	No	No
TINEMAHA (Inyo Co.) 9 mi. S of Big Pine	$10	3900'	All Year	Vault Toilets	Yes	No	No
BAKER CREEK (Inyo Co.) 0.5 mi. N of Big Pine	$10	4300'	All Year	Vault Toilets	No	No	No
SAGE FLAT Glacier Lodge Road	$13	7400'	Late April to November	Vault Toilets	Yes	No	No
UPPER SAGE FLAT Glacier Lodge Road	$13	7600'	Late April to November	Vault Toilets	Yes	No	No
BIG PINE CREEK Glacier Lodge Road	$13	7700'	Late April to November	Flush Toilets	Yes	Yes	Yes
PALISADE GLACIER/ CLYDE GLACIER (group only) Glacier Lodge Road	$6	8300'	Late April to November	Flush Toilets	Yes	Yes	No
BIG TREES South Lake Road	$14	7500'	Late April to mid-September	Flush Toilets	Yes	No	No
FORKS South Lake Road	$14	7800'	Late-April to mid-September	Flush Toilets	Yes	No	Yes
FOUR JEFFREY South Lake Road	$14	8100'	Late April to November	Flush Toilets	Yes	No	No
INTAKE 2 Lake Sabrina Road	$14	8200'	Late May to November	Flush Toilets	Yes	Yes	No
BISHOP PARK Lake Sabrina Road	$14	8400'	Late May to November	Flush Toilets	Yes	No	No
SABRINA Lake Sabrina Road	$14	9000'	Late May to November	Flush Toilets	Yes	Yes	Yes
WILLOW South Lake Road	$13	9000'	Mid-June to mid-September	Vault Toilets	No	Yes	No
NORTH LAKE (No Trailers or Rv's) North Lake	$14	9500'	Mid-June to mid-September	Vault Toilets	Yes	Yes	No

Sequoia Kings Pack Trains
PO Box 209
Independence, CA 93526
(800) 962-0775
www.395.com/berners/

Pine Creek Pack Station
PO Box 968
Bishop, CA 93515
(800) 962-0775
www.395.com/berners/

RANGER STATION: Inyo National Forest White Mountain Ranger Station is located in the north part of Bishop. Walk-in wilderness permits may be picked up during normal office hours, and bear canisters can be purchased or rented. A broad selection of books and maps is also available for sale.

Mailing address:

White Mountain Ranger District
798 N. Main (U.S. 395)
Bishop, CA 93514
(760) 873-2485

WILDERNESS PERMITS: Quotas are in effect between May 1 and November 1. While 60 percent of a quota is available by advanced reservation, the remaining 40 percent is available on a first-come, first served basis (no fee). A non-refundable, $5 per person fee is required for each member of your party for advance reservations. Reservations may be made up to 6 months before your trip. For wilderness permits, call the reservation line at (760) 873-2483. You may also send your application and arrangements for paying the fee by fax at (760) 873-2484 or by regular mail to:

Inyo National Forest
Wilderness Permit Office
873 North Main Street
Bishop, CA 93514

Advance reservations may be picked up at the ranger station the day before departure.
For more information, visit the Forest Service Web site at www.fs.fed.us/r5/inyo.

GOOD TO KNOW BEFORE YOU GO:
1. Even though you won't find gas for bargain prices in Bishop, it will be a lot less expensive there than in the smaller towns of Big Pine, Independence, and Lone Pine.

TABOOSE CREEK TRAILHEAD

TRIP **46**

Taboose Pass Trail

S ↗ BP

DISTANCE: 10 miles to JMT;
11.75 miles to Bench Lake

ELEVATION: 5425/11,418/10,805,
+6170'/-790'
5425/11,418/10,560,
+6205'/-1065'

SEASON: Mid-July to mid-October

USE: Light

MAPS: *Fish Springs, Aberdeen, Mt. Pinchot*

TRAIL LOG:

7.4	Taboose Pass
10.0	John Muir Trail Jct.
11.75	Bench Lake

INTRODUCTION: The Taboose Pass Trail is the northern entry in the "three not to see" category, along with sister trails over Baxter and Sawmill passes (Trips 44, 45). A low elevation start, lack of shade, and poorly maintained trail combine to make this a trip for only those in great shape who don't mind extreme heat and lousy trail conditions. However, for those who aren't vanquished by the grueling climb before reaching the pass, the sweeping view over a sloping, flower-splashed meadow is one of the most impressive in the High Sierra. In addition, the easy stroll over to lovely Bench Lake is certainly a pleasant experience, but the lake can be reached more easily from the Muir Trail rather than via the steep 7.5-mile climb from a trailhead near the bottom of Owens Valley.

DIRECTIONS TO THE TRAILHEAD: Approximately 12 miles south of Big Pine, leave U.S. 395 and turn west onto paved

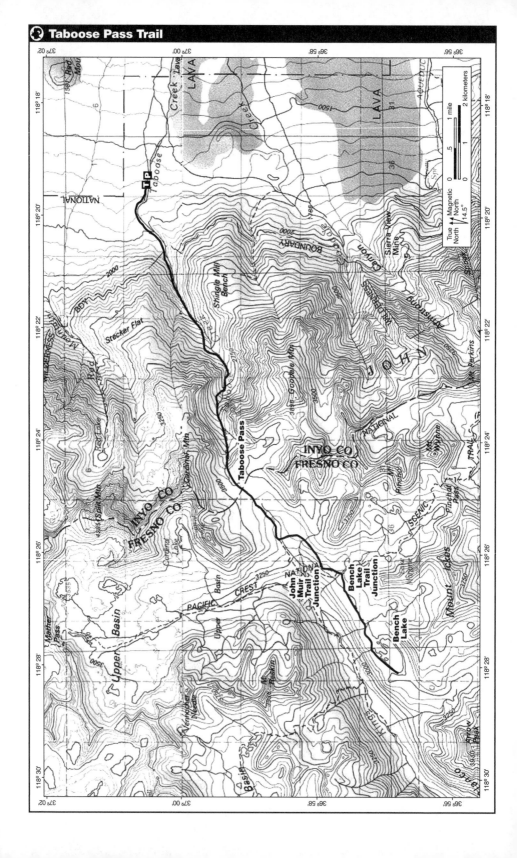

Taboose Creek Road. Proceed 1.1 miles to a four-way junction with Tinemaha Road, and continue straight ahead as the pavement turns to dirt. At 3.5 miles from U.S. 395, bear right at a Y-junction and follow deteriorating FS Road 11S04 another 1.5 miles to a corral. Unless you are driving a durable 4WD vehicle, you should park near the corral, as the final 0.5 mile to the trailhead is over very rough road.

DESCRIPTION: The first part of the journey involves a steadily rising ascent following Taboose Creek through a sea of sagebrush toward the deep gash of Taboose Creek canyon. Once you reach the canyon, you follow the tumbling, willow-lined stream up to a set of switchbacks, after which you traverse to a ford your reach after 3.5 miles. The trail continues its zigzagging climb up the canyon, passing a number of benches and fording the creek several more times before passing timberline. Meadows, wildflowers, and tarns lend an alpine feel to the basin below the pass. At 7.4 miles, you reach the boulder field of Taboose Pass

(11,418') and the boundary of Kings Canyon National Park. The sweeping views southwest to the deep cleft of the South Fork Kings River, west to the shimmering surface of Bench Lake backdropped by the symmetry of Arrow Peak, and west to the towering summit of Mt. Ruskin are all extraordinary.

A more gradual descent greets you on the west side of the pass, as you stroll through gardens of greenery and flowers. After stepping across a rivulet, you encounter an obscure junction. Take the left-hand fork and continue the mild descent, crossing more streams along the way, including one that drains a set of tarns to the east. You pass through a thickening forest of lodgepole pines, and then drop down to a junction with the John Muir Trail (10,805'±) in a broad sloping meadow, 10 miles from the trailhead.

Turning left (south) on the JMT, you step across a small stream, pass the signed lateral to the seasonal ranger station, and come to the ford of the creek that drains Lake Marjorie. Immediately beyond the

Independence Peak and the route to Robinson Lake

creek is a junction with the faint Bench Lake Trail.

At the junction, you head southwest away from the JMT across a flower-laden meadow, then begin a traverse across a granite bench beneath scattered lodgepole pines. Just over a mile from the junction, you ford a shallow stream and pass a pair of ponds before reaching the northeast shore of Bench Lake (10,558'). The trail continues to the west end of the lake before disappearing. Plenty of good campsites are nestled beneath lodgepole pines along the northwest shore. Rainbow and brown trout will entice any anglers in your group. The sight of Arrow Peak from the lakeshore is considered one of the premier views in the High Sierra.

Maintained trail may end at Bench Lake, but a couple of intriguing cross-country routes continue into the trailless backcountry beyond. The first leaves the northwest side of the lake and arcs south around to Arrow Pass (0.7 mile southeast of Arrow Peak), then descends the drainage on the south side of the pass to the trail along Woods Creek at the north end of Paradise Valley.

The second is more difficult and may require the use of an ice axe. Initially, the route is the same until you reach the basin just northeast of Arrow Pass. Instead of crossing Arrow Pass, ascend southeast from the basin to the head of a canyon and climb a steep chute (usually snow-covered) to Explorer Pass (0.9 mile northeast of Pyramid Peak). Drop from the pass heading south and then southeast into the basin east of Pyramid Peak. Follow a stream past a trio of small tarns to the north shore of beautiful Window Peak Lake, where you will find excellent campsites. From the lake, follow alongside the outlet to an intersection with the JMT, approximately 1.0 mile from the Woods Creek crossing.

From Arrow Pass, both Arrow Peak and Pyramid Peak are class 2 climbs. From Explorer Pass, a more moderate class 3

route follows the northeast ridge of Pyramid Peak to the summit.

R **PERMITS:** Wilderness permit required for overnight stays (quota: 13 per day).

CAMPFIRES: Fires permitted along Taboose Creek. Not permitted above 10,000 feet in Kings Canyon National Park.

RED CREEK TRAILHEAD

TRIP **47**

Red Lake

S / DH/BP

DISTANCE: 4.5 miles one way

ELEVATION: 6575/10,460, +4200'/-275'

SEASON: Late June to mid-October

USE: Very light

MAPS: *Fish Springs, Split Mountain*

INTRODUCTION: A long drive over dirt roads, followed by a steep, sweltering climb —why would anyone bother with a trip to Red Lake? The rewards for such an arduous journey are solitude and scenery. So

few people are drawn to Red Lake that for a long time the Forest Service didn't even have a quota for this trail. In 2002, all trails in the Inyo National Forest received quotas whether needed or not. The few who do make the effort are rewarded with a superbly picturesque lake backdropped by the impressive eastern face of Split Mtn., its twin summits separated by a narrow cleft. A high percentage of those who visit Red Lake are mountaineers bound for the easiest ascent of a "fourteener" in the Sierra, not including Mt. Whitney.

There are a few recommendations for this trail that will hopefully make your trip more enjoyable. First, make sure your vehicle is roadworthy. Second, get an early start to avoid the steep climb when temperatures are highest. Finally, pack along plenty of water for the ascent. With these few precautions, you may actually enjoy going where few others dare to tread.

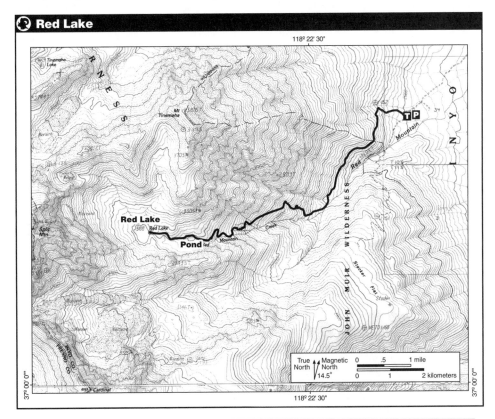

Red Lake

DIRECTIONS TO THE TRAILHEAD: Following 12 miles of dirt road to the beginning of the trail is a large part of the adventure of this trip—plan on an hour to reach the trailhead from Big Pine. In the center of Big Pine, turn west from U.S. 395 onto Crocker Street (which becomes Glacier Lodge Road outside of town) and follow the two-lane, paved road 2.75 miles to McMurry Meadows Road (FS Road 9S03) and turn left. Immediately after the turn onto the dirt road, bear left, bypassing a 4WD road coming in from the right (south). After a very brief climb, veer right and pass under a power line. Continue on well-traveled McMurry Meadows Road, ignoring lesser roads along the way. At 5.75 miles from Glacier Lodge Road, a lesser-used road on the right heads north. This is the route to the trailhead for Birch Lake (see Trip 48).

Continue on McMurry Meadows Road, crossing Birch Creek immediately after the junction with the road to the Birch Lake trailhead. Pass McMurry Meadows to a Y-junction near the 7-mile mark, where you bear left. A crude sign just beyond the

junction marked RED LAKE TRAIL is a reassuring note. A 0.25-mile long descent leads to the crossing of Fuller Creek and a T-junction beyond. Turn left and parallel the creek downstream on rougher road. Cross back to the creek's north bank and continue down the drainage to a major intersection, 9.0 miles from Glacier Lodge Road, where a locked gate blocks your forward progress.

Turn right at the intersection and head south for 0.75 mile, crossing Fuller Creek and Tinemaha Creek, to a T-junction. Turn right (west) and follow FS Road 10S01 another 2 miles to where the road forks. A small sign directs you left toward the trailhead parking area and right toward the beginning of the trail.

DESCRIPTION: Begin your hike by following the north branch of the road uphill toward the start of a single-track trail near a water diversion structure. Although the south branch of the road heads for a short distance directly toward Red Mountain Creek, there is no continuation of road or

Split Mountain rises above a pond along the Red Lake Trail

even trail up the steep, brush-choked canyon. You climb moderately steeply up the hillside, paralleling a spring-fed tributary of Red Mountain Creek. Beyond a series of short switchbacks, you continue the steady climb, soon bending south to cross a seasonal drainage and the sagebrush-covered hillside. Without the customary fanfare of a sign, you pass uneventfully into the John Muir Wilderness and follow the trail on a curving ascent into the Red Mountain Creek canyon, where the trail momentarily assumes a more gently ascending grade. Before steep climbing resumes, the trail briefly comes alongside the creek, approximately 1.5 miles from the trailhead.

A steep, zigzagging ascent leads away from the creek, up a gully, and across a seasonal stream toward some cliffs. After a moderate stretch of trail, the steeper climb continues as you cross a rocky wash and zigzag up the hillside to a thicket of vegetation, where a cool, refreshing stream courses through a cleft of rock. A few lonely pines make an appearance, granting you some hope that all of this climbing will eventually lead to more mountain-like terrain above. You soon cross another stream lined with dense vegetation, step over a rocky wash, and emerge on the slope above Red Mountain Creek once more. Just as you near the willow-lined stream, a switchback leads you away on a lengthy diagonal ascent across the hillside. Views east of the Owens Valley and the Inyo Mountains beyond improve as you climb farther up the trail. Another switchback leads you back to the canyon and a fine view to the west of Split Mtn. After more climbing, the trail levels off and, gratefully, you reach an unnamed pond, 3.75 miles from the trailhead. Here the view of Split Mtn. across the surface of the pond is quite impressive. At the pond's far end, a number of decent campsites will tempt backpackers after the stiff climb.

The trail passes half way around the north shore of the pond before petering out in some talus, reappearing briefly beyond the pond (more campsites), and then disappearing for good beneath a talus slide. A 0.25-mile scramble takes you to the east shore of Red Lake (10,459').

Surrounded by pockets of willow and widely scattered whitebark and foxtail pines, Red Lake rests dramatically below the steep talus slope and vertical walls of the east face of Split Mtn. (14,058'). Crude campsites suggest that the camping is better back down the trail along the creek or near the pond. Anglers may wish to ply the waters in search of golden trout.

⊙ For most hikers and backpackers, Red Mountain Creek canyon has no viable options for further wanderings. However, competent cross-country trekkers can cross the Sierra crest via a class 2-route over Red Lake Pass, 0.4 mile north of Split Mtn., to Upper Basin.

⊙ Mountaineers can ascend Split Mtn. from the pass via the relatively easy North Slope route.

R PERMITS: Wilderness permit required for overnight stays (quota: 10 per day).
CAMPFIRES: Permitted.

TRIP 48

Birch Lake

S ↗ DH / BP

DISTANCE: 5.5 miles one way

ELEVATION: 6485/10,800, +4615'/-300'

SEASON: Late June to mid-October

USE: Very light

MAPS: *Fish Springs, Split Mountain*

INTRODUCTION: Dirt road access, a low-elevation trailhead, and an infrequently maintained trail combine to dissuade most hikers and backpackers from even considering the trip to Birch Lake. Despite these perceived drawbacks, Birch Lake is quite scenic, nestled near the Sierra crest in the broad canyon of aspen-lined Birch Creek, between The Thumb and Birch Mtn. The sketchy trail dead-ends below the lake, making this trip well suited for either a dayhike or an overnight backpack.

DIRECTIONS TO THE TRAILHEAD: In the center of Big Pine, turn west from U.S. 395 onto Crocker Street (which becomes

Glacier Lodge Road outside of town) and follow the two-lane, paved road 2.75 miles to McMurry Meadows Road (FS Road 9S03) and turn left. Immediately after the turn onto the dirt road, bear left, bypassing a 4WD road coming in from the right (south). After a very brief climb, veer right and pass under a power line. Continue on well-traveled McMurry Meadows Road, ignoring lesser roads along the way. At 5.75 miles from Glacier Lodge Road, just before the crossing of Birch Creek, turn right (north) onto a lesser-used road and continue 0.6 mile to a T-junction. Bear right, drive another 0.1 mile and find limited parking near a closed gate.

DESCRIPTION: Initially, you follow a closed 4WD road about 100 yards to a trailhead sign and then continue up the road through a field of tall grass and occasional clumps of wild rose. Sagebrush-covered terrain alternates with meadows on the way to a Y-junction, 0.75 mile from the trailhead. Although the left-hand road heads toward Birch Creek, your route follows the right-hand branch up a seasonal drainage. Eventually, the road becomes a single-track trail that heads directly up a sandy wash. A switchback leads you out of the sandy wash onto more solid footing, from where you have fine views to the east of Owens Lake and the White Mountains. On a steady,

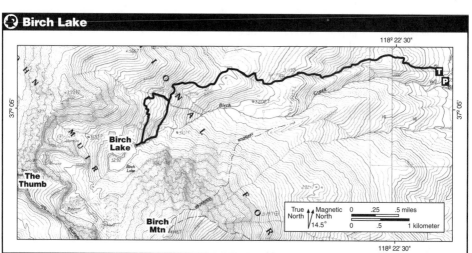

Birch Creek Canyon

winding climb you proceed over a hill and then a more moderate ascent leads you into the canyon of a seasonal tributary of Birch Creek. You follow this tributary by climbing moderately steeply past a tiny, spring-fed stream, then out of the drainage and up a grassy slope to an unsigned trail junction, 3.75 miles from the trailhead.

Bear left at the junction and follow the horseshoe curve of the trail around a side canyon. Follow by climbing up to the top of a rise with a spectacular view of the Owens Valley. Drop off the rise and descend into the next drainage. From this point the sketchy trail becomes hard to follow, splitting into two faint paths, each offering a slightly different approach to Birch Lake. The route as shown on the *Split Mountain* quad continues up the drainage and crosses the creek above a spring, and then heads south on a 0.75-mile traverse into the main canyon of Birch Creek just below the lake. The alternate route crosses the drainage immediately to head directly

over to the main canyon of Birch Creek well below the lake. Whichever of these two faint trails you decide to follow, both lead into the beautiful canyon of Birch Creek, where a number of primitive camp- sites can be found alongside the tumbling creek below the lake. To reach the lake, head upstream through the open canyon, then over talus to a meadow just below the lake. Birch Lake lies in a broad valley with excellent views up toward the Sierra crest. Anglers can test their skill on good-sized cutthroat trout.

🔲 Options are few for further wanderings in the Birch Creek drainage. A class 3 cross-country route provides access to the upper Palisade Creek drainage over Birch Creek Pass (12,800'), 0.4 mile south of The Thumb.

🔲 Mountaineers can climb Birch Mtn. (class 2) by ascending the moraine south of Birch Lake to the saddle southwest of the peak, and then climbing along the ridge to the summit. Overall, an ascent of The Thumb (class 2–3) is straightforward, once you surmount the cliff 0.5 mile southwest of the lake.

R **PERMITS:** Wilderness permit required for overnight stays (quota: 10).
   CAMPFIRES: Permitted.

TRIP **49**

South Fork Big Pine Creek to Brainerd Lake

S   ⟋   DH / BP / X

DISTANCE: 4.9 miles to Brainerd Lake; + 0.5 mile cross-country to Finger Lake

Elevation: 7750/10,790, +3740'/-700'

SEASON: Mid-July to early October

USE: Moderate

MAPS: *Coyote Flat, Split Mountain*

TRAIL LOG:
   3.8   Willow Lake Jct.
   4.9   Brainerd Lake
   5.4   Finger Lake

INTRODUCTION: Alpinists from all over the world come to test their skills on the bevy of 14,000-foot. peaks known as the Palisades. Splendid Sierra granite combined with dependably pleasant summer weather lure many mountaineers and technical climbers to the faces and ridges of these highly challenging and picturesque mountains. Hikers and backpackers have the opportunity to enjoy the splendid alpine scenery of the Middle Palisades on this trail up South Fork Big Pine Creek to Brainerd Lake, and to the off-trail backcountry beyond. This is definitely one trip where you'd better not forget your camera.

   Although the scenery is heavenly, parts of the steep ascent may seem to have less divine origins. The first half of the trip is a reasonable climb on decent trail up the moderate angle of South Fork Big Pine Creek, but the second half requires hikers and backpackers to surmount steep terrain on rough, poorly maintained trail. Those fortunate enough to survive the climb will

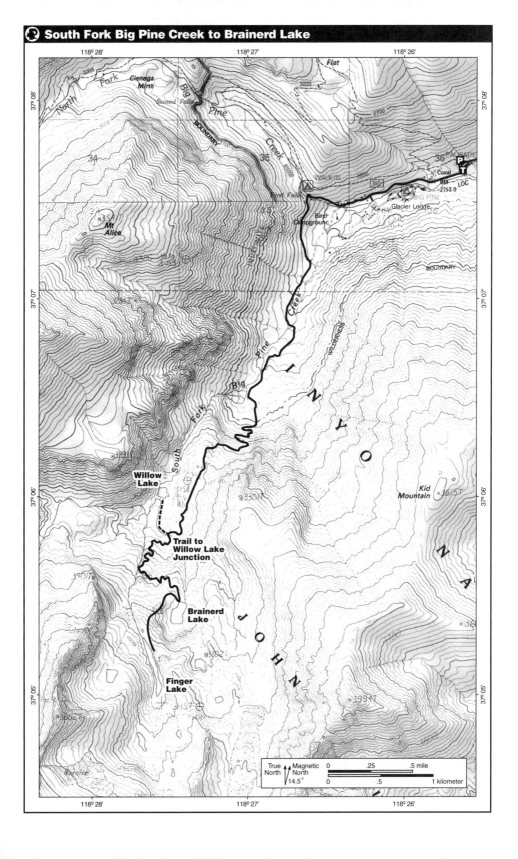

find superb "rooms with a view" at campsites near the shorelines of both Brainerd and Finger lakes.

DIRECTIONS TO THE TRAILHEAD: In the center of Big Pine, turn west from U.S. 395 onto Crocker Street (Glacier Lodge Road) and follow the two-lane, paved road past campgrounds to the overnight parking area, 9.2 miles from U.S. 395. Dayhikers may drive another 0.75 mile to the parking lot at the end of the road. Pit toilets are located near both the overnight and day-use trailheads.

DESCRIPTION: Rather than starting your journey from the overnight parking lot on the trail traversing the hillside north of the Glacier Lodge Road (see Trip 50), descend to the road and walk the pavement 0.75 mile to the dayhiker parking lot. As you walk through forest alongside Big Pine Creek, follow signs directing you past a closed steel gate and up a continuation of the road past some cabins. Soon the road turns into a single-track trail. You climb up a forested hillside on rock steps to a bridge

across the creek. From the bridge, continue 0.1 mile to a junction and bear left, across an open, sagebrush-covered slope. Enjoying striking views up the South Fork Big Pine Creek canyon of Norman Clyde Peak and Middle Palisade, you cross an old road and follow the course of South Fork Big Pine Creek. Cottonwoods line the creek, but along the trail you pass through a more arid area, where vegetation includes sagebrush and cactus. You continue up the canyon on a moderate grade, crossing a seasonal stream and proceeding across boulder-strewn slopes to a ford of the creek, lined with willow and birch, 1.7 miles from the backpackers parking area.

From the ford, you head upstream on a mild grade toward a hillside. Soon the grade of the trail increases and you begin a steep, winding ascent. Rocky switchbacks lead up through scattered limber pines to the base of nearly vertical bluffs. You traverse across the hillside before bending left and climbing steeply up a narrow cleft of rock to a crest. A short distance ahead awaits a splendid panorama of the southern

South Fork Big Pine Creek canyon

Palisades, stretching from Mt. Sill to The Thumb. This vista will rival any in the Sierra for stunning alpine scenery. From the viewpoint, you drop briefly into cover of lodgepole pines, pass a spring-fed rivulet, and then reach the T-junction with the lateral trail to Willow Lake, 3.8 miles from the overnight parking lot.

SIDE TRIP TO WILLOW LAKE: Willow Lake (9565') is just 0.3 mile from the main trail. Sediments are steadily transforming this body of water into more of a marshy meadow than a lake, and early in the summer the standing water creates a favorable environment for the breeding of mosquitoes. However, there are a couple of nice campsites beneath lodgepole pines here, in case you got a late start or are too pooped for the next stretch of climbing to Brainerd Lake. A class 2 cross-country route over Contact Pass can be used as a connection between the South and North Forks of Big Pine Creek. **END OF SIDE TRIP**

From the junction, make a short descent down to a crossing of the lushly vegetated outlet stream from Brainerd Lake. The climb resumes beyond the crossing as you make a winding ascent across lodgepole-covered slopes near the stream draining Finger Lake. Turning east, you pass a small pond and continue uphill via switchbacks to a hump of granite, from where you can see Willow Lake below. You pass a second pond, make a quick descent across a marshy meadow, and swing around a granite ledge as you make the final climb southeast to the lip of Brainerd Lake.

The opal-tinted, icy waters of Brainerd Lake (10,256), 5.0 miles from the trailhead, are tucked into a deep, glacier-carved bowl of granite. Steep cliffs nearly surround the lake, and snow oftentimes lingers in their narrow crevices well into late summer. The summits of the craggy, glacier-clad peaks of the Palisades loom over the top of cliffs thousands of feet above. A smattering of compact campsites are found near the outlet, sheltered by lodgepole and whitebark pines. Anglers may wish to test their luck on the brook trout that inhabit the lake.

Without question, the setting of Brainerd Lake is stunning, but to come all this way and not go beyond the lake would be to miss out on some even more extraordinary scenery. With a modicum of cross-country skills, you can quite easily make the 0.5-mile trek to Finger Lake. Follow a use-trail from near the outlet of Brainerd Lake on an arcing ascent above the cliffs around the northwest shore. Continue the climb toward the lake basin, following ducks as you weave through a field of boulders just before the lake. Finger Lake (10,787') conjures up images of a miniature Norwegian fjord, occupying as it does a narrow cleft in the rock that arcs toward the crest of the Palisades. Scattered pines dot the lakeshore, while tiny pockets of grasses and wildflowers attempt to soften the harshness of the otherwise rocky basin. A number of campsites are located just below the lake between the outlet and the trail.

A difficult, class 3 cross-country route requiring mountaineering equipment crosses the Sierra crest southwest of The Thumb at Southfork Pass (12,560'). However, for those whose wish is not to cross the crest but only to see one of the Sierra's largest glaciers, the cross-country route up the canyon above Finger Lake to the base of Middle Palisade is straightforward and not technically challenging. The ascent can be physically taxing, especially at this altitude, but the rewards of such dramatic alpine scenery more than compensate for the effort.

R **PERMITS:** Wilderness permit required for overnight stays (quota: 12 per day).

CAMPFIRES: Not permitted.

TRIP 50

North Fork Big Pine Creek to Big Pine Lakes

Ⓜ 𝒫 DH/BPx

DISTANCE: 12.5 miles semi-loop trip

ELEVATION: 7750/10,815, +3170'/-3170'

SEASON: Mid-July to early October

USE: Moderate to Heavy

MAPS: *Coyote Flat, Split Mountain, Mt. Thompson, North Palisade*

TRAIL LOG:

4.25	Black Lake Trail Jct.
4.25	First Lake
5.5	Third Lake
6.25	Glacier Trail Jct.
6.5	four-way Trail Jct.
7.25	Black Lake
8.25	North Fork Trail Jct.

INTRODUCTION: The North Fork Big Pine Creek Trail offers some of the best mountain scenery in the entire Sierra. Piercing the sky near the upper heights of the range, the Palisades comprise a craggy spine of tall peaks robed in scenic splendor as picturesque and dramatic as any in California, if not the entire western U.S. Clinging beneath the north faces of these rugged 13,000- to 14,000-foot peaks, glaciers, including the Palisade Glacier, largest in the Sierra, give the area an alpine feel. Even the lower peaks cast a bold and rugged presence, such as Temple Crag, which offers a classic challenge for technical climbers and a spectacular profile as seen from a variety of vantage points around the Big Pine Lakes basin. Nestled beneath the shadow of these giant peaks, the glacier-scoured Big Pine Lakes, with their milky-turquoise

waters, offer rewarding destinations for overnight stays. Many of these lakes are blessed with excellent vistas of the surrounding peaks and rugged terrain.

Such spectacular scenery is bound to inspire numerous visits by recreationists, and the area is definitely quite popular with hikers, backpackers, climbers, anglers, equestrians, and photographers. After the 5-mile hike up North Fork Big Pine Creek to the beginning of the Big Pine Lakes basin, most campers seem to congregate around First, Second, and Third lakes. Not only are they the first lakes encountered after the stiff climb, but mountaineers and rock climbers must pass by these lakes on their way to the majority of the climbing routes above. A greater degree of solitude can be found at some of the lakes off the main North Fork loop, such as Fifth, Sixth, Seventh, Summit, and Black lakes. Any one of the lakes provides a fine base camp for further wanderings to the other destinations in the basin or up the Glacier Trail. If time permits, a hike up this rocky path to the verdant ribbon of Sam Mack Meadow, and a continuation up the more primitive route to the edge of the Palisade Glacier, with a close-up view of the Palisades, are musts for anyone who visits the area.

DIRECTIONS TO THE TRAILHEAD: In the center of Big Pine, turn west from U.S. 395 onto Crocker Street (Glacier Lodge Road) and follow the two-lane, paved road past campgrounds to the overnight parking area, 9.2 miles from U.S. 395. Hikers may opt to drive to the day-use parking lot at the end of the road.

DESCRIPTION: From the overnight parking lot, follow the North Fork Big Pine Creek Trail on an upward traverse across a sagebrush-covered hillside, passing directly above the pack station.

Soon, impressive views of the Middle Palisades area, including Norman Clyde Peak and the Palisade Crest, appear up the South Fork Big Pine Creek canyon. A mile from the trailhead, as the trail bends northwest into the North Fork drainage, you

GLACIER LODGE

Across the highway, as you pass the pack station, are Big Pine Campground, cabins, a general store, and the foundation of the historic Glacier Lodge. The cabins and trailer park here are open. The lodge, however, which had been rebuilt after a 1969 avalanche destroyed it, burned to the ground in 1998.

pass above First Falls Walk-In Campground and quickly come to a signed Y-junction, where a trail angles through the campground and down to the day-use parking lot.

You continue the ascent through open terrain with a fine view of Second Falls a

mile up the canyon. Eventually, you reach a signed four-way junction. The right-hand trail heads uphill toward Baker Lake, and the trail on your left descends to the creek valley and follows a closed road, partially destroyed in the 1982 flood, back toward the day-use parking lot. You go straight.

As you proceed, the trail bends toward Second Falls, switchbacks up a hillside, crosses the John Muir Wilderness boundary, and then climbs a chasm. Above the falls, you climb moderately alongside the shady creek for a spell, wander back out into the open, and then encounter gently graded trail amid a dense stand of aspens and lodgepole pines occupying a flat known as Cienega Mirth (a combination of *cienaga*, a misspelled Spanish word, and *mirth*, a Scottish word, both meaning swampy place). A number of pleasant campsites are scattered about the area.

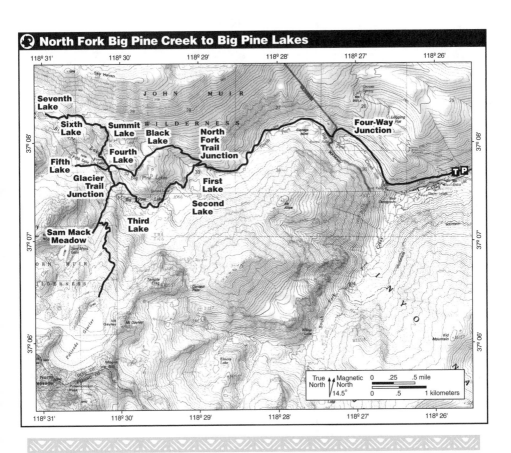

North Fork Big Pine Creek to Big Pine Lakes

THE LON CHANEY CABIN

In what may feel like the middle of nowhere sits a distinguished granite fieldstone cabin with a gabled roof and overhanging eaves. Currently being used by Forest Service rangers as a wilderness cabin, it was originally built in the 1920s by silent film star Lon Chaney Sr., who used it as a summer retreat for fishing, hunting, and relaxing. Listed on the National Register of Historic Places, the cabin was designed by Paul Revere Williams (1894–1980), the first African-American granted a fellowship by the American Institute of Architects.

A short way up the trail, just over 2.5 miles from the trailhead, you may be surprised to see a renovated cabin.

Beyond the cabin, you pass through an open area where you catch a glimpse of the rugged peaks up the canyon. The climb resumes as you wander to and away from the creek numerous times through areas of lush vegetation and light forest. You follow the trail as it curves west, offering occasional views of the dramatic northeast face of Temple Crag along the way. At 4.0 miles from the overnight parking area, you cross the willow-lined North Fork Big Pine Creek and climb more steeply via switchbacks, quickly coming to another crossing of the creek. More climbing leads to a signed junction with the Black Lake Trail, 4.25 miles from the overnight parking lot.

Follow the left-hand trail from the junction, signed LAKES 1–7, immediately cross the North Fork again, pass a couple of campsites, and continue the climb through scattered forest, granite slabs and boulders. Soon you hear the sound of a waterfall, and through the trees you catch a glimpse of the milky-turquoise, glacier-fed waters of First Lake (9975'±) below, 4.5 miles from the trailhead. A zigzagging ascent brings you to a spectacular overlook of Second Lake with the ramparts of Temple Crag behind.

Although Second Lake (10,059') is the largest in the chain of Big Pine Lakes, much of the shoreline is too steep to provide decent camping. A few isolated campsites are spread around Second Lake, but most campers are content with sites above the west shore of First Lake. Anglers can test their skill on rainbow, brook, and brown trout in both lakes.

A mildly graded trail leads you well above the north shore of Second Lake, where a sparse covering of forest permits fine views of the surrounding terrain. You'll see dramatic, precipitous flying buttresses rising toward the summit of Temple Crag, looming high above the shimmering water. These formations lure climbers from around the world. In stark contrast is the massive rock pile to the east of Second Lake known as Mt. Alice. (Steve Roper expressed his disdain for Mt. Alice in *Climbers Guide to the High Sierra* by calling it "one of the ugliest peaks in the Sierra

Angler at Second Lake

—a veritable pile of rubble.") Separating the two peaks is Contact Pass, where the distinction between darker and lighter shades of granite on either side is quite evident. A cross-country route over the pass provides a connection between the North and South forks of Big Pine Creek (see Options, below).

Beyond Second Lake, you come alongside its inlet creek and climb up through rocky terrain under a covering of lodgepole pines. You veer away from the creek and soon come to the north shore of Third Lake (10,249'), 5.5 miles from the overnight parking area. An even more impressive view of Temple Crag awaits, and this is perhaps the reason this lake is the most popular of the Big Pine Lakes among campers. Plenty of campsites are sprinkled about the lightly forested lakeshore, and anglers may be tempted by the brook and rainbow trout gliding through the water.

Leaving Third Lake, you follow switchbacks north up a hillside. Behind you is a view of Third Lake occupying a rocky bowl at the base of Temple Crag. To the south, the summits of the Palisades burst into view over the foreground ridge. The massive face of Mt. Robinson, with Aperture Peak peeking out behind, dominates the view to the southwest. The grade of the trail eases a bit as you pass a small meadow and step over the tiny creek draining Fourth Lake. Just beyond the creek, you reach a signed trail junction with the Glacier Trail near a grove of pines, 6.25 miles from the overnight parking area.

SIDE TRIP TO SAM MACK MEADOW AND PALISADE GLACIER: From the junction, head southwest through a willow-covered meadow and across the stream emanating from Fifth Lake, to a rocky slope where a moderately steep zigzagging ascent begins. You continue up the slope through widely scattered whitebark pines, passing a luxuriant spring-fed grotto carpeted with wildflowers along the way. Farther up the hillside the trail ascends alongside the creek through more flowers, including paintbrush, butter-

cup, shooting star, daisy, aster, and columbine. As the climb levels out and sedges appear, you crest the lip of a basin and stroll into the lower end of Sam Mack Meadow (11,035'±).

The long, thin band of verdant Sam Mack Meadow is hemmed in by steep walls of grayish granite and bisected by a sinuous creek tinged with glacial milk. Patches of snow cling to precipitous walls near the head of the canyon, lingering throughout the short summers common at this elevation. A few campsites are perched on the sloping, sandy bench adjacent to the meadows, surrounded by scattered clumps of dwarf pine. A footpath extends to the end of the meadows, but Sam Mack Lake is most easily reached via a cross-country route up the western lip of the canyon wall.

To head toward the Palisade Glacier, you must ford the creek near the lower end of Sam Mack Meadow. A small sign simply marked TRAIL pointed across the wide but shallow creek to the use-trail that ascends the east slope of the basin. Follow this trail on a winding course up the rocky hillside to a ridgecrest. Once at the crest, bend right (south) and continue to wind around boulders and over rocks amid scattered whitebark pines on the left side of the ridge. Excellent views of the Big Pine Lakes basin are plentiful along this part of the climb. Approximately 1.0 mile from Sam Mack Meadow, the route bends southeast and makes an ascending traverse over to a moraine. The path becomes less discernible as you climb more steeply over talus, boulders and rock slabs. Ducks may help guide you through this ascent, which ultimately leads to an overlook of the glacier and a stunning panorama of the Palisades. **END OF SIDE TRIP**

From the Glacier Trail junction, head northwest on a moderate climb, beside rocks, boulders, and scattered pines, with pleasant views of the Palisades. At 6.5 miles from the overnight parking lot, you come to a four-way junction, with the Black Lake Trail heading to the right and a lateral trail to Fifth Lake going left. The left-hand trail reaches Fifth Lake in 0.25 mile. The middle route, a continuation of the North Fork Trail, provides access to Sixth, Seventh, and Summit lakes. For the continuation of your loop, turn right on the Black Lake Trail. Dead ahead you see Fourth Lake, a forest-rimmed body of water lacking some of the incredible views offered by the other Big Pine Lakes, but with plenty of campsites nearby.

SIDE TRIP TO FIFTH LAKE: From the four-way junction, a short trail heads left through light pine forest to the creek draining Fifth Lake. You continue alongside this willow-lined creek on a mild climb to the east shore of the picturesque lake. Rugged mountains, including Mt. Robinson, Two Eagle Peak, and Aperture Peak, form a scenic arc around this sapphire lake. As if those peaks didn't provide a stunning enough backdrop, the more distant summits of Temple Crag, Mt. Gayley, Mt. Sill, and the Inconsolable Range add even more exquisite alpine scenery. A smattering of pines dot the shoreline and lower slopes of the lake basin, while grasses, sedges, and shrubs occupy small pockets of soil in between rock cliffs and talus slopes. Pleasant campsites are sprinkled around the inlet and farther around the shoreline. **END OF SIDE TRIP**

SIDE TRIP TO SIXTH AND SEVENTH LAKES AND SUMMIT LAKE: From the four-way junction, follow the trail straight (northwest) above the west shore of Fourth Lake and climb up the hillside above the lake past some campsites. The grade of ascent increases as you cross the willow-lined stream that flows into Fourth Lake. Near the stream an old, obscure path departs from the main trail and heads left (northwest) to Sixth Lake, but this path ends up being more of a cross-country route than a bona fide trail. Hiking in the opposite direction on a faint path quickly leads to a level ridge-top camping area with incredible views. **END OF SIDE TRIP**

> **FOURTH LAKE LODGE**
>
> The amazing vista of the Palisades, spanning from Temple Crag all the way to Mt. Winchell and including the Palisade Glacier, is the reason that Fourth Lake Lodge was built here in the 1920s. The Forest Service removed the lodge's stone house and eight wooden cabins after passage of the original Wilderness Act in 1964, leaving only a flat area and some scattered pieces of very small lumber.

From the creek, you continue the ascent and reach a signed trail junction, 0.5 mile from the four-way junction with the North Fork Trail. The left-hand trail heads to Sixth and Seventh lakes, and the right-hand trail goes to Summit Lake.

To reach Sixth Lake, turn north and climb moderately steeply on rocky trail via some switchbacks. The grade of ascent momentarily abates as you pass a pond surrounded by a small meadow. Beyond the meadow, you follow more switchbacks to the top of a lightly forested rise, where a short stroll away from the trail will take you to another incredible view of the Palisades. Drop off the rise to a meadow and cross a creek, then make a short climb that takes you over a rock hump to a smaller meadow. After more climbing the grade eases as Sixth Lake comes into view. A short descent leads to the lakeshore.

The ambience at Sixth Lake (11,088') is more pastoral than at most of the other Big Pine Lakes. Meadows surround the lake and low rises dotted with whitebark pines present a softer backdrop. The open terrain allows for fine views of Mt. Robinson, Two Eagle Peak, and Cloudripper, as well as the more distant Temple Crag and Mt. Gayley. Campsites are scattered above the lake on low rises.

Although no trail runs between Sixth and Seventh lakes, the route is easy over open meadowlands dotted with clumps of willow. Simply travel northwest and parallel the course of a stream for less than 0.25 mile to Seventh Lake's east shore. The lake itself is quite pleasant, tucked in an open basin below the slopes of Cloudripper. A few campsites appear here and there, sufficient to handle the few groups of campers who make it this far.

To reach Summit Lake, turn right (northeast) at the junction with the trail to Sixth Lake and make a moderate climb to the crest of a ridge. Soon you glimpse the lake through the trees and a quick descent takes you to the lakeshore, 0.5 mile from the junction. The roughly oval, forest-lined lake is perched on a bench above a steep drop that plummets toward Black Lake, which may account for its name. Campsites seem plentiful for the amount of use the lake receives. Brook trout will test the skill of anglers.

From the four-way junction with the trails to Fifth, Sixth, Seventh, and Summit lakes, follow the Black Lake Trail by turning northeast, skirting the south shore of Fourth Lake on a mild decline through scattered-to-light forest. Soon, a gentle ascent leads over a forested rise before a moderate descent takes you through a stand of lodgepole pines to Black Lake (10,690'±), 7.25 miles from the overnight parking lot. A number of fine campsites are around the lakeshore and above the trail. The lake is home to brook and rainbow trout.

A steeper descent leads away from Black Lake. Eventually, you leave the forest behind and break out into the open to views of Mt. Alice and Temple Crag across the North Fork canyon, and of Mt. Sill and North Palisade along the crest. Farther along the trail, several of the Big Pine Lakes also come into view. Long switchbacks lead across a sagebrush-covered slope dotted with mountain mahogany, wild rose, and occasional whitebark and lodgepole pines. One mile from Black Lake and 8.25 miles from the parking lot, you close the loop as you arrive at the junction with the North Fork Trail. From the junction, turn left and retrace your steps 4.25 miles to the trailhead.

O Options are many for the backpacker blessed with plenty of time to explore the hinterlands around North Fork Big Pine Creek. Aside from visiting all the lakes and traveling up the Glacier Trail to the Palisade Glacier, a number of cross-country routes will entice the off-trail enthusiast. From Third Lake a route crosses Contact Pass, providing a connection between the North Fork and South Fork drainages. A class 2–3 route over Jigsaw Pass in the Inconsolable Range provides a link between Fifth Lake and the Bishop Pass Trail. More-technical cross-country routes over Glacier Notch and Agassiz Col will appeal to mountaineer-types.

O The Palisades are a climber's paradise. No other area in the Sierra provides as many challenging routes up so many classic peaks. Unfortunately, less skilled peak baggers have fewer routes to choose from, as only a few non-technical climbs are available, including the south ridge of Mt. Agassiz from Agassiz Col and the east ridge of Cloudripper.

R **PERMITS:** Wilderness permit required for overnight stays (quota: 25 per day). **CAMPFIRES:** Not permitted.

TRIP 51

Bishop Pass Trail to Long, Saddlerock, and Bishop Lakes

Ⓜ ✒ DH/BP

DISTANCE: 4.3 miles one way to Bishop Lake

ELEVATION: 9845/11,325, +1740'/-260'

SEASON: Early July to mid-October

USE: Heavy

MAPS: *Mt. Thompson, North Palisade*

TRAIL LOG:

.75 Treasure Lakes Trail Jct.
1.9 Chocolate Lakes Trail Jct.
2.25 Long Lake
2.7 Chocolate Lakes Trail Jct.
3.75 Saddlerock Lake
4.3 Bishop Lake

INTRODUCTION: The Bishop Pass Trail provides backpackers with one of the least difficult ways over the Sierra crest and into Kings Canyon National Park (see Trip 52). The terrain south of Bishop Pass is highly popular with backpackers, hikers, equestrians, and anglers alike, with wilderness permits and parking spaces at a premium, especially on weekends. You won't find much solitude here without leaving the security of the trail. However, if you don't mind a little company, a bounty of picturesque lakes surrounded by stunning alpine peaks provide desirable destinations for either a day trip or an overnight visit. Rushing streams, vibrant wildflowers, verdant pocket meadows, and groves of pine forest provide the finishing touches to this classic eastern Sierra journey.

DIRECTIONS TO THE TRAILHEAD: From U.S. 395 in the center of Bishop, turn west onto Line Drive, which beyond the city limits becomes South Lake Road (Highway 168). Proceed southwest on South Lake Road 15 miles to a junction, where you turn left. Continue on the paved road another 6.75 miles to the end, near South Lake. Backpackers must park in the overnight lot. When this lot is full, additional parking is available 1.3 miles back down the road—a footpath connects the lower and upper lots. Dayhikers may park below the upper overnight parking lot in spaces marked NO OVERNIGHT PARKING. Restrooms and water are available near the trailhead.

DESCRIPTION: Begin your hike at the well-marked trailhead near the overnight parking lot, making a very short and steep descent through an area of lush vegetation. A mild climb follows as you pass well above the east shore of South Lake through young aspens and lodgepole pines. Soon you break out into the open to fine views of the terrain up the canyon and quickly begin a steeper ascent up a hillside. Enter the John Muir Wilderness and continue the climb to a Y-junction with the Treasure Lakes Trail, 0.75 mile from the trailhead (see Trip 54).

Veer to the left (southeast) from the junction and follow the Bishop Pass Trail through light lodgepole forest to a crossing of a small, flower-lined creek on a plank bridge. A moderate climb follows to an unmarked, faint trail junction, at 1.4 miles, with the partly cross-country route to seldom-visited Marie Lakes. Hikers in search of solitude can follow this route northeast to a marshy meadow and then steeply southeast to the lakes.

Just beyond this junction, you come alongside and then cross another small creek. Now you encounter a series of short switchbacks, which lead you over granite outcrops and boulders through scattered pines. At 1.9 miles you come to a marked Y-junction with the Chocolate Lakes Trail (see Trip 53).

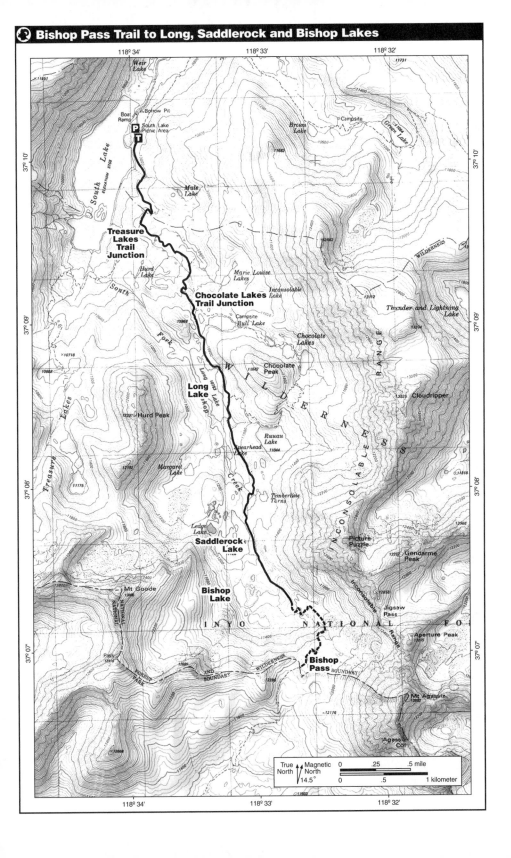

You continue on the Bishop Pass Trail from the junction and make an easy 0.25-mile stroll over to the north shore of aptly named Long Lake (10,753'). The elongated lake is surrounded by green meadows, granite boulders, and scattered trees. The crystal-blue waters are sprinkled with tiny islets and reflect the craggy images of Mt. Goode and Hurd Peak. The lovely scenery, close proximity to the South Lake trailhead, and decent population of rainbow, brook, and brown trout combine to make the lake a very popular destination with most backpackers, hikers, and anglers. Campsites abound around the overused lakeshore, particularly on the knoll near the south end of the lake. Long Lake seems to go on forever as you follow the trail along the east shore, occasionally right at the water's edge but sometimes a good distance away. Near the far end of the lake, 2.7 miles from the trailhead, you come to a marked T-junction with the south end of the Chocolate Lakes Trail.

Long Lake and Mt. Goode

Beyond the junction, you continue along the shore of Long Lake, cross the inlet stream from Ruwau Lake, and start to climb again through a light-to-scattered forest of whitebark pines. Through small grassy meadows, fields of rock, and patches of wildflowers you climb across the slope to the east of Spearhead Lake (10,750±). The lake is quite picturesque, with the spine of the Inconsolable Range as a backdrop. Limited campsites are scattered around the lake and fishing is reported as fair for rainbow and brook trout. Easy cross-country travel leads west from Spearhead Lake 0.3 mile to isolated Margaret Lake (10,970±).

A 0.5-mile climb from Spearhead Lake leads up a rocky slope to the lovely Timberline Tarns. Sparkling waterfalls and tumbling cascades greet you along the way. Although most campers bypass this area, a handful of excellent, out-of-the-way campsites nearby are worthwhile goals. An easy cross-country route from the easternmost tarn leads the way north to Ruwau Lake (see Trip 53).

From the tarns a short climb goes up to island-dotted Saddlerock Lake (11,128'), 3.75 miles from the trailhead. Nestled in a glacier-scoured basin at the foot of the northeast buttress of towering Mt. Goode, Saddlerock offers an austere haven for backpackers. Anglers can try their luck on rainbow and brook trout that inhabit its icy waters.

An unmarked use-trail from Saddlerock Lake over a low rise is the preferred route to irregular-shaped Bishop Lake (11,230±), because the Bishop Pass Trail travels up the hillside east of the lake. Good campsites can be found on the low rise just north of the lake. Rainbow and brook trout are also present in this lake.

Additional destinations accessible by trail are described in Trips 53–54. If you possess the time and energy, the strenuous ascent from Bishop Lake to Bishop Pass will reward you with grand views of Dusy Basin, the Black Divide, and an assortment of nearby peaks. Cross-country options from the vicinity of the trail-accessible lakes are limited to short forays to Marie Louise, Inconsolable, Margaret, and Ledge lakes.

⃞O Mountaineers interested in nontechnical ascents can attempt Mt. Goode from Bishop Lake or Mt. Agassiz from Bishop Pass.

⃞R **PERMITS:** Wilderness permit required for overnight stays (quota: 36 per day).

CAMPFIRES: Not permitted.

BEARS: Canisters required.

TRIP **52**

Bishop Pass Trail to Dusy Basin and LeConte Canyon

Ⓜ ⁄ BPx

DISTANCE: 7.5 miles one way to Dusy Basin; 13 miles one way to JMT in LeConte Canyon

ELEVATION: 9845/11,972/11,350, +2500'/-1550' 9845/11,972/8745, +2585'/-3680'

SEASON: Mid-July to early October

USE: Moderate to Heavy

MAPS: *Mt. Thompson, North Palisade*

TRAIL LOG:

6.0	Bishop Pass
7.5	Upper Dusy Basin
10.5	Dusy Branch Bridge
13.0	JMT Jct. LeConte Canyon

INTRODUCTION: Dusy Basin, where picturesque tarns encircled by lush meadows and sparkling granite slabs contrast vividly with a border of classic alpine peaks, is one of the prettiest alpine basins in the High Sierra. It's only 7.5 miles from the trailhead to the basin, but the moderately steep climb over a nearly 12,000-foot pass presents enough of a challenge that most backpacking parties take two days to reach Dusy Basin. With such an abundance of stunning scenery, at least one additional day should be spent exploring the nooks and crannies of this exquisite parkland. There is no designated, maintained trail across Dusy Basin, but the terrain is uncomplicated and the off-trail hiking is quite straightforward

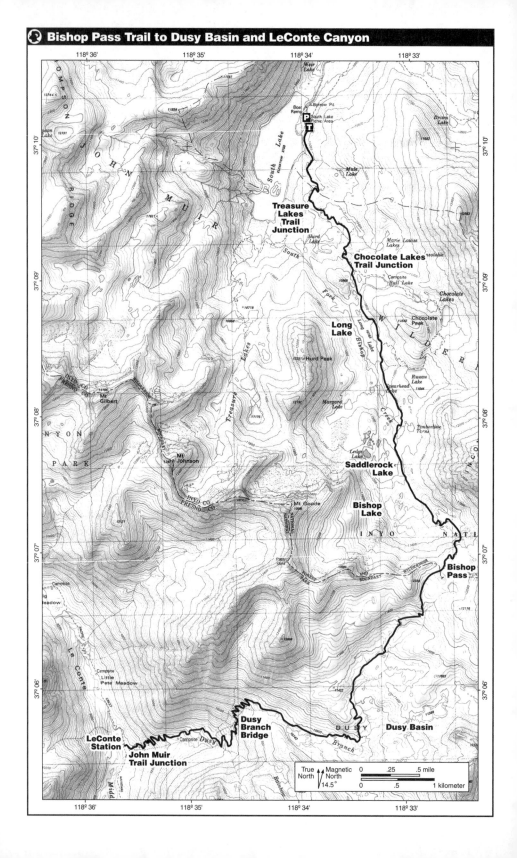

in the areas where use-trails have not already been established.

Extraordinary scenery coupled with relatively easy access from the South Lake trailhead makes Dusy Basin a popular destination for backpackers. Such popularity creates pressure for wilderness permits, particularly for trips beginning on or near weekends. The Park Service has attempted to ease the impact on the fragile alpine environment somewhat by banning stock from grazing or staying overnight in the basin. And, with a little effort, a reasonable amount of seclusion may be found by wandering across the basin far from the trail to remote campsites.

DIRECTIONS TO THE TRAILHEAD: From U.S. 395 in the center of Bishop, turn west onto Line Drive, which beyond the city limits becomes South Lake Road (Highway 168). Proceed southwest on South Lake Road 15 miles to a junction, where you turn left. Continue on the paved road another 6.75 miles to the end, near South Lake. Backpackers must park in the overnight lot. When this lot is full, additional parking is available 1.3 miles back down the road—a footpath connects the lower and upper lots. Dayhikers may park below the upper overnight parking lot in spaces marked NO OVERNIGHT PARKING. Restrooms and water are available near the trailhead.

DESCRIPTION: Begin your hike at the trailhead near the overnight parking lot, making a short, steep descent through an area of lush vegetation. A mild climb follows as you pass above the east shore of South Lake. Soon you break out into the open to fine views of the terrain up the canyon and quickly begin a steeper ascent. Enter the John Muir Wilderness and continue the climb to a Y-junction with the Treasure Lakes Trail, 0.75 mile from the trailhead (see Trip 54).

Veer to the left (southeast) from the junction and follow the Bishop Pass Trail to a creek crossing on a plank bridge. A moderate climb follows to an unmarked, faint

trail junction, at 1.4 miles, with the partly cross-country route to seldom-visited Marie Lakes. Just beyond this junction, you come alongside and then cross another small creek. Now you encounter a series of short switchbacks leading over granite outcrops and boulders through scattered pines. At 1.9 miles you come to a marked Y-junction with the Chocolate Lakes Trail (see Trip 53).

You continue on the Bishop Pass Trail from the junction and make an easy 0.25-mile stroll over to the north shore of Long Lake (10,753'). The elongated lake is a very popular destination with backpackers, hikers, and anglers. Campsites abound around the overused lakeshore, particularly on the knoll near the south end of the lake. You follow the trail along the east shore, occasionally right at the water's edge but at other times a good distance away. Near the far end of the lake, 2.7 miles from the trailhead, you come to a marked T-junction with the south end of the Chocolate Lakes Trail.

Beyond the junction, you continue along the shore of Long Lake, cross the inlet stream from Ruwau Lake, and start to climb again. You climb across the slope to the east of Spearhead Lake (10,750±). Limited campsites are scattered around the lake and fishing is reportedly fair for rainbow and brook trout. Easy cross-country travel leads west from Spearhead Lake 0.3 mile to isolated Margaret Lake (10,970±).

A 0.5-mile climb from Spearhead Lake leads to the lovely Timberline Tarns. Although most campers bypass this area, a handful of excellent, out-of-the-way campsites nearby are worthwhile goals. An easy cross-country route from the easternmost tarn leads the way north to Ruwau Lake (see Trip 53).

From the tarns a short climb goes up to Saddlerock Lake (11,128'), 3.75 miles from the trailhead, which offers an austere haven for backpackers. Anglers can try their luck on rainbow and brook trout.

An unmarked use-trail from Saddlerock Lake over a low rise is the preferred route to irregular-shaped Bishop Lake (11,230±), because the Bishop Pass Trail travels up the hillside east of the lake. Good campsites can be found on the low rise just north of the lake, which is also home to rainbow and brook trout.

Continuing up the Bishop Pass Trail, you pass timberline and enter the alpine zone as you follow rocky tread composed of red metamorphosed rock. Soon the grade increases as you reenter the domain of characteristic Sierra granite and climb the dramatic cirque wall toward the pass on a winding trail. Through a seemingly endless sea of boulders and slabs you continue the laborious ascent, perhaps pausing occasionally to catch your breath while enjoying the spectacular views of Mt. Goode and the spires of the Inconsolable Range. Depending on the previous winter's weather, you may encounter patches of snow across the trail on your way to the pass well into summer. Eventually you arrive at Bishop Pass (11,972'), 6.0 miles from the trailhead, where signs delineate the boundary of Kings Canyon National

Park. The westward vista from the pass is quite striking, with the meadow-rimmed tarns of Dusy Basin directly below you to the south, backdropped nicely by Giraud and Columbine peaks. To the southwest, beyond the deep chasm of LeConte Canyon, the Black Divide casts a regal profile. Flanking the pass to the northeast, Mt. Agassiz beckons energetic climbers toward its summit.

After the taxing uphill, you descend from the pass on sandy trail to some switchbacks. Here a fairly well-defined, short use-trail leads to the top of some cliffs, from where you have an excellent view of Dusy Basin and the surrounding peaks and ridges. Back on the main trail, you continue to wind downhill, encountering welcome patches of green meadow, an assortment of wildflowers, and some gurgling rivulets, at least until midseason when snowmelt is completed and the grasses, sedges, and flowers begin to fade and the watercourses start to dry up.

Along the descent, you have fine views of Dusy Basin's tarns and pocket meadows,

One of the many unnamed tarns in Dusy Basin

FRANK DUSY

Dusy Basin's namesake was a Canadian-born shepherd who drove his flocks into the Kings River backcountry, exploring the Middle Fork all the way to the Palisades. He was credited with the 1869 discovery of Tehipite Valley, a remote section of the Middle Fork canyon, and with taking the first photographs of the area 10 years later.

dramatically framed by the crags of the Palisades and Isosceles and Columbine peaks. Approximately 1.5 miles from the pass, a use-trail branches left away from the main trail and leads to the uppermost tarn (11,350±) in Dusy Basin. You can follow this trail to campsites around the first lake, or continue on the path to more secluded campsites near Lake 11388 or Lake 11425±. By remaining on the Bishop Pass Trail, you can descend about 0.75 mile to another use-trail, heading to campsites around the lower tarns.

Wherever you stay, Dusy Basin is an exquisitely beautiful area. Small pockets of luxuriant meadow and sparkling granite slabs border azure-colored tarns and tiny, crystalline streams. The surrounding mountains create a splendid backdrop, with rugged spires piercing the rarified air and precipitous faces and knife-edged ridges providing challenges for the heartiest mountaineers. The delicate alpine vegetation is quite fragile, so camps should be located only in sandy areas devoid of plant life. While traveling in the basin, follow the least damaging routes so as to avoid the plant life as much as possible.

Plenty of campsites are available throughout the basin, but as is usually the case, campers seem to congregate close to the trail. Possibilities for seclusion increase around the tarns farthest from the trail. Even if you don't plan on camping there,

the beauty of the area demands that you at least explore the remote corners of the basin sans backpack. Anglers may test their abilities on the golden and brook trout that reside in the tarns and connecting streams. Dusy Basin is famous not only with backpackers; photographers are drawn to its visual delights in almost equal numbers. Alpenglow on the western face of the Palisades can create a dreamlike conclusion to a beautiful sunset.

Those bound for the John Muir Trail should continue the scenic descent from Dusy Basin on the Bishop Pass Trail. Widely scattered whitebark pines grace the upper end of the basin but become slightly less scattered as you lose elevation. Interspersed between granite slabs and boulders are pockets of verdant meadow, clumps of willow and heather, and wild- flowers, including shooting star, penstemon, aster and buttercup. These greet you along the trail, which follows the winding Dusy Branch as it dances into LeConte Canyon. Beyond Lake 10742, you follow the trail to the edge of Dusy Basin and gaze into the deep declivity of the canyon.

With a constant view of the imposing wall of granite across LeConte Canyon, you begin the steep, switchbacking drop toward the Middle Fork Kings River. On the descent, you near a small creek highlighted by a splash of color from nearby wildflowers, and then continue to zigzag down to the wooden Dusy Branch bridge, 10.5 miles from the trailhead. The bridge, perched well above the plunging creek, provides a nice spot for a momentary rest while enjoying the fine vista of the precipitous granite barrier forming the walls of the canyon.

More switchbacks follow as the stiff descent continues. At various points, you have an excellent view of Dusy Branch spilling from Dusy Basin down a near-vertical wall of granite. Gazing down the hillside below, you can see where an avalanche from years past took out a large stand of trees. You plunge down the trail to a lightly forested bench and a pair of crossings over the multi-branched creek. Among nearby trees are several excellent campsites along the creek. Beyond the crossings, you proceed down the canyon wall through light-to-scattered lodgepole forest, interrupted briefly by an open stretch of chaparral; here you have a dramatic view of the canyon and towering Langille Peak. As the end of the descent approaches, this open terrain gives way to a light covering of forest shading the floor of the canyon. You reach a signed junction with the John Muir Trail, 13 miles from the trailhead at South Lake. Campsites are spread near the trail on either side of the LeConte Canyon Ranger Station.

Dusy Basin is so beautiful that a visit here is surely incomplete without at least one day spent wandering amid its meadows and tarns.

An adventurous but straightforward cross-country loop leads you from Dusy Basin over Knapsack Pass (11,680'±), through Palisade Basin, and back to Dusy Basin over Thunderbolt Pass (12,360'±). The route is not technically demanding, but ascending and descending from the passes over slopes filled with talus can make the hiking a bit tedious at times. From lower Dusy Basin, head east toward the saddle directly south of Columbine Peak, ascending a gully. The gully's bottom section is filled with brush and the upper section with rock. A use-trail once made the climb much easier, but it was partially destroyed by a rockslide some years ago. Traverse east from the saddle and then descend to Barrett Lakes. From the uppermost lake, you climb north over talus toward the distinct saddle immediately southeast of Thunderbolt Peak. Descend from the saddle over more talus to the uppermost lake in Dusy Basin.

Extended backpack routes are easily created from Dusy Basin through neighboring Palisade Basin and over Potluck Pass (12,120'±), connecting with the John Muir Trail near the lower Palisade Lake. From there an uncomplicated loop trip back to Dusy Basin follows the JMT north to LeConte Canyon and then east up the Bishop Pass Trail (37 miles round trip— 6.0 miles off-trail).

Wildflowers near Thunderbolt Pass, accessible from lower Dusy Basin

If Dusy Basin is too crowded for your liking, the narrow canyon holding Rainbow Lakes provides a more secluded alternative. These seldom-visited lakes are quite scenic, nestled into glacier-scoured bowls beneath the north face of Giraud Peak. To reach the lakes, leave the Bishop Pass Trail near the lower end of Dusy Basin, about 0.3 mile northwest of Lake 10742, and traverse cross-country 0.5 mile to the first lake (10,720'±). Brook trout are reported to inhabit the two largest lakes.

While all the impressive peaks of the Palisades require technical climbing, mountaineers will find class 2 challenges from Bishop Pass on either Mt. Agassiz to the southeast or, via a longer ascent, on Mt. Goode to the northwest. Columbine Peak, on the southeast edge of Dusy Basin, is also class 2 from Knapsack Pass. Also Class 2 is an ascent of the east ridge of Giraud Peak via the peak immediately northeast.

Once on the JMT, your options are numerous, especially if you can make arrangements for pickup at another trailhead. With a limited distance between trailheads, the multi-day trip northwest along the JMT to the Piute Pass Trail (see Trip 60) and then east over Piute Pass to North Lake is a relatively popular journey. Cross-country enthusiasts can accomplish the same goal over a shorter distance by crossing the Glacier Divide at either Snow-Tongue Pass or Alpine Col, and then connecting with the Piute Pass Trail in Humphreys Basin. Journeying southbound on the JMT, backpackers can connect to a variety of eastside trailheads. Further options exist for trans-Sierra hikes, but these require much more complex logistics.

PERMITS: Wilderness permit required for overnight stays (quota: 36 per day).
  CAMPFIRES: Not permitted.
  BEARS: Canisters required.
  STOCK: No stock allowed in Dusy Basin.

SOUTH LAKE TRAILHEAD

TRIP **53**

Chocolate Lakes Loop

M ♫ DH/BP

DISTANCE: 7.0 miles

ELEVATION: 9845/11,325, +1690'/-1690'

SEASON: Early July to mid-October

USE: Light (Chocolate Lakes Trail); Moderate to Heavy (Bishop Pass Trail)

MAP: *Mt. Thompson*

TRAIL LOG:
  2.0   Bishop Pass Trail Jct.
  2.25 Bull Lake
  2.8   Middle Chocolate Lake
  3.9   Ruwau Lake
  4.5   Bishop Pass Trail Jct.

INTRODUCTION: The relatively short semi-loop around aptly named Chocolate Peak branches off the beaten Bishop Pass Trail and leads to a string of picturesque lakes. The rewards include not only the outstanding scenery, but also a sense of relative seclusion, away from the steady stream of hikers, backpackers, and equestrians on the quite heavily used Bishop Pass Trail. Unfortunately, backpackers wishing to spend a night or two in the Chocolate Lakes area must compete for the same 36 wilderness permits issued per day to those bound for overnight camps on the more popular trail. The 7-mile total distance is well suited for a dayhike, for which permits are not necessary. However, be forewarned that portions of the trail between the Chocolate Lakes and Ruwau Lake are rough—indistinct in parts and indiscernible in others—although the route finding is fairly straightforward. On a brighter note, anglers should find the fishing quite good.

DIRECTIONS TO THE TRAILHEAD: From U.S. 395 in the center of Bishop, turn west onto Line Drive, which beyond the city limits becomes South Lake Road (Highway 168). Proceed southwest on South Lake Road 15 miles to a junction, where you turn left. Continue on the paved road another 6.75 miles to the end, near South Lake. Backpackers must park in the overnight lot. When this lot is full, additional parking is available 1.3 miles back down the road—a footpath connects the lower and upper lots. Dayhikers may park below the upper overnight parking lot in spaces marked NO OVERNIGHT PARKING. Restrooms and water are available near the trailhead.

DESCRIPTION: Begin your hike at the trailhead near the overnight parking lot, making a short, steep descent through an area of lush vegetation. A mild climb follows as

you pass above the east shore of South Lake. Soon you break out into the open to fine views of the terrain up the canyon and quickly begin a steeper ascent. Enter the John Muir Wilderness and continue the climb to a Y-junction with the Treasure Lakes Trail, 0.75 mile from the trailhead (see Trip 54).

Veer to the left (southeast) from the junction and follow the Bishop Pass Trail to a creek crossing on a plank bridge. A moderate climb follows to an unmarked, faint trail junction, at 1.4 miles, with the partly cross-country route to seldom-visited Marie Lakes. Just beyond this junction, you come alongside and then cross another small creek. Now you encounter a series of short switchbacks leading over granite outcrops and boulders through scattered pines. At 1.9 miles you come to a marked Y-junction with the Chocolate Lakes Trail (see Trip 53).

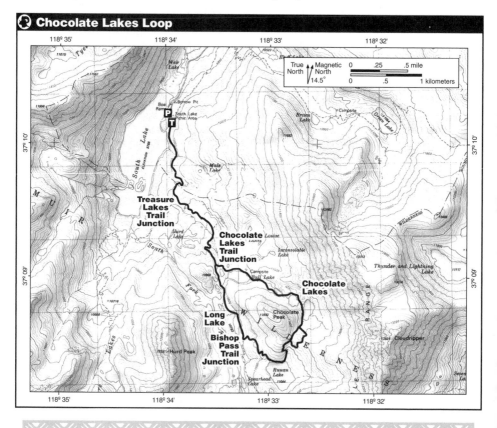

Chocolate Lakes Loop

One of the Chocolate Lakes

You turn left at the junction, cross a talus slide, climb up a steep draw to a meadow, and quickly arrive at Bull Lake (10,775±). The shoreline of the pretty lake is blanketed with a light forest of whitebark pines, wildflowers, and scattered clumps of willow. Plenty of campsites are just off the trail. Anglers can try their luck on the resident brook trout.

You follow the trail around the north shore of Bull Lake, cross the inlet, and climb moderately steeply alongside the creek through a display of wildflowers, including columbine, shooting star, and paintbrush. As the Inconsolable Range comes into view, you climb into a rocky basin past a shallow, seemingly insignificant pond, which turns out to be lower Chocolate Lake (10,950'±). Above the lower lake, you cross the creek again and climb up to Middle Chocolate Lake (11,060'±), 2.8 miles from the trailhead. Campsites are scattered around the hillside above the north shore. Continuing up the trail, you switchback up the hillside, cross a willow-lined creek, and climb to the next lake, largest of the three Chocolate Lakes

(11,075'±). Surrounded by grasses, shrubs, and few trees, the lake sits at the base of a talus slope with fine views of the nearby peaks and ridges. Decent campsites are spread around the lakeshore. Fishing is reportedly good for brook trout at all three Chocolate Lakes.

The trail continues to circumnavigate Chocolate Peak as you climb moderately steeply away from the upper lake over rocky terrain. The *Mt. Thompson* quad shows two trails leading out of the Chocolate Lakes basin, over the ridgecrest, and down to Ruwau Lake. Both trails are unmaintained and rough, with sections that virtually disappear for considerable distances. You have the option of heading straight for the ridgecrest on a steep, tightly zigzagging climb, or of following a route of longer switchbacks that reaches the crest just southeast of a craggy knob. From the crest you have fine views of the surrounding terrain. Whichever uphill route you choose, avoid the temptation to descend the talus-filled gully on the far side of the crest. The two routes merge at an ill-defined point and then follow a faint trail down the hillside above and west of this gully. The trail becomes more defined as you descend, eventually arriving at the north shore of Ruwau Lake (11,044'), 3.9 miles from the trailhead.

Ruwau Lake is perhaps the most scenic of the lakes along the Chocolate Lakes Loop. It is sandwiched between Chocolate Peak and the Inconsolable Range, and graced from all angles with views of craggy peaks and ridges. On hot afternoons, slabs on a tiny island near the north shore will entice sunbathers and swimmers willing to share the icy, crystalline waters with the resident rainbow trout. Whitebark pines shade campsites on a low hill above the north shore and near the outlet. Around the remainder of the shoreline, willow thickets and an assortment of wildflowers provide adornment. Although the lake is only 0.5 mile from the Bishop Pass Trail, it seems far enough off the beaten path to provide a reasonable helping of solitude and serenity.

To continue toward the Bishop Pass Trail, follow the path along the north shore of Ruwau Lake toward the outlet. Through heather and scattered pines, you turn away from the lake and proceed northwest on a slight descent. After a brief climb, the trail descends in earnest as you make a steep, winding drop toward Long Lake. At the bottom of the hillside, you meet the Bishop Lake Trail at a signed junction, 4.5 miles from the trailhead.

From the junction, you turn right (north) and proceed on a gentle grade through scattered forest past wildflowers and a marshy pond. Soon, a part of aptly named Long Lake appears to your left. You have a fine view of Mt. Goode rising to the southwest. A short climb over a low hump brings you directly alongside the picturesque lake. Beyond the north end of Long Lake, your descent increases, the forest thickens, and soon you encounter the junction with the Chocolate Lakes Trail, closing your loop. From this junction, retrace your steps 1.9 miles to the trailhead.

The Chocolate Lakes Loop can be combined with the Bishop Pass Trail (see Trips 51–52) for a number of extended journeys. An easy cross-country route from Ruwau Lake to the Timberline Tarns provides a more direct course toward Bishop Pass than the trail down to Long Lake. Work your way around the west shore of Ruwau Lake and then up an obvious gully at the lake's south end via a use-trail and intermittent boulder scrambles. From the top of the gully, drop down toward some small ponds, where you pick up a more distinct path. Follow this winding trail over a low rise and down toward Timberline Tarns, a stream crossing, and a connection with the Bishop Pass Trail.

A class 2 climbing route follows the southeast slope of Chocolate Peak up to fine views from its 11,682-foot summit. Cloudripper and Picture Puzzle peak in the Inconsolable Range are class 3 ascents.

PERMITS: Wilderness permit required for overnight stays (quota: 36 per day).

CAMPFIRES: Not permitted.

BEARS: Canisters required.

SOUTH LAKE TRAILHEAD

TRIP 54

Treasure Lakes

Ⓜ ↗ DH/BP

DISTANCE: 3.8 miles one way to Lake 11175

ELEVATION: 9845/11,185, +1765'/-450'

Season: Early July to mid-October

USE: Moderate

MAP: *Mt. Thompson*

TRAIL LOG:

0.75	Treasure Lakes Trail Jct.
2.8	Lake 10668
3.8	Lake 11175

INTRODUCTION: The Treasure Lakes Trail quickly leads away from the normal hubbub along the Bishop Pass Trail to a group of relatively secluded lakes in a granite basin near the Sierra crest. Over the short journey, you pass through three different plant zones—montane, subalpine, and alpine. The lakes are quite scenic, offering campers serene settings for pitching a tent, and providing anglers with excellent fishing for golden trout. Some route finding and a bit of boulderhopping are necessary to reach the upper lakes, but these should be easy for all but beginning backpackers. Although the trail is open to equestrians, the absence of a path over rocky terrain discourages horse use above the first two lakes, increasing the chances for an undisturbed visit. A straightforward cross-country route provides an alternative to simply backtracking to the trailhead (see Options, below).

DIRECTIONS TO THE TRAILHEAD: From U.S. 395 in the center of Bishop, turn west onto Line Drive, which beyond the city limits becomes South Lake Road (Highway

168). Proceed southwest on South Lake Road 15 miles to a junction, where you turn left. Continue on the paved road another 6.75 miles to the end, near South Lake. Backpackers must park in the overnight lot. When this lot is full, additional parking is available 1.3 miles back down the road—a footpath connects the lower and upper lots. Dayhikers may park below the upper overnight parking lot in spaces marked NO OVERNIGHT PARKING. Restrooms and water are available near the trailhead.

DESCRIPTION: Begin your hike at the well-marked trailhead near the overnight parking lot, making a short but steep descent through an area of lush vegetation. A mild climb follows as you pass well above the east shore of South Lake through young aspens and lodgepole pines. Soon you break out into the open to fine views of the terrain up the canyon and quickly begin a steeper ascent up a hillside. Enter the John Muir Wilderness and continue the climb to a Y-junction between the Bishop Pass Trail and the Treasure Lakes Trail, 0.75 mile from the trailhead.

Bear right (south) at the junction and head through scattered-to-light lodgepole pine forest to an easy crossing over two small streams. The mild descent continues as South Lake pops into view below you, and Mt. Johnson, Mt. Gilbert, Mt. Thompson, and Hurd Peak are revealed to the southwest. Soon you follow the trail on an arcing descent to three crossings over South Fork Bishop Creek and its two tributaries, where willows, grasses, and wildflowers line the drainages.

Now the real climbing begins, briefly interrupted by a short decline where the trail crosses Treasure Creek. Beyond the creek, you follow the trail on a winding, moderately steep climb beside granite boulders, over slabs, and through a mixed forest of lodgepole and whitebark pines. You work your way back to the creek, cross it, and continue the winding climb through a thinning cover of whitebark pines. After

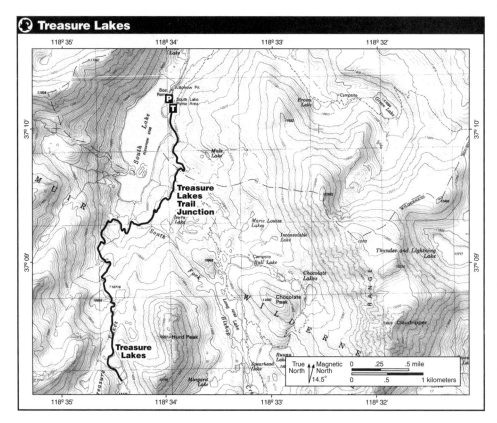

Treasure Lakes

passing a small pond, you switchback up a slope to Lake 10668, 2.8 miles from the trailhead.

The first and largest of the Treasure Lakes is dotted with small rock islands and bordered by boggy turf along the north shore. As you proceed up the gentle trail above the east shore, you pass a number of exposed campsites nestled beneath clumps of pines.

A steep wall of rock on the opposite shore rises up to Peak 12047 and provides a dramatic backdrop to the placid waters of the lake. Toward the south end, a use-trail branches left from the main trail past more campsites to the Treasure Lake directly east of Lake 10668. Smaller and somewhat less scenic, this lake has a handful of campsites scattered around the shore.

Continuing south on the main trail from Lake 10668, you cross the stream connecting the first two lakes and work

your way alongside a creek coursing down a rock-filled gully. Clumps of willow and small patches of meadow sprinkled with monkey flower soften the stark surroundings. Where the creek divides into two channels, follow the more gradual cleft to the right through large blocks of talus. Up canyon, Mt. Johnson and the long ridge between Mt. Johnson and Mt. Goode add to the rugged alpine atmosphere. Route finding from here is straightforward over the rocky terrain as you traverse east over a low ridge to the left-hand fork, where the trio of lakes is cradled into the deep cirque west of Peak 12192. There are excellent campsites amid whitebark pines near the northwest shore of the first lake. All three lakes should provide anglers with good fishing for golden trout. You reach the last lake in the chain, Lake 11175, at 3.8 miles from the trailhead

Rather than retrace all of your steps back to the trailhead, you can create a semi-loop trip by following a relatively easy cross-country route from Lake 11175. First, climb southeast up to the prominent saddle 550 feet above the lake. From the saddle descend northeast approximately 100 yards and angle over to a tiny creek. Follow the creek briefly and then head directly for Margaret Lake. Pick up a use-trail near the lake's northwest shore and head northeast to the south end of Long Lake. You ford the South Fork Bishop Creek, pass some campsites, and soon intersect the Bishop Pass Trail.

A more difficult (class 2) cross-country route, requiring use of an ice axe, heads up the right-hand canyon past the western-most Treasure Lake and up a snow/ice chute to Treasure Col, directly northeast of Mt. Johnson. From there, steep and loose rock leads to easier travel along a creek to cliffs above Big Pete Meadow, where more route finding is required in order to reach the John Muir Trail in the meadow below.

From here, the easiest return to the South Lake trailhead is via the JMT southbound to a connection with the Bishop Pass Trail in LeConte Canyon, and then over Bishop Pass, reversing the description in Trip 52.

Mountaineers can ascend a class 2 route from the uppermost Treasure Lake (11,625'±) to the summit of Mt. Johnson (12,871'). The southeast slope of Mt. Gilbert (13,106') is class 2 from Treasure Col, but as stated above, an ice axe is necessary to negotiate the chute on the northeast side of the col.

PERMITS: Wilderness permit required for overnight stays (quota: 13 per day).
CAMPFIRES: Not permitted.
BEARS: Canisters required.

One of the Treasure Lakes

SOUTH LAKE TRAILHEAD

TRIP **55**

Tyee Lakes

Ⓜ ↗ DH/BP

DISTANCE: 3.9 miles one way

ELEVATION: 9090/11,600, +2520'/-10'

SEASON: Mid-July to mid-October

USE: Light

MAP: Mt. Thompson

TRAIL LOG:

1.75 Cindy Lake
3.0   Clara Lake
4.0   Table Mountain View

INTRODUCTION: A little-used trail provides a short but steep route to a group of delightful lakes set in a high granite basin well east of the Sierra crest. The 3-mile

journey to the upper lake is well suited for either a dayhike, complete with swimming and a picnic lunch, or an overnight backpack. Anglers should find plenty of brook trout in all of the Tyee Lakes. The 0.75-mile, 600-foot climb from Clara Lake to the view from the plateau on Table Mtn. is certainly worth the effort. Inexplicably, the Tyee Lakes were named for a famed brand of salmon eggs. The origin of the various first names (Cindy, John, Jim, Ted, Clara, and Melissa) applied to the lakes is unknown.

DIRECTIONS TO THE TRAILHEAD: From U.S. 395 in the center of Bishop, turn west onto Line Drive, which beyond the city limits becomes South Lake Road (Highway 168). Proceed southwest on South Lake Road 15 miles to a junction. Turn left, remaining on the South Lake Road, and proceed 5.0 miles to the trailhead. Parking is available on the gravel shoulder.

DESCRIPTION: You begin the hike by crossing an impressive arched, wooden bridge over South Fork Bishop Creek. Just beyond

Bridge over South Fork Bishop Creek, along the Tyee Lakes Trail

Tyee Lakes

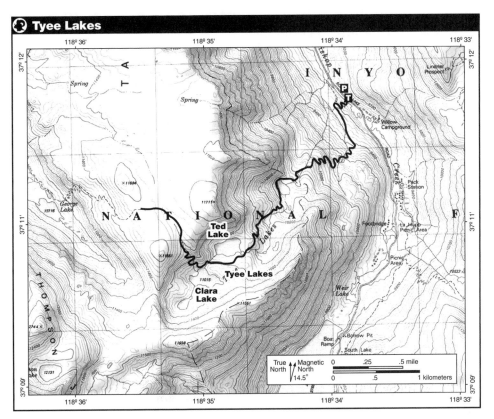

the bridge, you begin a moderate, zigzag-ging climb up the sagebrush-covered hill-side above the creek through intermittent pockets of young aspens and lodgepole pines. The steady climb continues as you cross the outlet from Tyee Lakes at 1.5 miles. The grade eases as you enter the John Muir Wilderness, round a hill, and encounter Cindy Lake (10,300'±), at 1.75 miles. A couple of fair campsites are near the stream below the lake. A pleasant beach on the west shore invites sunbathers and swimmers, but marshy meadow, willows, and pockets of aspen border the rest of the lake. Rising brook trout will entice anglers, although much of the lakeshore is difficult to access.

You arc around the first lake, cross over a trickling stream that dribbles into the lake, and resume the climb. A number of switchbacks lead you steeply uphill to the second lake, John Lake (10,595'±).

Surrounded by grasses, this lake is the smallest and shallowest of the Tyee Lakes. Across the outlet, a few pine-sheltered campsites occupy a hump of granite. Brook trout inhabit these waters also.

The trail leaves the west shore of John Lake and begins a moderately steep climb through whitebark pine over a granite bench. Switchbacks lead you to a viewpoint amid dwarf pines and scattered boulders, from where you have a bird's-eye vista of John Lake and other lakes to the east of the trail (the largest one is Jim Lake). Then, a more moderate climb leads across Tyee Creek and past a small pond to the fourth lake, Ted Lake (10,900'±). This lake is one of the larger Tyee Lakes and provides good campsites amid scattered whitebark pines. Talus cascades down the hillside above the far shore.

You skirt the south side of the lake away from the shoreline and then begin to climb moderately steeply up and over the talus-covered hillside over to the narrow cleft of the stream connecting Ted Lake with its upstairs neighbor. Cross the stream and climb up the cleft toward the next lake. You reach the fifth lake, Clara Lake (11,015'), at 3.0 miles from the trailhead.

Clara Lake is also one of the larger Tyee Lakes. Rugged cliffs form a splendid backdrop and a few scattered whitebark pines eke out an existence near timberline. Campsites appear above the northeast shore among the trees, and in a sandy area near the northwest shore. Unlike in the lower lakes, rainbow cohabitate with the characteristic brook trout at Clara. The last Tyee Lake, Melissa Lake (11,030'±) is easily reached by a short cross-country jaunt from Clara Lake's southwest shore.

From Clara Lake, it's a nearly 2-mile round-trip climb to the Table Mtn. vista point, but the dramatic view is worth the hike. Then, as you continue, the trail follows a winding course up the gorge of the delightful creek draining into Clara Lake. Near the head of the drainage the trail becomes indistinct, but the route is obvious —simply head west for the top of the plateau between Peaks 11684 and 11651, passing through a profusion of corn lily (in season) along the way.

With shuttle arrangements, you can continue from Clara Lake northwest over Table Mtn. and past George Lake to the Lake Sabrina trailhead. Views are excellent from Table Mtn., and George Lake provides some good campsites.

PERMITS: Wilderness permit required for overnight stays (quota: 13 per day).
CAMPFIRES: Not permitted.

LAKE SABRINA TRAILHEAD

TRIP **56**

Sabrina Basin

M ↗ DH / BP / BPx

DISTANCE: 6.8 miles to Hungry Packer Lake

ELEVATION: 9080/11,145, +2860'/-680'

SEASON: Mid-July to mid-October

USE: Moderate

MAPS: *Mt. Thompson, Mt. Darwin*

TRAIL LOG:

1.25	George Lake Trail Jct.
3.0	Blue Lake
3.25	Donkey Lake Trail Jct.
4.7	Dingleberry Lake
5.5	Midnight Lake Jct.
6.8	Hungry Packer Lake

INTRODUCTION: The main quandary when contemplating a trip to Sabrina Basin is whether you have enough time to visit all of its scenic lakes, because there is a bountiful number and nary a rotten apple in the bunch. An array of options—well-traveled trails, less-traveled use-trails, and a few cross-country routes—means you can select potential lake destinations compatible with your skill level and your desire for solitude. With so many lakes to choose from, "getting away from it all" should be fairly straightforward, especially if you're willing to veer off the beaten path a little.

The lakes in the upper basin are particularly scenic, nestled into granite bowls, encircled by steep rock cliffs, and with the towering Sierra crest as a backdrop. Along the way you will encounter delightful meadows, wildflowers, cascading streams, and picturesque waterfalls. The open nature of the basin provides striking panoramas throughout your journey. Whether you are just out for a day, a week,

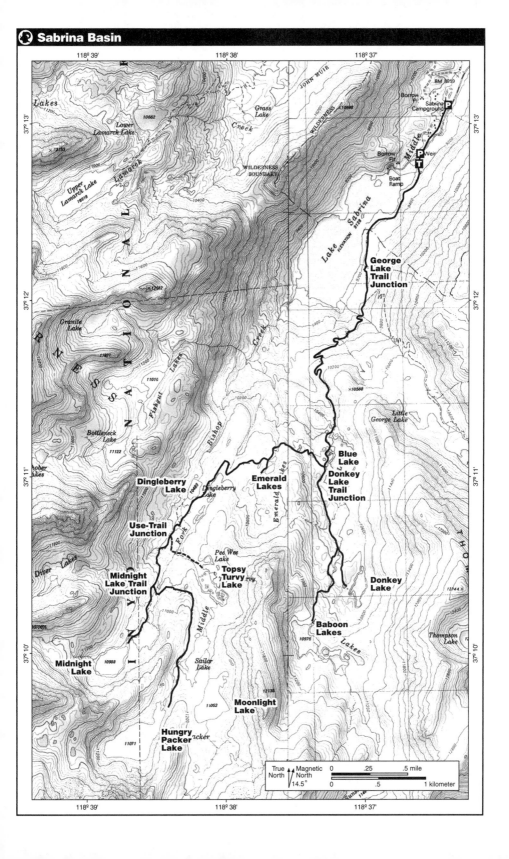

or somewhere in between, Sabrina Basin has much to offer.

DIRECTIONS TO THE TRAILHEAD: From U.S. 395 in the center of Bishop, turn west onto Line Drive, which beyond the city limits becomes South Lake Road (Highway 168). Proceed 18 miles, past the South Lake junction, to the North Lake turnoff and the overnight parking area for the Lake Sabrina trailhead. The actual trailhead is another 0.5 mile up the road, just below the lake. Day-use parking is available there, but all overnight users must park in the lot at the North Lake turnoff.

DESCRIPTION: From the trailhead, briefly follow the course of an old road through a cover of aspens until a single-track trail leads you around a corner to a fine view up Middle Fork Bishop Creek canyon and across open sagebrush-covered slopes dotted with junipers, Jeffrey pines, aspens, lodgepole pines, mountain mahogany, and western white pines. Immediately below you is the blue expanse of Lake Sabrina, with Middle Fork Bishop Creek cascading into a small cove at the lake's far end. Farther up the Middle Fork canyon, the rugged Sierra crest is crowned by the 13,000-foot summits of Mt. Darwin, Mt. Haeckel, Mt. Wallace, and Mt. Powell. You traverse across a hillside, past the John Muir Wilderness boundary to about the midway point of the lake, and then climb steadily up the slope. Near the end of the lake, 1.25 miles from the trailhead, you reach the junction with the trail to George Lake. Just beyond the junction, you come to a ford of George Lake's refreshing outlet stream.

Entering a light forest of lodgepole pines, you climb moderately via switchbacks up the hillside south of Lake Sabrina, crossing another creek on the way. Sporadic openings in the forest allow splendid views back to Lake Sabrina and on toward the Sierra crest. More switchbacks, interspersed with sets of granite steps, lead you up the hillside, through a rocky ravine, and to a small pond, where the climb abates. Near the pond, you spy the north shore of Blue Lake. You pass a couple of campsites and ford the outlet stream immediately below the lake, 3.0 miles from trailhead.

Blue Lake (10,388') is very photogenic, with an irregular shoreline bordered by weather-beaten lodgepole pines and granite benches, and the lake itself backdropped nicely by the craggy, undulating crest of Thompson Ridge. Plenty of campsites are spread around the shore, but choose your site wisely as some are obviously too close to the lake by Forest Service regulations. Anglers may try their luck on brook and rainbow trout. Follow the trail along the west shore to a three-way junction with the Donkey Lake Trail near the midpoint of the lake, 3.25 miles from the trailhead.

SIDE TRIP TO BABOON AND DONKEY LAKES: From the junction, head south through lodgepole pines and past granite slabs, well away from the shoreline of Blue Lake. You cross a seasonal stream and continue a mild climb to an unmarked junction with a faint path that heads south-southwest to the Baboon Lakes. The trail disappears completely before reaching the lakes, but the route finding is straightforward, paralleling the outlet creek to the largest lake (10,976'). Anglers may test their skill on rainbow trout in this lake, and on both rainbow and brook in the upper lakes. Adventurous cross-country types can extend their journey to Sunset Lake (11,464'), beneath the glacier-clad north face of Mt. Thompson.

To reach Donkey Lake, continue south from the unmarked junction a short distance to a crossing of the creek draining Baboon Lakes. You proceed on faint trail around outcrops, past a small pool, and through a notch on to Donkey Lake (10,590'±), tucked into a narrow cleft at the base of Thompson Ridge. Anglers can expect decent fishing for brook trout. **END OF SIDE TRIP**

Turn right (northwest) from the junction with the trail to Baboon and Donkey lakes, and proceed on mild trail over a low saddle, across a rocky slope, and then up granite ledges to a grassy valley dotted with lodgepole pines. At 3.75 miles from the trailhead, you cross the creek that drains the small ponds that are known as Emerald Lakes. Beyond the creek, the trail curves around the marshy meadow adjacent to the lower lakes and then comes to a faint use-trail on your left, which provides access to the larger lakes. Fine campsites can be found at the westernmost lake, where fishing is reported to be good for brook and rainbow trout.

On the main trail, you climb away from Emerald Lakes up granite steps and over granite slabs along the west side of a low ridge. Eventually, you wind down off this ridge and come to the southeast shore of Dingleberry Lake (10,489'), 4.7 miles from the trailhead. The lake is squeezed between cliffs and slabs of a low ridge on one side and the steep wall of Peak 13253's east ridge on the other. Campsites are at either end of the lake along the creek, but wet meadows on the south end are a haven for mosquitoes in early season.

Beyond the south end of Dingleberry Lake, the foot and stock trails split for separate fords of Middle Fork Bishop Creek. After the ford, you reconnect with the stock trail and climb alongside a tributary to a picturesque meadow, where the serpentine stream winds lazily through grasses, willows, and wildflowers. Across the valley, a dazzling waterfall plunges from Topsy Turvy Lake. In the midst of the meadow, you encounter a faint use-trail that heads left toward campsites at Pee Wee and Topsy Turvy lakes. At the head of the meadow, you resume the climb over numerous low granite benches to the signed Midnight Lake Trail junction, 5.5 miles from the trailhead.

⃝ SIDE TRIP TO MIDNIGHT LAKE: From the junction, veer right and after a short climb drop down to cross the stream draining Hell Diver Lakes. Mildly graded trail leads past a good-sized tarn and across the tributary draining Midnight Lake to steeper

Midnight Lake, with Mt. Darwin rising on the far shore

climbing over rock slabs. Eventually the grades eases again as you crest the lip of a basin and quickly stroll over to the north shore of Midnight Lake (10,988'), 0.5 mile from the junction.

This teardrop-shaped lake reposes in a granite bowl surrounded by talus slopes and steep, rugged cliffs, where patches of snow cling to shaded crevices and a waterfall cascades 300 feet toward the lake. Reigning over the Sierra crest, 13,831-foot Mt. Darwin looms in the background above the shimmering water. Near timberline, widely scattered lodgepole pines find tenuous holds in cracks of the granite hummocks lining the outlet. The steep lakeshore inhibits camping at the lake, but campsites can be found scattered along the creek between the lake and the tarn below. Although sites for human habitation are limited, the resident brook trout seem to fare quite well at Midnight Lake. **END OF SIDE TRIP**

From the Midnight Lake Trail junction, turn southeast and cross a pair of willow-and-flower-lined creeks. On a mild-to-moderate climb, you arc around a spur ridge and then head south through scattered whitebark pine to a sloping meadow filled with willow, heather, and an assortment of wildflowers interspersed among sparkling granite slabs. A short climb leads to a stunningly picturesque basin brimming with crystalline streams and splendid cascades, with the aptly named Picture Peak accenting the scene up the canyon. Approximately 0.75 mile from the junction, you encounter a use-trail veering southeast toward Moonlight Lake.

SIDE TRIP TO MOONLIGHT LAKE: Moonlight Lake is best approached via the use-trail below (north of) Sailor Lake, as a vast talus field inhibits the access from the main trail to Hungry Packer Lake above. Follow the use-trail to a ford of the outlet creek from Sailor Lake, cross the meadow below Sailor Lake, and then ascend alongside Moonlight Lake's outlet to the northwest shore of the rockbound lake (11,052').

Campsites are limited to exposed locations along the outlet and to the south end of a low rise above the west shore. In spite of the seemingly lifeless surroundings, the lake has a healthy population of brook trout. **END OF SIDE TRIP**

From the junction with the use-trail to Moonlight Lake, continue south on the main trail west of Sailor Lake (10,850'±).

The scenic lake nestles in the open, nearly treeless basin, bordered by sloping granite shelves and slabs (naturally suited for afternoon naps) and pockets of verdant meadow. A number of fine, although exposed, campsites are scattered around the basin. Anglers will find brook and rainbow trout in the lake and creek.

You proceed up the main trail, with the scenic north face of Picture Peak drawing you like a scenic beacon. You reach the north shore of Hungry Packer Lake (11,071'), a narrow finger of water, 6.8 miles from the trailhead. From here the view of the alpine peak across the serene surface of the lake lives up to its billing. Picture Peak towers over the far shore, and other steep cliffs sweep around the basin on either side. During snowmelt, thin ribbons of water cascade steeply over those cliffs, while throughout the summer patches of snow cling to clefts in the north face of Picture Peak. A granite peninsula on the northwest shore is too close to the water for camping, but its slightly sloping slabs

---

SAILOR LAKE

Sailor Lake was supposedly named for a frequent client of the Lake Sabrina Lodge who was found asleep one day by packers, apparently recovering from the effects of too much drink. Some older maps used the appellation "Drunken Sailor Lake," which is a bit more colorful, but the shorter name is the accepted one.

are fine for afternoon sunbathing. Camp-sites are confined to spots around the outlet. Rainbow trout will test the skill of anglers.

[O] With such a bounty of lakes, Sabrina Basin offers plenty of opportunities for exploration. A number of days could be spent just visiting the lakes easily accessible from the main trail. Cross-country routes extend the number of opportunities to more far-flung destinations such as Fishgut or Hell Diver lakes. What is perhaps the most noteworthy route ascends the ridge east of Hungry Packer Lake to the boulder-strewn canyon above Moonlight Lake, and then up to austere Echo Lake (11,602'), just north of the Sierra crest below Clyde Spires.

[O] From upper Sabrina Basin, experienced cross-country enthusiasts have a trio of strenuous off-trail options for crossing the Sierra crest to connections with the John Muir Trail. Echo Pass and Haeckel Col are both rated class 3, the former requiring an ice axe. The least difficult crossing is the class 2 route over Wallace Col (12,960'), which ascends the ridge east of Hungry Packer Lake to a bench directly west of Echo Lake and then climbs over Wallace Col (the broad saddle south of Mt. Wallace). Descend west from the col over loose rock past tarns to the JMT near Sapphire Lake in Evolution Basin.

[O] Non-technical climbing routes from a base camp in Sabrina Basin are few and far between. The one exception is a class 2 route up the north slope of Mt. Wallace (13,377'). From the bench west of Echo Lake mentioned above, head northwest into the cirque between Mt. Haeckel and Mt. Wallace and proceed to the summit.

[R] **PERMITS:** Wilderness permit required for overnight stays (quota: 33 per day).

CAMPFIRES: Not permitted.

TRIP **57**

George Lake

(M) ✒ **DH / BP**

DISTANCE: 3.3 miles one way

ELEVATION: 9080/10,735, +2025'/-170'

SEASON: Early July to mid-October

USE: Light

MAP: *Mt. Thompson*

TRAIL LOG:

1.25	George Lake Trail Jct.
3.3	George Lake

INTRODUCTION: Although George Lake may not be the most picturesque lake accessible from Sabrina Basin Trail, it certainly is one of the least crowded. This is a bit mysterious, considering the short distance required to reach the shore of this delightful body of water. Although anglers will make the 3.3-mile journey to the lakeshore in search of some decent fishing, most backpackers bypass the lake altogether in favor of reaching more popular territory farther up the main trail in Sabrina Basin, which makes George Lake an attractive possibility for either a dayhike or an overnight backpack.

DIRECTIONS TO THE TRAILHEAD: From U.S. 395 in the center of Bishop, turn west onto Line Drive, which beyond the city limits becomes South Lake Road (Highway 168). Proceed 18 miles, past the South Lake junction, to the North Lake turnoff and the overnight parking area for the Lake Sabrina trailhead. The actual trailhead is another 0.5 mile up the road, just below the lake. Day-use parking is available there, but all overnight users must park in the lot at the North Lake turnoff.

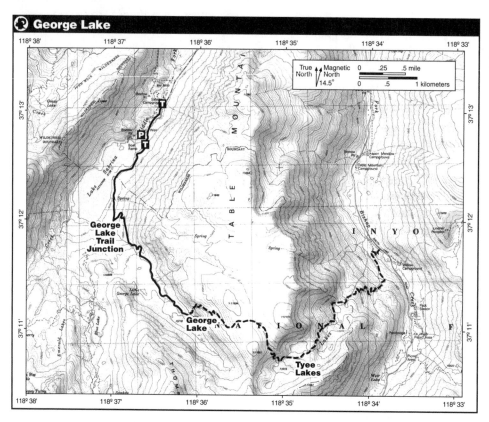

DESCRIPTION: From the trailhead, briefly follow the course of an old road through a cover of aspens until a single-track trail leads you around a corner to a fine view up Middle Fork Bishop Creek canyon. Immediately below you is the blue expanse of Lake Sabrina, with Middle Fork Bishop Creek cascading into a small cove at the lake's far end. Farther up the Middle Fork canyon, the rugged Sierra crest is crowned by the 13,000-foot summits of Mt. Darwin, Mt. Haeckel, Mt. Wallace, and Mt. Powell. You traverse across a hillside, past the John Muir Wilderness boundary to about the midway point of the lake, and then climb steadily up the slope. Near the end of the lake, 1.25 miles from the trailhead, you reach the junction with the trail to George Lake.

Turn left (northeast) at the junction and follow the George Lake Trail as it switchbacks moderately steeply up the exposed hillside. Approximately 0.5 mile from the junction, a scattering of whitebark pines begin to appear. Farther up the trail, you make a couple of crossings over George Creek. Continue the winding climb up the hillside until a milder ascent greets you, where the forest cover thickens near the lower end of a valley. You proceed on a pleasant grade up this valley, crossing the creek near the head of a pleasant meadow, 2.5 miles from the trailhead. Follow the west bank of George Creek for about 0.25 mile to where the trail veers left, crosses the creek once more, and climbs above the creek to circumvent a willow-choked meadow. Another 0.5 mile of trail brings you to George Lake (10,716').

Fine campsites are scattered around the north shore of the lake. Once the day-hiking anglers who frequent the lake depart, you should enjoy a healthy dose of solitude. The hours around sunrise and sunset should provide uncrowded fishing for brook and rainbow trout.

[O] Although the trail from George Lake over Table Mtn. to Tyee Lakes is faint, even nonexistent in parts, the route is straight-forward. With arrangements for pickup, you can enjoy an 8-mile hike from Lake Sabrina to the Tyee Lakes trailhead on South Lake Road. If arrangements can't be made, a dayhike to the great view atop the plateau on Table Mtn. is worth the extra effort. Halfway around the lakeshore, follow the main trail by turning east, away from the lake, and then climb switchbacks on an increasingly steep grade up the side of the canyon. Beyond the lip of the canyon the ascent eases slightly as you continue toward the crest of Table Mtn. Near the top, you follow nearly level trail to a high point with fine views of the Sierra crest and the surrounding countryside. To reach South Lake Road, reverse the description in Trip 55.

[R] **PERMITS:** Wilderness permit required for overnight stays (quota: 8 per day).

CAMPFIRES: Permitted (although legal, campfires are discouraged at George Lake due to lack of wood).

Lake Sabrina, Middle Fork Lakes Trail

NORTH LAKE TRAILHEAD

TRIP **58**

Lamarck Lakes

Ⓜ ⟋ DH / BP

DISTANCE: 2.2 miles one way to Lower Lamarck Lake; 2.7 miles one way to Upper Lamarck Lake

ELEVATION: 9255/10,920, +1700'/-35'

SEASON: Early July to mid-October

USE: Light

MAPS: *Mt. Darwin*

TRAIL LOG:

1.0	Grass Lake Jct.
2.2	Lower Lamarck Lake
2.7	Upper Lamarck Lake

INTRODUCTION: The Lamarck Lakes Trail offers hikers and backpackers a short route to a pair of lakes with rugged mountain scenery. While the distance is short, making the trail well suited for the weekend hiker or backpacker, the elevation gain of 1700 feet requires a reasonable amount of exertion. The maintained trail dead-ends at Upper Lamarck Lake, which may account for its relatively light use, but off-trail options include the rarely visited Wonder Lakes, as well as the classic cross-country route over Lamarck Col as described in Trip 59.

DIRECTIONS TO THE TRAILHEAD: From U.S. 395 in the center of Bishop, turn west onto Line Drive, which beyond the city limits becomes South Lake Road (Highway 168). Proceed 18 miles up the highway, past the South Lake junction, to the North Lake turnoff. Dayhikers follow this single-lane gravel road 1.0 mile to the day-use parking area. Backpackers must travel another 0.6 mile to the right-hand turn on the road leading to the dual overnight park-

ing lots (pit toilets), directly west of North Lake. Dayhikers and backpackers alike must walk up the continuation of the North Lake Campground access road from their cars to the trailhead.

DESCRIPTION: You begin your journey by walking the North Lake Campground access road to the campground, which is 1.0 mile from the day-use parking area and 0.7 mile from the overnight parking lots. Just past a sign at the campground entrance is the trailhead, designated by a trail sign, a John Muir Wilderness signboard, and the beginning of single-track trail. You follow this trail through aspens and pines, around a restroom, and then past campsites to a junction near the far end of the campground.

Bear left at the junction and cross a trio of willow-lined branches of North Fork Bishop Creek on plank bridges. Beyond the crossings, you climb moderately steeply up a hillside via switchbacks, passing beneath aspen and lodgepole pine cover. Limber pines join the mix as you approach a signed junction, 1.0 mile from the trailhead. The trail straight ahead travels 0.2 mile to aptly named Grass Lake, which as the season progresses becomes less of a lake and more of a meadow.

At the junction, you veer right, toward Lamarck Lakes, and continue to climb, initially through more pines. Switchbacks resume where the trail becomes steep, rocky, and exposed near some cliffs, from where you have views of Grass Lake and North Lake. Eventually, you leave the views behind and proceed through light forest, continuing the climb up another set of switchbacks. You pass above a small pond to your right, and then soon spy the lake ahead. A short drop brings you to a crossing of the outlet stream and Lower Lamarck Lake (10,662'), 2.2 miles from the trailhead.

Lower Lamarck Lake is quite scenic, nestled beneath steep granite cliffs and backdropped by the triangular summit of Peak 12153. Clumps of limber pine shade

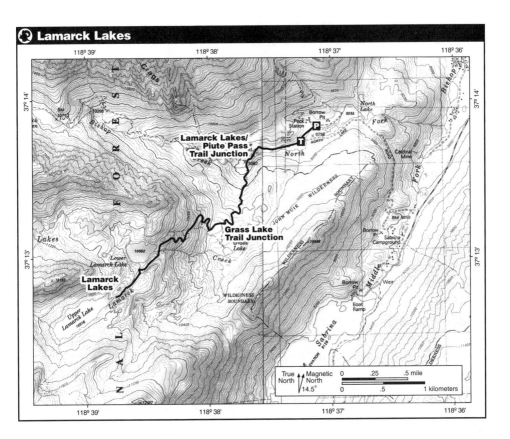

Lamarck Lakes

numerous heavily used campsites near the outlet stream and slightly less-used sites above the northeast shore. Fishing is reported to be fair for rainbow and brook trout.

From the lower lake you follow the trail through the rocky wash of Lamarck Creek. A series of short switchbacks takes you above and then down again to the creek, which you soon cross. The path follows the northwest side of the creek through tiny meadows dotted with pine to the outlet of Upper Lamarck Lake, 2.7 miles from the trailhead.

Upper Lamarck Lake, tucked in a narrow, steep-walled canyon, is much longer than its lower neighbor. The starkness of the upper lake and its surroundings make the area seem less hospitable than the lower lake. The only break in the cliffs and talus surrounding the lake is found where some

stunted pines cling desperately to the shallow soil on a rise above the southeast shore. Fine campsites are on this rise and also near some small tarns east of the lake. Upper Lamarck Lake harbors brook and rainbow trout.

Lower Lamarck Lake makes a fine base camp for off-trail forays west to a series of neighboring lakes and tarns known as Wonder Lakes.

IF YOU WERE WONDERING...

A packer sent into the high country to plant fish in the 1930s named the Wonder Lakes. After a difficult time getting his stock to the lakes, the story goes that he wondered how he had gotten the job done.

A trail follows the shoreline of Lower Lamarck Lake to its northwest side, where a steep climb is necessary to exit the basin. A faint use-trail, occasionally marked by ducks, follows the left side of the outlet stream over rock slabs to the beginning of the Wonder Lakes. The lakes are surrounded by meadows, scattered pockets of pines, and granite slabs and ramps. Steep cliffs and glacial moraines add a decidedly alpine character to the area. Less-developed campsites around the lower lakes provide a more secluded alternative to those at Lower Lamarck Lake. Anglers will find small brook trout in the lower lakes.

○ For a description of the route over Lamarck Col see Trip 59.

R **PERMITS:** Wilderness permit required for overnight stays (quota: 10 per day).
    CAMPFIRES: Not permitted.

The austere surroundings of Upper Lamarck Lake

TRIP 59

Evolution Basin via Lamarck Col

S ↗ BPx

DISTANCE: 10 miles one way to Evolution Lake

ELEVATION: 9255/12,920/10,852, +4505'/-1595'

SEASON: Late July to late September

USE: Light

MAP: *Mt. Darwin*

TRAIL LOG:

2.7	Upper Lamarck Lake
5.3	Lamarck Col
7.0	Lake 11592
7.6	Darwin Bench
8.6	JMT
9.4	Evolution Lake

INTRODUCTION: A classic glacier-scoured canyon, jagged peaks, and a string of crystalline alpine lakes combine to make Evolution Basin one of the premier destinations in the High Sierra. The lengthy distance one must overcome by trail just to reach the basin is perhaps the only thing that keeps such a spectacularly beautiful area from being overrun by adoring fans. By maintained trail, the closest trailheads are at North Lake, 30 miles away, and at South Lake, 23 miles away. However, armed with a spirit of adventure and rudimentary navigational skills, backpackers can shorten the distance to 10 miles by combining established trail with a cross-country route over Lamarck Col.

Actually, very little of this route can truly be classified as cross-country, since for most of the way backpackers follow a well-defined use-trail. From the Lamarck Lakes

Trail, a boot-beaten path has been established to the permanent snowfield just below 12,920 foot Lamarck Col. After you surmount the snowfield and cross the col, the next mile is by far the most difficult section. Here backpackers must negotiate a tedious 1,000-foot descent to Darwin Canyon, clambering over boulders and negotiating an extensive, ankle-twisting talus field without the aid of a trail. The lakes in the canyon signal relief—stay along their north sides. Along the shore of Lake 11623, the middle lake, a use-trail reappears and continues through Darwin Canyon, across verdant, pond-dotted Darwin Bench, and down the north wall of the canyon above Evolution Valley to a connection with the "superhighway" of the John Muir Trail.

The route to Lamarck Col is physically demanding, gaining over 3600 feet in 5.0 miles. In addition, the 12,920-foot elevation presents the dual concerns of acclimatization and the potential for afternoon lightning storms, which are not uncommon in the High Sierra. The small, permanent snowfield on the northeast side of the col may require the skill to wield an ice axe. As previously mentioned, the initial descent from the col requires extra care over steep, boulder-and-talus-strewn slopes, particularly for those who experience fatigue after carrying a loaded backpack from North Lake in one day. Although not as difficult as many cross-country routes across the Sierra crest, the route over Lamarck Col should not be undertaken lightly.

While Evolution Basin is the ultimate goal of this trip, there are some additional highlights along the way, and some beyond the basin, to consider. The austere lakes in Darwin Canyon are scenic in their own right, and offer a degree of solitude that is rare for this section of the High Sierra. Above the lakes, the towering cliffs of Mt. Mendel and Mt. Darwin, with ice-filled couloirs and clinging pocket glaciers, create an ambience as alpine as any in the range. The Darwin Bench is only 400 vertical feet below the lakes, but that's enough of an

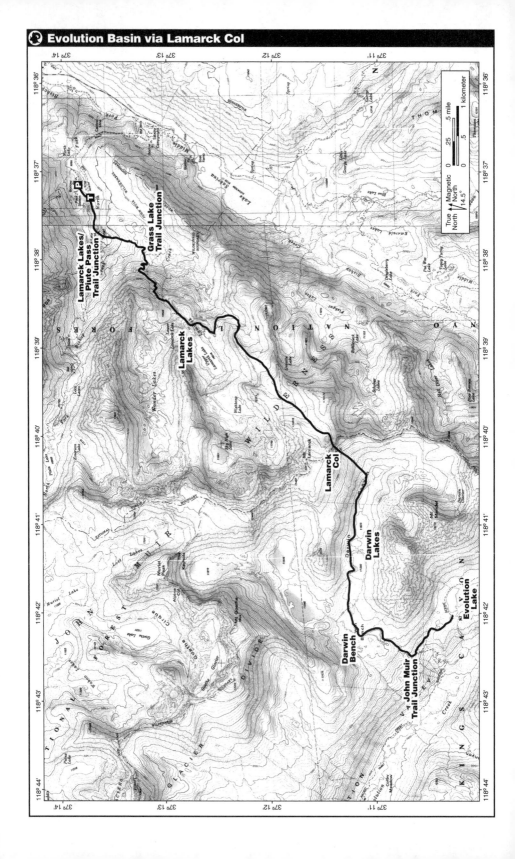

altitude change to create a distinctly different subalpine environment, composed of delightful tarns surrounded by low humps of granite interspersed with pockets of wildflower-filled meadows. There are a limited number of underdeveloped campsites at the lower Darwin Canyon lakes and around Darwin Bench. For suggestions for scenic wanderings beyond Evolution Basin, see Options, below.

DIRECTIONS TO THE TRAILHEAD: From U.S. 395 in the center of Bishop, turn west onto Line Drive, which beyond the city limits becomes South Lake Road (Highway 168). Proceed 18 miles up the highway, past the South Lake junction, to the North Lake turnoff. Dayhikers follow this single-lane gravel road 1.0 mile to the day-use parking area. Backpackers must travel another 0.6 mile to the right-hand turn on the road leading to the dual overnight parking lots (pit toilets), directly west of North Lake. Dayhikers and backpackers alike must walk up the continuation of the North Lake Campground access road from their cars to the trailhead.

DESCRIPTION: You begin your journey by walking the North Lake Campground access road to the campground, which is 1.0 mile from the day-use parking area and 0.7 mile from the overnight parking lots. Just past a sign at the campground entrance is the trailhead, designated by a trail sign, a John Muir Wilderness signboard, and the beginning of single-track trail. You follow this trail through aspens and pines, around a restroom, and then past campsites to a junction near the far end of the campground.

Bear left at the junction and cross a trio of branches of North Fork Bishop Creek on plank bridges. Beyond the crossings, you climb moderately steeply up a hillside via switchbacks, coming to a signed junction 1.0 mile from the trailhead. The trail straight ahead travels 0.2 mile to Grass Lake.

At the junction, you veer right, toward Lamarck Lakes, and continue to climb.

Switchbacks resume as the trail becomes steep, rocky, and exposed, near some cliffs, from where you have views of Grass Lake and North Lake. Eventually, you leave the views behind and proceed through light forest, continuing the climb up another set of switchbacks. You pass above a small pond to your right, and then soon spy the lake ahead. A short drop brings you to a crossing of the outlet stream and Lower Lamarck Lake (10,662'), 2.2 miles from the trailhead. Here, clumps of limber pine shade numerous heavily used campsites near the outlet stream and slightly less-used sites above the northeast shore.

From the lower lake you follow the trail through the rocky wash of Lamarck Creek. A series of short switchbacks takes you above and then down again to the creek, which you soon cross. The path follows the northwest side of the creek through tiny meadows dotted with pine to the outlet of Upper Lamarck Lake, which is 2.7 miles from the trailhead.

Leave the Lamarck Lakes Trail several hundred yards before reaching Upper Lamarck Lake, veer left to cross Lamarck Creek, and make a short climb, following a use-trail up the rise to the southeast. You continue up this trail past campsites and a small pond to a sloping meadow with a gurgling stream. With the aid of sporadic ducks, you make a winding climb alongside this stream before crossing it and continuing a serpentine ascent beside boulders and rocks, up a steep hillside. As you reach the crest of a ridge there are good views of Grass Lake, Lower and Upper Lamarck lakes, North Lake, Lake Sabrina, parts of the Owens Valley, and the White Mountains beyond.

The grade eases as you follow the trail around the left side of the ridge through widely scattered pines to a lushly vegetated hillside watered by seasonal streams. Leaving this oasis behind, the trail zigzags more steeply up an arid hillside, followed by an ascending traverse. More climbing is necessary to surmount another hill, after which the trail leads into a sloping valley below the Sierra crest. You proceed up this sloping valley toward the perennial snowfield just below the col. Cross the snowfield and continue up over rock to Lamarck Col (12,920'), 5.3 miles from the trailhead.  This lofty aerie provides a stunning view of Mt. Mendel, Mt. Darwin, and the Darwin glacier, as well as of the Darwin Canyon lakes and down into the deep cleft of Evolution Valley.

Aside from the brief crossing of the snowfield on the northeast side of the col, in an average season you should be able to follow a well-defined trail all the way from Lamarck Creek to Lamarck Col. However, the descent to the Darwin Lakes is a different matter, as you will have to pick your way down the boulder-and-talus-filled slopes without the aid of a trail. The route to the lakes is clear and not particularly difficult from a route finding perspective, but the actual descent is quite tedious while you're carrying a full pack. The going is easier once you reach Lake 11623, the middle lake, where you pick up the faint path that runs along the north shore of the Darwin Canyon lakes. A few decent camp-

sites are located near the shore of Lake 11592, 6.9 miles from the trailhead.

You continue along the faint path, following the creek that drains Darwin Canyon, to the beautiful tarn-dotted Darwin Bench (11,225'±), 7.6 miles from the trailhead. After the time-consuming descent of the barren, rock-filled slopes below the col, this area is a verdant oasis of vegetation. Little-used campsites scattered around the bench offer beautiful vistas across Evolution Valley.

Leave Darwin Bench and swing south on a 0.75-mile descent over a series of granite benches until you intersect the John Muir Trail, 8.6 miles from the trailhead. The goal is to meet the JMT near the top of the switchbacks climbing out of Evolution Valley, around 10,700 feet. From here, Evolution Lake is an easy 0.8-mile stroll southeast on the well-constructed JMT. Good campsites can be found near the small peninsula on the northwest shore (see Trip 62).

Multi-day options from Evolution Basin abound, including a variety of short and long loops back to North Lake. The

Evolution Lake, on the John Muir Trail

easiest alternative is to go northwest on the JMT 12.25 miles from Evolution Lake through Evolution Valley to a junction with the Piute Pass Trail. Go northeast and then east another 17.5 miles through Piute Canyon and Humphreys Basin to the trailhead (see Trips 62 & 60).

O Experienced cross-country travelers have even more options. After spending a day or two visiting the string of large alpine lakes in Evolution Basin, you could simply choose to return the way you came over Lamarck Col. However, for more variety, you could accept the challenge of a more technically difficult cross-country route over the Glacier Divide via either The Keyhole (class 3), Alpine Col (class 2), or Snow-Tongue Pass (class 2–3) to a connection with the Piute Pass Trail in Humphreys Basin.

O While in the heart of Evolution Basin, you could extend your visit on various cross-country loops, including a straightforward route through McGee Lakes and McGee Canyon that connects with the JMT (see Trip 62). More involved off-trail loop trips lead into the stark beauty of Ionian Basin. For a longer adventure, consider continuing through Ionian Basin to Martha Lake and then return to the JMT via the lightly used Goddard Canyon Trail (see Trips 62 & 38). From there you can head northwest on the JMT to the Piute Pass Trail, or go southeast through Evolution Valley to Evolution Lake and back to the trailhead over Lamarck Col (or via one of the options mentioned above).

O Mountaineers have a pair of ascents to consider. From Lamarck Col, Mt. Lamarck (13,417') is a straightforward class 2 climb. The south slope of Mt. Goethe (13,264') is a mere class 1 ascent from the isthmus between Lakes 11540 and 11546, in the basin just northwest of Darwin Canyon.

R PERMITS: Wilderness permit required for overnight stays (quota: 10 per day).
CAMPFIRES: Not permitted.

NORTH LAKE TRAILHEAD

TRIP 60

Piute Pass Trail to Humphreys Basin and the John Muir Trail

Ⓜ🅢 ⟋ DH/BP/BPx

DISTANCE: 6.8 miles to Humphreys Basin; 16.8 miles to the John Muir Trail

ELEVATION: 9255/11,423/10,800, +2175'/-645' 9255/11,423/8075, +2600/-3795

SEASON: Mid-July to Early October

USE: Moderate

MAPS: *Mt. Darwin, Mt. Tom, Mt. Hilgard, Mt. Henry*

TRAIL LOG:

2.2	Loch Leven
3.3	Piute Lake
4.6	Piute Pass
7.1	Lower Golden Trout Lake
11.8	Hutchinson Meadow, Pine Creek Pass Trail Jct.
16.8	JMT

INTRODUCTION: Just north of the Glacier Divide, which forms the northern boundary of Kings Canyon National Park, is a large, lake-dotted alpine basin that rivals any in the Sierra for sweeping beauty. Most of the effort required to reach this mountain splendor is expended in a moderate 5.3-mile climb along a well-maintained trail from North Lake (9255') to Piute Pass (11,423'). From the pass, a gentle descent propels travelers toward a bountiful assortment of pristine lakes scattered across the wide expanse of Humphreys Basin. Since the Piute Pass Trail is the only maintained path through the basin, reaching most of its

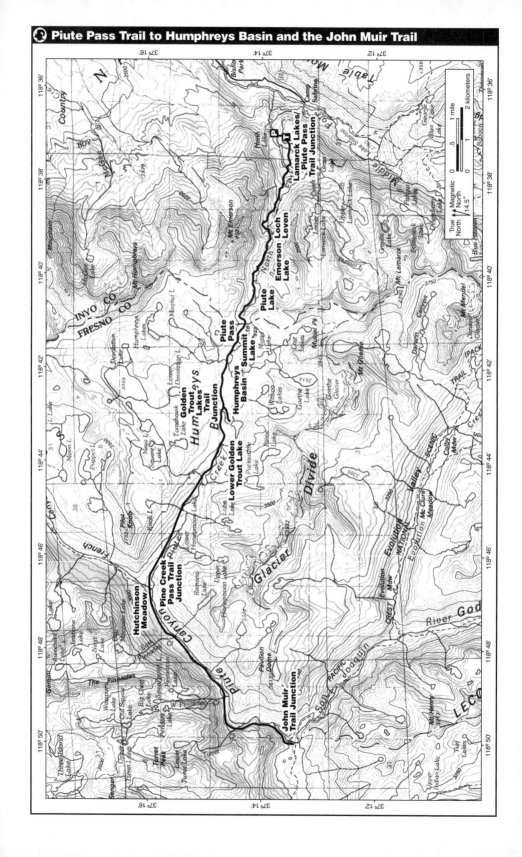

lakes will require you to follow use-trails or to travel cross-country. A base camp in Humphreys Basin may well be an off-trail enthusiast's nirvana, as the area is ripe for numerous explorations and the open terrain is fairly easy to negotiate. Piercing the skyline above the basin is a fine assortment of rugged Sierra peaks, culminating in 13,986-foot Mt. Humphreys, whose airy summit is a feather in any mountaineer's cap (the least difficult route to the top is rated class 4).

With elevations near 11,000 feet, Humphreys Basin will necessitate some acclimatization by those who reside at low altitudes. Spending the first night at one of the many Forest Service campgrounds east of the crest should be helpful. In addition, the open terrain at this altitude may pose a potential problem during lightning storms, which can develop rather quickly and are not uncommon during summer afternoons.

DIRECTIONS TO THE TRAILHEAD: From U.S. 395 in the center of Bishop, turn west onto Line Drive, which beyond the city limits becomes South Lake Road (Highway 168). Proceed 18 miles up the highway, past the South Lake junction, to the North Lake turnoff. Dayhikers follow this single-lane gravel road 1.0 mile to the day-use parking area. Backpackers must travel another 0.6 mile to the right-hand turn on the road leading to the dual overnight parking lots (pit toilets), directly west of North Lake. Dayhikers and backpackers alike must walk up the continuation of the North Lake Campground access road from their cars to the trailhead.

DESCRIPTION: You begin your journey by walking the North Lake Campground access road to the campground, either 1.0 mile from the day-use parking area or 0.7 mile from the overnight parking lots (mileages noted in the description and trail log start from the campground trailhead). Just past a sign at the campground entrance is the trailhead, designated by a trail sign, a John Muir Wilderness signboard, and the beginning of single-track trail. You follow

this trail through aspens and pines, around a restroom, and then past campsites to a junction near the far end of the campground.

Veer right on the Piute Pass Trail, soon passing into the John Muir Wilderness. You climb gently through aspen groves, stands of lodgepole pine, and patches of meadow dotted with wildflowers in season. Beyond two crossings of North Fork Bishop Creek, the grade of the trail increases to moderate as a series of switchbacks lead you above the canyon floor. A long, gently ascending traverse follows. You have fine views of the North Fork's waterfall plunging steeply out of the basin above, and of Peak 12691 on the left and Mt. Emerson and the multi-hued Piute Crags on the right. Rock steps and more switchbacks await as the moderate climb resumes, taking you up the narrowing canyon through diminishing amounts of lodgepole and then limber pine. At 2.2 miles from the trailhead you surmount the canyon headwall and reach the shore of Loch Leven (10,700'). Picnic spots and campsites are scattered around the lake, and fishing is fair for brook and rainbow trout.

Leaving Loch Leven behind, you make a short, moderate climb through scattered lodgepole and whitebark pines until the grade briefly eases near some ponds. However, more climbing is needed to take you up into the next basin. At 3.3 miles from the trailhead you arrive at the northeastern shore of Piute Lake (10,958'), where meadows, willows, and scattered clumps of whitebark pine greet you. Anglers can test their skill on brook and rainbow trout.

Campsites near the trail at Piute Lake are badly overused. Look for other possibilities scattered around the lakeshore, but try to find a site that affords protection from the strong winds that frequent this mostly open basin. For those desirous of more solitude, a 0.3-mile cross-country scramble southeast from the east shore of Piute Lake leads up a steep slope to rockbound Emerson Lake (11,219').

From Piute Lake you follow the trail northwest toward timberline, climbing over granite slabs and passing through meadow-lands sliced by refreshing brooks and dotted with tiny ponds. A final traverse leads to Piute Pass (11,423'), 4.6 miles from the trailhead. At the pass your stiff climb is rewarded by stunning views both near and far. Immediately below and west is the wide expanse of scenic, lake-dotted Humphreys Basin, towered over to the southwest by the rugged crest of the Glacier Divide, including Muriel Peak and Mt. Goethe. To the north, the dramatic summit of Mt. Humphreys tops out just shy of 14,000 feet. To the west are Pilot Knob and the deep cleft of the South Fork San Joaquin River.

If decision making is not your long suit, you will surely be in trouble in Humphreys Basin, as myriad lakes tempt adventurers in every direction. A modicum of navigational skills enables you to travel easily across the open terrain of the basin to a wide variety of scenic destinations. Enjoying the numerous ponds, tarns, and lakes could consume several days of splendid activity. With a willingness to leave the security of the trail come ample opportunities for solitude and exploration.

If you're headed toward Muriel Lake, find the faint use-trail heading southwest from just below the pass. Otherwise, follow the Piute Pass Trail on a winding descent around hummocks of granite and past tiny brooks coursing through meadows toward austere Summit Lake (11,225'), where anglers may find brook trout gliding through the pale blue waters. The route of the trail passes well above the level of the lake and continues on a gentle grade across the basin. Approximately 1.5 miles from the pass, you reach a junction where use-trails branch both north and southwest. The more heavily traveled path, to the southwest, heads nearly a mile to the popular Golden Trout Lakes, where camping is not allowed within 500 feet of Lower Golden Trout Lake (10,786'). The northern path leads up to large, aptly named Desolation Lake (11,375'), a fine base camp for short jaunts to smaller neighboring lakes.

Goethe Lake, in Humphreys Basin, from Alpine Col

The Piute Pass Trail is a gateway into some of Kings Canyon's most impressive terrain. By continuing westward, you can descend through a lodgepole pine forest that progressively thickens with the corresponding drop in elevation. Soon you reach a series of subalpine gardens that line Piute Creek and carpet the floor of Piute Canyon. A wide array of wildflowers splash color across the green meadowlands from early to midsummer in all but the driest of years. At 11.8 miles from the trailhead, you cross the braided creek draining French Canyon and come to fine campsites in Hutchinson Meadow (9438') and a junction with the Pine Creek Pass Trail heading north. From the picturesque meadow you have excellent views of Pilot Knob and other nearby peaks. Anglers will find the fishing good for rainbow and golden trout in both Piute and French Canyon creeks.

Away from Hutchinson Meadow, you descend mildly through lodgepole pines to a ford of East Pinnacles Creek. Beyond the creek the grade of descent increases as you follow the often rocky, sometimes winding trail toward the South Fork San Joaquin River, with plunging Piute Creek as your companion. After an easy ford of West Pinnacles Creek and bridged crossings over a pair of gullies, the trail bends south and soon crosses multi-channeled Turret Creek. Eventually the lodgepole forest gives way to chaparral, granting fine views of Pavilion Dome to the east. You continue the rocky descent along Piute Creek to a junction with the John Muir Trail, 5.0 miles from Hutchinson Meadow and 16.8 miles from the trailhead. Plenty of good campsites are near the junction.

O In Humphreys Basin off the main trail, there are too many options for side trips to cover in this limited space. Truly, this area is a cross-country enthusiast's delight. Just about every lake in the basin is relatively easy to reach and offers extraordinary scenery. Generally, the terrain south of the trail in the shadow of the Glacier Divide offers steep-walled cirques filled with talus, whereas the landscape north of the trail is more rolling and open. With a little creativity, adventurous off-trail types can extend their wanderings south across the Glacier Divide into Kings Canyon National Park, or north through very scenic terrain within the John Muir Wilderness.

O Armed with plenty of time, you can head southeast from the junction on the JMT to either beautiful Evolution Valley (see Trip 62) or less-traveled Goddard Canyon. In Goddard Canyon, a route takes you to Martha Lake (see Trip 38), the western gateway to the off-trail paradise of Ionian Basin. A classic Sierra excursion follows the JMT south to Evolution Basin, over Lamarck Col, and back to the trailhead at North Lake, a journey of 38.5 total miles (see Trips 59 and 62).

R **PERMITS:** Wilderness permits required for overnight stays (quota: 39 per day).

CAMPFIRES: Not permitted.

CAMPING: No camping within 500 feet of Lower Golden Trout Lake.

JOHN MUIR TRAIL

TRIP **61**

John Muir Trail: Kearsarge Pass Trail to Bishop Pass Trail

Ⓜ️Ⓢ ✝ BPx

DISTANCE: 42 miles; +7.0 miles from Onion Valley trailhead; +13 miles to South Lake trailhead

ELEVATION: 10,865/11,978/8547/12,130/ 10,098/12,100/8020/8710, +8600'/-10,700'

SEASON: Late July to early October

MAPS: *Mt. Clarence King, Mt. Pinchot, Split Mountain, North Palisade*

TRAIL LOG:

0.0	Kearsarge Pass Trail/ JMT Jct.
2.3	Glen Pass
5.0	Rae Lakes/60 Lakes Basin Jct.
7.0	Baxter Pass Trail Jct.
10.5	Woods Creek Crossing Paradise Valley Trail Jct.
11.25	Explorer Pass Route
14.0	Sawmill Pass Trail Jct.
18.0	Pinchot Pass
20.75	Bench Lake Trail Jct./Taboose Pass Trail Jct.
22.5	South Fork Kings River Crossing Muro Blanco/Cartridge Pass Routes
23.75	Vennacher Col Route
28.0	Mather Pass
31.25	Lower Palisade Lake/Cirque Pass Route
35.0	Deer Meadow/Cataract Creek Route
38.25	Middle Fork Kings River Middle Fork Trail Jct.
39.25	Grouse Meadows
42.0	Bishop Pass Trail Jct.

INTRODUCTION: This stretch of the route between the Kearsarge Pass and Bishop Pass trails is one of the most scenic along the 210-mile John Muir Trail. Backpackers will have to cross three 12,000-foot passes —Glen, Pinchot, and Mather—along the way, providing fine vantage points from which to observe the length and breadth of the High Sierra. In addition, they will encounter three "holes," deep canyons including the crossings of Woods Creek and the South Fork Kings River, as well as an extended journey along the Middle Fork Kings River through LeConte Canyon. A number of picturesque basins provide rich scenery and a plethora of enticing campsites. Striking alpine peaks, exquisite lakes, rushing rivers, tumbling creeks, wildflower-covered meadows, and magnificent forests will delight wilderness lovers throughout the length of this trip. Encompassing a wide range of elevation, this journey exposes backpackers to a correspondingly wide range of bio-zones, including montane, subalpine, and alpine.

Aside from the usual concerns of a long-distance High Sierra backpack, a few additional matters should be considered. Winters of average-to-above-average snowfall may drape the high passes with blankets of snow that persist throughout most of the summer. When such conditions exist, the skilled use of an ice axe may be necessary to successfully negotiate the passes. In addition, the unbridged river and creek crossings along the JMT may be unsafe during the height of snowmelt. Before embarking on this trip, check with the Park Service about current conditions.

DIRECTIONS TO THE TRAILHEAD:
START: For access to the JMT via the Kearsarge Pass Trail, follow directions in Trip 39 to the Onion Valley Trailhead.

END: For access to the South Lake Trailhead, reverse the description in Trips 51 and 52.

DESCRIPTION: The first leg of your journey involves getting to Rae Lakes Basin, as described in Trip 41, which follows the

Kearsarge Pass Trail from Onion Valley to a junction with the JMT, and then over Glen Pass to Rae Lakes basin. Backpackers can also access Rae Lakes from the west via the 13.5-mile Bubbs Creek Trail to a junction with the JMT (see Trip 36).

Beyond the lower Rae Lake, you follow the trail on a slight decline north across a hillside dotted with widely scattered lodgepole pines. Pass a pond and come above the east shore of meadow-rimmed Arrowhead Lake (10,292'), backdropped by a fine view of King Spur. Near the far shore, where the JMT reaches the lake, a use-trail branches away to potential campsites with bear boxes nearby.

Just past a small waterfall below Arrowhead Lake, you make a log crossing over the outlet and soon spy the next lake below. A brief descent leads you by steep cliffs and the willow-choked inlet to Dollar Lake (10,205'±). Granite outcroppings and groves of lodgepole pines share the west shore, and a large talus slope rises up from the lake's east side to Diamond Peak at the Sierra crest. As from Rae Lakes, fine views

from here of Fin Dome and the King Spur add a sublime sense of alpine beauty to the setting. A limited number of campsites are at Dollar Lake, but a sign encourages overnighters to go south on the trail to better sites around Arrowhead Lake. The one-night camping limit for the Rae Lakes basin includes Arrowhead and Dollar lakes. Near Dollar Lake's north shore, an old post marks the inconspicuous junction with the Baxter Pass Trail, 7.0 miles from the Kearsarge Pass Trail junction. Solitude-seekers may elect to climb 2.25 miles north and then east away from the JMT to fair campsites at the largest Baxter Lake (see Trip 44).

You leave the Rae Lakes area behind and follow a gentle trail alongside South Fork Woods Creek through pleasant terrain composed of meadows, boulders, and widely scattered lodgepole pines. A mile-long descent leads through thickening forest to a crossing of the wildflower-and-willow-lined creek draining Sixty Lake Basin, where a couple of small campsites are nearby. You pass through the gate of a

Rae Lakes and Fin Dome

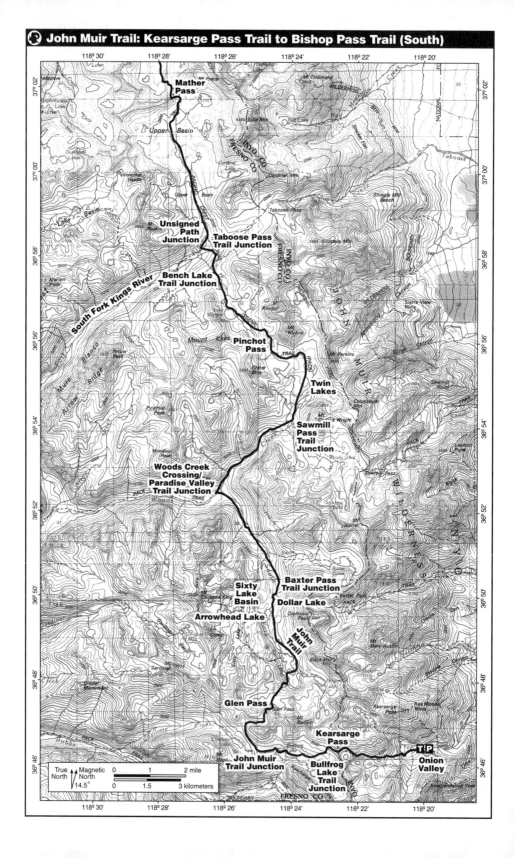

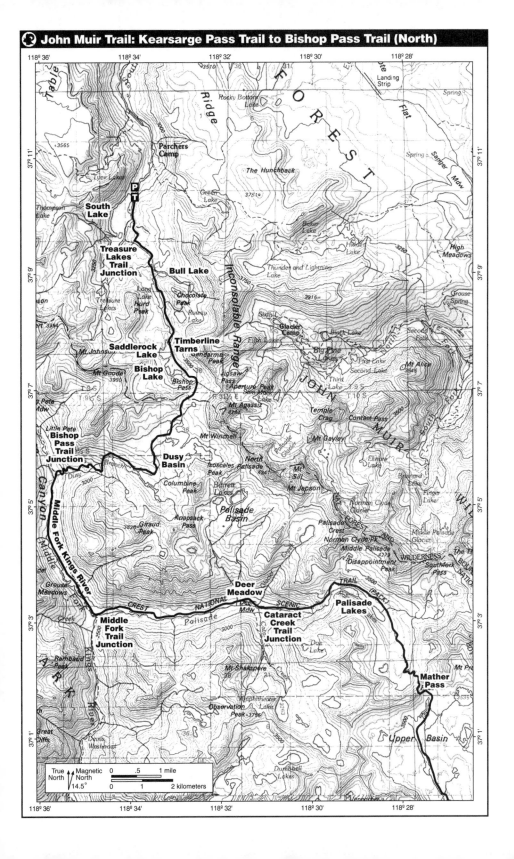

Upper Tyndall Creek Basin, on the John Muir Trail

barbed-wire fence, descend a rocky ridge, and come to a boggy meadow. Beyond the meadow, you proceed on the JMT amid open, rocky terrain to the small stream rushing down from Lake 10315 (3144 on the *Mt. Clarence King* map). You continue the steady descent well above the level of the South Fork, passing through stretches of lush vegetation, sagebrush-covered slopes, and a light forest composed of aspens, red firs, and lodgepole pines. The trail leads around the north end of King Spur and down to Woods Creek (8492'), 10.5 miles from the Kearsarge Pass Trail junction.

Numerous campsites nestle beneath red firs, lodgepole pines, aspens, and alders on either side of Woods Creek, a major stop along the JMT and the Rae Lakes Loop, so don't expect to have the place to yourself. A pit toilet is a short distance away from the trail on a hillside above the north bank. Although campfires are permitted, most of the firewood has been picked over by the hordes of campers who find temporary shelter here during the summer months. An

impressive suspension bridge has been constructed high above Woods Creek to avoid the kind of torrents that washed out previous structures.

Beyond the bridge, on the north side of Woods Creek, you reach a well-signed junction with the Paradise Valley Trail, which leads to Cedar Grove, 15 miles away. Continuing northbound on the JMT, you climb away from the deep cleft of Woods Creek through manzanita and scattered Jeffrey pines. You come alongside the creek cascading mightily across sloping slabs of granite. The wildly churning waters produce dramatic spouts and fountains, particularly during the height of snowmelt. Where you step across a flower-lined tributary, the forest of Jeffrey pines and junipers gives way to an open vista up the canyon, including a lovely cascade emanating from Window Lake. You soon step across the creek from Window Lake, 0.75 mile from the Woods Creek crossing. The Explorer Pass cross-country route begins here, leading to Window Lake in 1.25 miles (see Options). As you continue up the canyon, take the time to gaze behind you at the deep cleft of Woods Creek and the mighty ramparts of King Spur. Beyond a barbed-wire fence, 12 miles from the Kearsarge Pass Trail junction, you come to the ford of White Fork Woods Creek. Potentially difficult in early summer, you should be able to boulderhop this stream easily later in the season.

The moderate climb continues through a lush area of wildflowers, ferns, willows, and aspens to a set of switchbacks that lead you higher up the hillside. Crossing a brook lined with an array of wildflowers, you enter lodgepole forest, passing above a pair of fair campsites. In the midst of more switchbacks, you climb into the no-fires zone and then break out into the open to a view of Mt. Cedric Wright. The winding trail leads to a creek crossing and the inconspicuous junction with the Sawmill Pass Trail (10,347'), 14 miles from the Kearsarge Pass Trail junction. You may find only a stick poking out of a small cairn to mark the junction. Fine campsites can be found near the creek, or around Woods Lake (10,760'±), 1.75 miles up the Sawmill Pass Trail from the JMT.

From the junction, you follow the mildly graded JMT west of Mt. Cedric Wright for about 0.5 mile to a use-trail leading to Twin Lakes (10,595'±). The short path leads to the lakes, set in an open, view-packed bowl below the rocky northwest slope of Mt. Cedric Wright. Scattered pines offer partial shade to fair campsites above the west shores of both lakes. Despite lying just east of the JMT, the campsites appear to be only lightly used.

Back on the JMT, you climb moderately through open terrain filled with grasses, sedges, and scattered clumps of whitebark pine, until the grade eases momentarily near a pond. A few fair campsites are found on a low hill east of the trail overlooking the pond. Past the pond a moderately graded climb resumes through open terrain, which allows for expansive views of the upper Woods Creek drainage, including the barren, rust-colored slopes of Mt. Wynne

to the northwest. Unnamed tarns short distances off the trail provide alternate destinations for exploration and lonesome camping.

As you enter the realm above timberline, the trail curves west around a rocky hillside into a side canyon sprinkled with delightful tarns rimmed by small pockets of tundra-like meadows. Soon you say farewell to the meadows and climb moderately across barren territory of boulders and talus below the pass ahead. The switchbacking ascent leads you to Pinchot Pass (12,110'), 18 miles from the Kearsarge Pass Trail junction, where splendid vistas greet you. The view northwest reveals a string of sparkling tarns set in the stark canyon descending toward the South Fork Kings River. In the northwest distance rise the dark, brooding summits of the Palisades. Behind you, south beyond the serrated face of Mt. Cedric Wright, lies a sea of endless peaks.

You follow a rocky, zigzagging descent across the barren slope below Pinchot Pass. Before you reach the first tarn, the grade of the trail mellows a tad, and patches of grass and a refreshing creek herald a welcome return to more hospitable climes. You pass above the tarn on a winding, moderate descent across sandy slopes, broken by pockets of grassy meadow and scattered wildflowers. You proceed past a small pond and over a small creek to Lake Marjorie (11,132'), 1.25 miles from the pass, nicely framed by steep, dark gray slopes plunging from Mt. Ickes. A few Spartan campsites are spread around the shoreline among scattered dwarf whitebark pines.

Continuing the march toward the South Fork, your descent leads past lovely tarns, each with a few pleasant campsites nearby. Along the way you cross a number of small creeks surrounded by a progressively increasing amount of vegetation. Whitebark pines give way to lodgepole pines near the last tarn in the chain, where the inlet cascades over granite blocks before sinuously drifting through green meadows above the south shore. Passing along the west shore of the tarn, you reach an impressive view of Cirque Crest across the deep divide of the South Fork canyon. A moderate descent leads you through lush meadows and shrubs to a junction on your left with the faint Bench Lake Trail (10,794'), 20.75 miles from the Kearsarge Pass Trail junction (see Trip 46). Even though a small sign denotes the junction, the little-used path to Bench Lake can easily be missed if you're not paying attention.

About 25 yards past the junction, the JMT leads to a ford of the creek. Just beyond, a sign points toward a seasonal ranger station just up the hillside. Away from the creek you enter light lodgepole forest and quickly come to a signed junction with the upper Taboose Pass Trail (10,794'). A moderate-to-steep descent follows as you wind down into the South Fork Kings River canyon. As you approach the river, the roar of pounding water reverberates across the deep cleft. In the middle of the switchbacking descent, you cross a tributary stream and continue to the bottom of the forested canyon. You reach the South Fork Kings River (10,840') at 22.5 miles from the Kearsarge Pass Trail junction. Once at the South Fork, you must negotiate your way across its churning waters using a combination of well-placed rocks and logs, or else find a convenient place to ford. An islet just downstream divides the river into two channels, and here may provide the safest crossing, although the ford can be quite difficult in early season. Limited camping is available near the river, but better sites are only a short distance away, north up the JMT.

After the long descent from Pinchot Pass to the South Fork, you now begin the 5.5-mile ascent toward Mather Pass. A short distance beyond the crossing of the South Fork is a faint path heading downstream, which off-trail enthusiasts may follow for trips through Muro Blanco, or to a connection with the route over Cartridge Pass. Remaining on the JMT, you ascend the drainage of the South Fork as it bends north, crossing a couple of flower-lined streams along the way. Near the second stream, about 0.3 mile from the crossing, an unsigned path leads right to fair campsites nestled beneath lodgepole pines near the banks of the South Fork. Past the campsites, the path crosses the river and climbs toward Taboose Pass.

Beyond this unsigned path, you continue the ascent on the JMT through wildflower-covered meadows and groves of lodgepole pine. Approximately 0.75 mile from the crossing of South Fork Kings River, you encounter a stream draining the basin below Vennacher Needle, where a cross-country route heads for Vennacher Col (see Options, below). You continue up the JMT, with ever-expanding views of Upper Basin and distant Mather Pass. You cross numerous steams and rivulets as you proceed up the trail, passing through exquisite terrain, composed of tranquil, wildflower-carpeted meadows, clumps of shrubs, scattered whitebark pines, and granite boulders and slabs. The ever-widening basin is enclosed by steep, craggy ridges on three sides, culminating in the rugged Sierra crest to the east. Cardinal Mtn. (13,397'), Split Mtn. (14,058'), and Mt. Prater (13,329') stand guard along the crest, towering over the scenic basin.

At 25 miles from the Kearsarge Pass Trail junction, you cross South Fork Kings River and continue the ascent through the Upper Basin. As you march on toward timberline and the pass ahead, the few widely scattered whitebark pines at this elevation appear more like shrubs than trees. Along the way, you step over numerous rivulets and pass lovely tarns, in constant view of the seemingly impassable headwall below the pass. Larger, more distant tarns emit their siren call, beckoning the unhurried traveler to leave the security of the trail and explore the far reaches of the basin, which offers austere yet dramatically scenic locales for campsites.

You approach Mather Pass from the east, sweeping around the base of the wall below the pass on a long ascending traverse. With an incredible view as your constant companion, you next follow a series of switchbacks up the slope that leads to rockbound Mather Pass (12,100'), 28 miles from the Kearsarge Pass Trail junction. Gazing north from the pass, you see the dark-gray 14,000-foot spires of the Palisades piercing the azure Sierra sky. In the canyon to the northwest, dark-colored tarns and the uppermost Palisade Lake contrast vividly with the surrounding granite of the basin. Last looks south to Upper Basin, east to Split Mtn., and northeast to Mt. Prater are stunning as well.

From Mather Pass, you wind on rocky trail down the talus-covered slope. Signs of life appear on the descent—pockets of grasses, sedges, and wildflowers between fields of boulders. You cross a number of flower-lined brooks and streams during the descent, and encounter widely scattered pines again as you lose elevation. Along the way, you have excellent views of Palisade Lakes and the surrounding peaks and ridges. About 2.3 miles from the pass, you come well above the northeast shore of upper Palisade Lake. Soon you cross a pic-

turesque stream cascading steeply toward the lake through a willow-and-flower-lined glade. Just beyond the stream are small campsites near the trail, offering great views but little privacy. You continue across a hillside toward the far end of the upper lake into an area of lush vegetation near a pair of tiny rivulets.

Above the lower lake, you proceed across the hillside on a series of granite benches interspersed with pockets of vegetation. After stepping across another charming rivulet, which dances across the trail and tumbles down the slope toward the lower lake, you follow the trail around slabs and cliffs to a series of short switchbacks that bring you alongside the lakeshore near the far end of Lower Palisade Lake, 31.75 miles from the Kearsarge Pass Trail junction. If you wish to camp near the lake, look for sites at the east end. Near the west end of the lake, you step across a stream from a scenic waterfall that pours down the face of a rock wall above.

Tarn below Arrow Peak, on the Explorer Pass cross-country route

Leaving the lower Palisade Lake, you quickly encounter a small, delightful side canyon where yet another stream cascades down the hillside and flows through clumps of willow and tiny pockets of wildflower-covered meadow before joining Palisade Creek. Campers may find a few cozy sites spread around the floor of this petite basin. A cross-country route leaves the JMT in this side canyon on an ascent over Cirque Pass (12,000'±) and on toward Palisade Basin (see Trip 52). A short, pleasant stroll leads around the edge of the basin to the beginning of a major descent.

You ease into the descent as you follow the trail briefly above Palisade Creek, which plummets from the basin holding the two Palisade Lakes by means of short waterfalls, cataracts, and cascades. You proceed down the trail on a winding descent sandwiched between low humps of granite, with occasional glimpses of the plunging creek. You pass over a granite outcropping, from where you have an incredible view of the deep cleft of the canyon 1,500 feet below and of the towering peaks along the crest above. Mt. Shakespeare is southwest, Devils Crags, the Black Divide, and the Citadel rise sharply to the west, while 12,608-foot Giraud Peak dominates the skyline to the northwest.

You follow the trail around some cliffs to the start of a series of tight switchbacks, known as the "Golden Staircase," carved out of the granite on the north face of the canyon. The fact that this portion of the 200-mile JMT was the last completed comes as no surprise to those who experience this section of the trail firsthand. Near the bottom of the descent, you pass through a lushly vegetated hillside, kept well watered by a series of seeps. You continue down the rocky trail, switchbacking occasionally until you reach the floor of the canyon, where you meet young aspens, lodgepole pines, and red firs.

The cool shade of the forest is a welcome relief from the heat of the day, and your feet are sure to appreciate the dirt path carpeted with pine needles after the rocky descent of the Golden Staircase. You pass a nice distribution of forested campsites along the creek, cross multi-braided Glacier Creek, and stroll above Deer Meadow (8860'), which today bears little resemblance to an actual meadow, since the flat is filled with a light forest of lodgepole pines. You reach an unmarked junction with the Cataract Creek Trail at 35 miles from the Kearsarge Pass Trail junction. Just beyond the junction you'll find some good campsites.

On a moderate descent, you cross the multi-branched outlet draining Palisade Basin and continue down the Palisade Creek canyon. The first break in the timber is the result of a large avalanche that destroyed some fair-sized trees. The forest is composed primarily of lodgepole pines in the upper end of the canyon, joined by aspens, white firs, and Jeffrey pines as you proceed downstream. Manzanita, snowbrush, sagebrush, and young aspens cover the ground between the trees. About 2 miles from Deer Meadow, you enter a large clearing bordered by aspens and willows, known unofficially as Stillwater Meadow. Palisade Creek glides lazily through this peaceful flat, reportedly providing good fishing for golden trout. Good campsites are found near the far end of the clearing.

You continue the descent away from Stillwater Meadow as the gradient increases over the next mile. You wind down past the supports for the bridge that used to span Palisade Creek, which provided access to the Middle Fork Trail. The bridge was destroyed by flooding in the early 1980s and is not slated for replacement. Your descent terminates near the meeting of Palisade Creek and the Middle Fork Kings River (8020'), 38.25 miles from the Kearsarge Pass Trail junction. A small, forested flat provides good camping near the tumbling rapids of the Middle Fork. From the flat, a short use-trail leads to a ford across the broad channel of Palisade Creek, providing access to the Middle Fork Trail. When the creek is running high and swift, backpackers may find a better spot at which to ford the creek above the former bridge — plan on getting your feet wet regardless of where you cross the creek. Any crossing of Palisade Creek is potentially dangerous and should be attempted only when conditions allow for safe passage.

Northwest at the confluence, a stiff climb soon leads to a more moderate ascent through light forest as you follow the course of the Middle Fork Kings River. You cross the stream draining a trio of unnamed lakes below the southeast face of Giraud Peak, and then pass through an open hillside covered with sagebrush to Grouse Meadows (8250'), 1.0 mile from the confluence of the Middle Fork and Palisade Creek. Grouse Meadows is quite scenic — the Middle Fork assumes a sedate, meandering course through an expansive field of lush grassland, backdropped by the near-vertical granite walls of LeConte Canyon, a scene strikingly reminiscent of Yosemite Valley. A number of campsites offer fine views of the meadows and the river, although these sites are heavily used, and the mosquitoes can be bothersome in early season.

Beyond the serene grasslands of Grouse Meadows, the placid river begins to pick up speed again, and you climb mildly up the trail through scattered-to-light forest. As you continue the gentle ascent, the effects of an old avalanche and a past forest fire combine with natural breaks in the forest to provide occasional views of the surrounding terrain. Towering over LeConte Canyon, the mighty granite ramparts of the Citadel combine with the cascading stream from Ladder Lake to paint a dramatic mountain portrait on the west side of the valley. Where the trail draws nearer to the Middle Fork, shooting cascades of white water catapult across granite slabs. Farther up the trail, watery ribbons of the Dusy Branch slide gracefully down the sloping face of an extensive granite slab on the deep canyon's eastern wall. Near the crossing of the Dusy Branch, campsites are just off the trail. A bridge leads across the creek past more campsites to the signed junction with the Bishop Pass Trail, 42 miles from the Kearsarge Pass Trail junction. Nearby, the LeConte Ranger Station is just a short walk up a lateral to your left.

From the Bishop Pass Trail junction, reverse the description in Trips 51 and 52 to follow the Bishop Pass Trail 13 miles to the South Lake trailhead. Or you can continue up the JMT, as described in Trip 62.

EXPLORER PASS CROSS-COUNTRY ROUTE: Off-trail enthusiasts may want to forsake the JMT 0.75 mile above the crossing of Woods Creek to follow a cross-country route up to Window Lake, over Explorer Pass, and down to Bench Lake. Leave the JMT where it crosses the outlet from Window Lake and climb up the brush-filled slope east of the creek and south of a small lake to fine campsites at Window Lake. Follow the rocky drainage north from the lake on the east bank of the stream to Explorer Pass (12,250'±). A class 3 chute, often snow-filled, on the northwest side of the pass is the crux of the route. Once past this difficult section, descend the valley below and then traverse northeast to forest-rimmed Bench Lake. To return to the JMT, follow the Bench Lake Trail 1.5 miles east (see Trip 46).

CARTRIDGE PASS CROSS-COUNTRY ROUTE: Leave the JMT on the north bank of the South Fork Kings River and head downstream for 2 miles to the small brook that drains a pair of good-sized tarns below Cartridge Pass (stream doesn't appear on the *Mt. Pinchot* quad). Climb along the east bank of this stream to tarns, then ascend talus slopes to Cartridge Pass (11,680'±). Make a steep, rocky descent to easier talus and then drop into exquisite Lakes Basin. Two routes exit the basin. The first follows a 4.5-mile cross-country descent of Cartridge Creek from Marion Lake northwest to the Middle Fork Kings River Trail. From there, the trail can be followed 4.5 miles north to the JMT, just after a potentially difficult ford of Palisade Creek. The second route heads north from the basin, passing by Dumbell and

Amphitheater Lakes before descending the abandoned trail down Cataract Creek to the JMT at Deer Meadow, which, like the first route, also requires a potentially difficult ford of Palisade Creek.

◯ CIRQUE, POTLUCK AND KNAPSACK PASSES CROSS-COUNTRY ROUTE: Cross-country enthusiasts can take a shortcut to the Bishop Pass Trail by leaving the JMT just beyond the northwest end of lower Palisade Lake. Ascend northwest over a series of granite ledges to the west of a small tarn near the head of the cirque above. Climb to the broad saddle of Cirque Pass (12,000'±) and then descend to the lake below (11,672'), where you will find some good campsites. Cross Glacier Creek near the southwest shore and climb over scree and granite ledges to Potluck Pass (12,120'±). From the pass, follow a slightly descending traverse to a flat saddle directly northeast of Peak 12005, and then drop to the northeast shore of the largest Barrett Lake (shown as Lake 11523 on the *North Palisade* quad). Look for secluded campsites above the north and northeast shores. Pass south of Lake 11468 and traverse the south slope of Columbine Peak to Knapsack Pass (11,680'±). Descend the rocky gully west of the pass to the lower lakes in Dusy Basin, where plenty of excellent campsites await. An easy traverse northwest across the basin leads to the Bishop Pass Trail.

Ⓡ PERMITS: Wilderness permit required for overnight stays (quota: 60 per day).

CAMPFIRES: Not permitted above 10,000 feet.

CAMPING: One-night limit at Charlotte Lake and in Rae Lakes basin.

.

TRIP **62**

John Muir Trail: Bishop Pass Trail to Piute Pass Trail

Ⓜ / BPx

DISTANCE: 25.75 miles; +13 miles from South Lake trailhead; +17.5 miles to North Lake trailhead

ELEVATION: 8710/11,955/8050, +4200'/-4870'

SEASON: Late July to early October

USE: Moderate to High

MAPS: *North Palisade, Mt. Goddard, Mt. Darwin, Mt. Henry*

TRAIL LOG:

0.0	Bishop Pass Trail Jct.
0.5	Little Pete Meadow
1.75	Big Pete Meadow
7.0	Helen Lake
	Ionian Basin Routes
8.0	Muir Pass
10.0	Wanda Lake
11.75	Sapphire Lake
	McGee Lakes Route
14.0	Evolution Lake
15.0	Lamarck Col/The Keyhole/Alpine Col & Snow-Tongue Pass Routes
17.25	Colby Meadow
18.0	McClure Meadow
	McGee Lakes Route
20.25	Evolution Meadow
20.75	Packsaddle Pass & Lobe Pass Routes
22.25	S. Fork San Joaquin River Goddard Canyon Trail Jct.
24.5	Aspen Meadows
25.75	Piute Pass Trail Jct.

INTRODUCTION: This 25-mile stretch of the John Muir Trail passes through the remarkably scenic Evolution Basin, where a narrow, rockbound canyon holds a string of jeweled alpine lakes in the shadow of towering peaks. Unofficially referred to as the Evolution Group, Mt. Huxley, Mt. Fiske, Mt. Wallace, Mt. Haeckel, Mt. Spencer, Mt. Darwin and Mt. Mendel reign over the region. Six of these summits reach above 13,000 feet, with 12,431-foot Mt. Spencer the lone exception. Although Theodore S. Solomons, charter member of the Sierra Club and JMT visionary, named the peaks in 1895 for contemporary proponents of evolutionary theory, such appellations fall quite short of capturing the majesty of the area. Subalpine Evolution Valley is the picturesque equivalent of alpine Evolution Basin, where the verdant grasslands of Colby, McClure, and Evolution meadows are interspersed with serene lodgepole pine forest. The sinuous course of Evolution Creek flowing gracefully through its namesake valley complements the pastoral ambience found in the meadows.

If Evolution Basin and Valley were the only treasures found along this section of the JMT, the trip would be well worth undertaking. However, additional gems await your discovery. From the Bishop Pass Trail junction, the JMT passes through the deep cleft of LeConte Canyon beneath the massive exfoliated granite face of Langille Peak and the dark shadow of the Black Divide. Beyond the canyon, a rigorous climb leads past picturesque tarns and austere Helen Lake to 11,955-foot Muir Pass. The area around Muir Pass is the gateway for off-trail routes to the extraordinary Ionian Basin (see Options, below). From the pass, a descent leads into the magnificent Evolution country, and then along the roaring course of the South Fork San Joaquin River through a deep chasm to the Piute Pass Trail Junction. If wildflower-laden meadows, glacier-carved canyons, roaring creeks, striking alpine peaks, and crystalline lakes are the ultimate features of a classic backcountry experience, then this journey will not disappoint.

Evolution Lake in Evolution Basin

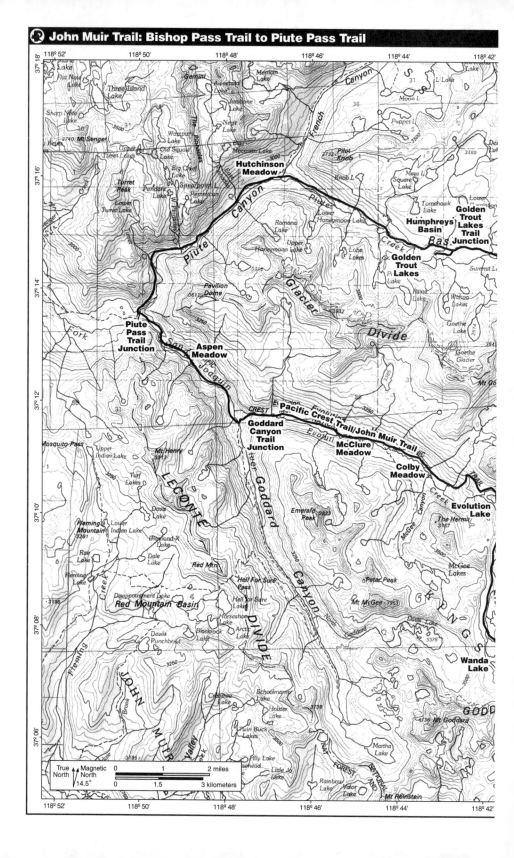

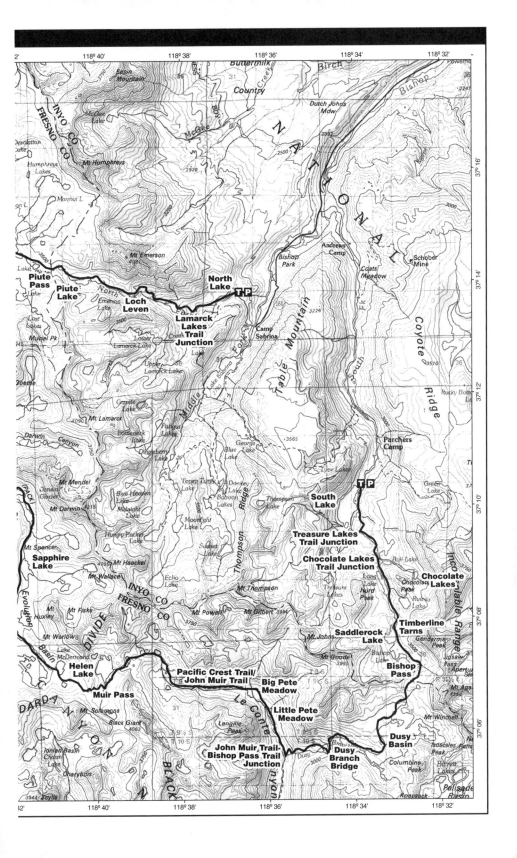

By utilizing the Bishop Pass and Piute Pass trails to access the JMT, a 56-mile semi-loop trip can be followed, one that presents travelers with the additional blessings of Dusy and Humphreys basins (see Trips 51, 52 and 60). The short distance between the trailheads at South Lake and North Lake—only 12 miles—makes the logistics of a car shuttle fairly reasonable.

Following well-maintained trails for the entire distance, this trip presents no major route-finding challenges. However, the usual factors associated with high-altitude journeys in the Sierra must be considered, including the potential for snow-covered slopes near the passes and difficult fords across streams, especially in early season.

DIRECTIONS TO THE TRAILHEAD:

START: For access to the South Lake trailhead, follow directions in Trip 51.

END: For access to the North Lake trailhead, follow directions in Trip 58.

DESCRIPTION: The first leg of your journey involves getting to the junction of the John Muir Trail and the Bishop Pass Trail. The shortest and most direct route follows the Bishop Pass Trail 13 miles west from the South Lake trailhead (see Trips 51 and 52).

From the Bishop Pass Trail junction in LeConte Canyon, head northbound on the JMT on a mild grade through light forest, passing numerous campsites above the east bank of the Middle Fork Kings River, near the ranger station. The grade of ascent increases as you leave the forest behind, and you gaze at the towering profile of 12,018-foot Langille Peak looming over the canyon. Until late summer, a prolific display of wildflowers lines the trail. At Little Pete Meadow, 0.5 mile from the junction, the climb eases and the river mellows, meandering through a sloping, grass-covered meadow surrounded by sagebrush and scattered groves of lodgepole pines and mountain hemlocks. A number of adequate campsites are sprinkled around the meadow, shaded by the conifers. Fishing in the river is reported to be good for rainbow, brook, and golden trout.

Above the meadow, you resume the climb through open terrain with nice views up the canyon of the now cascading river. After crossing a couple of streams, you drop into a lush wildflower garden intermixed with young aspens, pass through a gap in a drift fence, and climb through scattered pines to Big Pete Meadow, 1.75 miles from the Bishop Pass Trail junction. where the JMT turns west, this mostly forested meadow harbors a number of campsites.

Near the far end of Big Pete Meadow, you hop over streams and pass through an area of extensive damage left from a past avalanche. Massive Langille Peak continues to dominate the view. About 0.25 mile from the meadow, you pass more campsites as you closely follow the river in and out of the shade of a light forest. Now you climb moderately to moderately steeply between walls of granite, which can feel like an oven during the heat of the day. Above a talus slope, you skirt the side of the canyon and climb up above granite slabs to a fine view of a waterfall on the turbulent Middle Fork. You follow the trail across a luxuriant, seep-watered hillside amid a bounty of wildflowers to a series of rocky switchbacks that climb above the falls and into a small basin filled with verdant meadows and delightful tarns.

The grade of the trail momentarily eases as you stroll through this small, picturesque basin past intermittent stands of lodgepole, western white, and whitebark pines, and scattered mountain hemlocks. After crossing a small stream, a short climb leads to campsites nestled beneath trees near the trail. Another set of switchbacks leads up to views of a pond-filled basin, where primitive campsites can be found scattered around the pond's shorelines. After crossing the dwindling Middle Fork, you wander around a tangle of rock humps and low ridges to the largest tarn below Helen Lake. Overnighters can set up camp on the rock shelf at the south shore, or on the hillside to the southwest amid widely scattered trees.

Saying farewell to the last whitebark pines, you follow the trail away from the tarn to a section of washed-out trail, where you recross the Middle Fork. The trail improves above the far bank, following the stream briefly before veering away, climbing over slabs, and crossing the tiny, meadow-rimmed outlet from the tarn just below Helen Lake. Away from the shallow tarn, you continue the ascent on a winding course through rock-strewn terrain. In the middle of the climb, a short use-trail leads to a view-filled campsite on a forested knoll, the last decent place to pitch a tent east of Muir Pass. You climb up the trail, generally following Helen Lake's outlet stream, to desolate Helen Lake (11,617'), 7.0 miles from the Bishop Pass Trail junction. Although Helen Lake, named for one of John Muir's two daughters, possesses a stark beauty, backpackers in search of a place to camp will be woefully disappointed by the marginal sites in this rocky basin near the convergence of the Black and Goddard divides. Although the environs are poorly suited for humans, a healthy population of golden trout seems to find the lake a quite reasonable residence. A cross-country route from the vicinity of the lake leads into the mysterious realms of the Ionian Basin, over Black Giant Pass (see Options).

You follow the JMT around the south shore of Helen Lake past some tarns and begin a steady climb toward the pass. A

MUIR HUT

The beehive-shaped stone hut was constructed by the Sierra Club and dedicated in 1933 to the memory of John Muir, the organization's most famous member, cofounder, and original president. The hut was built to honor Muir but also to "offer protection and safety to storm-bound travelers." In keeping with this spirit, travelers may use the hut temporarily during inclement weather.

0.25-mile winding ascent across the often snow-covered, rocky slope leads to Muir Pass (11,955'), 8.0 miles from the Bishop Pass Trail junction. Visitors will revel in the extraordinary views from this notch in the Goddard Divide, although their immediate attention may be drawn to the interesting structure nearby.

Although Muir Hut may be used for temporary shelter, camping at Muir Pass is prohibited due to human waste concerns. From the pass, the Solomons Pass cross-country route leads into the heart of Ionian Basin.

The descent from Muir Pass begins moderately and then eases as you make a mild descent across the upper part of Evolution Basin. Less than a mile from the pass, you encounter lonely Lake McDermand (11,650'±), passing by its west shore on the way to massive Wanda Lake (11,426'), 10 miles from the Bishop Pass Trail junction. Wanda Lake was named for Muir's other daughter. Spartan campsites near the outlet seem devoid of life except for diminutive alpine vegetation, but the views more than compensate for the austere surroundings. Glacier-clad Mt. Goddard rises sharply up into the southwest sky, crowning the multi-hued Goddard Divide. Mt. Huxley, Mt. Spencer, Mt. Darwin and Mt. Mendel fill the horizon to the north. Near the outlet, a cross-country route takes off-trail enthusiasts over Davis Lake Pass to Davis Lake and onward into Goddard Canyon.

In the shadow of Mt. Huxley, the JMT continues a mild descent along the course of Evolution Creek, fording the creek and continuing past the next unnamed gem in the chain of lakes. You enter the glacier-polished basin of Sapphire Lake (10,966') and drop down to campsites at the north end. Proceeding through the deep cleft of the canyon, a short descent takes you to the last lake in the chain.

The JMT follows the east side of Evolution Lake (10,852'), which is tucked into a long, narrow chasm at the north end of Evolution Basin, towered over by the

Lush meadows in Evolution Valley

hulks of 13,831-foot Mt. Darwin and 13,710-foot Mt. Mendel. Verdant strips of meadow soften the otherwise granite-laden bowl. Near the far end of the lake, you crest a low rise and swing around the north end of a large cove to a small, elevated peninsula. On the peninsula are a number of scenic campsites amid widely scattered, stunted whitebark pines. Before leaving the lake, the majesty of Evolution Basin is worth a final, admiring glance before you begin the descent toward Evolution Valley. This slender basin, graced with a string of jeweled lakes and a procession of magnificent peaks, provides one of the most glorious views in the High Sierra.

From Evolution Lake, follow sandy trail past some tarns and over granite slabs to switchbacks leading down into Evolution Valley. At the top of these switchbacks, cross-country routes leave the JMT on climbs toward three high passes on the Glacier Divide—The Keyhole, Alpine Col, and Snow-Tongue Pass (see Trip 60)—and one on the Sierra crest—Lamarck Col (see Trip 59). A thickening forest of lodge-pole pine coincides with the drop in elevation as you zigzag down the wall of the canyon. Through sporadic gaps in the forest, you have fine views across the deep cleft. During the descent, a couple of flower-lined streams spill across the trail. Nearing the floor of the canyon, you pass below a thundering waterfall on the creek draining Darwin Bench and, after a few more switchbacks, wind around to cross that creek.

Now you proceed down the valley on a mildly graded trail through stands of scattered pines, across small pockets of meadow, and beside granite slabs and boulders, eventually reaching Colby Meadow (9840'), 17.25 miles from the Bishop Pass Trail junction. Good campsites nestle beneath lodgepole pines around the edge of the meadow, and fishing is good in nearby Evolution Creek for golden trout. The meadow affords nice views of the valley, the winding creek, and the surrounding peaks.

Continuing on the JMT, you follow a mild path over a couple of creeks and through light forest for 0.75 mile to the beginning of McClure Meadow (9620'±), the largest of the meadows in Evolution Valley. The McGee Lakes cross-country route leaves the east end of the meadow, crosses Evolution Creek, and proceeds up McGee Creek. Numerous campsites are spread around the fringe of McClure Meadow, some providing excellent views of lazy Evolution Creek flowing sinuously through the verdant clearing. On a low rise north of the trail is the McClure Meadow Ranger Station, the summer home for a seasonal ranger who patrols this section of Kings Canyon National Park. Beyond the cabin, you continue on a mild path past more campsites to the end of the meadow at the tumbling creek.

For the next couple of miles, you follow the JMT in and out of more lodgepole forest and over a trio of streams draining the south side of Glacier Divide. Through breaks in the forest, you have sporadic views of the surroundings, including a major avalanche swath and a picturesque waterfall below Emerald Peak. Near the west end of Evolution Valley, 20.25 miles from the Bishop Pass Trail junction, you reach Evolution Meadow (9210'±). The JMT skirts the meadow through lodgepole pine forest, passing a number of sheltered campsites on the way. Beyond the west end of the meadow, at 20.75 miles, you come to a crossing of a twin-channeled creek. A pair of cross-country routes follow this creek upward to cross Glacier Divide at Packsaddle Pass and Lobe Pass. From the stream crossing, you curve south to ford Evolution Creek. Except at the height of snowmelt, the crossing of the broad channel is not particularly difficult, although the creek is usually deep enough to get your feet and lower legs wet.

After the ford, you briefly follow the gently graded trail along the south bank to where the creek suddenly begins a raucous plunge, tumbling over slabs and careening through boulders, on its way to converge with the South Fork San Joaquin River. The trail seemingly matches the fall of the stream with a zigzagging descent down an exposed west-facing wall, providing nice views of the canyon and river below. Near the bottom of the descent, you enter the welcome shade of a mixed forest of aspens, lodgepole pines, and cedars. At 22.25 miles, you cross a wooden bridge spanning the South Fork San Joaquin River (8425'±) and come to the signed junction with the Goddard Canyon Trail (see Trip 38). Good campsites are spread around the junction on either side of the refreshing river. Here you turn right.

Continuing northbound on the JMT, you follow the river through mixed forest, soon crossing and then paralleling the stream draining the canyon east of Mt. Henry. A mixed bag of vegetation greets you over the next mile as you wander in and out of scattered forest and across open slopes covered with sagebrush, currant, and an assortment of wildflowers, including lupine, paintbrush, penstemon, pennyroyal, cinquefoil, and Mariposa lily. At 23.25 miles, just before you cross another bridge over the South Fork, a short spur trail leads left above the south bank of the river to good campsites beneath a dense grove of pines.

Downstream from the bridge, the canyon becomes a narrow gorge, propelling the river powerfully through the slim, rocky chasm. You proceed alongside the raging waters until more placid surroundings appear about a mile from the bridge. Just beyond a stream crossing you arrive at Aspen Meadow (8235'±), 24.5 miles from the Bishop Pass Trail junction. Actually more of a grove than a meadow, the aspen-covered flat is sprinkled with some pines as well. A few sheltered campsites are nearby.

Away from Aspen Meadow, you proceed downstream alongside the South Fork through mostly open, rocky terrain, following the trail as it bends north around John Muir Rock. You veer away from the river and proceed through widely scattered conifers to a lightly forested flat harboring a number of campsites. Just before a steel bridge spanning Piute Creek, a sign announces your departure from Kings Canyon National Park. Across the bridge, you reach a signed junction with the Piute Pass Trail (8075'±), 25.75 miles from the Bishop Pass Trail junction.

From the junction, you can reverse the description in Trip 60 and follow the Piute Pass Trail 17.5 miles to the North Lake trailhead, or you can continue along the JMT to reach various departure points (see Trip 38).

☐ **IONIAN BASIN CROSS-COUNTRY ROUTES:** The Ionian Basin is an area of the High Sierra much coveted by cross-country enthusiasts and mountaineers alike. Known for its stark, above-timberline beauty, the convoluted terrain is filled with austere lakes and surrounded by impressive peaks. The long distance from trailheads and the arduous terrain insure that the region remains relatively uncrowded. A number of classic Sierra treks pass through Ionian Basin, including one from Helen Lake to Martha Lake in Goddard Canyon (see below), and two more difficult routes down the Enchanted Gorge and Goddard Creek (you're on your own).

☐ **BLACK GIANT PASS:** Black Giant Pass offers accomplished cross-country enthusiasts access to Ionian Basin. Leave the JMT at the south end of Helen Lake and climb just east of Lake 11939 to the pass, a broad saddle (12,225'±) 0.5 mile west of Black Giant. Descend from the pass to Lake 11828, then turn west and pass numerous lakelets to Chasm Lake (11,011'). From Chasm Lake, a number of possibilities are available for further wanderings. A short return to the JMT can be accomplished by climbing northwest 0.5 mile to Lake 11592. From there, you can travel northeast over Solomons Pass (see below) to Muir Pass, or head northwest over Wanda Pass (see below) and around the west side of Wanda Lake to the JMT.

☐ **GODDARD CREEK PASS:** To continue toward Martha Lake from Chasm Lake, climb around Peak 11978 and follow the

south shore of Lake 11837 to a short climb up to a rocky saddle southwest of the lake. Proceed west to Lake 11818 and then follow the lakeshore to the middle of the lake, where the two peninsulas nearly touch. Boulderhop to the far side and climb northeast past the north shore of an unnamed lake to Goddard Creek Pass (12,240'±), 0.75 mile directly south of Mt. Goddard. From the pass, descend rocky slopes to the east shore of Martha Lake. To follow the Goddard Canyon Trail, see Trip 38.

☐ **SOLOMONS PASS:** From Muir Pass, make a gradual ascent southwest 0.5 mile to the saddle (12,440'±) 0.3-mile directly west of Mt. Solomons. In most years, you will have to cross a permanent snowfield on the northeast side below the pass. Descend southwest over rocky slopes to Lake 11592.

☐ **WANDA PASS:** Find your way to Lake 11592, by either the Black Giant Pass or Solomons Pass routes. From the lake, climb northwest 0.5 mile to Wanda Pass (12,440'±), the obvious saddle in the Glacier Divide 0.25 mile east of Peak 12976. Head down toward the west shore of Wanda Lake and meet the JMT near its outlet, 1.75 miles from the pass.

☐ **MCGEE LAKES CROSS-COUNTRY ROUTE:** Leave the JMT at the east end of McClure Meadow and ford Evolution Creek, which may be difficult in early season. Pass through dense lodgepole pine forest heading southeast toward McGee Canyon, where you may see traces of an old trail. Eventually, you come alongside McGee Creek and continue upstream to McGee Lakes. Excellent campsites can be found along the north shores of the two largest lakes. From the upper lake, head east past two small tarns to a distinct notch in the skyline ridge directly west of Sapphire Lake. Make a short, steep descent to the JMT at Sapphire Lake. An alternate exit from McGee Lakes continues south from Lake 10821 past two tarns before arcing east past a third to a gap above Lake

11293. From the gap, a short drop leads back to the JMT on the west side of Lake 11293 in Evolution Basin.

⊙ **PACKSADDLE PASS CROSS-COUNTRY ROUTE:** From Evolution Meadow, climb easy slopes north and northeast 2.5 miles to the pass (12,440'±), which is 0.25 mile southeast of a point marked *Divide 12900* on the *Mt. Henry* quad. Descend steeply for the first 300 feet below the pass, and then continue down easier terrain alongside a creek toward Packsaddle Lake (10,663').

⊙ **LOBE PASS CROSS-COUNTRY ROUTE:** This route also leaves Evolution Meadow and climbs north along the creek toward Lake 11236 below the Glacier Divide. From the lake, ascend north and then east 0.5 mile to Lobe Pass (12,320'), which is 0.3 mile northwest of Peak 12722 (on the *Mt. Henry* quad). Descend steep slopes from the pass and then easier slopes through a canyon to Lobe Lakes (10,775'±).

⊙ **OTHER OPTIONS:**

- **LAMARCK COL:** See Trip 59.
- **ALPINE COL, THE KEYHOLE, AND SNOW-TONGUE PASS:** See Trip 60.

R **PERMITS:** Wilderness permit required for overnight stays (quota: 36 per day).

CAMPFIRES: Not permitted above 10,000 feet.

Appendices

APPENDIX I

Backpacks Features Chart

Note: Time of year headings represent the average point in the season when trails become snow free. Times may very from year to year depending on variables, such as the amount of snow that fell in the previous winter and how fast that snow melts in the spring.

Backpacks Features — West Side							
		Ratings 1–10				Length in	Elevation
Best Time / Trip	Route	Scenery	Solitude	Difficulty	Days	Miles	Gain/Loss
EARLY MAY							
3. Redwood Mountain— Hart Trail	↻	8	7	Ⓜ	2	7.25	+2065/-2065
4. Redwood Mountain— Sugar Bowl	↻	8	7	Ⓜ	2	6.6	+2130/-2130
MID-JUNE							
5. Stony Creek Trail to Jennie Lake	↗	7	8	Ⓢ	2	5.75	+2875/-405
6. Jennie Lakes Loop	↻	7	7	Ⓜ	2–4	17.8	+4135/-4135
25. Sphinx Creek	↗	7	6	ⓂⓈ	2	6.2	+3745/-215
LATE JUNE							
37. Rae Lake	↗	7	8	Ⓜ	2–3	12	+2840/-1040
37. Hell-for-Sure Lake	↗	9	8	Ⓜ	3–5	15	+4035/-1375
EARLY JULY							
7. Seville Lake	↗	7	9	Ⓜ	2	6.6	+1455/-955
27. East Lake & Lake Reflection	↗	9	8	Ⓜ	2–3	11.6	+4665/-230
32. East Kennedy Lake	↗	8	6	ⓂⓈ	2–3	11	+7280/-1690
33. Copper Creek Trail to Granite Basin	↗	8	7	Ⓜ	2–3	9.5	+5735/-685
MID-JULY							
8. Rowell Meadow to Giant Forest	↗	10	9	Ⓜ	4–7	38	+9450/-10675

Best Time/Trip	Route	Ratings 1–10 Scenery	Solitude	Difficulty	Days	Length in Miles	Elevation Gain/Loss
26. Circle of Solitude	↻	10	9	MS	5–10	68	+18,700/-18,700
28. Charlotte Lake	↗	8	5	M	2–3	14.5	+5890/-535
34. State & Horseshoe Lakes	↗	7	6	M	3–4	18	+7735/-2275
36. Rae Lakes Loop	↻	10	2	MS	3–5	38.9	+3870/-400
38. Martha Lake	↗	10	9	M	4–6	23	+4830/-1175

Backpacks Features – East Side

Best Time/Trip	Route	Ratings 1–10 Scenery	Solitude	Difficulty	Days	Length in Miles	Elevation Gain/Loss
LATE JUNE							
47. Red Lake	↗	8	10	S	2	4.5	+4200/-275
48. Birch Lake	↗	8	10	S	2	5.5	+4615/-300
MID-JULY							
39. Robinson Lake	↗	7	8	M	2	1.5	+1335/-5
40. Kearsarge Lakes	↗	8	4	M	2	5.5	+2685/-1415
41. Charlotte & Rae Lakes	↗	10	3	MS	3–5	12	+4050/-2685
42. Trans-Sierra Trek	↗	8	5	MS	2–3	20.5	+2845/-4140
43. Golden Trout Lakes	↗	7	7	M	2	2.5	+2295/-80
44. Baxter Pass	↗	6	10	S	2–3	11	+6650/-2430
45. Sawmill Pass	↗	6	10	S	2–3	12.5	+7315/-1560
46. Taboose Pass Trail	↗	7	10	S	2–3	10	+6170/-790
46. Bench Lake	↗	8	10	S	3–4	11.75	+6205/-1065
49. Brainerd Lake	↗	10	6	S	2–3	4.9	+3740/-700
50. Big Pine Lakes	↺	10	4	M	2–4	12.5	+3170/-3170
51. Long, Saddlerock & Bishop Lakes	↗	8	3	M	2–3	4.3	+1740/-260
52. Dusy Basin	↗	10	4	M	2–5	7.5	+2500/-1550
52. LeConte Canyon	↗	10	5	M	3–5	13	+2585/-3680

| Best Time/Trip | Route | Ratings 1–10 | | Difficulty | Length in | | Elevation |
		Scenery	Solitude		Days	Miles	Gain/Loss
53. Chocolate Lakes Loop	⟳	7	6	Ⓜ	2–3	7	+1690/-1690
54. Treasure Lakes	↗	6	7	Ⓜ	2	3.8	+1765/-450
55. Tyee Lakes	↗	5	7	Ⓜ	2	3.9	+2520/-10
56. Sabrina Basin	↗	9	4	Ⓜ	2–4	6.8	+2860/-680
57. George Lake	↗	4	8	Ⓜ	2	3.3	+2025/-170
58. Lamarck Lakes	↗	8	6	Ⓜ	2	2.7	+1700/-35
59. Evolution Basin	↗	10	7	Ⓢ /X	2–4	10	+4505/-1595
60. Piute Pass to the John Muir Trail	↗	9	5	Ⓜ Ⓢ/X	2–4	16.8	+2175/-645
61. John Muir Trail-Kearsarge Pass Trail to Bishop Pass Trail	↗	10	5	Ⓜ Ⓢ	5–8	42+20	+8600/-10700
62. John Muir Trail-Bishop Pass Trail to Paiute Pass Trail	↗	10	7	Ⓜ Ⓢ	4–7	26+31	+4200/-4870

APPENDIX **II**

Day Hikes Features Chart

Note: Time of year headings represent the average point in the season when trails become snow free. Times may very from year to year depending on variables, such as the amount of snow that fell in the previous winter and how fast that snow melts in the spring.

		Ratings 1–10			Length in	Elevation
Best Time/Trip	Route	Scenery	Solitude	Difficulty	Miles	Gain/Loss
EARLY MAY TO MID-MAY						
3. Redwood Mountain— Hart Loop	↻	7	7	**M**	7.25	+2065/-2065
4. Redwood Mountain— Sugar Bowl	↻	7	7	**M**	6.6	+2130/-2130
18. General Grant Tree Trail	↻	8	1	**E**	0.5	negligible
21. Roaring River Falls	↗	7	2	**E**	0.25	negligible
22. River Trail	↗	5	3	**E**	2.5	+35/-225
23. Zumwalt Meadow Nature Trail	↻	6	2	**E**	1.5	negligible
24. Kanawyer Loop Trail	↻	6	3	**E**	4.7	+265/-265
29. Deer Cove Trail	↗	5	9	**M**	3.4	+2720/-620
30. Cedar Grove Overlook	↗	6	6	**MS**	2.4	+1525/-115
31. Hotel & Lewis Creeks Loop	↻/↗	7	7	**MS**	6.4/5.0	+1920/-2035
35. Mist Falls	↗	7	4	**M**	3.9	+765/-0
LATE MAY						
2. Buena Vista Peak	↗	7	4	**E**	1	+475/-0
11. Chicago Stump	↗	7	9	**E**	0.3	negligible
12. Boole Tree	↻	7	9	**E**	2.25	+740/-740
13. Big Stump Grove	↻	6	5	**E**	2	+325/-325
14. Hitchcock Meadow	↗	5	7	**E**	0.6	+20/-290

Best Time / Trip	Route	Ratings 1–10		Difficulty	Length in Miles	Elevation Gain/Loss
		Scenery	Solitude			
15. Sunset Loop Trail	↻	6	6	Ⓜ	5.75	+1885/-1885
17. North Grove Loop	↻	6	7	Ⓔ	1.5	+355/-355
19. Park Ridge Lookout	↻	8	5	Ⓔ	5.6	+1430/-1430
EARLY JUNE						
1. Big Baldy	↗	7	6	Ⓜ	2.2	+1000/-420
10. Evans Grove	↗	6	10	Ⓜ	2	+595/-920
20. Don Cecil Trail to Lookout Peak	↗	8	7	ⓂⓈ	5	+4000/225
MID-JUNE						
5. Stony Creek Trail to Jenny Lake	↗	7	8	Ⓢ	5.75	+2875/-405
16. Azalea-Manzanita Loop	↻	7	5	Ⓜ	4.6	+1200/-1200
25. Sphinx Creek	↗	7	6	ⓂⓈ	6.2	+3745/-215
EARLY JULY						
7. Seville Lake	↗	7	9	Ⓜ	6.6	+1455/-955
9. Mitchell Peak	↗	8	9	Ⓜ	3.25	+2090/-55

Dayhikes Features – East Side

Best Time / Trip	Route	Ratings 1–10		Difficulty	Length in Miles	Elevation Gain/Loss
		Scenery	Solitude			
LATE JUNE						
47. Red Lake	↗	8	10	Ⓢ	4.5	+4200/-275
48. Birch Lake	↗	8	10	Ⓢ	5.5	+4615/-300
MID-JULY						
39. Robinson Lake	↗	7	7	Ⓜ	1.5	+1335/-5
40. Kearsarge & Bullfrog Lakes	↗	8	5	Ⓜ	5.5	+2685/-1415
42. Trans-Sierra Trek	↗	8	5	ⓂⓈ	20.5	+2845/-4140
43. Golden Trout Lakes	↗	7	7	Ⓜ	2.5	+2295/-80

Best Time/Trip	Route	Ratings 1–10			Length in Miles	Elevation Gain/Loss
		Scenery	Solitude	Difficulty		
49. Brainerd Lake	↗	10	6	Ⓢ	4.9	+3740/-700
50. Big Pine Lakes	↺	10	4	Ⓜ	12.5	+3170/-3170
51. Long, Saddlerock & Bishop Lakes	↗	8	2	Ⓜ	4.3	+1740/-260
53. Chocolate Lakes Loop	↺	7	6	Ⓜ	7.0	+1690/-1690
54. Treasure Lakes	↗	6	7	Ⓜ	3.8	+1765/-450
55. Tyee Lakes	↗	5	7	Ⓜ	3.9	+2520/-10
56. Sabrina Basin	↗	9	4	Ⓜ	6.8	+2860/-680
57. George Lake	↗	4	8	Ⓜ	3.3	+2025/-170
58. Lamarck Lakes	↗	8	6	Ⓜ	2.7	+1700/-35
60. Humphreys Basin	↗	9	5	Ⓜ	6.8	+2175/-645

Appendix

Highest Sierra Nevada Peaks and
Largest Giant Sequoias in Sequoia and Kings Canyon

Highest Peaks in the Sierra Nevada					
Rank			Elevation		
CA	Sierra	Name	Feet	Meters	USGS 7.5 min. map
1.	1.	Mt. Whitney	14,494	4418	Mount Whitney
2.	2.	Mt. Williamson	14,375	4382	Mt. Williamson
4.	3.	North Palisade	14,242	4334	North Palisade
6.	4.	Mt. Sill	14,153	4314	North Palisade
7.	5.	Mt. Russell	14,086	4293	Mount Whitney
8.	6.	Split Mountain	14,058	4285	Split Mtn.
9.	7.	Middle Palisade	14,040	4279	Split Mtn.
10.	8.	Mt. Langley	14,028	4275	Mt. Langley
11.	9.	Mt. Tyndall	14,018	4273	Mt. Williamson
12.	10.	Mt. Muir	14,009	4270	Mount Whitney
13.	11.	Thunderbolt Peak	14,003	4268	North Palisade

Several "points" in the Sierra are higher than some of the mountains listed above, but are not considered to be actual peaks. Among these sub-peaks are Keeler Needle (14,272), Starlight Peak (14,220), West Horn of Mt. Williamson (14,160), East Horn of Mt. Williamson (14,125), and Polemonium Peak (14,000).

Largest Giant Sequoias in Sequoia and Kings Canyon

Rank CA	Seq/Kings	Name	Volume (cu ft)	Height (ft)	Circumference (ft)	Location
1.	1.	General Sherman	52,508	274.9	102.6	Giant Forest
2.	2.	Washington	47,850	254.7	101.1	Giant Forest
3.	3.	General Grant	46,608	268.1	107.6	Grant Grove
4.	4.	President	45,148	240.9	93.0	Giant Forest
5.	5.	Lincoln	44,471	255.8	98.3	Giant Forest
8.	6.	Boole	42,472	268.8	113.0	Converse Basin
9.	7.	Franklin	41,280	223.8	94.8	Giant Forest
10.	8.	King Arthur	40,656	270.3	104.2	Garfield Grove
11.	9.	Monroe	40,104	247.8	91.3	Giant Forest
12.	10.	Robert E. Lee	40,102	254.7	88.3	Grant Grove
13.	11.	John Adams	38,956	250.6	83.3	Giant Forest
14.	12.	Ishi Giant	38,156	248.1	105.1	Kennedy Grove
15.	13.	Unnamed	37,295	243.8	93.0	Giant Forest
17.	14.	Unnamed	36,292	239.4	75.5	Giant Forest
18.	15.	Unnamed	36,228	281.5	95.1	Giant Forest
21.	16.	Pershing	35,855	246.0	91.2	Giant Forest
22.	17.	Diamond	35,292	286.0	95.3	Atwell Grove
24.	18.	Roosevelt	35,013	260.0	80.0	Redwood Mtn.
26.	19.	(AD)	34,706	242.4	99.0	Atwell Grove
27.	20.	Hart	34,407	277.9	75.3	Redwood Mtn.
29.	21.	Chief Sequoyah	33,608	228.2	90.4	Giant Forest

APPENDIX IV

The Bear Facts and Other Animal Concerns

Bears

The last grizzly bear in the Sierra Nevada was shot near Horse Corral Meadows in the early 1900s. Since then, the common American black bear has been the only species of bear in the range. Despite their name, black bears range in color from jet black to cinnamon. They are very quick and agile animals, and often quite large — mature males can weigh as much as 300 pounds. Black bears are active both day and night, and have highly developed senses of smell. Usually found on the west slope of the Sierra, between 5000 and 8500 feet, black bears occasionally travel to higher elevations. Although they are considered omnivores, black bears subsist mainly on vegetation and typically are not aggressive animals, especially toward humans. Bears who have not become familiar with humans tend to be shy and retiring, avoiding contact at virtually any cost. However, black bears that grow accustomed to human food and garbage through our carelessness can become destructive and potentially dangerous animals.

Once bears discover food or garbage from coolers, cars, or backpacks, it is extremely hard to recondition them. Bears that frequent developed campgrounds tend to be the boldest and potentially most dangerous ones. Relocating such animals to backcountry areas has not proven effective, as bears generally find their way back to civilization, or become highly aggressive toward recreationists. "Problem bears" eventually have to be destroyed.

Despite a reputation for being stupid animals, bears have figured out ways to render our attempts at deceiving them useless. The standard way to protect food from bears in the backcountry was the counter-balance method of hanging food, but this method no longer works. Nowadays, if you attempt to protect your cache by hanging a stuff sack full of food from a tree limb a bear may climb the tree to snap the cord, simply break the branch, or dive-bomb the sack; or a mother bear will send a cub up the tree to the same end. The counter-balance method had drawbacks from the beginning for campers near or above timberline, where the trees are either too small or absent entirely. Several years ago the park managers for Yosemite and Sequoia/Kings Canyon, along with the surrounding forest managers, embarked on a plan to help minimize encounters between bears and backcountry users. Popular backcountry campsites provide bear-proof lockers; bear-proof canisters are required in the most heavily used areas and strongly encouraged elsewhere. Hopefully, this plan will help break the association between humans and food by making it impossible for the bears to obtain human food that is stored in lockers and canisters. The plan requires the cooperation of all who use the backcountry and park campsites. It is the responsibility of park visitors to store food so that it is inaccessible to bears and to deposit garbage in the appropriate receptacles, so that bears do not become accustomed to food and garbage and thus to prevent the destruction that might result. The canisters add a couple of pounds to backpackers' loads, but that burden is offset by the security the canisters provide. The presence of bears needn't discourage anyone from hiking or backpacking in the Sierra.

The following guidelines should enhance your experience and help protect the bears.

CAMPGROUNDS

- Leave extra or unnecessary food and scented items at home.
- Store all food, food containers, and scented items in bear lockers and latch them securely.

Locations of Backcountry Bear Lockers (subject to change)

Kings Canyon	Sequoia

Kings Canyon

Bubbs Creek Area *(1)*
Sphinx Creek *(2)*
Charlotte Creek *(1)*
Junction Meadow (lower) *(1)*
Junction Meadow (East Creek) *(1)*
East Lake *(1)*
Vidette Meadow *(2)*
JMT (9900´±) *(1)*
JMT/Center Basin Junction *(1)*
Charlotte & Kearsarge Lakes *(1)*
Charlotte Lake *(1)*
Kearsarge Lakes *(1)*
Copper Creek *(1)*
Lower Tent Meadow *(1)*
Lewis Creek *(1)*
Frypan Meadow *(1)*
Sugarloaf Valley/Roaring River *(1)*
Ranger Lake *(1)*
Seville Lake *(1)*
Lost Lake *(1)*
Sugarloaf Meadow *(1)*
Roaring River Ranger Station *(1)*
Comanche Meadow *(1)*
Woods Creek *(1)*
Lower Paradise Valley *(1)*
Middle Paradise Valley *(1)*
Upper Paradise Valley *(1)*
JMT-Woods Creek Crossing *(1)*
Arrowhead Lake *(1)*
Lower Rae Lake *(1)*
Upper Rae Lake *(1)*

Sequoia

Hockett Plateau *(1)*
Hockett Meadow *(1)*
South Fork Meadow/Rock Camp *(1)*
Hidden Camp/Lower South Fork Meadow *(1)*
Upper Camp/South Fork Pasture *(2)*
Kern Canyon *(1)*
Lower Funston Meadow *(1)*
Upper Funston Meadow *(2)*
Kern Hot Springs *(2)*
Junction Meadow *(1)*
Little Five Lakes/Cliff Creek/Chagoopa *(1)*
Moraine Lake *(1)*
Cliff Creek/Timber Gap Junction *(1)*
Pinto Lake *(1)*
Big Five Lakes *(1)*
Big Arroyo Crossing *(1)*
Lost Canyon/Big Five Junction *(1)*
Lodgepole Backcountry *(1)*
HST-Mehrten Creek *(1)*
HST-9 Mile Creek Crossing *(1)*
Bearpaw Meadow *(4)*
Upper Hamilton Lake *(3)*
Emerald Lake *(2)*
Pear Lake *(2)*
Clover Creek *(1)*
JO Pass/Twin Lakes Junction *(1)*
Twin Lakes *(2)*
HST-Buck Creek Crossing *(1)*
Rock Creek *(1)*
PCT-Lower Rock Creek Crossing *(1)*
Lower Rock Creek Lake *(1)*
Lower Soldier Lake *(1)*
Tyndall/Crabtree Area *(1)*
JMT-Tyndall Creek *(1)*
Tyndall Creek Frog Ponds *(1)*
JMT-Wallace Creek *(1)*
Lower Crabtree Meadow *(1)*
Crabtree Ranger Station *(1)*
Mineral King *(1)*
Monarch Lake *(2)*
Franklin Lake *(3)*

- Dispose of all trash in bear-proof garbage cans or dumpsters.
- Do not leave food out at an unattended campsite.

BACKCOUNTRY

- Don't leave your pack unattended while on the trail.
- Once in camp, empty your pack and open all flaps and pockets.
- Keep all food, trash, and scented items in a bear-proof locker or canister.
- Pack out all trash.

EVERYWHERE

- Don't allow bears to approach your food—make noise, wave your arms, throw rocks. Be bold, but keep a safe distance and use good judgment.
- If a bear gets into your food, you are responsible for cleaning up the mess.
- Never attempt to retrieve food from a bear.
- Never approach a bear, especially a cub.
- Report any incidents or injuries to the appropriate agency.

TRAILS THAT REQUIRE USE OF BEAR CANISTERS

- Mt. Whitney Trail (Trip 59) (Inyo National Forest)
- Kearsarge Pass Trail (east of Kearsarge Pass) (Trip 62) (Inyo National Forest)
- Bishop Pass Trail (including Dusy & Palisade Basins) (Kings Canyon National Park)

Other Animal Concerns

COUGARS: The chances of seeing a cougar, or mountain lion, in the backcountry are extremely small, as cougars are typically shy and avoid human contact at nearly all costs. It is more likely that one has seen you, especially if you've hiked much in the western foothills. Unlike black bears, mountain lions are strictly carnivorous. Mule deer is the main staple of their diet; when hunting for venison is poor, they sup-

plement with smaller animals. A typical lion is estimated to kill 36 deer per year, and the health of the deer population is directly linked to the predatory nature of these cats as they thin the herd of its weaker members. In the unlikely event of an encounter with one of these big cats, keep in mind the following guidelines:

- Never hike alone, especially in the foothills.
- If you encounter a cat, don't run, as they might mistake you for prey.
- Make yourself appear as large as possible—don't crouch or try to hide.
- Hold your ground or back away slowly while facing the cat.
- Don't leave small children unattended; pick them up if a cat approaches.
- If the lion seems aggressive, make noise, wave your arms, and throw rocks.
- If the animal attacks, fight back.
- Report any encounters to a ranger as soon as possible.

MARMOTS: These fuzzy, chirping rodents hardly seem threatening to humans. However, members of their clan have been known to wreak havoc on cars at Mineral King by chewing on engine parts such as rubber hoses, wires, and even radiators. Many a vehicle has been disabled in spring and early summer, leaving drivers stranded until they can arrange for repairs or for a long, arduous tow to Three Rivers. If you plan on visiting Mineral King during spring or early summer, check with park rangers about the best places to leave your car and what measures to take to minimize this potential hazard. By midsummer, their curious cravings for engine parts seem to disappear.

Marmots in other areas of the park, particularly near popular campsites, have been known to chew through backpacking equipment in search of a treat. Store your food in bear lockers and hang your belongings from a tree when leaving your campsite unattended for any length of time.

RATTLESNAKES: Although rattlesnakes are common to the foothills community on the west side of the Sierra and the pinyon-sagebrush zone on the east side, human encounters with them are relatively rare. Actual bites are even more infrequent, and are almost never fatal in adults. While rattlers live in a wide range of environments, pay special attention when hiking along streams and creeks below 6000 feet. These reptiles seek sun when the air temperature is cold and retreat to shade in hot weather; they are typically nocturnal for most of the summer hiking season. Rattlers are not aggressive and will seek an escape route unless cornered. If you happen upon one, quickly back away. If bitten, seek medical attention.

TICKS: Ticks are most common in the lower elevations of the foothills zone; their numbers are highest in spring, especially after wet winters. Ticks are rarely a problem at higher elevations in the southern Sierra during the normal hiking season.

These blood-sucking pests would be just another nuisance if they weren't also carriers of Lyme disease and Rocky Mountain spotted fever. Although rare in the southern Sierra, these tick-born conditions can be serious if not treated by antibiotics. If you have been bitten by at tick, watch for flu-like symptoms, headache, rash, fever, or joint pain, and consult your physician if you develop any of these symptoms.

Myths, old wives tales, and urban legends abound about how to remove ticks. The medically accepted method advises using a pair of tweezers to get a good hold on the pest, and then applying gentle traction to back the tick out of the flesh. Check the wound to make sure the head hasn't been left behind. After removal of the whole tick, thoroughly wash the wound with soap and water, and apply of an antibiotic ointment. Monitor your health for the next several days afterward to detect any symptoms of serious illness. Prevention is the best medicine, so observe the following measures when traveling in tick country:

- Use an effective insect repellent on skin and clothing and apply liberally.
- Wear long-sleeved shirts and tuck pant legs into socks.
- Inspect your entire body for bites at least once each day while in the backcountry.
- Check clothing thoroughly for any loose ticks.

MOSQUITOES: While not a major health concern, pesky mosquitoes can ruin a peaceful day in the mountains. Fortunately, the mosquito cycle in the Sierra Nevada builds for a short time in early summer, peaks for about two weeks, and then steadily diminishes; the peak varies from year to year, yet usually coincides with the climax of wildflower season.

Mosquitoes seem to prefer some humans over others. For those people who mosquitoes do find attractive, supposed deterrents are the modern era's snake oil, from sleeping beneath a pyramid, ingesting a boatload of vitamin B, bathing in a vat of hand lotion, lighting aroma-therapy candles, or emitting a high-pierced electronic shriek heard only by bugs and aliens. Although the only sure-fire protection against the ubiquitous mosquito is to stay home, which isn't much of an alternative, the following suggestions might help you enjoy the backcountry during the perpetual buzz of peak mosquito season.

- Use an insect repellent with DEET as the active ingredient and reapply often.
- Wear a long-sleeved shirt and long pants.
- Wear a mosquito head net for extreme conditions.
- Select a mildly wind-prone campsite away from wet or marshy areas.
- Don't forget your tent.

APPENDIX **V**

Minimum Impact Stock Regulations

While "no trace" camping is standard practice in the wilderness, you can also minimize your impact on the land and help to preserve wilderness access privileges by properly caring for your stock animals. Everyone in your party should be familiar with the following guidelines and regulations for wilderness stock use. You will receive a copy of these regulations when you pick up your wilderness permit.

PLANNING YOUR TRIP

- The *Forage Area Guide* describes the designated forage areas and grazing regulations. It is available through the Wilderness Office. Use it to select areas where your stock can graze with minimum impact. An on-line copy of the *Forage Area Guide* will be available in the future.

- Opening dates have been established to protect meadows from stock impacts while they are wet and soft. Grazing is not permitted prior to these dates.

- Take only as many animals as necessary to make your trip successful. Use light-weight, compact equipment to minimize the number of pack animals you'll need. Maximum number of stock allowed per party is 20. Some areas have lower limits.

ON THE TRAIL

- Stock are restricted to maintained trails in most areas. You may travel up to half a mile from trails to reach a campsite. Off-trail stock use is permitted only in certain areas—see the *Forage Area Guide*.

- Shortcutting trails and switchbacks is prohibited. Reduce impacts by riding in the center of the trail. Avoiding sandy,

muddy or rocky spots by riding off-trail causes additional damage to the trail. Ride over, not around, water bars, causeways, and riprap. Move trail obstacles instead of skirting them. Double-rope (put a lead rope around both sides of the animal ahead) string animals that habitually walk off-trail. Notify a ranger of obstacles or problems.

- Use tact and courtesy with hikers when asking for the right-of-way. Ask hikers to step off the trail on the downhill side in plain view and to remain still until stock have passed.

- Dead stock must be moved at least 300′ from trails, campsites and water within 72 hours. If any of your stock dies in the backcountry, notify a ranger as soon as possible for help in properly disposing of the animal.

IN CAMP

- Stock should be confined as little as possible. Restless, restrained animals trample vegetation, paw up tree roots and debark trees.

- However, stock must be restrained at all times prior to the grazing opening dates and in areas closed to grazing. Carry substitute feed (processed hay pellets, cubes or weed-free hay) in these areas. Use nosebags or lay feed out on a tarp, not on the ground.

- When confinement is necessary, use existing hitch rails or a hitch line with "tree-saver" straps between two trees or rocks on a flat, hard, non-vegetated site at least 100′ away from the trail, water and camp. Hobble animals that paw excessively.

- Tie animals to trees only when packing or unpacking stock. Never tie to a tree smaller than 6 inches in diameter.

- Water stock downstream and well away from campsites. Avoid fragile stream banks and lakeshores.

GRAZING

- Be sure that forage and water near your camp can support the needs of your stock. Avoid places that have already been heavily grazed, and don't stay too long in one area. Overgrazing weakens grasses, allows weeds to grow, leaves nothing for the next party, and ruins the beauty of the meadows. Some areas have length-of-stay limits; check the *Forage Area Guide* or grazing regulations.

- Drift fences have been provided in many areas to help hold stock. When turning your stock loose to graze, examine the terrain to predict where they'll go. Use bells only on lead animals. Hobbles may be used, but will become less effective with time. Picketing and portable electric fences are permitted as long as they are moved frequently enough to prevent trampling and overgrazing. If you use these methods, try restraining only enough animals to keep the rest from straying. To minimize risk of injury, introduce stock to hobbles, picketing, and electric fences at home, before entering the wilderness.

- Your stock will be easier to catch if they are trained beforehand to expect grain.

LEAVING CAMP

- Carry a rake to fill in pawed-up areas and scatter all manure piles when you leave camp. Remove all manure from within 100′ of the campsite to reduce odors and insect problems, and to maintain the appearance of the site.

- Pack out everything you packed in! Leave nothing behind!

AFTER YOUR TRIP

- The Park Service welcomes your comments on the condition of the wilderness and your wilderness experience.

- Effective management of stock use requires accurate data on patterns of use. Please return the Stock Use Reporting Card (available from the Wilderness Office or wherever you obtain your wilderness permit) to the nearest ranger station, or mail it to:

Wilderness Office
Sequoia & Kings Canyon
National Parks
Three Rivers, CA 93271
(559) 565-3761

APPENDIX **VI**

Nonprofit Organizations

Sequoia Natural History Association

The Sequoia Natural History Association is a non profit organization dedicated to the enhancement of visitor experiences in Sequoia and Kings Canyon national parks. The SNHA is committed to promoting awareness of the parks through educational programs, publications, and financial support. The SNHA participates in the following activities:

- Operation of the park's visitor center bookstores
- Operation of the Sequoia Field Institute and Beetle Rock Education Center
- Free and low-cost school programs
- Publication of the Sequoia and Kings Canyon National Parks newspaper
- Tours of Crystal Cave
- Operation of the Pear Lake Ski Hut
- Purchasing supplies for ranger programs
- Financing active protection of black bears
- Field seminar courses
- Funding visitor center and trail exhibits
- Information staff at visitor centers
- Publishing books and maps of the parks
- Funding scientific research within the parks

MEMBERSHIP CATEGORIES

Individual	$25/year
Family	$30/year
Supporter	$50/year
Business	$150/year
Sponsor	$500/year
John Muir Circle	$1000/year

MEMBERSHIP BENEFITS

- 15% discount on mail order and visitor center purchases
- 50% off ticket price for Crystal Cave tours
- 20% discount at Pear Lake Ski Hut
- Discounts on field seminars
- Special members only sales
- Discounts on books and maps at many other national park visitor centers
- Low-cost internet access
- Membership newsletter
- Seasonal copies of the park visitors guide
- Invitation to members' annual picnic

SNHA
HCR 89 — Box 10
Three Rivers, CA 93271-9792
(559) 565-3759
(559) 565-3728 (fax)
snha@sequoiahistory.org (email)
www.sequoiahistory.org

The Sequoia Fund

The Sequoia Fund is the primary non profit fundraising organization for Sequoia and Kings Canyon national parks and Devils Postpile National Monument. Their mission is to support projects that enhance the restoration, conservation, and enjoyment of these parks. The fund has raised over $500,000 for park projects, including the Beetle Rock Environmental Education Center and the Bradley Meadow Interpretive Loop Trail.

The Sequoia Fund
PO Box 3047
Visalia, CA 93278-3047
(559) 739-1668
(559) 739-1680 (fax)
savethetrees@sequoiafund.org (email)
www.sequoiafund.org

APPENDIX

List of Abbreviations

List of Abbreviations	
CCC	Civilian Conservation Corps
DNPS	Delaware North Park Services
FS	Forest Service
GSNM	Giant Sequoia National Monument
HST	High Sierra Trail
INF	Inyo National Forest
JMT	John Muir Trail
KCNP	Kings Canyon National Park
KCPS	Kings Canyon Park Services Co.
NPS	National Park Service
PCT	Pacific Crest Trail
quad(s)	quadrangle (usually refers to 7.5 minute USGS maps)
RD	Ranger District
S&KCNP	Sequoia and Kings Canyon national parks
SNHA	Sequoia Natural History Association
SNP	Sequoia National Park
USFS	United States Forest Service
USGS	United States Geological Survey

APPENDIX **VIII**

Quick Guide to Frequently Called Numbers and Websites

General	
Campground Reservations (NPS)	(800) 365-2267
Campground Reservations (USFS)	(877) 444-6777
Caltrans (Road Conditions)	(800) 427-7623
The Map Center	(510) 841-MAPS (6277)
Wilderness Press	(800) 443-7227

Inyo National Forest	
Information	(760) 873-2400
Mt. Whitney RD	(760) 876-6200
White Mountain RD	(760) 873-2500
Wilderness Permits	(760) 873-2483; Fax (760) 873-2484

Lodging	
DNPS	(888) 252-5757
Kings Canyon Lodge	(866) KCANYON (522-6966)
KCPS	(559) 335-5500
Montecito-Sequoia Lodge	(800) 227-9900
Silver City Resort	(559) 561-3223 or (805) 528-2730 (winter)

Sequoia & Kings Canyon national parks	
Information	(559) 565-3341
Wilderness Permits	(559) 565-3708; Fax (559) 565-4239
The Sequoia Fund	(559) 739-1668; Fax (559) 739-1680
Sequoia Natural History Assoc.	(559) 565-3759; Fax (559) 565-3728
Sequoia National Forest Information	(559) 338-2251
Hume Lake RD	(559) 338-2251

Sierra National Forest	
Information	(559) 855-5360
Pineridge RD	(559) 855-5360
USGS	(800) ASK-USGS (275-8747)
Field Station	(559) 565-3171

Websites	
Caltrans (road conditions)	www.dot.ca.gov/hq/roadinfo/
Inyo National Forest	www.fs.fed.us/r5/inyo/
Lodging (DNPS)	www.visitsequoia.com
Lodging (KCPS)	www.sequoia-kingscayon.com
Montecito-Sequoia Lodge	www.montecitosequoia.com
Sequoia & Kings Canyon national parks	http://nps.gov/seki/
The Sequoia Fund	www.sequoiafund.org
Sequoia National Forest	www.fs.fed.us/r5/sequoia/
Sequoia Natural History Assoc.	www.sequoiahistory.org
Sierra National Forest	www.fs.fed.us/r5/sierra/
Silver City Resort	www.silvercityresort.com
USGS	www.usgs.gov/
Wilderness Permits (INF)	www.fs.fed.us/r5/inyo/passespermits/index.html
Wilderness Press	www.wildernesspress.com

Bibliography and Suggested Reading

Arnot, Phil. 1996. *High Sierra, John Muir's Range of Light*. San Carlos, CA: Wide World Publishing/Tetra.

Backhurst, Paul, Editor. 2001. *Backpacking California*. Berkeley, CA: Wilderness Press.

Browning, Peter. 1991. *Place Names of the Sierra Nevada*. Berkeley, CA: Wilderness Press.

Cutter, Ralph. 1991. *Sierra Trout Guide*. Portland, OR: Frank Amato Publications.

Dilslayer, Larry M. and William C. Tweed. 1990. *Challenge of the Big Trees*. Three Rivers, CA: Sequoia Natural History Association.

Farquhar, Francis P. 1965. *History of the Sierra Nevada*. Berkeley, CA: University of California Press.

Felzer, Ron. 1992. *High Sierra Hiking Guide: Mineral King*. 3rd Ed. Berkeley, CA: Wilderness Press.

Horn, Elizabeth L. 1998. *Sierra Nevada Wildflowers*. Missoula, MT: Mountain Press Publishing Co.

Jackson, Louise A. 1988. Buelah, *A Biography of the Mineral King Valley of California*. Tucson, AZ: Westernlore Press.

Jenkins, J.C. and Ruby Johnson Jenkins. 1992. *Exploring the Southern Sierra: East Side*, 3rd Ed. Berkeley, CA: Wilderness Press.

Jenkins, J.C. and Ruby Johnson Jenkins. 1995. *Exploring the Southern Sierra: West Side*, 3rd Ed. Berkeley, CA: Wilderness Press.

Johnston, Verna R. 1994. *California Forests and Woodlands, A Natural History*. Berkeley, CA: University of California Press.

Johnston, Verna R. 1998. *Sierra Nevada, The Naturalist's Companion*, Revised Edition. Berkeley, CA: University of California Press.

Krist, John. 1993. *50 Best Short Hikes in Yosemite and Sequoia/Kings Canyon*. Berkeley, CA: Wilderness Press.

Moore, James G. 2000. *Exploring the Highest Sierra*. Stanford, CA: Stanford University Press.

Morey, Kathy. 2002. *Hot Showers, Soft Beds, and Dayhikes in the Sierra Nevada*, 2nd Ed. Berkeley, CA: Wilderness Press.

Petrides, George A. and Olivia Petrides. 1998. *Western Trees*. New York: Houghton Mifflin.

Robinson, John W. and Andy Selters. 1986. *High Sierra Hiking Guide: Mt. Goddard.* 3rd Ed. Berkeley, CA: Wilderness Press.

Robinson, John W. 1974. *High Sierra Hiking Guide: Mt. Pinchot.* Berkeley, CA: Wilderness Press.

Roper, Steve. 1976. *The Climber's Guide to the High Sierra.* San Francisco, CA: Sierra Club Books.

Roper, Steve. 1997. *Sierra High Route, Traversing Timberline Country.* Seattle, WA: The Mountaineers.

Schaffer, Jeffrey P., Ben Schifrin, Thomas Winnett and Ruby Johnson Jenkins. 2002. *Pacific Crest Trail: Southern California.* Berkeley, CA: Wilderness Press.

Secor, R.J. 1992. *The High Sierra, Peaks, Passes, and Trails.* Seattle, WA: The Mountaineers.

Selters, Andy. 1987. *High Sierra Hiking Guide: Triple Divide Peak,* 2nd Ed. Berkeley, CA: Wilderness Press.

Smith, Genny, Ed. 2000. *Sierra East, Edge of the Great Basin.* Berkeley, CA: University of California Press.

Sorensen, Steve. 1991. *Day Hiking Sequoia,* 2nd Ed. Three Rivers, CA: Fuyu Press.

Spring, Vicky. 1995. *100 Hikes in California's Central Sierra & Coast Range.* Seattle, WA: The Mountaineers.

Stone, Robert. 2000. *Day Hikes in Sequoia and Kings Canyon National Parks.* Red Lodge, MT: Day Hike Books, Inc.

Strong, Douglas H. 2000. *From Pioneers to Preservationists, A Brief History of Sequoia and Kings Canyon National Parks.* Three Rivers, CA: Sequoia Natural History Association.

Tweed, William. 1986. *Beneath the Giants, A Guide to the Moro Rock-Crescent Meadow Road of Sequoia National Park.* Three Rivers, CA: Sequoia Natural History Association.

Tweed, William.1986. *Kaweah Remembered.* Three Rivers, CA: Sequoia Natural History Association.

Weeden, Norman F. 1996. *A Sierra Nevada Flora,* 4th Ed. Berkeley, CA: Wilderness Press.

Whitney, Stephen. 1979. *A Sierra Club Naturalist's Guide.* San Francisco, CA: Sierra Club.

Winnett, Thomas with Melanie Findling. 1994. *Backpacking Basics,* 4th Ed. Berkeley, CA: Wilderness Press.

Winnett, Thomas and Kathy Morey. 1998. *Guide to the John Muir Trail.* Berkeley, CA: Wilderness Press.

Winnett, Thomas. 2001. *Hikers Guide to the High Sierra: Mt. Whitney.* 3rd Ed. Berkeley, CA: Wilderness Press.

Winnett, Thomas, Jason Winnett, Kathy Morey and Lyn Haber. 2001. *Sierra South, 100 Backcountry Trips in California's Sierra,* 7th Ed. Berkeley, CA: Wilderness Press.

Wuerthner, George. 1993. *California's Sierra Nevada.* Helena, MT: American & World Geographic Publishing.

INDEX

15
20
35
30

About the Author

Mike was raised in the suburbs of east Portland, Oregon, in the shadow of Mt. Hood (whenever the cloudy Pacific Northwest skies cleared enough to allow such things as shadows). His mother never learned to drive, so walking was a way of life for her, as it was for her young son in tow. As a teenager with access to a car, Mike took advantage of his new mobility to explore further afield, and began hiking, backpacking, and climbing in the Cascades of Oregon and Washington. He continued these interests as a young adult with a group of buddies from Seattle Pacific University. After acquiring a BA from SPU, he married his wife, Robin, and settled down in Seattle for a couple of years while continuing his outdoor pursuits.

Mike and his wife soon left the greenery of the Pacific Northwest to relocate to the high desert of Reno, Nevada. The mountains lured Mike first to the Tahoe Sierra, and later down the thoroughfare of U.S. 395 to the east side of the High Sierra. The aesthetic beauty of the Sierra, combined with the typically sunny California skies, opened the door to many fine adventures. However, his forays were not limited to the Sierra, as over the years several extended trips led him away from Reno to numerous wild areas across the West.

In the early 1990s, Mike left his last "real" job with an engineering firm, and began writing about the places he had visited. His first project for Wilderness Press was an update and expansion of Luther Linkhart's classic guide, *The Trinity Alps*, which became a third edition in 1994 (now an updated fourth edition). *Nevada Wilderness Areas and Great Basin National Park* appeared in 1997, followed by the *Snowshoe Trails* series (Tahoe in 1998, Yosemite in 1999, and California in 2001). Mike was also a contributor to *Backpacking California*, published in 2001. In addition to his work with Wilderness Press, he has written articles for *Sunset*, *Backpacker*, and the *Reno Gazette-Journal*. As a part-time instructor, Mike passes on his accrued outdoor wisdom to students in hiking, backpacking and snowshoeing classes at Truckee Meadows Community College.

Current projects include, *Afoot and Afield in Reno and Lake Tahoe*, *Backpacking Nevada*, and *Top Trails™ Lake Tahoe*.

Mike continues to live in Reno with Robin and their two boys, David and Stephen, along with their yellow lab, Barkley.